The Chinese
and the Japanese

Essays in Political and Cultural Interactions

Sponsored by the Joint Committee

on Contemporary China

of the American Council of Learned Societies

and the Social Science Research Council

The Chinese
and the Japanese

Essays in Political and Cultural Interactions

Edited by Akira Iriye

CONTRIBUTORS

MADELEINE CHI	MARIUS B. JANSEN
SAMUEL C. CHU	SUSAN H. MARSH
LLOYD E. EASTMAN	TAKAFUSA NAKAMURA
HARRY D. HAROOTUNIAN	BONNIE B. OH
BUNSŌ HASHIKAWA	SHUMPEI OKAMOTO
MASARU IKEI	JOHN E. SCHRECKER
AKIRA IRIYE	YUE-HIM TAM
NORIKO KAMACHI	ERNEST P. YOUNG

PRINCETON UNIVERSITY PRESS

PRINCETON, NEW JERSEY

091913

CONTENTS

[v]

CONTENTS

ACKNOWLEDGMENTS

I WOULD like, first of all, to thank the Joint Committee on China of the Social Science Research Council and the American Council of Learned Societies for providing support, intellectual as well as financial, for a project in modern Chinese-Japanese relations, out of which this volume has grown. The project participants first held a workshop in Chicago in May 1974, and then a research conference at Portsmouth, New Hampshire, in June 1976. Some of their essays are here printed in revised form. I am indebted to them and to the other participants—John Hunter Boyle, Hilary Conroy, James B. Crowley, and Lin Min-te—for all their efforts to make this a unique and stimulating undertaking.

Nearly four years have elapsed since these essays were presented in their original form. These years have seen momentous changes in Chinese-Japanese relations. It is to be hoped that this book will contribute to an understanding of these changes. In this same period, the essays in the book have been revised, edited, and re-edited several times. I am grateful to all who have had a hand in the process, particularly the staffs of the Social Science Research Council and the Princeton University Press, their anonymous outside reviewers, Anthony Cheung, my research assistant, and Anne Ch'ien, who held the project together at my end as secretary/coordinator.

June 1979   Akira Iriye

CONTRIBUTORS

Madeleine Chi is on the staff of the Office of the Historian, the Department of State. She has taught at Manhattanville College and published *China Diplomacy, 1914-1918* (1970).

Samuel C. Chu is professor of history at Ohio State University, having also taught at Bucknell University and the University of Pittsburgh. He is the author of *Reformer in Modern China: Chang Ch'ien, 1853-1926* (1965), and is working on a history of the Sino-Japanese War, 1894-95.

Lloyd E. Eastman, professor of history at the University of Illinois, Champaign-Urbana, has taught at Connecticut College and Ohio State University. He is the author of *Throne and Mandarins: China's Search for a Policy during the Sino-French Controversy, 1880-1885* (1967), and *The Abortive Revolution: China Under Nationalist Rule, 1927-1937* (1974). He is currently working on wartime China.

Harry D. Harootunian is Max Palevsky Professor of History and Civilizations at the University of Chicago. He has taught at several other institutions, including the University of Rochester and the University of Wisconsin. He is the author of *Toward Restoration: The Growth of Political Consciousness in Tokugawa Japan* (1970), and *Between Religion and Politics: Studies in Tokugawa Nativism* (in press). He has coedited a number of books, including *Modern Japanese Leadership: Transition and Change* (1966) and *Japan in Crisis: Essays on Taisho Democracy* (1974).

Bunzō Hashikawa, professor of modern Japanese history at Meiji University, is the author of numerous books, among which are (in Japanese): *Modern Japanese Political Thought* (1968), *On the Japanese Romantics* (1973), *The Yellow Peril* (1976), and *The Dream of Asian Liberation* (1978).

Masaru Ikei is a professor in the Faculty of Law, Keio University. A specialist in modern Japanese diplomatic history and Sino-Japanese relations, he has published a number of monographs dealing with these subjects, as well as a survey of modern Japanese foreign policy and a history of baseball in Japan.

Akira Iriye, professor and chairman of the department of history at the University of Chicago, has also taught at Harvard University, the University of California (Santa Cruz), and the University of Rochester. His publications include *After Imperialism: The Search for a New Order in the Far East, 1921-1931* (1965), *Across the Pacific: An Inner History of American-East Asian Relations* (1967), *Pacific Estrangement: Japanese and American Expansion, 1897-1911* (1972), *The Cold War in Asia: A Historical Introduction* (1974), and *From Nationalism to Internationalism: U.S. Foreign Policy to 1914* (1977).

Marius B. Jansen taught at the University of Washington before moving to Princeton University, where he is professor of history. He has published a number of books, including *The Japanese and Sun Yat-sen* (1954), *Sakamoto Ryōma and the Meiji Restoration* (1961), and *Japan and China: From War to Peace, 1894-1972* (1975). He is currently editing a volume of the *Cambridge History of Japan*.

Noriko Kamachi is associate professor of history at the University of Michigan, Dearborn. She is coauthor (with John K. Fairbank and Ichiko Chūzō) of *Japanese Studies of Modern China since 1953* (1975), and has published several articles in the field of Chinese-Japanese relations. She is at work on a history of Chinese communities in Japan.

Susan H. Marsh is assistant professor of political science at Providence College and a research associate of the political science department at Brown University.

Takafusa Nakamura is professor of statistics and economics at the University of Tokyo. His publications include (in Japanese) "The May 30th Incident" (1964), *The Contemporary Japanese Economy* (1968), and *The Future of the Japanese Economy* (1975).

Bonnie B. Oh is assistant professor of history at Loyola University, Chicago. Previously she taught at Marquette University. Her essays have been published in the *Journal of Social Science and Humanities*. She is writing a study of Chinese-Korean relations before the Sino-Japanese War of 1894-95.

Shumpei Okamoto, professor of history at Temple University, has published *The Japanese Oligarchy and the Russo-Japanese War*

(1970). He is also coeditor, with Dorothy Borg, of *Pearl Harbor as History: Japanese-American Relations, 1931-1941* (1973).

John E. Schrecker teaches history at Brandeis University. He is the author of *Imperialism and Chinese Nationalism* (1971) and the coeditor of *Reform in Nineteenth-Century China* (1976). He is currently completing a reinterpretive study entitled *The Rise of Socialist China.*

Yue-him Tam, who received his doctorate from Princeton University, is lecturer in history and dean of students at New Asia College, the Chinese University of Hong Kong. He is preparing a book-length study of Naitō Konan.

Ernest P. Young, professor of history at the University of Michigan, has also taught at Dartmouth College. His publications include *The Presidency of Yuan Shih-k'ai: Liberalism and Dictatorship in Early Republican China* (1977). He is currently engaged in a study of Chinese conceptions of Japan in the twentieth century.

The Chinese
and the Japanese

Essays in Political and Cultural Interactions

INTRODUCTION

AKIRA IRIYE

THE CHINESE and the Japanese have lived as Asian neighbors for nearly two thousand years. Being geographically so close and yet psychologically quite remote despite their common cultural roots, the two peoples have developed a sense at once of commonality and disparity, interdependence and autonomy, mutual respect and suspicion, attraction and repulsion, and admiration and condescension toward one another. They have talked of their shared heritage and their identity as Asians, but they have not hesitated to seek outside assistance to fight against one another. They have contributed to each other's cultural and modern transformation, but their patterns of development have been vastly dissimilar. Throughout, the fact of their existence and the patterns of their association have been among the most enduring features of the history of East Asia.

This phenomenon deserves extensive study, and yet it has not been adequately explored by historians of modern East Asia. There are China specialists and Japan specialists, but few, if any, China-and-Japan specialists. Because it is a laborious process to establish a degree of competence for the history of a civilization as complex as Chinese or Japanese, specialists in Chinese history and Japanese history have tended to work within the confines of their respective fields, and have rarely had an opportunity to engage in a collaborative effort to study the two peoples' interactions. In China and Japan, moreover, it has been extremely difficult—some would even say impossible—to transcend personal experience or to avoid applying political dogmas and ethical standards to the study of the modern history of Chinese-Japanese relations. Most works published in China and Japan on the subject have been not so much scholarly monographs as personal statements, evidence of how a particular author intellectually and psychologically relates himself to events of the recent past. Dispassionate scholarship has seemed irrelevant, if not obscene, to a generation of Japanese writers whose lives have been intimately associated with the aggressive acts their country perpetrated upon China, and to Chinese writers who could not, even if they would, dissociate the

[3]

sense of humiliation and outrage they felt toward the Japanese from scholarly studies of the relations between the two countries. This may explain why the few existing monographs that do deal with the modern history of Sino-Japanese relations have been written by Western historians. But Western scholars, too, have recently tended to shy away from the study of China's and Japan's foreign affairs, viewing them as superficial, a relic of the traditional scholarship that stressed the West's "impact" on Asia and the latter's "response" to the West.

These historiographical handicaps, however, need not stymie a serious effort to examine what the Chinese and the Japanese have meant to each other. Such a study necessitates much more than a narrative of government-to-government relations. Far more important is the exploration of ways in which ideas, institutions, and individuals of one country contributed to social change, cultural definition, and intellectual discourse in the other. The sixteen essays in this volume all seek to make a contribution to the understanding of the modern history of China and Japan by analyzing their points of contact, whether physical or symbolic. The authors stress different themes and employ various approaches, but they share a keen awareness of the baffling ambiguities inherent in the history of the two countries' interactions in modern times.

The first five essays deal with the period through the end of the nineteenth century. Harootunian's is an important study of how "China" helped Japanese self-definition in the eighteenth and nineteenth centuries. He shows that there was a progression of thought from the modality of continuity to that of contiguity, that is, from viewing China and Japan as inherently similar to considering them (and all countries in the world by implication) distinct entities. The loss of China's centrality in Japanese discourse, Harootunian argues, prepared the Japanese intellectually to cope with the urgent problems brought about by the contact with the West. One such problem was Korea. The essay by Oh details how, for the Japanese, Korea became a test case of their self-conscious liberation from Chinese tradition. The Chinese, on the other hand, sought to uphold their time-honored position of superiority; but paradoxically, as the Oh essay shows, in doing so they were putting an end to their traditional hands-off policy in the Korean peninsula. By 1894, Sino-Japanese rivalries in Korea, and their implications for Korean domestic politics, had reached a stage where it appeared that either one or the other would have to establish undisputed authority over the peninsular kingdom. Underneath this surface drama, however, one should not lose sight of other aspects of Sino-Japanese relations. The essay by Kamachi points out the roles played by Chinese residents in Japan in the latter's modernization. They were agents of Westernization in a still over-whelmingly traditional nation. Moreover, Chinese self-perception was a product of the changing Japanese attitudes toward them. On the other hand, Chu's essay on another class of Chinese—scholar-officials —reveals a general indifference to Japan, and no serious intellectual engagement among them about its meaning. Even so, both the Chinese merchants living in Japan and officials in China were eventually forced to come to terms with the growing self-confidence and even arrogance on the part of the Japanese. Whether they liked it or not, Japan was beginning to affect the life and thought of the Chinese. Indeed, by the late 1890's, as Schrecker's speculative but suggestive essay indicates, some Chinese reformers were making use of the Meiji Restoration as an example of internal reconstruction which they believed held valuable lessons for their own country. Japan was beginning to play a role in Chinese transformation, and it is revealing that it was affecting China's political and intellectual discourse just as China had defined the perimeters of Tokugawa political thought.

From this time on Chinese and Japanese would make increasing use of one another, whether for personal gain, group interests, or loftier objectives. Jansen's study of Konoe Atsumaro suggests that Japan's cultural diplomacy in China at the turn of the century, with its explicit espousal of pan-Asian solidarity, was an exercise in elitist cooperation between upper-class Chinese and Japanese. Konoe was an organizer of semi-public and semi-private groups in Japan whose objective was to maintain social cohesion in the middle of change. Young's essay gives examples of more mundane dealings between Chinese politicians and generals and their Japanese counterparts at a time when China was thrown into turmoil after the passing of the Ch'ing dynasty. The Young essay, as well as Chi's study of Ts'ao Ju-lin, suggest how easy it was for ambitious Chinese politicians to avail themselves of the Japanese connection, persuading themselves that it was no more criminal to make use of Japanese assistance than to turn to some other countries, even if it meant making significant concessions to Japan. The rigid framework of Japanese imperialism and Chinese nationalism breaks down because these Chinese considered themselves nationalists and even argued that China's cause was best served, and the more odious aspects of Japanese policy mitigated, by entering into special ties with Japan.

Japan, however, was not a monolithic entity. If anything, as the essays by Tam, Okamoto, and Ikei reveal, many approaches to China were possible. Naitō Konan, the historian, was concerned with the problem of culture and power. As Tam shows, Naitō asked how the Chinese could seek to maintain their cultural integrity in the midst of foreign influences. The answer was to stress Japan's unique mission in China as the inheritor of Chinese culture and the center of a new Asian civilization that was to be generated through Sino-Japanese cooperation and to supersede the decaying Occidental civilization. Japan's task in China, then, was essentially a cultural one. For Ishibashi Tanzan, a journalist, on the other hand, Japanese behavior in China was important as an indicator of Japan's own development. Okamoto's essay stresses Ishibashi's call for a peaceful and reformist Japan that eschewed imperialism for peace and coprosperity. Overseas expansionism was antithetical to internal reforms, and thus if Japan were to develop as a liberal and peaceful country, it should refrain from aggressive acts in China. The opposite of such views was the position of General Ugaki Kazushige, the subject of Ikei's study. Ugaki was the archetypical imperialist with no interest in or concern for China per se; China was important merely as an object of Japanese needs. It was not surprising, moreover, that in the 1920's Ugaki should have come to advocate joint action with Western powers to combat radical nationalism in China. Although this was precisely what men like Naitō and Ishibashi opposed, Japanese dealings with China revealed that, on the whole, Japan behaved as one of the advanced industrial powers in China, viewing it as a field for political and economic exploitation and development.

Joint action among the industrial powers became more difficult after 1929, when the world economic crisis shattered the framework of capitalist internationalism. There grew a strong tendency on the part of each power to seek a unilateral solution to its economic problems and to establish an autarkic sphere for economic and political control. Japan was no exception; in fact it took the lead in destroying the structure of cooperative international order and in weakening the domestic interests and constituents that had identified with that order. The 1930's were characterized by the ascendancy in Japan of those who sought a new order at home and in Asia, and by a complex pattern of response to it on the part of Chinese. The Nakamura essay details not only Japanese penetration of north China, but also an intense rivalry among various Japanese groups for exploiting the new opportunities. Japanese domination over China, therefore, was giving rise to the question of which Japanese groups were to control that domination. Thus a new order in north China was accompanied by new arrangements in Manchuria. The story also involved the Chinese. The Iriye essay on the Hsin-min hui (People's Renovation Society) and Eastman's study of clandestine and officially sanctioned dealings between Chinese and Japanese during the war suggest that on China's part, too, the 1930's were giving rise to new groupings and new opportunities. Chinese society, as distinct from the state, had somehow to function during the turmoils of war. While the government formally proclaimed resistance to Japanese aggression and while millions loyally carried on the war effort, others had little personal sense of involvement. Instead, they found in collaboration with Japan a way to reconstruct social order and reaffirm cultural integrity. Marsh's study of one collaborationist (Chou Fo-hai) indeed argues that collaboration with an alien invader had been traditional behavior in Chinese politics. Collaborators were individuals who were trying to maintain systemic order when the state had failed to do so.

These are controversial interpretations, and should probably be balanced by studies of Chinese individuals and groups who chose to fight against Japan. Since this side of the story is better known, however, it seems justifiable to dwell at some length on the meaning of collaboration, as Marsh does. We need not forget or rationalize the story of Japanese atrocities and damages inflicted upon the Chinese population to try to understand the efforts of some Chinese to preserve national integrity through collaboration with the enemy. All this, however, needs to be put in perspective, and the reflective piece by Hashikawa, one of Japan's leading students of Sino-Japanese relations, provides a fitting conclusion to the study. He traces the evolution of Japanese views of China from the nineteenth century to the 1930's, reminding the reader once again that the question of China has been a central concern of the Japanese.

Together these essays constitute the story of two highly self-conscious peoples as they have made use of one another in terms of specific intellectual strategies, economic opportunities, political choices, and personal needs. Because they have had a highly literate tradition, they have left mountains of written evidence to express their sentiments and ideas. It is only by studying them closely that one may gain a sense of their dilemmas as well as a measure of their solutions. These essays show how futile it is to study modern East Asian history without coming to grips with the ways in which Chinese and Japanese chose to deal with each other. This is an ongoing story. The issues will continue to baffle the two peoples for decades to come. They should concern all students of modern East Asia.

CHAPTER I

The Functions of China in Tokugawa Thought

———

HARRY D. HAROOTUNIAN

THIS ESSAY examines some of the central questions posed by
Tokugawa writers, especially nativists (*kokugakusha*), in terms of
the functions they assigned to China in their perceptions. Such an
examination will disclose something about the kinds of deeper
strategies they used to structure their perceptions, and tell us more
about Japanese consciousness than about what Japanese actually knew
or felt about China. It is one of the ironies of this problem that China
faded from serious discourse precisely at that moment when Japanese
were in a position to gain firsthand and empirical information about
the country.

The use of China to dramatize other issues suggests something
about the way thinkers resort to highly complex and ritualized
strategies for repression, sublimation, and deflection of thought or
emotion from its true object. Their intellectual responses do not represent a world whose true nature is given to them in direct perception;
rather we find that they occupy a world that is perceived through
codes that have been already prepared for them, and into which
they are indoctrinated by processes of socialization that are themselves manifestations of the code.[1] It is the mode of relating to the
world that determines the nature of classification systems as well as
the boundaries used in the mapping of places that objects will
"naturally" occupy. The use of China in discourse had nothing to do
with the way Japanese perceived China, but it had everything to do

---

[1] This view is considerably different from the one proposed by Uete Michiari in
Nihon kindai shisō no keisei (Tokyo, 1974), where we are told that such shifting
images are firmly rooted in views related to the politics of international relations and
to the survival of the fittest (p. 234).

with the way by which writers related the world of things in specific modalities. Thinkers' views of China were not strongly connected to changing perceptions prompted by direct experience, though the acquisition of news and information might help in the resolution of a specific problem. More often the acquisition of new knowledge concerning China was used to confirm an opinion already held. The news of British activities in China and information about the Taiping Rebellion entered Japan in increments; they never inspired the formulation of a new attitude toward China, but only validated a function that writers had already agreed upon.

"Dehistoricization" of China: Inner and Outer

Obviously, the central function of China in Tokugawa thought had been fixed by Confucianism. In thought and social life China functioned metaphorically; it was associated with moral concepts such as *tendō* (heavenly way), the five relationships, duty and designations (*meibun*), and indeed civilization itself. But it was not, for these purposes, necessarily a civilization bound by history or geography. China was referred to as *chūka*, the central florescence, or *chūgoku*, the central kingdom; the former term, favored by Tokugawa writers, permitted greater disassociation from specific times and places. Even nativists, despite their heated denunciations of Confucians (Hirata Atsutane's classic "stinking *zusha*"), were no exception in observing this convention. The overall result was, of course, a kind of reverence for China, but a China removed from any real historicity. China was, after all, the home of the sages and the Four Books, the standard of thousands in their ascent to civilized life. An early Confucian, Nakae Tōju, wrote that before and after Confucius there was nothing, while a later writer, Itō Jinsai, proposed that *chūka*, because of what it meant, was the highest and most exalted of places. The most apparent purpose of this metaphorical function was to dramatize the juxtaposition of inner and outer (*naigai*), civilization and barbarism. At one level such oppositions provided the principles for a classification scheme, and writers often listed sets of associations that belonged in each category; such a scheme also represented a rather crude view of international society, though consciousness of such an order appeared only later. The more basic function of *chūka* was to emphasize the centrality of ethical conduct and its acquisition. By extension there could only be those who possessed it and those who did not.

In Tokugawa Japan this type of metaphor resulted in a kind of vulgarization that valued the outer (China) and denigrated the inner (Japan). This was an ironic, if not paradoxical, reversal, since in its original meaning inner referred to civilization, while outer was identified with the world of the barbarian. But in moral terms outer behavior always took precedence over inner impulse (unless one was a member of the Wang Yang-ming persuasion). However, in Tokugawa social life, perhaps a better or less sublimated indicator into attitudes than high thought, outer referred simply to China. The terms for "import" and "imported goods," as they were used in Tokugawa speech, were *hakurai* and *hakuraihin*, respectively, and referred to ship-borne goods brought to Nagasaki from China and Holland. Yet when people spoke of *hakuraihin* they meant only goods produced in China. In time this identification gave way to considerations of value, and Chinese imports came to mean "elegant products." Imports themselves acquired the invariable association of excellence over comparable products produced in Japan. This conceit probably informed other areas of Tokugawa life. Chinese doctrine and culture were esteemed over native accomplishments, often at the expense of forgetting about Japan itself. Hiraga Gennai, an eccentric who lived in the eighteenth century (1726-1779) and who was a professed enthusiast of "Dutch Learning" (*rangaku*), was prompted to call attention to this China-worship in one of his novels (*gesaku*). Through the agency of one of his fictional characters, Hiraga denounced the contemporary rage for things Chinese. He wrote, "frog-scholars, schooled in wells and ponds, are shaped according to Chinese favoritism. They call Japan, where we have been born, the land of the Eastern Barbarians and argue that Amaterasu is no different from the evening star (Venus). . . . Because they calculate the rice stipends . . . with the measurements of the Chou period, we have come to resent the sages in our times. Ruling in the Chinese fashion is like looking at road-side prohibition edicts. . . . The customs of Japan are different from those of China; the Chinese emperor (*tenshi*) is like a migratory worker, for if he does not have 'spirit' he is replaced. The realm is not the realm of one person but belongs to the realm itself. And it is for this reason that the rulership of the realm in China has been snatched by force, and there have been 10,-000 breaches of etiquette. In China sages abound, and doctrine is honored everywhere. But because Japan's realm has protected virtue and principle naturally, there has been lasting peace even though there have been no sages."[2]

Hiraga was a student of the nativist scholar Kamo Mabuchi, whose own denunciations of China he echoed. Yet Hiraga's observations about contemporary sinophilia among the leadership simply illustrates the structural relationship between how China functioned in thought, and what it meant in more popular usage. In both cases China served to dramatize standards of excellence and refinement. In thinkers such as Kumazawa Banzan, Yamaga Sokō, Arai Hakuseki, and Ogyū Sorai, China evoked specific cultural and moral associations, and served as a principle to classify and differentiate. Kumazawa Banzan, in the *Shūgi washo* (1672), saw the "realm of the central florescence" as the source of civilization, and contrasted it with the surrounding barbarians:[3] "*chūka* was the parent to the children, who were the eastern, southern, western and northern barbarians, as the mountain was parent to the river's children."[4] It was the very centrality itself that defined civilization:[5] "*chūka* is the central kingdom (realm) of heaven and earth; it is at the center of the four seas. There are six realms in the south, seven in the west, eight in the north, nine in the east and all constitute the four seas. In the south people are called *ban* and they have the shape of insects; in the west they are called *jū* and they resemble dogs; in the north there are the *teki* who appear as beasts; and in the east there are the *i* who have the shape of men."[6] Banzan argued that in the four seas the countries that made up the eastern barbarians (i.e., Japan, Korea, etc.) were the most superior; in fact, outside of *chūka*, Japan ranked highest.

Writers like Kumazawa, armed with this conception of centrality, were able to define the area of moral rulership and map out the boundaries between civilization and barbarism in terms of gradations. To be near the center was not a geographical but a civilizational fact. Such a classification was ultimately expressed in terms of a basic opposition between "flowery" and "barbarian" (usually expressed in the imagery of nature, such as animals, beasts, and insects), and between "inner" (*nai*) and "outer" (*gai*). This is certainly one of the meanings in Hiraga's condemnation of sinophiles who refer to Japan, "the country where we have been born," as the eastern barbarian region.

---

[2] Hiraga Gennai, "Fūryū Shidōken-den," in Nihon Koten Bungaku Taikei, *Furai sannishō* (Tokyo, 1974), vol. 55, pp. 216-17.

[3] Nihon Shisō Taikei, *Kumazawa Banzan* (Tokyo, 1971), vol. 30, pp. 17ff.

[4] Ibid., p. 135.   [5] Ibid., p. 106.   [6] Ibid., pp. 148-49.

Despite Kumazawa's assurances that in the eastern realms the *i* appeared in the shape of men, he was quick to admit that at the time of creation the *i* were formed as birds and beasts. Notions of refinement referred to inner, to central florescence, surrounded by an outer world of barbarism, whereas the outer world, at least in this usage, was identified with nature, something wild, unrefined, and uncivilized. Internally, this conception called for a differentiation between the "revered" and the "despised," the "high" and the "low." Because political leadership was identified with moral doctrine, the scope of rule was not only spatially and horizontally different but also socially and vertically distinct. The flowery-barbarian dichotomy was not applied to the broad realm (*tenka*), but was used in Japan to designate the notion of territory (*kokka* or *kuni*), which was usually associated with domains; in other words conventional usage linked this classification to the organization of political space.[7]

Because China had pioneered lasting human achievements and formed the high civilization to which the Japanese felt they had come late in the history of the race, it was not surprising that there existed in Japan a strong consciousness of reverence for China as the source of creativity and civilization. Thus, the civilization/barbarism opposition might result in still another opposition: the distinction between great and small countries. Kumazawa remarked in the *Shūgi washo* that while there was a "great country," which he identified with China, "Japan is a small country. The reason for this is because its spiritual powers are thin and weak."[8] One can also recall Yamaga Sokō's (1622-1685) confessions in his autobiographical *Haisho zampitsu* (1667): "I once thought Japan was small and thus inferior . . . to China. . . . This was not my idea alone; scholars of every age have thought so and devoted themselves to the study of Chinese. But we have believed too much in what we have heard and not enough in what our eyes could see; we have ignored what is near at hand in our search for what is distant."[9]

None of this is to suggest that Japanese in the Tokugawa period thought of themselves as barbarians. Reverence for the central florescence meant reverence for China. However, as Sorai, himself

[7] In lieu of any real grounds for differentiation among the various peoples in the human species, this conception of *ka-i* functioned as a kind of sanction for traditional Chinese foreign policy.

[8] *Kumazawa Banzan*, vol. 30, p. 80.

[9] Hirose Yutaka, ed., *Yamaga Sokō zenshū* (Tokyo, 1940), vol. 12, p. 592.

[13]

denounced as the "barbarian Sorai" for his sinophilia, showed, this feeling was directed at the great sages of antiquity (Yao, Shun, T'ang, Wu), and respect for the achievement of the system of "rites and music." It did not mean indiscriminate adulation for all things Chinese; nor did it relate to the China of the day. For those who revered the central florescence, and not China of a specific historical time, *chūka* as a metaphor was in time transformed to designate Japan itself. This was especially true of writers such as Yamazaki Ansai and Yamaga, and to a lesser degree of nativists themselves. But for the latter the problem was different because the function of China had already changed. The attitudes that nativists inherited tended toward a reverence for Japan which, in turn, reflected more basic philosophic orientations. These orientations, marked by late seventeenth century writers such as Yamaga and Itō Jinsai, shifted the object of thought to the primacy of human passions and sentiment—dispositions long denounced by Neo-Confucians as invitations to immorality and selfishness.

This shift was expressed in more explicit language and represented some fundamental reconsiderations in political theory. Yamaga Sokō, for example, argued for a kind of imperial loyalism (*sonnō-ron*) based on the belief that the legitimacy of authority relationships rested upon the unbroken continuity of *taigi meibun*—the great principle of duties and loyalty symbolized in the imperial house. Indeed, it was in this context that he argued that Japan, rather than China, represented the "true" central realm of civilization. His *Haisho zampitsu* suggested reasons for such a view: (1) the imperial line, "legitimate descendents of the Sun Goddess, had ruled since the age of the gods . . . without interruption"; (2) Japan, owing to its tradition of martial arts and the excellence of its military accomplishments, had successfully won recognition of its superiority from other countries such as the "Three Kingdoms of Han" (Korea) and had never been conquered by a foreign invader; and (3) because of the preservation of such cardinal virtues as wisdom, humanity, and valor, "Japan greatly excels China in each of them and undoubtedly merits the name of middle kingdom (*chūchō*) far more than China."[10] That it took him so long to understand this truth represented a failure of perception that he and his contemporaries shared, according to Yamaga. In his major work on the problem of the central kingdom, the *Chūchō jijitsu* (True facts about the Central Kingdom), he explained: "When one

[10] Ibid., pp. 592-93.

looks upon the blue sky without investigating, one does not see its greatness; when one looks upon fields without thought of furrows and ridges, one does not know its width and breadth. It has become a long-time habit. . . . What a fool I have been, born in the land of the central kingdom and civilization, that I have not yet perceived its beauty. I have cultivated chiefly a taste for foreign classics (*gaicho*, probably Chinese) and adulation of these foreigners."[11] In a spasm of self-recrimination he asked rhetorically: "How could I have been so shortsighted? How could I have lost my resolve so easily? Is one to like the stranger and to esteem the different?" In *Haisho zampitsu* Yamaga explained that such a failure was rooted in the epistemological inadequacies of Neo-Confucianism itself. "While I was engaged in the study of the Ch'eng-Chu system . . . I was given too much to the practice of sustained reverence and quiet sitting, and found myself becoming too taciturn and grave. . . . The approach of Lao Tzu, Chuang Tzu, and Zen offered far more life and freedom. . . . From that point on I followed the impulse of my own nature."[12] Yet, Sokō admitted, he had problems in understanding everyday matters. Such concerns, he had been taught to believe, were of little importance, and it was best to take them on their own terms. But he acknowledged that an overwhelming involvement in daily, practical affairs necessitated a means to understand their nature. His failure to make sense of the quotidian life was linked to his dependence upon reading later commentaries on the classics rather than the classics themselves. It was difficult to make sense of the affairs of daily life through the mediation of Sung commentaries; what was required was a direct engagement of the classics, just as it was important to engage life itself directly. But life itself in the late seventeenth century seemed to be hard to explain in terms of Neo-Confucian modes of understanding. It was in this context that he emphasized the importance of a method of examining the original classics as if they were given directly to experience.

Yamaga's method yielded an awareness of the centrality of practicality and activity, a cognitive shift that subsequently informed his reconsideration of what constituted the central florescence. The discovery of "real facts" permitted Yamaga to transform *chūka* into a metaphor for Japan. Confucianists, he argued in the *Chūchō jijitsu*, had called China the "central kingdom" and acknowledged Japan as the region of the Eastern barbarians. Yamaga, however, proposed to

[11] Ibid., vol. 13, p. 7.
[12] Ibid., vol. 12 (*Haisho zampitsu*), pp. 577-78.

identify civilization with Japan. "Its waters and lands are superior to all others; its virtue and martial values have conquered all others."[13] The unique nature of Japan's soil and water was merely a manifestation of divine creation through the agency of the deities. Indeed this divinity accounted for Japan's centrality, for the imperial succession was in fact coeval with heaven and earth. This was what *chūgoku* meant; centrality was the promise of divinity.[14]

Yamazaki Ansai (1618-1683) shared something of Sokō's disposition to see the central kingdom differently, and agreed that it was incorrect to see China as the central florescence. In the *Nihonshoki*, he argued, China had been referred to as the "western land." But it was one of Yamazaki's pupils, Asami Keisai (1652-1711), who revealed the same kind of shift in orientation that Yamaga had earlier exemplified. In his *Seikan igen* (a work later favored by Bakumatsu activists as a kind of classic of loyalism), Asami sought to clear up the "confusions of contemporary Confucians over the discrimination of inner and outer, revered and despised." The confusion was inspired, he claimed, by the practice of referring to China as the central kingdom, and by calling Japan the land of the Eastern barbarians. The argument, he believed, stemmed from those who read Chinese books and who literally trembled with fright over the fact they had been born in a barbaric land. Yet, he urged, centrality was where one found the cardinal virtues (*taigi*). "But if Japan is called the central kingdom, then will there be the inclination to use the word barbarian? These terms come from Chinese books. When one of these terms is used to describe our country, one is invariably imitating the Chinese. If one designates our country as inner (*nai*) and foreign countries (*iteki*) as outer (*gai*), and discriminates between the two realms, the pedigree does not change regardless of the direction." Asami argued that his opposition really grew out of Chinese convention; to talk about *chūgoku* evoked its opposite—barbarian. But such distinctions, he said, had nothing to do with "loyalty, duties and designations, legitimacy, or the master-retainer principle," and merely represented errors compounded by Confucianists. He despaired: "those who read Chinese books descend into all kinds of riot and rebellion [*ranzoku*, literally, gangsters]. They ought to be lamented and better informed. . . . They are led astray in this manner because of the existence of such

[13] Ibid., vol. 13 (*Chūchō jijitsu*), pp. 7, 11ff.
[14] Ibid., pp. 15-32.

characters [ideographs] as *chūgoku/iteki* in Confucian books. When one does not read such books, one is not led into error."[15]

One of the consequences of this kind of orientation was that while the actual differentiation between *chūka* and *iteki*·had nothing to do with race or territory, there was a strong tendency to identify the various barbarians with the peoples who lived within the orbit of the historical empire of China. When this idea became an object of discourse, it obviously underwent modification and retained its historical associations only. Dazai Shundai, a student of Ogyū's, put it in the following way in his *Keizairoku*: "The four groups of barbarians are called *iteki*; they are ranked under the central florescence because they are without benefit of rite and ritual. Even for men in *chūka*, if they are without rite and ritual they are the same as the *iteki*. For men among the four groups of barbarians, if they possess rite and ritual, they are no different from men in the central florescence." Dazai discloses the comparative ease with which Japanese writers were able to seize upon the *chūka*/barbarian opposition as a functional device; coupled with the concurrent recognition that the ideology of *ka-i* possessed no tangible corporeality, the fixed boundaries of civilization and barbarism were easily overcome. Yamaga Sokō identified Japan as a true manifestation of civilization, while Asami and Dazai could look beyond any fixed point and find civilization and barbarism wherever certain conditions existed or were absent. But this transformation was also being effected by nativist scholars who reversed the criteria for civilization and barbarism; nature, which had marked barbarism, would become the standard of civilization, whereas culture and morality would be seen as its polar opposite. They thus sought to show that Japan might serve as a metaphor for civilization of a different kind.

The Nativist Transformation

In the writings of Kamo Mabuchi, Motoori Norinaga, and, to some degree, Hirata Atsutane and his followers, notably Ōkuni Takamasa, China functioned as a reminder of Japan's centrality. In fact, the premises governing the *chūka*/barbarian opposition were reversed; the resulting classification represented transformations from one side of the opposition to the other. Much of this was made possible by

---

[15] Quoted in Kiyohara Sadao, *Kokushi to Nihon seishin no kengen* (Tokyo, 1943), p. 260.

resorting to a new kind of linguistic strategy; nativism, in its call for a return to the pure meaning of words, acknowledged the failure of representing reality with "Chinese" words. Indeed, their whole quest was to dramatize how language itself, elevated to a privileged position by Confucians, serving the task of representation, ascribed to itself a transparency it could never hope to achieve. Discontent took the form of a new "human science" which they called *kokugaku*. In other words, nativists, like many of their Confucian colleagues, had perceived the problem of ascribing to language a privileged status as instrument of representation, and thus the disparity between the world and the knowledge men might have of it. They assumed that language was a thing like other things, with no special position, since all were the creation of the deities; since language was like anything else, to assign it the task of representing the world of things, as though it might perform this task adequately, was a profound mistake. This criticism of language was manifest in their attack on Chinese learning and in their ultimate celebration of "wonder," silence, the things that could not be said or explained.

The nativists thus sought to return to pure metaphor, to similitude by means of metonymic reduction, by using what the French writer Jacques Lacan elsewhere has called "the power of 'reference back' of signification in order to invest it with the desire aimed at this which it supports."[16] This was how they sought to characterize reality in metaphorical identification and to put words back in their proper place. With this strategy, nativists like Kamo and Motoori were able to see the world in terms of phenomena/noumena, light and dark, visible and invisible; in other words, in terms of pairings which represented oppositions between what was real and tangible and what was not, and in which phenomena were seen as functions of noumena, death as an aspect of life (a concealment), and evil as the absence of good (impurities that could be cleansed). In this sense Japan functioned as the opposite of China, just as what was essentially pure and real (nature) functioned as the opposite of what was artificial and mediocre (civilization, including the privileged position of language as a means of representation), and as what was authentic functioned as the opposite of what was inauthentic. Despite the nativist denunciation of the "Chinese spirit" (*Karagokoro*), the attack was not prompted simply by an inherent dislike of China, but rather by the

---

[16] Jacques Lacan, *The Language of the Self* (New York, 1968), p. 114.

[18]

linguistic strategy itself. Their view of China was merely another way of saying that life could no longer be represented by words in eighteenth-century Japan.

The obvious consequence of this strategy was to see Chinese as different from Japanese, and therefore to designate all Japanese as similar to each other by virtue of their common origins. Kamo Mabuchi's (1697-1769) *Kokuikō* (written in 1765), dramatized this strategy by concentrating on the meaning of China. For him barbarian had no real meaning; the conception of respectable/despicable was purposeless. "If those from barbarian lands . . . emerged to become emperors of China and all submitted to them, is it not foolish to call barbarians lowly and common?"[17] These were simply surface teachings and did not penetrate the heart. The reason for such superficiality, Kamo reasoned, was that China, compared to Japan, was ruled by artificial principles, rather than by a natural conformity with the heart of heaven and earth. Kamo agreed that because the Chinese ruled by invention and artifice, and subsequently by deceit itself, the term for *despised* (*iyashimetarukoto*) referred to the Chinese, not to the so-called barbarian. The teachings of the Chinese subjected people to unnatural restraints; the nativists' purpose was to show what was refined.

Underlining Kamo's judgments was, of course, a cognitive mode that sought to understand and thus represent the world as it was, as it was given, in wonder, in silence if necessary, rather than through the device of abstract principles and words.[18] Such speculative devices as mediations in the task of representation merely introduced disorder which, for Kamo, meant distinctions and differentiations, differences which no longer could be comprehended in the modality of similitude. "That which says man is different from the birds and the beasts is, in human terms, self praise and contempt for others. This too is characteristic of the Chinese. The Chinese despise the realms of the worlds [literally, the four directions] as barbarian realms, which is an incorrect usage of the word *ebisu*. Are not all things that live within the universe insects? Among them why should man alone be esteemed? Why should man alone be different?"[19] Kamo apparently attributed the Chinese conception of man to the linguistic confusion wrought by categorization and differentiation; the privileged status

---

[17] Kamo Mabuchi, *Kokuikō*, in Nihon Shisō Taikei, *Kinsei shintōron: zenki kokugaku* (Tokyo, 1972), vol. 39, p. 376.

[18] Ibid., p. 378. [19] Ibid., p. 379; also pp. 386, 387.

of man was comparable to the status occupied by language as a representational mode. In this connection Kamo contended that rational understanding, which he identified with the Chinese spirit, inevitably led to differences (due to the position of language), to misunderstanding and disorder. He found evidence for this conviction by examining the usefulness of Chinese characters as instruments for representation, and concluded that it was not only too burdensome for the mind to recall so many of them, but that they acted as a kind of screen obscuring real intent and real meaning. They were, in the idiom of modern linguistics, too opaque.[20] The importance of Kamo's strategy was to demonstrate how received oppositions such as refinement/roughness and civilization/barbarism were confusions produced by the Chinese reliance on theory and abstraction. Yet such dispositions were related to the language itself. While songs and poetry were important as essential sources to pure and unsullied sentiment (which had been straitjacketed by Sung theorists[21]), men had been led astray, he believed, by the sparkle of scholarship at the expense of truer forms of learning, that were at once more natural and penetrating than anything the Chinese ever produced.

"What then existed in China in an older age?" Kamo asked rhetorically, and answered with an even more rhetorical question: "Since men later fabricated them [the achievements of ancient China], do they believe that we must have fabricated our history here in Japan?"[22] The implications of the question revealed Kamo's point: the accomplishments of China's antiquity were mere inventions of men seeking power and control, who, through writing and philosophy, had sought to make these achievements appear as natural endowments of heaven and earth. By contrast, Japanese had no need to resort to mere invention and trickery, since, as the poems of the *Manyō* showed, the ancient spirit was in "harmony with the heart of heaven and earth." Ironically, Kamo's denunciation of the Chinese for resorting to sham and deception did not prevent him from invoking the authority of Lao Tzu, whose conception of being in harmony with heaven and earth Kamo considered to conform to the antique Japanese experience. For this experience was marked by a sense of genuine "uprightness" manifest in the early songs. The songs themselves seemed to confirm the Taoist conceit against thought, the belief that many things simply could not be said or represented, since,

[20] Ibid., pp. 380-81.   [21] Ibid., p. 382.   [22] Ibid.

Kamo argued, they used very few words; there were also fewer things to cloud up one's mind and heart. "In such an age," he announced, "when there were so few words and things, [the disposition] of the heart was straight. There was no use for difficult doctrines." Here too, Kamo returned to the contemporary problem of consciousness, the problem of difference and differentiation. In time, he wrote, the heart of man gradually grew divisive, and this introduced disorder and evil, the very characteristics which had become synonymous with China. In this connection, he reasoned that evil, despite the presence of rectitude, should not remain concealed; exposure of evil might produce momentary confusion, but it would also guarantee inevitable expiration because "the teachings of good are never completely absent." But in China, the opposite had been the case. There, since the human heart was disposed toward deception and evil, the chances for a "great evil" had not only appeared frequently but had plunged the land into regular cycles of disorder, despite the availability of profound doctrines.[23] And it was this Chinese spirit that had redirected the Japanese into the unnatural path of deception and disorder.

Kamo's anxieties turned on what was natural as against what was not. He reversed the received order of the basic Chinese opposition between nature and culture, and found greatest value, which the Chinese had identified with culture, in nature. Since Chinese teachings were not in accord with nature, "they . . . interfere with the continuity of nature [literally, harden nature]."[24] Therefore, the Chinese emphasis upon a morality marked by "benevolence," "honesty," and "knowledge" went against the thrust of nature itself, the movement of the seasons for example, and introduced dangerous discontinuities and rigidities, distinctions and differences that had nothing to do with reality. "It was better," Kamo acknowledged, "to follow the heart of heaven and earth without [recourse to] names."[25] What he seemed to imply is that the Chinese practice of naming, produced by language, theory, and speculation, was itself the reason for the proliferation of differences that had come to cloud the minds of contemporary Japanese. The purpose of this analysis was indeed the promise of a new scholarly discipline that would reveal a more authentic mode of cognition. According to Kamo, cognition as disclosed in the antique poetic experience offered his contemporaries the proper guidelines to map the space of governance. Differences, he

[23] Ibid.   [24] Ibid.   [25] Ibid., p. 384.

[21]

observed, led people into divided purpose; but the upright heart, as he wrote in the last pages of *Kokuikō*, "required little" and was founded on simplicity, the surest defense against the entanglements of division. In the end, China functioned to persuade men to return to wholeness and similitude.

It was this principle of the upright heart, the undivided heart, that informed the purpose of Motoori Norinaga's *Naobi no mitama*. Motoori (1730-1801), the most gifted practitioner of the nativist persuasion, studied with Kamo and undoubtedly brought the study of national learning to its most mature level. Scattered denunciations of China and Confucianism appeared throughout his writings, but *Naobi no mitama*, completed sometime between 1764 and 1772, dealt explicitly with the problem of China, and illustrated the function it was to play in Motoori's consciousness. While his own strategy did not differ from Kamo's, and while they shared a comparable purpose of apprehending the world of things in the modality of similitude, *Naobi no mitama* refined and often enlarged themes that Kamo had only raised. The problem Motoori tried to dramatize was how to rule well. China, he observed, offered a significant example of disorder and illegitimacy, despite the reverence accorded to the Chinese political model by Tokugawa Confucianists; it was, he wrote, a "wrestling arena for wicked *kami*."[26] In China, where custom had become depraved and hearts corrupt, men had been inspired to make revolution. "Thus it happens," he noted, "that even people of lowly origins become rulers. . . . Hence those who are above make provisions so that they are not destroyed by those who are below; while those who are below plot to seize control from those who are above."[27] Indeed, holiness was simply the condition of success, veneration the reward of power. "Thus the so-called holy ones (*seijin*) were nothing more than successful rebels."[28]

In a cynical tone Motoori went on to say that success in maintaining control in China conferred the status of holiness upon the leader. But it would be wrong, he warned, to see these "holy men" as *kami*, as many had believed them to be—for intentionality was vastly different between *kami* and *seijin*. "What these holy men in China devised was the so-called Way. But that which they called the Way had only two goals: to snatch away the realm from others, and to take

[26] Yoshikawa Kōjirō, ed., *Motoori Norinaga shū*, vol. 15 of *Nihon no shisō* (Tokyo, 1969), p. 285.
[27] Ibid.   [28] Ibid., p. 296.

care that their control would not be seized by others."[29] Elsewhere, Motoori argued that the heavenly mandate was simply a contrivance of the *seijin* to destroy the rulers of ancient China and was thus a mask for seizure and illegitimacy. He asked, mockingly and in disbelief, "Could heaven really have spirit and reason?"[30] Motoori's argument struck at the problem of legitimacy (as if to make a distinction from authority); its thrust was to show that the Way, as proposed by the Chinese, was simply an elaborate concealment to justify the ultimate right of "revolution." (I use the term "revolution" merely to indicate, in Motoori's usage, disorder and the change of political rule.) Indeed, the Way remained a "fruitless rumor" among later Confucians. The content of the Way, made up of high-sounding values such as good will, integrity, propriety and modesty, love of parents, respect for kin, loyalty to ruler, and faith in humans, was nothing more than a device to control the people. Chinese elevated the Way to the level of a law for all time to come, but was it ever anything more than the law of that age which invented it?[31]

It was, Motoori believed, a special characteristic of the Chinese to view this antique achievement as the highest kind of wisdom. But rather than understanding the world of things with a pure heart, the Chinese relied upon invention, writing, and making, which ultimately obliged them to pursue everything down to the smallest detail. The result was, of course, further proliferation of differences that set people quarreling with one another and ultimately against each other.[32] To rule in China meant to invite division and disorder; for China, unlike Japan, had known nothing but disorder. "But even scholars in Japan have not yet grasped this [fact] and continue to envy the so-called Way of China," he noted.[33] Chinese intellectual divisiveness had spilled over into Japan, where those who believed there was a Way battled incessantly with those who did not. The trouble was the attraction of Chinese books and the status of scholarship in things Chinese, and particularly the importance of the written word as a representational mediation, and the kind of prestige its mastery conferred. The result was not simply to turn Japanese away from their own traditions as an object of study, but also to prevent them from gaining an adequate understanding of reality. Japan, Motoori concluded, gloomily I suspect, had become China. Indeed,

[29] Ibid., pp. 285-86.　　　　[30] Ibid., p. 292.
[31] Ibid., p. 287.　　　　　　[32] Ibid., p. 288.
[33] Ibid., p. 289.

so thorough was this cultural assimilation that only through religious festivals were ancient Japanese customs and usages preserved. But saturation with Chineseness per se was even more dangerous than the mere obliteration of ancient customs and practices. For Chinese custom had penetrated the very heart of the ordinary person and had diverted his intentions from the will of the emperor. The consequence was a proliferation of differences once more, in the form of each individual following his own impertinent heart.

Motoori hoped to offer some explanation for the randomness of unhappy events. He despaired of Chinese efforts to relate such occurrences to the will of heaven. He attributed failure in the world to the behavior of the *kami*. There was no order or meaning to the distribution of good and evil as it was spread throughout history. And Motoori warned of attempts to understand such phenomena by means of language and principle (theory); all such efforts merely illustrated the limitations of human understanding.[34] Motoori denounced the Chinese belief in "rationality"; it was wonder and silence that promised true understanding and reunification with the intention of the emperor. This was, I believe, what Motoori meant by the upright heart. By contrast, China and its history showed only a long, painful record of usurpations, divided intention, upheaval and invasion. Moreover, the right to establish order and the arrangement of society belonged only to those who seized control and maintained their personal power. Here, Motoori noted the irony of peoples who were called barbarian by the Chinese, but who, once they had seized power, were referred to as the sons of heaven.[35] The absence of any agreed rules concerning rank and status had made the Chinese appear to be closer in their ways to birds and beasts than even those whom they had consigned to that condition, the barbarian peoples surrounding *chūka*.

Ultimately, it was Motoori's purpose to offer his contemporaries the certainty of happiness (*anshin*). The example of China, he argued persistently, demonstrated the prevalence of unhappiness and deception, confusion and disorder, all products of the disposition to understand and explain things in terms of words and principles. To act apart from one's true endowment was to court unhappiness; happiness was naturalness, and its achievement depended upon abandoning teachings and doctrines. "If one wishes to penetrate still further into the spirit of the true Way, then one must purify oneself from the

---

[34] Ibid., p. 294.   [35] Ibid., p. 299.

[24]

filthy spirit of Chinese writings and proceed to the study of the ancient texts [of Japan] with the pure spirit of the sacred land. If that is achieved one will come to know, gradually, that we are not obligated to accept the Way of China. But to know this is to receive the Way of the *kami* itself."[36]

In the end the nativists transformed China to mean the Other; China, which had served metaphorically to convey the sense of civilization as juxtaposed with the rudeness of nature, was transformed into its opposite. Nativists who were to follow in this idiom, notably Hirata Atsutane (1776-1843) and his Neo-Shinto school, turned away from China as a problematique to engage other, more pressing questions of the time. Yet all accepted the vision of China as enunciated by Kamo and Motoori; even Hirata, whose energies went into offering resolutions of problems of social order, did not find it difficult to rank Japan above all countries, not just China. In those texts where he specifically talked about China, such as *Kodō tai-i* and the *Taidō wakumon*, Hirata merely sustained the nativist diatribe against Chinese political practice. The latter text is, in fact, in the mode of Motoori's *Naobi no mitama* and represents a rather long "history" of Chinese political misfortune which he, Hirata, hoped might serve as a demonstration to instruct his contemporaries in the dangers of China worship. Indeed, his *Kamōsho*, written early in the nineteenth century as a bombast against Dazai Shundai's *Bendōsho*, a work noted for its veneration of China, and *Saiseki gairon* (1822) were virulent attacks on China for not having fulfilled the great moral principles of discrimination and for having celebrated a model of political disorder. Hirata's explanations centered around the effort to show that Japan was the source of value and civilization. In the *Kodō tai-i*, for example, he returned to the linguistic argument proposed earlier by Kamo. However, he wanted to show that the ancient Japanese histories were not mere imitations of the Chinese style of writing dynastic accounts. Rather, the Japanese histories (*Nihonshoki, Kojiki*) were records of the age of the gods acted out long before the first Chinese histories were written. At the time the events took place, later to be recorded in the national chronicles, "intent [*kokoro*], deed and word were mutually unified . . . but because they were recast in Chinese words there is much about the true facts of antiquity that we have lost. Still, the *Kojiki*, . . . since it has recorded and transmitted antiquity as it was, has unified intent, deed,

[36] Ibid., p. 312.

and word and remains the first record of the true facts of high antiquity and of ancient words."[37] Hirata's argument aimed at showing that dependence upon Chinese words and concepts could lead only to the very confusions and distortions that characterized Chinese texts. Indeed, Chinese practice separated intention, deed, and word from each other, and elevated the latter to a position of privilege over the former two. Such practice not only distorted the true record, but forced people to "forget about the ancient spirit of Japan." The importance of knowing about antiquity in its true and essential character, Hirata argued, was to be reminded again that Japan, not China, was the real source of civilization. One of the confusions spread by the use of Chinese language had been to see China as inner (*nai*) and Japan as outer (*gai*); yet, Hirata wrote, this was clearly incorrect.[38] Much of this kind of argumentation was preparatory to the assertion that Japan was not simply the most superior country in the world but, owing to the creative energies of the *kami*, was also the source of value and invention. In *Kodō tai-i* (and elsewhere, in *Idō tai-i*, "A summary of the way of medicine") Hirata put forward the curious interpretation that the fourth generation deities, Ōnamochi no kami and Sukunabikona no kami, originated medicine during the age of the gods, and transmitted it to China, from whence it was reimported to Japan.[39]

In the writings of Ōkuni Takamasa (1792-1871), especially in *Shinshin kōhōron*, it was through precisely this kind of argumentation, emphasizing the creative originality of the Japanese deities, that the nativist conception of China was brought to a final resolution. Yet Ōkuni shared with many of his late Tokugawa contemporaries, who were not nativists, the growing belief that China was really not so important for serious discourse; but this, as I will try to show later, grew out of a different kind of strategy.

In *Shinshin kōhōron* (written in 1866 or 1867) Ōkuni confessed to his discovery of "Hyūgo of Holland, who was interested in studies relating to the public law of all nations [international law, *bankoku kōhō*]." Ōkuni was no doubt referring to Hugo Grotius' writings on international law. The occasion for this reference was the Chinese practice which, instead of viewing the nations of the world in terms of some irreducible principle, saw "all nations in terms of two

[37] Muromatsu Iwao et al., eds., *Hirata Atsutane zenshū* (Tokyo, 1912), vol. 1, pp. 18-19.
[38] Ibid.   [39] Ibid., also *Idō tai-i*.

[categories], *chūka* and barbarian, which, for the Chinese, meant honoring their own country and slighting all other countries."[40] Elsewhere, in *Gakuunron*, Ōkuni condemned the Chinese designation of Japan as a dependency or "vassal state" (*zokkoku*). When Ōkuni referred to China in his own writings, he no longer used *chūgoku* or *chūka* but rather *shina*, to designate differentiation but not privilege. Ōkuni was irked by the way the Chinese promoted hierarchical distinction between countries as if it were a "public law" rather than a mere private theory, as it really was. Moreover, Ōkuni claimed, such ideas as the "son of heaven" and "royal family" were also simply expressions of opinion that had no substance. The Chinese called their emperor the son of heaven, but the establishment of an emperor was really due to the "coming and going of the two deities Ōnamochi no kami and Sukunabikona no kami. After the two deities established the principle of kingship, the Chinese descended into pillage and banditry but continued to call their kings sons of heaven."[41] While the term *tenshi* (son of heaven), when used in Japan, had appeared to be an imitation of the Chinese usage, it was, according to Ōkuni, in fact used much earlier in Japan. This argument was Ōkuni's way of getting at the problem of "public law" and announcing that what the West understood as an international law of nations regulating the order of countries and their relations to each other was no more valid than the Chinese idea of *chūka*/barbarian.

The Western conception of *bankoku kōhō* involved the right format but the wrong content. According to Ōkuni, Japan was the source of international law; and Japan's own creation offered the true principles by which to order and regulate the conduct of nations in the world. It was necessary to rank nations in terms of an order, according to a law, but such a law could be found only in Japanese *shintō*.[42] In this connection, Ōkuni argued that true ethics began in Japan, not China, and spread subsequently throughout the several nations. China's rulers, he asserted, recalling Motoori, had deceived and lied. "When one today compares ancient Japan to ancient China," he continued, "Japan was thick and straight; China was thin and bent. The proof of this lies in the Classics of the Chinese dynasties such as the Hsia, Yin, and Chou, where there are no words for loyalty and filiality. . . . In Japan, even though there were no words for loyalty

[40] Ōkuni Takamasa, *Shinshin kōhōron*, in Nihon Shisō Taikei, *Hirata Atsutane, Tomo Nobuyuki, Ōkuni Takamasa* (Tokyo, 1973), vol., 50, p. 497.
[41] Ibid.   [42] Ibid., p. 498.

and filiality, there were in truth parent and sovereign. Since men in Japan were thick and straight, the imperial rule has remained unbroken from the age of the gods down to the present."[43] Ōkuni's argument rested upon the earlier equation between "intention," "deed," and "word" that marked Hirata's *Kodō tai-i*. In antiquity there had been intention and deed; they had been one and the same thing, and the words to express them had also been the same.

Ōkuni justified this theory by reference to the creation myths to which Hirata had only recently given new cosmological expression. He simply expanded the argument that the universe had been created by the *musubi no kami* (creative deities): "The spirit called Ama no minakanushi no kami in Japan is called God [*tenshu*] in the Western regions and is equated with the heavenly sovereigns [*tentei, t'ien-ti*] in China. Following this, those who are called Takami musubi no kami and Kamumi musubi no kami [the two creative deities] in Japan are called the creators [*zōbutsusha*] in China. These heavenly emperors and creators were divided between Izanagi no mikoto and Izanami no mikoto, who gave birth to the 10,000 countries of the world."[44] Thus, according to Ōkuni, despite apparent terminological differences concerning the origin of things, all countries were linked together by homology owing to their common creation.[45] Any order of nations must be based upon this "public" fact. "Japan is the base and thus commands respect; the several countries are the branches and thus are to be despised."[46] Of course, Ōkuni observed, there were many Confucians in Japan who believed that China since ancient times had been the home of the archetypical sages (*sen-ō*); and Westerners too had argued that all sages were inferior to Roman emperors (because they were lawgivers). But in reality only Japan, among all nations, could lay claim to a direct and unbroken succession of rulership from the time of creation. Those "who have agreed to follow the men of China have divided [the world] between *chūka* and barbarian realms," and they have presumed to call the emperors of China sons of heaven. "Once this doctrine crossed over to Japan it elevated China to the level of central florescence and our Japan was considered barbarian. The perversity of Confucianists yielded only one kind of expulsionism [*jōi*]."[47]

Since this view was narrow-minded, petty, and ultimately wrong,

[43] Ibid., pp. 508-509.
[45] Ibid., p. 500.
[47] Ibid., p. 504.

[44] Ibid., pp. 498-99, 501.
[46] Ibid., p. 499.

Ōkuni proposed that as the principles of a true international order had originated in Japan, there were really two kinds of *jōi*: "small expulsionism which depends upon military activity" and "great expulsionism which depends upon the principle of respect and justice." Respect and justice were owed to Japan by virtue of its divine appointment and the common origin of things and nations. Ōkuni's argument on expulsionism had, in part, already been anticipated by Yokoi Shōnan a decade or so earlier, and revealed the outlines of a new and different kind of problematique facing writers and activists in Bakumatsu Japan.

Bakumatsu Japan as Epilogue:
Rehistoricization and the "Disappearance" of China in Discourse

Perhaps it is a bit too strong to suggest simply that China disappeared from discourse in the late Tokugawa period. But in a sense, China, by losing its privileged position in discourse, did "disappear" as an object of serious consideration. While, as we have seen, nativist writers sought to show China as a source of difference and thus discord, they nevertheless continued to accord the subject a principal place in their work. Yet, as I have tried to suggest, this function grew out of a prior strategy to apprehend the world in the modality of similitude. Such an attempt failed in the end, even with the nativist effort to return language to the world of things and deeds, as being merely one thing among a number of things—and gave way to both its own system of transformation (via the recognized impossibility of accounting for new things in this modality) and to discontinuities introduced by the coming of Western states to Japan. But it would be wrong, I think, to place too much emphasis upon the relationship between changes in consciousness and the impact of outside events in the time they occurred. Japanese writers in the late Tokugawa period had first to make sense of China in terms of the epistemological and linguistic strategies available to them. Thus China was seen increasingly as simply an instance of decline. Ōkuni, by referring to China as *shina*, had already shown how far it had been removed from its earlier identification with civilization and excellence. For most late Tokugawa writers, China was simply one more country among the nations of the world, constituting differentiation in one sense, as England, America, or France represented differences, but a nation just the same, like all others. To reach this kind of conclusion was possible only insofar as writers could appeal to a different modality

[29]

of representation. By late Tokugawa times the search for similitudes had given way to the acknowledged primacy of differences; the problem that thought had already begun to set for itself was the resolution of differentness. And it did so by disposing the world of things in the modality of contiguity, not of continuity—that is, in categories of order and measurement, conceived in spatial terms. Representation sought discriminations, that is, identities, which established the inevitability of the connections between all successive degrees of a series.

To see China as *shina*, and as an instance of decline, was merely the result of seeing things in a series of contiguities leading to political misfortune. The real problem was not China, nor indeed any country per se, but the connections and linkages, origins and effects, in a series, the relationship between signs and what they signified in the hope that by knowing them they might yield to control. This is surely the meaning of Sakuma Shōzan's (1811-1864) appeal to the imagery of the *I Ching* to explain disorder. "If we grasp the currents and developments of the times," he wrote, "we will be able to fore-tell disorder." In this passage Sakuma resorted to a play on words which, if read differently, evoked the lesson of the *I Ching* that too much use of a bowl or vessel would "give rise to worms" and thus decay.[48] Moreover, this was the purpose behind the intensity of con-cern for the "investigation of things" (*kakubutsu kyūri*) which characterized his own efforts and those of so many of his contem-poraries in the late Tokugawa period. With Sakuma, as with Hashimoto Sanai and Yokoi Shōnan, metaphysical surety, not em-pirical certainty, defined the modality. Yet this new disposition led to a search for empirical verification in measurement.

Among all, Sakuma, I believe, disclosed most clearly the contours of the new strategy and what it meant for discourse. The result was a method in which things were investigated and thus were seen in their particularity, in their identity, in their differentness, but also in a series of contiguities.

In a Chinese poem written in 1844, Sakuma proposed that both Westerners and Chinese were, for Japanese, foreign or different. If this were the case, how could Chinese learning, or indeed China itself, be called "within" (*nai*) and judged good, while Western learning be called "outer" (*gai*) and judged bad? Sakuma's insistence on Japan's differentness, its independence (one was a condition of the

---

[48] Shinano Kyōikukai, ed., *Shōzan zenshū* (Nagano, 1922), vol. 1, p. 304.

other), indeed the differentness of all nations, would permit inquiry into the "conditions of the world," without fear of privileged spheres.

To release inquiry into the world from its moorings in rigid categories imposed by Chinese learning, it was essential for Japanese to draw out their own individuality from the Orient. Such a liberation, founded on the full acceptance of differences that had to be explained, involved a repudiation of the earlier Mito insistence on the civilization/barbarism opposition that so many late Tokugawa writers accepted without question. Much of this sentiment was expressed in Sakuma's *Seiken roku*, where he described his reactions and disgust upon reading Wei Yüan's *Hai-kuo t'u-chih*. Sakuma could sympathize with Wei's efforts to assist China in its new needs, but he was quick to call attention to the conceits that prevented Wei and the Chinese from meeting the problems of defense. But the issue was not simply defense, but understanding. The Chinese, Sakuma remarked, could not take the West seriously.[49] By this he meant that the Ch'ing state had failed because it had not understood the meaning of Western skills and what their mastery really required. Sakuma's well-known phrase, "Oriental morality for the base, Western skills for use," meant not the priority of the one over the other, but rather their equivalence. That is, they were to be connected in terms of uses and functions, to complete "a circular pattern so that half of the earth should not be missing," as he said in the second half of his famous slogan.

China had not been prepared for the first Anglo-Chinese War, due to seeing the world in terms of the civilization/barbarism opposition, in which the Chinese were obliged not only to rate themselves as superior in knowledge but also to see foreigners as unworthy of serious consideration. Indeed, Sakuma would point to China time and time again as an example of how older strategies of cognition had failed. The decline of the Ch'ing state was simply a dramatic manifestation of this mind-set.

In this context, Sakuma proposed the idea that mathematics was the only basis for all learning and investigation. Even Sun Tzu, he tried to show, had recognized the importance of "measurement." It was evident that mathematics was the means by which to order things in specific, spatial sequences, to define their relationships and connections. It was the science par excellence for establishing contiguities between different things, that is, relating different things to each

[49] Ibid., pp. 13-14.

other. This is what Sakuma ultimately meant when he deployed the Neo-Confucian conception of investigation of things (*kakubutsu kyūri*).

It was this technique that permitted Sakuma to see things in their differentness, their individuality: to see Japan as simply part of a larger order, or a commonwealth of countries. Japan, he asserted, should no longer be associated with Oriental culture. Rather Japan was merely that which is "ours" united to a new kind of reality. By conforming to the true principles, which were accepted by the "several countries of the five continents," Sakuma argued, Japan would in fact revive the lesson that had been formulated by Sung thinkers when they had advised men "to investigate all things on earth if understanding is to be achieved." (This interpretation itself was a dramatic repudiation of the received idea that one principle illuminated the ten thousand things.)

This new conception was demonstrated in Sakuma's ultimate denunciation of the *chūka*/barbarian opposition, which Mito writers, and a number of shogunal officials, had not yet abandoned in their dealings with the representatives of Western nations. Irritated by continued usage of the term barbarian in official documents, he wrote: "Now that we have frequent contact with foreign countries, I wish that official correspondence would be drafted with more special care . . . for the appellations used are not at all suitable for these countries." As an earlier adept of the Mito learning, he knew that such usage was inspired by Chinese practice and was intended to dramatize the difference between civilization and barbarism. But the Chinese were mistaken, as he argued in *Seiken roku*, and now that he was proceeding from a new strategy, he could say that barbarian "countries possess arts, learning, legal systems and culture superior to those of the Chinese."[50] To Yanagawa Seigan, elegant littérateur in the Chinese style and self-styled "loyalist," he explained his position: "The foreigner today has come out ahead of the Chinese in learning and skills. He has clarified and explained things which the Classics have not yet illuminated."[51] How new this view was in the late Tokugawa can best be illustrated by calling attention to Aizawa Seishisai's contention in the *Shinron*, the classic text of the Mito school, written in 1825. Aizawa pointed out that in certain cases "name and loyalty are darkened," and that one such case was "Ming and Ch'ing China which still calls itself *chūka*," and where the "*kokutai*

[50] Ibid., pp. 244-45.   [51] Ibid., vol. 2, p. 487.

has been defiled." But Japan was independent and preserved the name of civilization.[52] In other words, Aizawa, unable to see the principle of difference, was content to argue that despite China's own failings, Japan represented the last sanctuary of *chūka*.

Even more than Sakuma Shōzan, Yokoi Shōnan (1809-1869) was prepared to see China simply as an example of what Japan should avoid. Yokoi, perhaps unlike Sakuma, was moved more by events on the continent and what they revealed. China, he believed, had not followed through in the investigative techniques established by the sages of the Three Dynasties. And it was the discovery of such techniques that truly corresponded to the Way found in all civilized countries. Yokoi had already, in 1853, shaken off much of the dust of the Mito argument, and while he was still disposed to see things in terms of the civilization/barbarism opposition, he had changed the meaning of what really constituted the content of each. The world was divided between countries that pursued virtue and those that did not. Yokoi objected to the kind of principles that earlier had differentiated between *chūka* and barbarian, and concluded that Japan, as well as other nations, possessed virtue. But virtue meant the desire to open trade and communication with another country; this was a sign of civilization, not barbarism.[53] It was, Yokoi believed, private management, not public law, that drove countries such as China and Japan to discourage contact and relations with other nations. The result of this short-sightedness, now stalking contemporary China, was the doom that awaited Japan:

> Ever since ancient times, the Chinese have slighted the barbarians and accorded them the status of birds and beasts. At the end of Tao-kuang's reign, the Chinese were badly beaten by the British during the Opium War and thus, unavoidably, were forced to sign a peace treaty. But the Chinese did not keep their promises and continued in their ways, showing at all times their contempt toward the British. . . . They committed additional insolence by assassinating a British consul, and this merely angered the British all the more. Four months later [the British] were joined by the French and struck out against these wrongs and faithlessness. The allies, in the end, occupied Peking . . . and China became an empire in name only.[54]

[52] Aizawa Seishisai, *Shinron*, in Nihon Shisō Taikei, *Mitogaku* (Tokyo, 1973), vol. 53, p. 67.
[53] Yamazaki Masashige, ed., *Yokoi Shōnan ikō* (Tokyo, 1943), p. 11.
[54] Ibid., p. 40.

Escape from this kind of self-centeredness was provided by the ideal of a benevolent polity (*jinsei*) and by the examples of the Three Dynasties, Yao, Shun, and a new member of this universal pantheon, George Washington, who, Yokoi said, understood the true principle of "public interest" that bound all nations together. Whereas Sakuma believed that investigative principles comparable to measurement had been worked out in the Sung, Yokoi moved the pedigree back to the Three Dynasties. But in both cases China, as a metaphor for civilization, had disappeared in favor of a conception of a world community in which universal principles made possible linkages and connections between different states.

Finally, the specter of a ruined China, long removed from claims to civilization (a conception that itself was consigned to the rubbish heap of a useless history) and now under the control of the very barbarians once despised, was the subject of Takasugi Shinsaku's (1838-1867) *Yushin goroku*, written in the spring of 1862. Takasugi was an activist and loyalist from Chōshū, whose leadership in the civil wars would no doubt have earned for him a leading position in the Meiji government had he not died of illness in 1867. He had been a troublesome student of Yoshida Shōin's, an associate and close friend of Kusaka Genzui's, a leader of the Chōshū loyalists in Kyoto in the early 1860's, and one of the leaders of the "conscription" forces in Chōshū during the first and second punitive wars with the bakufu.

In the spring of 1862, Takasugi was taken away from radical loyalist activity and sent to China, to serve as an attendant to a shogunal official, on the ship *Senzai Maru*, bound for Shanghai on a desperate mission to investigate trade possibilities in China. During the trip Takasugi kept an elaborate diary, divided into five separate records, representing the five episodes of the trip. While he stayed only two months in Shanghai, he seems to have spoken to an army of people (even though he knew no spoken Chinese or English; in the case of the former he has left us records of his encounters in which the communicative medium was written Chinese). Takasugi was a sensitive and, I believe, dispassionate witness to the virtual collapse of the Ch'ing state. The entries in the diary offer abundant testimony that although it seemed to rain nearly every day during his stay in Shanghai, Takasugi was uncomplaining and greatly interested in what he saw and was able to evaluate. The city, he observed, showed signs of strain from Western incursions and the Taiping rebellion that was still being suppressed by the dynasty.

Moreover, he noted China's dependence upon the English, especially for arms and skills, in the struggle with the "long-haired rebels."[55] The wealth of the city was concentrated in the hands of foreign merchants who were interested only in "private profit."

In Shanghai, Takasugi also saw Chinese who should have held positions of authority (according to his record of a discussion with a Chinese named Li I-chou)[56] who instead were impoverished and working in the most menial jobs. "In viewing earnestly the conditions [of the city], I have observed Chinese serving foreigners, and Englishmen strutting along the streets of the city. The Chinese are avoided in the streets and their ways have been replaced. In reality, though the territory of Shanghai is part of China, it should be said to belong to the English and the French."[57] Takasugi expressed his fears in a short poem addressed to himself: "Will it not be like this in our country?" What was worse, he noted, was Chinese reliance upon Western powers. He remarked, in the diary, that even though the Chinese possessed Wei Yüan's *Hai-kuo t'u-chih* (illustrated gazetteer of maritime countries), they had failed to plan a defense capable of protecting the country from within and without. In fact, the Chinese lacked any understanding of Western armaments. Two wars had been fought with the foreigners and lost. Owing to obstinacy and idleness, "they did not know how to absorb the new foreign studies." The Chinese in the Shanghai area, faced with a large-scale rebellion, had simply been driven into the arms of the British and the French—an observation Takasugi made several times. Takasugi and his companions returned to Nagasaki in July of 1862, but before departing from Shanghai they had decided that it was unwise for the Japanese to attack or reject foreign culture as unworthy, as had the Chinese. Rather, Takasugi advocated the establishment of industries and a new program of foreign trade between Japan and the rest of the world as the surest means of avoiding the colonial status into which China had sunk. He concluded, predictably I think, that the decline of the Ch'ing state resulted from the Chinese "not knowing ways to resist the foreigner."

Just before he left for Shanghai, Takasugi had written a remarkable poem in Chinese: "To begin to follow Western words, one must pledge oneself to abstain from reading books in Chinese and Japa-

[55] Naramoto Tatsuya, ed., *Takasugi Shinsaku zenshū* (Tokyo, 1974), vol. 2, pp. 161-62. Especially entry for June 14.
[56] Ibid., pp. 195-204. The conversation is recorded in Chinese.
[57] Ibid., p. 173.

nese."[58] It is ironic that just at the moment when China was being "rehistoricized," Takasugi should have given expression to a view that formed a fitting climax to the whole process of China's "dehistoricization" in Tokugawa intellectual discourse. The effect of this development on subsequent Japanese perceptions of China can hardly be exaggerated.

[58] Ibid., p. 400. This is a Chinese poem written by Takasugi sometime in the spring of 1862, just as he entered a foreign language school in Nagasaki in preparation for his trip to Shanghai.

CHAPTER II

SINO-JAPANESE RIVALRY
IN KOREA, 1876-1885

━━━

BONNIE B. OH

IN 1885 a treaty was signed between China and Japan that allowed them equal rights of military interference in Korea.[1] This ended the first phase of modern Sino-Japanese interactions over Korea. It had begun when Japan attempted to modernize its antiquated mode of relationship with the hermit kingdom. Korean intransigence in refusing to deal with the new Japan had provoked the angry outcry of *seikanron* in Japan in 1873,[2] and resulted in the gunboat diplomacy which forced the Treaty of Kanghwa on Korea in 1876.[3] The treaty was an open, formal challenge to traditional Chinese-Korean relations and gave rise to an intense rivalry between China and Japan over Korea. This rivalry lasted almost two decades, until the Sino-Japanese War of 1894-95 settled the question through force of arms. But it was during the eight years between 1876 and 1884 that patterns for this keen rivalry and for Korean response were set. The two countries invariably used arguments that suited them, China insisting on the tributary relationship and Japan on modern treaties; took turns in advancing and retreating; and jointly intervened whenever there were internal disturbances in Korea. Koreans reacted by procrastination, by appeasement, and by what they thought was temporary capitulation.

In this short period, China's policy underwent two changes: first

---

[1] The Tientsin Convention (also known as the Li-Itō Convention). For the text, see Carnegie Endowment for International Peace, *Korea, Treaties and Agreements* (Washington, D.C., 1921), pp. 7-8.

[2] Tabohashi Kiyoshi, *Kindai Nis-Sen kankei no kenkyū* (Keijo, 1940), vol. 1, pp. 133-97.

[3] *Treaties, Regulations, etc., Between Corea and Other Powers 1876-1889* (Shanghai, 1891), p. 1.

from noninterference to giving advice and assistance, and then to active interference in Korean politics. Japan moderated its initial policy of applying pressure to have Korea implement all the treaty terms, and began emphasizing efforts "to influence, direct and stimulate reform in Korea."[4] There was considerable diversity in the Korean response to external challenges, but this diversity, unlike that in bakumatsu Japan, could not constructively influence the government's policies, due to the extremely centralized nature of Korean politics. In time, opposing opinions were brutally suppressed by the government, which was itself torn among rival factions bent upon political domination. In order to strengthen its position, each group would rely on the support of foreign countries—China, Japan, and occasionally other powers—and constantly shifted sides according to political expediency.

The Opening of Korea by Japan

Because of their geographic proximity, Korea had always had contact with Japan. But unlike its relations with China, Korea's relations with Japan were those between equal neighbors. This relationship was succinctly described as *kyorin* (befriending the neighboring country), whereas Korea's relationship with China was known as *sadae* (serving the great). *Kyorin* may be regarded as a scale model of the tributary system in which Korea was the overlord over Tsushima *han* of Japan, the only agent permitted to communicate with the magistrate of Tongnae in the southeastern tip of Korea. It was conducted in strict observance of Confucian decorum and intricate formalities, including such practices as avoiding the use of characters in the personal names of kings of the Yi dynasty and Tsushima's use of the seal conferred upon it by the Korean government.[5] Tsushima found this practice humiliating but continued it because of its economic advantages.

Following the Meiji Restoration, Japan's management of Korean affairs was formally transferred to the foreign office, and upon the suggestion of the daimyō of Tsushima, the Japanese government sought to reform the old practices and establish a direct route of intercourse with Korea. An advance messenger bearing a letter was sent in late 1868 to warn the magistrate of Tongnae of the intended

---

[4] Marius B. Jansen, *Japan and China: From War to Peace, 1894-1972* (Chicago, 1975), p. 114.

[5] *Nis-Sen tsūkō shi* (Fusan, 1915), vol. 1, pp. 649-53.

change, to obtain the approval of the new seal, and to inform him of the coming of the ambassador. The letter read in part:

> In our country times have changed completely. Political power has been restored to the imperial house [kōshitsu].[6] A special ambassador shall bring you news of that event. . . . I was summoned by imperial edict [choku][7] to manage diplomatic affairs with your country . . . and also grant the official warrant and seal. The letter which the ambassador will bring bears the *new seal*.[8]

But Korea was then under the rule of the Taewŏn'gun (Grand Prince), the de facto regent and the father of the king,[9] who pursued a firm closed-door policy. The magistrate at Tongnae would not even accept the letter because of its improper style and the new seal, and would not let the ambassador proceed to Seoul. For the next few years numerous meetings were held at Tongnae, but all in vain. They only led to a deterioration of feelings on both sides.

Late in 1872 Hanabusa Yoshitada, vice-minister of foreign affairs, was instructed to go to Korea. He was sent aboard a warship, accompanied by a steamship carrying two infantry platoons. This reflected the rising feeling of belligerency on the part of samurai in Japan.[10] The appearance of steamships and the show of force only further stiffened the Korean attitude, for they reminded the Koreans of the dreaded Western invaders. This time the men aboard were from Tokyo, the seat of the new Japanese government, with which Koreans desired no relations.[11] The magistrate of Tongnae ordered all Koreans to boycott the market in the Japanese settlement, called the Japan House. Formal relations between Japan and Korea seemed to be at an end.

Koreans considered the Westernized Japanese shameless and felt

[6] *Huang-shih* in Chinese and *huang-sil* in Korean.

[7] *Ch'ih* in Chinese and *chik* in Korean.

[8] Emphasis mine.

[9] Ching Young Ch'oe, *The Rule of the Taewŏn'gun, 1864-1873* (Cambridge, Mass., 1972).

[10] A Sada Hauchi suggested in 1870 that Japan should send thirty battalions of samurai to Korea to demonstrate imperial glory. Sada's memorial, May 15, 1870, *Nihon gaikō bunsho* (Hereafter cited as *NGB*; Tokyo, 1936-56), vol. 3, pp. 138-40. These belligerent feelings climaxed in early 1873 when a Yokoyama Yasumu committed suicide after presenting a memorial to the emperor urging revenge for Korean insults. The memorial is quoted in Ōkawa Nobuyoshi, ed., *Dai Saigō zenshū* (Tokyo, 1926-27), vol. 3, p. 717.

[11] Korea, Pibyŏnsa and Uijŏngbu, comp., *Tongnae kyerok* (Seoul, 1849-89), October 21, 1872.

that they should no longer even be called Japanese because of changes in their appearance and customs. Judging by its recent behavior, the warnings continued, the country was lawless, whereas there was still law in Korea. Therefore,

> If those who are living in the Japan House want to do things according to law, they shall never be troubled. If they do things against the law, they shall be constrained . . . and shall take the consequences for whatever may happen.[12]

This proclamation resembles Commissioner Lin Tse-hsü's exhortations to Queen Victoria in 1839, in which he said, "if they [the English] wish to do business . . . [they] are required to obey our statutes. . . ."[13] Like the Chinese commissioner in 1839, Koreans felt justified in insisting on Japanese observance of traditional law.

Difficulty between Korea and Japan in this period was actually a conflict between tradition and modernity. If the old indirect way of intercourse was unacceptable to Japan in the process of modernization, Japan's proposals for change were even more unthinkable to the Koreans under the Taewŏn'gun's rule, which was aimed at restoring the traditional order and repelling the barbarians with a staunch anti-foreign stand and closed-door policy. To the Taewŏn'gun Japan appeared a traitor to Eastern civilization, no better than the detestable Western barbarians who had given him trouble in the 1860's. But most of all, the Koreans could not let the Japanese use the terms *huang* (emperor) and *ch'ih* (imperial order), which they considered to be reserved exclusively for Chinese emperors. The elevation of the Japanese ruler to the same rank as the Chinese emperor implied, of course, the inferior position of the Korean king to the Japanese ruler, which the ritual-conscious Korean Confucian officials could not tolerate.[14]

Korean intransigence aroused the spirit of the less restrained Japanese officers and officials temporarily in charge during the absence of other high officials as members of the Iwakura mission, and precipitated the bitter *seikanron* or "conquer-Korean-argument" in Japan in 1873.[15] Its advocates' main argument was that Korea was important for the future security of Japan. Despite the heated debate, however,

---

[12] *NGB*, vol. 6, pp. 280-83, doc. 119.

[13] John K. Fairbank and Ssu-yu Teng, *China's Response to the West* (Cambridge, Mass., 1954), p. 27.

[14] Ch'oe, *Taewŏn'gun*, pp. 130ff.

[15] Tabohashi, *Nis-Sen kankei*, vol. 1, pp. 133-97; *NGB*, vol. 9, pp. 690-97.

no immediate punitive expedition against Korea took place. The jingoistic group eventually lost out to the moderates, who, returning from a world tour, took the more realistic view that Japan could not yet undertake overseas military expeditions.

In the same year, an important political change took place in Korea also. The Taewŏn'gun, who had maintained tight control over the government since 1863, was pressured out of power. He had instituted numerous reforms while pursuing the closed-door policy; but while the reforms were aimed at rejuvenating the declining dynasty by restoring the traditional order, his means were often nontraditional and came under severe attack from many Confucian scholars.[16] Kojong's queen began recruiting these dissident scholar-officials and her relatives for an eventual showdown with her father-in-law, whose rule she resented especially after the king had reached maturity of sixteen *se* (*sui* in Chinese) in 1866. The opposition to the Taewŏn'gun had begun to brew earlier, but it was not until late 1873 that open attacks on the king's father began. It is doubtful that the *seikanron* in Japan was directly responsible for the Taewŏn'gun's downfall, because the documents attacking him concentrated entirely on his internal policies.[17]

The fall of the Taewŏn'gun did not portend as drastic a change as might be expected or has been believed.[18] Even in foreign affairs there was little change during the first year of the Mins' rise to power. It was only upon receiving a warning from China about a rumored Japanese invasion of Korea and after the violent death of the Min clan chief Min Sung-ho that the Korean government changed its policy toward Japan. Korean fears and Japanese concern over the rumored imminent return of the Taewŏn'gun drew the two governments together. But even then the Korean government procrastinated so long[19] that by the end of 1875 the Japanese government had become convinced that nothing less than a real danger of invasion, close

---

[16] Ch'oe Ik-hyŏn (1833-1906) memorialized the throne in 1866 against the Taewŏn'gun's massive program of palace reconstruction and issuing of worthless *tangbaekchŏn* (only 1/5 of the legal value of the regular currency in use and only 1/20 of the face value of the metal) to finance his internal reform projects. Yi Hi-sung et al., eds., *Han'guk inmyŏng tae sajŏn* (Seoul, 1967), p. 957; Song Sang-do, *Kiro sup'il* (Seoul, 1955), pp. 95-104; Ch'oe, *Taewŏn'gun*, p. 177.

[17] Ch'oe, *Taewŏn'gun*, pp. 167-68.

[18] Because of the Mins' strong anti-Taewŏn'gun stand, they have been credited with more reforms than were actually undertaken by them. Tabohashi, *Nis-Sen kankei*, vol. 1, pp. 133-35; *NGB*, vol. 8, p. 101, July 2, 1875.

[19] *NGB*, vol. 8, p. 101, July 2, 1875. The Min appointees to the Tongnae were little different in their anti-Japanese attitude.

to the capital of Korea, would compel the Koreans to abandon their old stand. An incident had to be contrived to open fire in order to convince them of the danger of invasion and the futility of their resistance. It was for this purpose that a group of Japanese warships was dispatched again to Korea, this time near the Inch'ŏn harbor, close to the capital, in September 1875.

Three warships were sent in utmost secrecy, and one of them, *Unyō*, appeared on the western coast near Seoul on September 20. What followed was the celebrated *Unyō* incident in which the first artillery shots were exchanged between the poorly equipped Korean coast guards and the Japanese warship.[20] The exaggerated report of the *Unyō* incident aroused another wave of popular outrage in Japan which demanded immediate retaliation against Korea. Even some of the former anti-*seikanron* leaders urged positive action from the Japanese government, which obliged by dispatching a military expedition to deal directly with the Koreans. Simultaneously, the Japanese government sent a separate mission, headed by Mori Arinori, to China, first of all to inform the Chinese government of the purposes and strictly peaceful intentions of the mission to Korea, secondly to seek Chinese cooperation to influence Korea, and finally to clarify China's view on the status of Korea.[21]

As might be expected, the third objective of Mori's mission— defining the status of Korea—took most of his time with the Chinese officials. They took the same position they had expounded earlier to the Western powers, namely that Korea was an independent as well as a tributary state.[22] When Mori boldly asked what the attitude of China would be in the event of an outbreak of armed hostilities between Japan and Korea, Prince Kung, the head of the Tsungli Yamen, replied, "although China does not interfere with Korea's governmental affairs, *China is always concerned with the safety of Korea.*"[23] In another letter to Mori, Prince Kung invoked the Sino-Japanese treaty of 1871 and claimed that, being a tributary of China, *Korea belonged to China.*[24] Mori maintained, on the other hand, that the Japanese government considered Korea independent enough to be able to negotiate alone.[25]

Mori decided to draw on the influence of Li Hung-chang, the imperial commissioner of the northern ports. Since 1870, Li had mas-

[20] Ibid., vol. 11, pp. 129-33.
[21] Tabohashi, *Nis-Sen kankei*, vol. 1, pp. 516-18.
[22] *NGB*, vol. 12, pp. 144-45.   [23] Ibid., p. 165.
[24] Ibid., p. 167.   [25] Ibid.

terminded China's diplomatic and military affairs along the northern coast, and would continue to do so for the next quarter of a century.[26] His abilities as a diplomat were well known to foreign representatives at Peking, and few of them en route there failed to pay formal visits to him at his office at Tientsin, the maritime gateway to the capital of the Chinese empire.[27] So it was only natural that Mori would want to consult Li when his negotiations with the Tsungli Yamen reached a deadlock. Li expressed his desire to cooperate but warned that Japan should moderate its position. "If Japan should make war, not only Russia but China too would send troops to Korea."[28] However, he promised Mori that he would work for a satisfactory solution.

The motive behind Li's agreement to use his influence is worth noting. Even before Mori's visit, Li had sent a communication to the Tsungli Yamen in which he observed that both Japan and Korea were ill-disposed and thus war might easily ensue.[29] Korea was no match for Japan and probably would ask for assistance from China—as in the sixteenth century when Japan invaded Korea.[30] To avoid such a crisis, Li considered it advisable that the Yamen immediately dispatch a confidential communication to the government in Seoul, counseling it either to have forbearance and to receive the Japanese envoy with proper courtesy or to send an envoy to Japan to explain the entire incident so that resentment and suspicion might be dispelled and peace assured. As to whether or not Korea should start trade relations with Japan, Li thought it a matter that should be left to its own decision and that China was not in a position to intervene.[31]

[26] Kwang-ching Liu, "Li Hung-chang in Chihli: The Emergence of a Policy," in Immanuel C. Y. Hsü, ed., *Readings in Modern Chinese History* (New York, 1971), p. 237.

[27] Ibid.

[28] Li was referring to a rumor that Russia was moving its forces near the mouth of the Amur river. Li Hung-chang, *Li Wen-chung kung ch'üan-chi* (Nanking, 1905; Taipei reprint, 1962). The collection includes Li's memorials (*ts'ou-kao*), letters to friends and colleagues (*p'eng-liao han-kao*), letters to the admiralty (*hai-chün han-kao*), letters to the Tsungli Yamen (*i-shu han-kao*), and telegrams (*tien-kao*). Except for the *ts'ou-kao* and *tien-kao*, which have the same initials when abbreviated, all documents are quoted with initials, i.e., *ISHK*, etc. Li, *ISHK*, 4:38a, January 24, 1876.

[29] Ibid., 4:30b, January 19, 1876.

[30] Not to help the dependency would be slighting it, but to send troops to help Korea would arouse Japan, thus causing it to attack Korea. Li also was concerned that if Korea were invaded by Japan, Manchuria might become the next target. Thus, losing the dependency would have been a situation akin to the saying, "When lips are gone the teeth will be cold." Li, *ISHK*, 4:30b, January 19, 1876.

[31] Ibid., 4:30a-31b, January 19, 1876.

Li's recommendation, adopting a more positive policy toward Korea, was impelled primarily by concern for China's own security.[32] But Li had not realized the far-reaching implications of his proposal: by urging a change in the old "hands-off" policy in order to keep Korea in its traditional relationship with China, he was, in fact, undermining the traditional relationship itself.

While Mori Arinori was sounding out the Chinese government in Peking, the Japanese mission to Korea arrived at Kanghwa island at the end of January 1876. Surprisingly, the local Korean officials received them cordially. Two days later two Korean delegates were named and negotiations began on February 10.

After lengthy arguments from both sides concerning the responsibility for the *Unyō* incident, the Japanese delegates proposed the signing of a Western-style treaty, which they explained was necessary to assure lasting friendship between the two neighbors. After a few minor modifications were made in the Japanese-prepared text at the request of the Korean delegates and compromise reached on the use of a new seal of the king,[33] the treaty of amity known as the Treaty of Kanghwa was signed on February 27, 1876.

The treaty, consisting of twelve articles, opened three Korean ports for trade with Japan, provided for the establishment of diplomatic relations, and granted Japan the privilege of making a coastal survey.[34] Its single most important article was the first, which declared, "Corea being an independent state enjoys the same sovereign rights as does Japan."[35] Significantly, Korea used its own dynastic year, not the Chinese calendar year, in dating the document. The treaty was clearly conceived within the modern Western framework of international relations, although it is doubtful whether Korea or even China was fully aware of its implications and possible consequences. But Japan, in its attempt to challenge China's theoretical superiority in East Asia, found modern Western concepts of international relations useful as a wedge to separate Korea from China. As an Eastern state, Japan was cognizant of the extreme ambiguity of the terms expressing traditional relations in the Far East, such as *cha-ju chi-bang* (*tzu-chu chih-pang* in Chinese), and was able to exploit

[32] Li's positive policy at this time was nothing more than giving advice to Korea. But he was the first of the Chinese officials to see a real danger in Korea.

[33] A new seal was made for the occasion as a result of a compromise.

[34] Yi Pyŏng-do, *Han'guk sa taekwan* (Seoul, 1964), pp. 478-79.

[35] John M. Maki, *Selected Documents on Far Eastern Relations (1689-1951)* (Seattle, 1957), p. 102.

this convenient weakness. The phrase, which literally means "a self-governing area or state," could also be used to mean "an independent state." Because of the familiarity of the terms used in the most important provision, neither the Koreans nor the Chinese perceived any serious break in traditional Sino-Korean relations. China in fact considered it an affirmation of the long-established practice.[36]

Chinese Reaction to the Japanese Challenge, 1879-1882

China failed to respond swiftly to Japan's challenge to its unique position in Korea. This failure was due to many factors.[37] But most importantly it was caused by the fact that the affairs of Korea, a tributary state, were managed by the Board of Rites, which communicated with the Tsungli Yamen which in turn consulted the commissioner of northern ports on difficult problems. However, Li Hung-chang was not put in charge of Korea even after he, as commissioner, became responsible for the defense of the capital district of China and Manchuria, the homeland of the ruling dynasty. Still, he was concerned with the security of the Korean peninsula, regarding it as "the protective fence," the first line of defense for China. As Li and other responsible authorities perceived the problem, Korea could be preserved under Chinese domination by twofold measures:[38] by scrupulous maintenance of the status quo and by careful preservation of peace in the Far East. Two policy lines emerged. One, China should negotiate with foreign powers, urging them to recognize Korea's special relationship with China and pledge not to violate the former's territorial integrity. Two, China should advise and assist Korea to abandon its isolationism and instead conclude treaties with foreign powers. Both of Li's policy lines were implemented only gradually.

While the Chinese were undecided whether to intervene actively in the affairs of dependent states, the Japanese stepped up their activities by systematically implementing the 1876 treaty with Korea. But in 1879, when Japan formally annexed the Liu-ch'iu islands, Chinese policy toward Korea finally began to change.[39] In that

[36] T. C. Lin, "Lin Hung-chang: His Korea Policy," in Immanuel C. Y. Hsü, ed., *Readings*, pp. 278-79.

[37] In the late 1870's China was preoccupied with problems with Britain, France, and Russia.

[38] Lin, "Li Hung-chang," *Readings*, p. 273.

[39] The Liu-ch'iu (Ryūkyū in Japanese) islands had been a vassal of both China and Japan, to China since 1372 and to Japan since 1609. For more on the status of

year, the management of Korean affairs was transferred from the Board of Rites to the direct supervision and control of the commissioner of the northern ports and the minister to Japan.[40] From then on Li Hung-chang became the main authority on Korea. He was the official to whom the minister in Japan and, later, the commissioner of trade in Korea referred all matters concerning Korea.

In August, Li expressed his anxiety in his communication to the Tsungli Yamen:

> As the Liu-ch'ius have been annexed, Korea is in a position of imminent danger. In view of this and of the growing interest of the Occidental nations in Korea, we can no longer refrain from devising ways and means for the security of Korea.[41]

This concern over Korea was echoed by another prominent official in China, Ting Jih-ch'ang, governor-general in charge of the defense of the south.[42] Such public pronouncements by high officials in charge of foreign affairs also reflected *ch'ing-i*[43] criticism, which began in the 1860's and became louder as China steadily lost its former dependencies.

As soon as Li became the key official in charge of Korean policy, he began giving advice and assistance to Korea. He urged the Korean government to negotiate treaties with the Western powers so that Korea's international relations would become multinational, thus avoiding dominance by any one treaty power.[44] The first opportunity came in 1880 when the United States commissioned Commodore R. W. Shufeldt to attempt anew the establishment of treaty rela-

---

the islands, see Ueda Toshio, "Ryūkyū no kisoku o meguru Nis-Shin kōshō," *Tōyō bunka kenkyūjo kiyō*, vol. 2 (September 1950), pp. 151-201.

[40] *Ch'ing-chi wai-chiao shih-liao*, ed. and comp. by Wang Yen-wei and Wang Liang (Hereafter cited as *WCSL*; Peiping, 1935), 25:1-3, February 23, 1881.

[41] Li, *ISHK*, 9:34, August 29, 1879.

[42] Arthur W. Hummel, ed., *Eminent Chinese of the Ch'ing Period* (Washington, D.C., 1943), pp. 721-22. Ting Jih-ch'ang should be distinguished from Admiral Ting Ju-ch'ang.

[43] *Ch'ing-i* was a political tradition dedicated to the expression of elite opinion on public questions. As such, it is generally believed that *ch'ing-i* advocates appeared only in the second half of the 1870's, but there was a similar group of scholar-officials who, in the early 1860's, advocated an uncompromising war policy. Masataka Banno, *China and the West, 1858-1861: The Origins of the Tsungli Yamen* (Cambridge, Mass., 1964), p. 67; Lloyd Eastman, *Throne and Mandarins: China's Search for a Policy during the Sino-French Controversy, 1880-1885* (Cambridge, Mass., 1967), p. 4.

[44] Li, *ISHK*, 11:42-45, December 22, 1880.

tions with Korea. The United States government had first approached Japan to obtain its good offices for a favorable decision from the hermit kingdom. Informed that this approach had not been successful,[45] Li immediately sent a timely invitation to Shufeldt, offering to use his influence to secure a treaty from Korea.[46] He pointed out to the Korean government that an American treaty would be a counterbalance to that with Japan[47] and would thus serve as a model for Korea's relations with other countries. He further told the Koreans that the United States had no territorial ambitions in Korea.[48]

The treaty, which was negotiated and agreed upon mainly between Li Hung-chang and Shufeldt at Tientsin, was delivered to Korea aboard a Chinese naval vessel and signed by the Korean government on May 22, 1882.[49] This Treaty of Peace, Amity, Commerce, and Navigation between the United States and Korea, consisting of fourteen articles, established more than one precedent. Not only did it serve as a model upon which other Western nations would base their treaties, but it also became a point of departure from China's traditional policies toward Korea. With the conclusion of the treaty, Li Hung-chang put into effect a policy of giving advice and assistance and, by insisting upon a formal statement by the king, compelled other powers to recognize unequivocally China's sovereign position over Korea.[50]

Now that Korea had entered into international commercial relations, China became concerned that other countries having treaties with it might surpass Chinese trade there. China therefore sought to revise its old trade practices which hitherto had been limited to the Korean border. Two treaties were concluded, one concerning maritime trade and the other overland trade.[51] Both were arrangements made especially and exclusively for China and Korea, and were not to be applicable to other treaty powers. They were the results of China's attempt to express, in terms of modern treaties, the ambiguously defined age-old tributary relationship between the two countries. The

[45] Tyler Dennett, *Americans in East Asia* (New York, 1941), p. 436.
[46] Li, *ISHK*, 13:7-10, March 25 and 27, 1882.
[47] Ibid., 13:7b, March 27, 1882.
[48] Li, *ISHK*, 13:33-34, April 22, 1882.
[49] Maki, *Selected Documents*, p. 108.
[50] Li said that a written statement on Korea's vassal status was necessary because its omission might result in other powers forgetting about it and thus cause future troubles, Li, *ISHK*, 13:7-8, March 1882.
[51] Korea, *Treaties*, pp. 64-70.

preamble of the 1882 maritime trade regulations clearly announced to the world that China was Korea's suzerain and thus would enjoy privileges.

> Korea has long been ranked among the vassal states. All that pertains to the rites has been definitely regulated and no change is required there. But as various countries have now entered into trade relations [with Korea] by water, it becomes necessary [that] both countries enter into commercial relations. . . . Be it understood that they are made out of *China's favor for the vassal and shall not be subject to equal participation by other nations*.[52]

Li also attempted to help Korea reorganize and modernize its military forces so that it would be able to defend itself. Following Li's advice, the Korean government sent sixty-nine selected young men to Tientsin in 1881 to learn from Li's Anhwei army about the technology, machines, and skills of the modern military.[53] Li's new Korean policy would have had a good chance of succeeding, had there not been equally vigorous activities on the part of Japan and strong conservative opposition in Korea.

Korean Response

Internal opposition to the opening of Korea had been brewing ever since 1876, but from the end of 1879 it was led by the conservative Confucian scholars, who advocated *wijŏng ch'ŏksa* (preserve the correct and repel heresy) and expressed their views by presenting memorials to the court. After 1880, memorials became more numerous and the opposition more vocal as disturbing news continued to spread. In addition to the news of the first Japanese consul formally taking residence at Pusan[54] and to the opening of treaty negotiations with the United States, it was also reported that Russians were trespassing on the northern border and demanding treaty relations with Korea. Even more disturbing was the rumor circulating in Seoul in the summer of 1880 that the Korean government might conclude treaties of alliance with Japan and the United States. It originated in a small pamphlet called *Ch'ao-hsien ts'e-lüeh* (Korean strategy), written

---

[52] Li, *Telegrams*, 44:40. English translation in Lin, "Li Hung-chang," *Readings*, pp. 283-84.
[53] Yi Pyŏng-do, *Han'guk sa*, pp. 479-80.
[54] Korea, Kuksa P'yonch'an Wiwonheo, *Kojong sidae sa* (Seoul, 1970), vol. 2, pp. 151, 157; Li, *ISHK*, 11:42-45, December 22, 1880.

by a Chinese official in Tokyo, Huang Tsün-hsien, and brought home from Japan by Kim Hong-jip, the second *susinsa* to Japan.[55]

The pamphlet warned the Koreans of the Russians' southward movement and their possible designs on the peninsula. To defend against such aggression, Korea should consider allying itself not only with China but also with Japan and the United States. The last country, although a Western nation, was friendly and appeared to have no territorial ambitions; a close tie with it would help Korea ward off other Western encroachment.[56] A few hundred copies of the pamphlet were soon circulated among government officials and scholars. Many expressed basic agreement with the treatise but at the same time voiced their concern that there might be strong opposition.[57] Indeed, the pamphlet provoked a renewed attack on the government from conservative Confucian scholars[58] for not upholding the tradition of *wijŏng ch'ŏksa*.[59] Throughout most of 1881 they waged a desperate struggle against the government over what they considered to be its sell-out policy. Their campaign soon took on the air of a patriotic movement led by the literati. Memorials bearing over 100,000 seals were presented to the court by thousands of scholars who had poured into Seoul. By fall, the movement had even produced a martyr, Hong Jae-hak from Kangwon province.[60] But it soon became embroiled in factional politics involving an illegitimate son of the Taewŏn'gun who allegedly had schemed to depose the reigning king.[61]

Factional involvement and ill-planned political plots provided the Korean government with excuses to suppress the *wijŏng ch'ŏksa* movement ruthlessly. This marked an end of the conservative elite's leadership in antiforeign and antigovernment activities. Thereafter, the antigovernment movement came either from the masses or from the elite of a new breed, the progressive reformers. The *wijŏng ch'ŏksa* idea did not completely vanish, however, but survived in the militant national movement of *uibyŏng* (righteous army) in the early twentieth century.

---

[55] *Kojong sidae sa*, p. 182.

[56] Ibid., pp. 183-86; Kim Ki-su, *Susinsa ilki*, ed. Han'guk saryo ch'ongso (Seoul, 1974), pp. 160-71.

[57] *NGB*, vol. 13, pp. 394-96; Yi Sun-gun, *Han'guk sa* (Seoul, 1962-63), p. 431.

[58] Yi Kwangrin, *Han'guk kaehwa sasang yŏn'gu* (Seoul, 1974), p. 31.

[59] *Kojong sillok*, in *Yijo sillok* (Tokyo, 1960), vol. 17, November 3, 1880.

[60] Song, *Kiro sup'il*, pp. 8-14; *Kojong sidae sa*, p. 255.

[61] *Kojong sidae sa*, pp. 266, 269, 270.

The majority of Koreans in 1882 had many concerns and griev-
ances. The economy was in a state of bankruptcy, which people blamed
on the opening of the country to trade. But the government under the
domination of the Min clan was obliged to continue the unpopular
open-door policy, not only because the regime had inherited the policy,
but also because Li Hung-chang was urging its expansion. The news
of the conclusion of the Shufeldt treaty and rumors of more treaties
with other powers alarmed Koreans still opposed to the opening of
their country. But what touched off the fire was the reorganization of
the Korean army under the aegis of Japan and the poor treatment of
old army soldiers. Their patience reached a breaking point on July
23, 1882, when the long-awaited distribution of tribute rice was found
mixed with sand and amounted to a fraction of the totals due.[62] The
furious soldiers broke into the government granary and took the grain
for themselves. Several of them were arrested, and an attempt to petition for their pardon led to an armed conflict with the guards. The
old soldiers rushed to the house of Min Kyŏm-ho, the person in charge
of the government granaries, and destroyed a good part of it.[63]

The rebelling old soldiers persuaded the reluctant Taewŏn'gun to
be their leader,[64] and the former regent took the reins of government
once again. The rebels were now joined by the masses and attacked
the Japanese legation. Minister Hanabusa and his men fled in disguise
after setting the building afire. Both Japan and China sent forces to
Korea,[65] the latter ostensibly to investigate the causes of the disturbance and the former to exert pressure on Korea to accede to Japanese
demands for a formal apology and indemnity for the loss of Japanese
lives and the destruction of the legation building. The Taewŏn'gun,
now in power, considered the Japanese terms too harsh and refused
to accept them, and the talks deadlocked. Ironically, the Chinese took
command of the delicate situation and cleared the way for a peaceful
settlement between Korea and Japan by removing the Taewŏn'gun,
the obstacle to peace, from Korean politics.[66] The power of the
suzerain was unequivocally demonstrated. The Mins thereafter re-

[62] Yi Pyŏngdo, *Han'guk sa*, p. 483.

[63] Homer B. Hulbert, *The History of Korea* (Seoul, 1905; revised and edited
by Clarence Norwood Weems, New York, 1962), vol. 2, pp. 225-27.

[64] Yi Pyŏng-do, *Han'guk sa*, p. 484.

[65] Itō Hirobumi, ed., *Chōsen kōshō shiryō* (Tokyo, 1936), vol. 1, pp. 114-15;
Wang Hsin-chung, *Chung-Jih chia-wu chan-cheng chih wai-chiao pei-ching* (Peking,
1936), p. 36.

[66] Wang, *Chung-Jih chan-cheng*, p. 39.

mained at least outwardly grateful and subservient to China, resulting in Chinese domination of Korean politics. On the other hand, Japan suffered a reversal in its influence in Korea despite the apparent diplomatic victory of the Chemulp'o Treaty, which granted Japan important rights including that of stationing troops.

While the Imo mutiny of 1882 was the result of conservative Koreans' opposition to the rapid opening of their country, the coup d'état of 1884, known as Kapsin chŏng-pyŏn (political change of Kapsin year), was precipitated by progressive young Koreans who were impatient with the slow rate of change in their country in the face of numerous foreign challenges. The leaders of the coup were members of the so-called Independent Party. Taking advantage of China's preoccupation with problems in Annam, a Korean anti-Ch'ing force collaborated with the Japanese to overthrow the pro-Chinese government and remove China's influence in Korea.

The early independents were mostly pro-Japanese insofar as they were impressed with Japanese accomplishments. They hoped to adopt a reform program for Korea following the Japanese pattern, and sought assistance from Japan. These men represented the most radical of the modern political parties in late Yi Korea in that they advocated the most thorough reforms in the fastest possible way.[67] They found their friends and supporters among the Japanese liberals, whose motivations to help Korea differed according to their political inclinations and changed in the course of time. But at least in the beginning, they seem to have been motivated by the desire to share what they had learned from the Westerners.[68]

The party's leadership came from the membership of the first few missions to Japan after the conclusion of the treaty of 1876. Some members of the third mission, "Gentlemen's Observation Group," stayed longer to observe and study the progress of Japan. The ablest of these was Hong Yŏng-sik, the founder of the Independent Party. Pak Yŏng-hyo, brother-in-law of King Kojong and chief susinsa following the Imo mutiny,[69] was also impressed by Japanese progress and espoused the cause of reform. The most audacious of the re-

---

[67] Yi Ki-ha, Han'guk chŏngdang paldal sa (Seoul, 1960), p. 7.

[68] Fukuzawa Yukichi, the leader of the Japanese liberals in the early Meiji period, even composed a poem after meeting and talking with the young Korean reformers, reminiscing about his youthful years abroad for study in Western countries. Ishikawa Mikiakira, Fukuzawa Yukichi den (Tokyo, 1931-33), vol. 3, p. 289.

[69] Chŏng Kyo, Tae Han kyenyon sa (Seoul, 1957), p. 14.

formers was Kim Ok-kyun, who was not a member of the missions to Japan but went there later in 1882, perhaps with the king's blessing.[70] All were members of the *yangban* class,[71] and Kim came from the Andong Kim family, the formerly powerful consort family which had been replaced by the Min clan. Kim disliked the Mins, and particularly Min Yŏng-ik, Queen Min's nephew by adoption and her favorite.

The staunchest enemies of the Independents, of course, were the conservatives of the Queen Min faction, whose power became more firmly established after the 1882 mutiny and after the "kidnapping" of the Taewŏn'gun. Although retired since 1873, the former regent was considered the father of the nation and had become a symbol of resistance to foreign aggression. His abduction and captivity in China aroused indignation among Koreans.[72] The young Independent Party members, especially, considered it one of the most humiliating events in Korean history.[73] They also felt that the Mins' program of gradual reform under Chinese guidance was too slow, that their attitude was too submissive to China, and that their government reorganization yielded little improvement.

It soon became obvious that the young Independents were not powerful enough to influence major government policies or carry out their programs of innovation.[74] And yet, the young reformers were impatient to set Korea on a rapid course of reforms. The year 1884 seemed auspicious. China had withdrawn half its troops from Korea and was preoccupied with a conflict with France over Annam. The Japanese government was being severely criticized by liberals for its cautious policy,[75] and many hoped that it might decide to render assistance to the Korean reformers. And Kim Ok-kyun, who had been in Japan since late 1882 and become imbued with the dream of modernizing Korea along Japanese lines and possibly with Japanese aid,

[70] Ibid.; Harold F. Cook, *Korea's 1884 Incident: Its Background and Kim Ok-kyun's Elusive Dream* (Seoul, 1972), p. 37.

[71] *Yangban* literally means "two classes" of civil and military officials, and usually denotes the ruling class in a general sense. To call it aristocracy is a misnomer.

[72] Pak Chong-hwa, "Na ui hoegirok," *Han'guk ilbo*, September 20, 1970.

[73] Ishikawa, *Fukuzawa*, vol. 3, p. 290.

[74] Kim Ok-kyun, the most successful of the reformers in obtaining government positions through a regular route of passing examinations, still could not advance higher than a junior second-grade official, undoubtedly due to antipathy between the Yohung Min clan of the reigning queen and the Andong Kims of the formerly powerful consort families. Cook, *1884 Incident*, pp. 54-55.

[75] Conroy calls this "safe and sane policy." Hilary Conroy, *The Japanese Seizure of Korea* (Philadelphia, 1960), p. 127.

decided to return to Korea. He referred to Japan as the "Great Britain of the Orient," and wanted to make Korea into "an Asian France."[76]

Upon his return, Kim was cordially received by the king, but found the situation not as favorable for reform as he had anticipated. The pro-Chinese Min faction was firmly entrenched in power; Kim had been passed over for promotion while Min Yŏng-ik, his rival and junior by nine years, had reached the same rank as he and was holding as many as six positions concurrently. Although Chinese troops in Seoul had been reduced to 1,500, the modern Korean army under the control of four Korean commanders and Yüan Shih-k'ai was now four battalions strong. These factors led Kim and his friends to believe that their objective could not be achieved without the removal of those in power. He discussed this with the Japanese minister to Korea, Takezoe Shinichirō, who was undecided at first but later agreed with Kim.[77]

Beginning in November 1884 the atmosphere in Seoul became increasingly tense with the mobilization of Chinese and Japanese troops. By the end of the month, details of the coup were worked out with Takezoe's blessing and his promise to lend the conspirators 3,000,000 yen.[78] It was to be staged on December 4 at a dinner banquet celebrating the occasion of the completion of the new post office building to which all important government officials and foreign representatives would be invited. A fire would be set at the nearby palace of the heir-apparent to create confusion, during which the conservative officials would be assassinated. But the plot did not proceed as planned because the Seoul streets were heavily guarded by Chinese and Yüan-trained Korean soldiers. Only one of the high Korean officials, Min Yŏng-ik, was wounded, and the incident was immediately reported by Ch'en Shu-t'ang, the Chinese minister, to Yüan Shih-k'ai. Frustrated, the reformers requested help from Japanese troops stationed in the legation headquarters. Together they seized the King and killed many of his ministers. The reformers then organized a new government before dawn with Pak Yŏng-hyo as commander of the two battalions of the Left and Right.[79] The reformers' dream finally seemed to have

---

[76] Cook, *1884 Incident*, p. 86.

[77] Kim Ok-kyun, "Kapsin ilki," in Itō Hirobumi, ed., *Chōsen kōshō shiryō* (Tokyo, 1970), vol. 1, p. 447.

[78] Ibid.

[79] As prearranged, the rioters forced the king to write a message to the Japanese minister seeking his protection. Takezoe had been ready and came immediately with his legation guards. Wang, *Chung-Jih chan-cheng*, pp. 67-68.

been realized, but it was cut short by another prompt intervention of Chinese troops led by Yüan Shih-k'ai. The new government lasted only three days. The king was "rescued" by the Chinese forces, who shot the rebel-reformers on sight. Only a handful of surviving rioters, including Kim Ok-kyun, Pak Yŏng-hyo, Sŏ Jae-p'il, and their Japanese sympathizers, including Japanese minister Takezoe, fought their way to Inch'ŏn where they boarded a Japanese liner for Japan.

The king was moved to Yüan's camp where the latter helped him to reestablish the government. When the crisis had passed, the king moved to the palace, taking Yüan along with some Chinese troops as a palace guard. Yüan lived in the room next to the king. It may have been at this time that the king developed such confidence in Yüan that he would later ask the Chinese government to appoint him "resident-Chinese official" in Korea.[80]

The Sino-Japanese Settlement

The problems created by the Independents' coup of December 1884 were settled in two separate treaties, one between Korea and Japan (the Seoul Protocol) and the other between China and Japan (the Tientsin Convention). Korean-Japanese negotiations were conducted in the presence of six hundred well-armed Japanese soldiers who escorted Inoue Kaoru, the minister plenipotentiary. The Korean negotiators were threatened with imminent war in case of procrastination and cajoled with reduced demands to encourage swift acceptance. It was also reported that the Chinese were displeased with the unilateral Korean talks with Japan. Thus, within a week, the Koreans acceded to most of the Japanese demands, which included a formal letter of apology, an indemnity for Japanese victims and for the construction of a new legation building, and the maintenance of a thousand Japanese soldiers in Seoul.[81] The resulting agreement, the Seoul Protocol, was signed on January 9, 1885.[82]

Even after the Seoul Protocol, Japan continued to be anxious about China's position in Korea. Twice already (in 1882 and 1884), armed intervention by China had thwarted pro-Japanese aspirations, and a large number of Chinese and Japanese troops still stationed in Seoul were engaged in sporadic minor conflicts. Jingoistic anti-Chinese senti-

[80] Wang Yün-sheng, *Liu-shih-nien-lai Chung-kuo yü Jih-pen* (Tientsin, 1932), vol. 1, p. 220.
[81] Kim Chŏng-myŏng, ed., *Nik-Kan gaikō shiryō shūsei* (Tokyo, 1966-67), vol. 3, pp. 169-76, 178-89.
[82] For the text of the protocol, see *NGB*, vol. 28, pp. 348-49.

ment within Japan was also a cause of serious concern to the Japanese government and made it more urgent than ever that an accord be reached with China.[83] Itō Hirobumi was appointed ambassador plenipotentiary to China. Li Hung-chang represented the Chinese government. The negotiations, which began in a cordial atmosphere in Tientsin on April 3, 1885, soon reached an impasse over Japanese insistence on punishment of the Chinese military personnel and withdrawal of troops of both countries from Korea.[84] Li at first refused to consent to permanent withdrawal of Chinese troops on the grounds that China had the right to send troops to Korea in future internal disturbances, in view of the traditional ties between a suzerain and a dependent nation. In the end, however, both sides modified their positions to save the conference. Li agreed that both China and Japan should have the right to dispatch troops to Korea in an emergency provided that the other signatory was notified. Japan moderated its demands on the punishment of Chinese military personnel and accepted an official communication from Li promising punishment.

The Tientsin Convention (also called the Li-Ito Convention), signed on April 18, consisted of three articles, the most important of which was the third. This article specified that in case of a grave disturbance in Korea necessitating the sending of troops from China and/or Japan, the signatories should notify Korea and each other in writing of their intentions, and that after the conflict was settled the troops were to be withdrawn.

The Tientsin Convention appeared to have granted Japan all it wanted. China seemed to have given up the traditional relationship of a suzerain, while Japan was awarded an equal status vis-à-vis China in Korea; the principle of reciprocity with regard to the dispatch of troops and advisers was established by the Convention. But since neither nation could station troops in that country in peace-time, the traditional ties of dependence on China would in practice tend to bind Korea to her old suzerain; China would still have an official there who, if he had sufficient sagacity and ability, could exert great influence. Li found such a person in Yüan Shih-k'ai, a brash, forceful young man of twenty-six, well acquainted with Korea.

By 1885, the Korean policy of Li Hung-chang had undergone a change. Li's program of "opening Korea"—allowing Western powers to sign commercial treaties with Korea—only brought grief

[83] Tabohashi, *Nis-Sen kankei*, vol. 1, pp. 1066-67.
[84] *NGB*, vol. 18, pp. 262-63.

to China instead of heading off dangers from Japan as he had originally intended. Korea, therefore, had to be "closed" once more. Chinese suzerainty had to be established again for all time, and every foreign nation had to be encouraged to handle its Korean business with Li's office in Tientsin through Yüan Shih-k'ai in Korea. In the next decade, Li and Yüan successfully dealt with Japanese rivalry, numerous incidents of foreign encroachment, and Korean schemes to gain independence from China.

Conclusion

After the opening by Japan, Korea was like a "shrimp," as an old Korean saying goes, which was "caught in the fight among whales and got its back broken." Indeed, Korea could not respond swiftly and effectively enough to save itself as an independent entity. A number of factors impeded its successful response to external challenges, especially from China and Japan.

Korea was spared the Western powers' ventures and was opened instead by neighboring Japan, challenging China's traditional sovereign position. Once the hermit kingdom was opened, it immediately became the prey of its two neighbors, China and Japan, whose encroachment on Korea was much more intense than that of the Western powers on themselves. But Korea did not perceive that greater dangers would come from the neighboring countries. It underestimated Japanese strength and determination. It also was not fully cognizant of the peninsula's strategic importance to China. Japan, ever sensitive about its security, also regarded Korea as necessary for its national defense. For these reasons, the competition between the two countries over Korea was much keener than the Western powers' rivalry over China and Japan.

Korea of the 1870's and 1880's was not able to cope with such intense rivalry. It had been suffering under the rule of the tottering Yi dynasty for almost five hundred years. The country was also the most secluded of East Asian nations, and its seclusionist policy had been reinforced under the Taewŏn'gun's rule in the decade preceding the opening. The government had been torn asunder by various factions whose main differences were more political than ideological. The Mins who replaced the Taewŏn'gun in government were almost as conservative and seclusionist, but agreed to the opening of the country, partly to oppose their rival.

Pressured by Japan and by the antigovernment activities of elite factions and the masses, the Min-dominated government appeased the Japanese in the naive hope of later rectifying the situation. The Mins also undertook a moderate program of reform in a piecemeal fashion, partly as a measure of opposition to their adversaries and partly to accommodate Chinese wishes. China now adopted an active policy of interference in Korea, and the Mins were obliged to follow China's directives to stay in power. This course satisfied few Koreans: the government's program was too much for conservatives, who were ill-prepared for reform, and too little for the radical reformist elite, who desired complete independence and rapid modernization on the Japanese pattern. Modernization in Korea became embroiled with strife between pro-Chinese conservative and pro-Japanese reformist factions.

The reformers saw Korea's only salvation in achieving independence and bringing about rapid reform. Having little power and means to achieve this, however, they relied on Japan to oust China. Conservatives in power believed that the maintenance of the status quo was necessary to Korea's survival in the face of intense international rivalry and followed China's directives in gradual reform programs. The problem of Korean modernization thus became a central part of the rivalry between China and Japan, both of which were in the middle of modernization efforts themselves. The reformers' ill-conceived, hasty coup with Japanese blessing failed utterly and led to direct intervention by China and Japan. Chinese troops easily suppressed the coup, the reformers took refuge in Japan, and the pro-Chinese Mins were restored to power. The Mins felt more obliged than ever to the Chinese and acquiesced in China's increasing interference, while China and Japan made decisions on Korea's destiny.

Due to its geographical position, its historical relationships with China and Japan, and its own weaknesses, it was almost inevitable that Korea should become a source of contention between its two larger and stronger neighbors. During the decades of modernization in China and Japan and their own struggles against Western enroachment, to maintain or secure control of Korea became a measure of the success of Chinese and Japanese efforts to survive and to achieve power status.

CHAPTER III

The Chinese in Meiji Japan: Their Interactions with the Japanese before the Sino-Japanese War

═══════

NORIKO KAMACHI

DURING THE Meiji period, two kinds of Chinese lived in Japan: mercantile or laboring commoners who were more or less permanently settled there; and elite literati who were temporary residents— diplomats, students, travelers, and political refugees. The second group has received greater scrutiny from historians because it played conspicuous parts in China's national affairs. This study is concerned with the first group: its unique status and roles in Japanese society during the early decades of the Meiji era preceding the Sino-Japanese War of 1894-95, the period when Japan was not yet a full member of the modern world. Like China, Japan was bound by unequal treaties with the Western nations. Culturally, Japan had not been weaned from the influence of China's tradition. Chinese classics were still the basis of Japanese education and literature, although there was a craze for Western civilization. As Donald Keene has brilliantly demonstrated, one result of the Sino-Japanese War was the self-confidence that Japan's victory generated; another was the respect and admiration of the West for the triumph of the smaller and presumably weaker nation. The Japanese themselves were convinced that "the Chinese were backward, cowardly and even contemptible, unworthy heirs of a once-great tradition."[1] The status of the Chinese in Japan before the war reflected Japan's inferior position vis-à-vis the West, as well as its traditional ties with China.

[1] Donald Keene, "Sino-Japanese War of 1894-95 and Its Cultural Effects in Japan," in Donald H. Shively, ed., *Tradition and Modernization in Japanese Culture* (Princeton, 1971), p. 142.

Chinese communities in Japan in the modern era came into existence as a result of the opening of the country to the West. When the Western merchants who had been trading at China's treaty ports opened branch firms in Japan, they brought with them their Chinese employees and their families and servants. A still greater number of Chinese who were not employed by the Westerners followed them to Japan. Though the Chinese had no legal right to stay there until the first treaty between China and Japan was concluded in 1871, they obtained protection from the treaty power nationals, becoming their nominal dependents or servants by paying fees and subletting their lots within the foreign settlements. They outnumbered the Westerners in the treaty ports—Nagasaki, Yokohama, Kobe, Osaka, and Hakodate—and Chinese communities grew rapidly.[2]

The Nagasaki Chinese community was an outgrowth of the traditional trading establishment that had existed under the Tokugawa system. For the two hundred years during which the seclusion policy of the Bakufu was in effect, the Japanese government had allowed a limited number of Chinese merchants to trade at Nagasaki. These men were not permitted to bring their families, and after 1689 their living quarters were restricted to the Chinese enclosure (*Tōjin yashiki*). A sense of community gradually developed among them. They maintained the Buddhist temples built during the 1620's when Chinese merchants had had unrestricted entry and the right to live anywhere in the city. The Chinese commissioners (*Tōtsūji*), the officials who supervised the Chinese enclosure and assisted the government agency in business transactions were mostly descendants of the Chinese who had lived in Nagasaki before the enclosure was constructed and had chosen to become Japanese subjects. They mediated disputes among the Chinese in the enclosure, and were responsible for preventing criminal activities and especially the practice of the Christian religion. Although serious crimes such as *nukeni* (smuggling) had to be reported to the police, minor crimes were handled in the enclosure, and Japanese laws were not strictly applied there.[3]

After Nagasaki was opened in 1859, the Tokugawa authority lost

---

[2] Hishitani Buhei, "Nagasaki gaijin kyoryūchi ni okeru kakyō shinshitsu no keii ni tsuite," *Nagasaki daigaku gakugei gakubu shakai kagaku ronsō*, no. 12 (March 1963); M. Paske-Smith, *Western Barbarians in Japan and Formosa in Tokugawa Days* (Kobe, 1930), pp. 242-48.

[3] *Tsūkō ichiran* (Kokusho Kankōkai, 1913), chaps. 147-48; Nakamura Tadashi, "Sakoku jidai no zainichi kakyō, Tōtsūji ni tsuite," *Shigaku kenkyū*, nos. 77, 78, and 79 combined issue; Tōtsūji Kaisho Nichiroku Kenkyūkai, "Tōtsūji kaisho nichiroku no kenkyū," *Shigaku kenkyū*, no. 54 (April 1954), pp. 38-41.

control over the entry of Chinese to the city, and numerous Chinese with their families settled within the enclosure and in its vicinity, the districts of Hirobaba and Shinchi. The community that developed in this area consisted mainly of Fukienese and people from Kiangsu and Chekiang provinces; the bulk of the merchants who did business under the old system had come from these regions. Peculiarly, Cantonese had been excluded from the traditional trading establishment; hence there were no Cantonese even among the commissioners. The Cantonese community developed within the foreign settlement in the Ōura and Namihira districts. The Fukienese-Kiangsu-Chekiang community generally comprised the merchant class and their employees; the Cantonese community was a mixed group of laborers, artisans, and some merchants. The census of 1880 recorded 549 Chinese residents in Nagasaki: 490 men and 59 women.[4]

Yokohama had the largest Chinese community in Japan: the registered population in 1869 was 1,002; in 1880, 2,169 (1,863 men and 306 women); and in 1907, 3,644.[5] This community was predominantly Cantonese, but after the steamship lines were opened between Yokohama and Shanghai in 1875, a sizable number of migrants from Kiangsu, Chekiang, and Fukien arrived. The Chinese in Yokohama, rich and poor alike (except for those who lived in the compounds of Western firms), were concentrated in an area within the foreign settlement, later known as Nankin-machi (Chinatown). Most of their stores, which doubled as dwellings, dealt in foodstuffs and miscellaneous goods. The majority of the residents were laborers, many of whom did not have steady employment.[6]

After Kobe was opened in 1867, some ten or more Chinese merchants moved there from Nagasaki. In 1880, 516 Chinese (425 men and 91 women) were living in Kobe, and by 1911 the number had increased to about 1,800.[7] The Cantonese were an overwhelm-

---

[4] "Meiji 13 nen kakukyoryūchi zairyū gaikokujin kunibetsu," *Daiikkai Nippon teikoku tōkei nenkan* (1882), pp. 10-11. *Tōkei nenkan* gives the breakdown of foreign residents in each treaty port only in the first issue. In Nagasaki, original register books of the period from 1868 through 1878 are preserved at Nagasaki Kenritsu Nagasaki Toshokan (hereafter abbreviated as NKNT).

[5] Gaimushō, *Nihon gaikō bunsho* (Tokyo, 1949-), vol. 3, pp. 622, 627; Koizuka Ryū for Yokohama Shōkōkaigisho, *Yokohama kaikō gojūnen shi* (Yokohama, 1909), vol. 2, p. 54; *Daiikkai Nippon teikoku tōkei nenkan*, pp. 10-11.

[6] Uchida Naosaku, *Nihon kakyō shakai no kenkyū* (Tokyo, 1949), pp. 165-66; Koizuka, *Yokohama kaikō*, pp. 33-34; Usui Katsumi, "Yokohama kyoryūchi no Chūgokujin," in Yokohama-shi, comp., *Yokohama-shi shi* (Yokohama, 1963), vol. 3b, pp. 864-65.

[7] *Daiikkai Nippon teikoku tōkei nenkan*, pp. 10-11; Kanda Suematsu for Bōekikyoku, *Hanshin zairyū no kashō to sono bōeki jijō* (n.p., 1938), p. 145.

ing majority, although there were a significant number of migrants from central China and Fukien. Cantonese merchants in Kobe traded not only with south China but also had well-established trading networks in Hawaii, California, and Southeast Asia. They also handled most of Japan's trade with India (raw cotton from India became important from about 1875). In the mid-1870's they imported sugar and raw cotton from China, and exported copper, seafood, dried mushrooms, and other traditional goods. During the 1880's, matches became an important export item to China and Southeast Asia.[8]

In the Osaka community of Chinese who traded with north China, many had first settled in Kobe and branched out to Osaka. After 1890, when Osaka became Japan's major trading port with north China and Manchuria, the number of traders who visited it increased. It is estimated that by 1894 there were three to four hundred Chinese living there.[9]

After Hakodate was opened in 1859, the Cantonese came to settle, followed by Chekiang merchants, all of whom were engaged in the export of seafood. In 1880 there were thirty-three of them, and the number remained fairly stable for the rest of the Meiji era.[10]

In the life of Chinese communities, associations (*hui-so* or *kung-so*) or guilds (*hui-kuan*) played important roles in self-government and mutual help. These organizations provided a collective credit system, mediation of disputes within the community, defense against external adversaries, religious and social festivities, maintenance of a common burial ground, transportation of remains for permanent interment in China, and various types of charity. The immediate motivation that prompted Chinese residents in Japan to set up communal associations was their need for officially recognized self-governing units. In 1868 the Japanese government had announced that resident Chinese would be under its jurisdiction and that alien registration would be required. The announcement was based on an agreement of 1867 between the Bakufu and the treaty powers concerning foreign nationals whose governments had no treaty relations with Japan. Soon after, representatives of the Cantonese in Nagasaki petitioned the Nagasaki authorities for permission to organize a Cantonese association and to allow individuals to register through the association. They asked that the Chinese be permitted to govern themselves "according to the Chinese *tao* [laws and principles]." Should a Cantonese

---

[8] *Hanshin zairyū*, pp. 138-42.   [9] Ibid., pp. 11-15.
[10] *Daiikkai Nippon teikoku tōkei nenkan*, pp. 10-11; Uchida, *Nihon kakyō*, p. 168.

be involved in trouble with the Japanese authorities (for example, for evasion of customs duty), the association should be allowed to resolve the matter. In serious cases, the association would negotiate a settlement with the Japanese; in the case of a criminal act, search, arrest, and punishment of the offender would be the responsibility of the association. The Fukienese followed suit with a similar petition. Both associations were recognized by the Nagasaki government, and in 1874 Chinese representatives were officially appointed as headmen (*sōkan*) of their respective groups.[11] These associations assumed that they had the responsibility of preventing crime and the right of handling criminals within their respective communities. Thus, in March 1875, when the police arrested three Chinese for opium smoking, the associations filed joint protests stating that the associations should have been informed of the offense and entrusted with the arrest and punishment of the offenders.[12]

Soon after the government order of registration was issued, representatives of the Chinese residents in Yokohama petitioned for permission to form an assembly to supervise Chinese nationals, to which the Japanese agreed.[13] Likewise, in Kobe in 1869 a certain Kung Shen-fu was appointed by the Japanese as the headman of the Chinese residents. Kobe had many regionally based associations; around 1890 an organization was established for its entire Chinese community.[14]

The Chinese demand for self-government was legally supported by the provisions of the Sino-Japanese treaty of friendship of 1871, which entitled Chinese residents in Japan to the status of extraterritoriality. After the Chinese consuls arrived in 1878, the expatriate Chinese enjoyed the privilege of consular jurisdiction. The association continued to function, acting as adviser to the consuls in community affairs.[15]

Japanese popular sentiment toward the resident Chinese during the early Meiji period was a mixture of amity, envy, resentment, and contempt. The feeling of amity was a legacy from the Tokugawa past.

---

[11] A petition from Cantonese (n.d.) in "Gaimuka jimubo, Shinajin ōfuku, Meiji 1-2 nen," NKNT; Usui, "Yokohama kyoryūchi," p. 885.

[12] From Kuang-tung hui-so and Pa-min hui-so, March 1875, in "Gaimuka jimubo, Shinkoku jimmin shonegai, Meiji 8 nen," NKNT.

[13] Akimoto Masutoshi, "Kyoryūchi no jōtai," *Yokohama-shi shi* (Yokohama, 1961), vol. 3a, p. 374.

[14] Kōbe kaikō sanjūnen kinenkai, comp., *Kōbe kaikō sanjūnen shi* (Kobe, 1898), vol. 1, p. 371; Yamada Masao, "Hanshin Chūka kaikan no setsuritsu," *Shigaku kenkyū*, no. 57 (October 1954), pp. 44-54.

[15] Uchida, *Nihon kakyō*, pp. 250-51.

Many popular songs in Nagasaki reflected a friendly general attitude. The Chinese were called *Acha-san*, a term with overtones of respect and friendship. For example, a song of the Tokugawa era, "*Acha-san* visit their temple," depicts a Chinese merchants' procession to a temple. The custom was to cross the city in sedan chairs and halt for a rest on the Sian bridge, where they were surrounded by curious children to whom they distributed candies, zinc rings, and other favorite souvenirs from China. A Chinese song, "K'an-k'an hsi!" (Look!), sung by courtesans in the central Chinese dialect, was about a ring made of nine small rings. Such songs, with a Japanese verse attached, were very popular among the Japanese in Nagasaki.[16] In the late 1870's there was a craze for the moon guitar, and people in Nagasaki—from government officials to wives of shopkeepers—enthusiastically took lessons on this Chinese musical instrument. Friendly sentiments seemed most deeply rooted in the Nagasaki area; the term *Acha-san* continued in use even after the Sino-Japanese conflict.[17]

The Chinese merchants who traded at Nagasaki under the Tokugawa system were generally regarded as rich and generous. The giant cooking pot at Sōfukuji temple that was cast to feed the hungry during the great famines in the 1680's symbolized such a spirit, and the tradition continued into the Meiji period. In 1880, when a great fire broke out in the city, some Chinese joined the firefighters, an act that was commended in the local newspapers. During the famine of 1890, Fukien merchants donated 7,000 *koku* of rice and Cantonese merchants contributed 300 yen.[18] Because the Chinese were considered wealthy, destitute Japanese parents were glad to have them adopt their children, believing that the child would receive a good education and would eventually inherit the family business. The Nagasaki prefect in 1870 issued a warning against the practice of selling children under the guise of adoption.[19] In many ways, the Chinese in Nagasaki inherited not only the export-import business from their predecessors but also their reputation for generosity.

[16] Ōba Akira, *Nagasaki zuihitsu* (Nagasaki, 1928), pp. 99-100, 109-10; *Tōkyō sakigake*, August 31, 1877, in Meiji Hennenshi Hensankai, comp., *Shimbun shūsei Meiji hennenshi* (Tokyo, 1936), vol. 3, p. 288.

[17] Miyanaga Yoshio, *Hasu no mi*, cited by Hashikawa Bunzō in his paper "From Datsu-A to Tōa kyōdōtai" presented at the conference on "China and Japan: Modern Interactions" at Portsmouth, New Hampshire, 1976.

[18] From Consul Yü to the prefect of Nagasaki, KH 6(1880)/1/21, 5/23, in "Shin ryōji raikan todome, Meiji 11-16," NKNT.

[19] Announcement of Gaimukyoku, June 1870, in "Shinkokumin ōfuku, Meiji 3 nen," NKNT.

In the heyday of foreign traders in Yokohama and Kobe, Chinese compradors and merchants shared in the prosperity and prestige of Westerners. They were good customers at the best restaurants. Scenes of banquets with Westerners, with geisha and Chinese in colorful silk gowns, were favorite subjects for *nishikie* (woodblock print) artists.[20] In Kobe, the construction of the Chinese guild house in 1892 demonstrated the wealth of the merchants; the building was regarded as the most magnificent structure in the city, and sightseers came from afar to see it.[21]

Though it is seldom recalled today, the Chinese contributed to Japan's westernization on a practical level with various skills they had learned from Westerners. Tailors from Shanghai helped westernize Japanese dress. The Chinese in Nagasaki were the first to import kerosense and oil lamps to Japan. In 1874, when gas lights were novel, leaders of the Chinese community in the city volunteered to install street lights and were given government permission. They also proposed to build an orphanage after the Western model.[22] In the late 1870's some Chinese were invited to Shizuoka and Nagoya to teach the Japanese the processing of black tea. By about 1887, in the tea-firing factories in the foreign settlement in Yokohama, all the supervisors, technicians of tea coloring, and firemen were Chinese.[23] A potter from Huichow probably taught the Japanese how to make porcelain for export. In Tokyo the government employed Chinese technicians at an agricultural laboratory to conduct experiments on the artificial incubation of ducks.[24]

The rate of intermarriage is generally regarded as an important indicator of assimilation. In the case of the Chinese in Japan, records in Nagasaki indicate that there were twenty-two marriages between Chinese men and Japanese women between 1873 and 1899.[25] At this time, permission from the prefect and the home minister was required

[20] Yokohama Shiyakusho, *Yokohama-shi shi kō, Fūzoku hen* (Yokohama, 1932), pp. 346-47.

[21] *Hanshin zairyū*, p. 141; Yamada, "Hanshin Chūka kaikan," pp. 48-49.

[22] *Hanshin zairyū*, p. 132: from the presidents of Pa-min hui-so and Kuang-tung hui-so (n.d.) to Nagasaki prefect, in "Gaimuka jimubo, Meiji 7 nen, Shina jūmin shonegai todome"; from Lin Yün-k'uei, May 1870, "Gaimuka jimubo, Shinkokujin ōfuku, Meiji 3 nen," NKNT.

[23] *Yokohama-shi shi kō, Fūzoku hen*, pp. 580-82.

[24] *Yūbin hōchi*, August 8, 1878, in *Shimbun shūsei*, vol. 3, p. 270; from Niu Ch'un-shan to Nagasaki prefect, December 1870, "Gaimuka jimubo, Shinkokujin ōfuku, Meiji 3 nen"; from Consul Yü to Nagasaki prefect, KH 9(1883)/4/5, in "Shin ryōji raikan todome, Meiji 11-16," NKNT; *Yūbin hōchi*, May 10, 1877, in *Shimbun shūsei*, vol. 2, p. 528.

[25] "Naigaijin kyokon jimmeibo, Meiji 22 nen 5 gatsu shirabe, Gaimuka," NKNT.

for intermarriage. It was widely known, however, that many un-official liaisons existed; consequently, there were many children of mixed parentage in Chinese communities. Su Man-shu, a famous Chinese writer born in Yokohama of a Chinese father and a Japanese mother, recalled that half his classmates in the Ta-t'ung school in Yokohama in 1899 were of mixed blood.[26]

The Japanese resented the business association and collaboration of the Chinese merchants with the Western traders who dominated Japan's foreign trade. During the first ten years of the Meiji era, over 95 percent of Japan's export-import trade was handled by foreigners. Although the percentage gradually decreased, in 1900 it was still as high as 60 percent. Taking full advantage of extraterritoriality, superior capital endowment, and the lack of a Japanese information network on overseas markets, the Westerners maintained the upper hand in fixing prices and other terms in trade negotiations.[27] Foreign domination of trade was a matter of serious concern for the Japanese. It was believed to be a major cause of the deficits that plagued Japan during the early decades of Meiji rule, and a movement for the recovery of trading rights arose as part of efforts toward revision of unequal treaties.

The tough, shrewd Chinese compradors who were employed by Western firms added to the bitterness of the Japanese. As managers (*bantō*, as they were called in Japan), they had direct contact with the Japanese in business transactions. Since the Japanese lacked experience in foreign trade, they were easily manipulated by the astute compradors, who collected fees of 1 to 2 percent for arranging purchases of export goods, a custom the Japanese regarded as corrupt.[28]

Chinese warehouse keepers also collected fees for measuring and weighing goods. Their methods of measurement were objectionable to the Japanese: they used small scales and did not count fractions.[29] They were also accused of taking illicit fringe benefits in handling imported goods. Fabrics (Japan's major import in early Meiji) were compressed between iron slats for shipping in order to reduce volume and for protection. But when the goods were delivered to

[26] Feng Tzu-yu, *Ko-min i-shih* (Chungking, 1944), vol. 1, p. 166.

[27] "Yushutsunyū buppin kakaku naigaishō betsu," in *Daiikkai Nippon teikoku tōkei nenkan*, p. 296; *Dai 20 kai teikoku tōkei nenkan*, p. 532; *Yokohama kaikō*, vol. 1, p. 483, vol. 2, pp. 536, 650-52.

[28] *Hanshin zairyū*, pp. 140-41, 151, 277-81; Yen-p'ing Hao, *The Comprador in Nineteenth Century China: Bridge between East and West* (Cambridge, Mass., 1970), pp. 54-59, 63.

[29] *Kōbe kaikō*, vol. 2, p. 651; *Yokohama kaikō*, vol. 2, p. 537.

Japanese buyers at Western firms, the warehouse keepers removed the slats to sell for their own profit. The buyers complained that they had to bear not only the higher cost of transportation but a higher risk of damage. Only after protracted negotiations and organized protest were the Western firms persuaded to stop the practice.[30]

Chinese merchants enjoyed an almost exclusive monopoly in Japan's China trade in early Meiji. Only after the Sino-Japanese War, when Japan began to export industrial products, were native merchants increasingly involved in trade. By about 1905, the ratio of Japanese to foreign merchants reached one to one, and it was in the area of China trade that the Japanese first made significant advances.[31]

From the early Meiji period, Japanese newspapers reported on Chinese residents in tones of contempt and sarcasm. Chinese were often called the pejorative *chan-chan sensei* (Mr. Pigtail). Reporting on the arrival of China's first diplomatic delegation to Japan in 1877, *Yokohama mainichi* noted the filth and lack of discipline among the crew of the *Haian* which carried the delegation.[32] A street incident reported in 1877 in *Yomiuri* described a contretemps between two peddlers that further illustrates the Japanese opinion of the Chinese. A collision occurred between a Chinese cookie peddler and a Japanese noodle peddler, and some of the noodles fell in the mud. The Chinese was blamed for the accident and was fined half the price of the spoiled noodles. Thereupon he picked them off the ground, saying he had paid for them and would take them home. The newspaper commented sarcastically that the man must have thought it wasteful to leave the muddy noodles.[33]

The Chinese naturally resented such demeaning allegations and thought that the presence of a consul might improve the situation.[34] In 1881 the Hakodate community sued the local newspaper for libel

---

[30] *Yokohama kaikō*, vol. 2, pp. 643-44.

[31] In 1889, the Japanese consul to Hankow pointed out that, in the preceding year, out of 11.42 million yen worth of exports to China, 9.90 million, and out of 10.36 million yen worth of imports from China, 9.60 million, were handled by Chinese and other foreign nationals, and that the major export items were seafood and coal. *Nihon gaikō bunsho*, vol. 22, p. 590; from Itō to Okuma, March 20, 1889, *Hanshin zairyū*, p. 142; Nagasaki Shiyakusho, *Nagasaki shisei gojūnen shi* (Nagasaki, 1939), pp. 145-51.

[32] *Yokohama mainichi*, December 20, 1877, cited by Usui, "Yokohama kyoryūchi," p. 888.

[33] *Yomiuri*, May 26, 1876, in *Shimbun shūsei*, vol. 2, p. 540.

[34] Wu Ju-lin, comp., *Li Wen-chung kung ch'üan-chi: I shu han-kao* (Shanghai, 1921; Taipei, 1962 reprint), 4:24, KH 1(1875)/8/25.

for calling a Chinese *chan-chan* in reporting on an affair between a Chinese cook and a Japanese woman. The community felt that the use of this derogatory term "slandered the glory of the great Ch'ing empire and the honor of the Chinese people," and a suit was filed with the public prosecutor. The case was dropped after the editor testified that *chan-chan* referred only to a specific individual who had committed adultery and that it did not refer to Chinese in general.[35]

Despite mutual resentment between the Chinese and Japanese in the treaty ports, no serious violence was reported. The frictions noted above, while they indicate that the Chinese lived in close contact with the Japanese, do tend to show that there was no racial antagonism comparable to that in California. However, the records of the communications between the first Chinese consul at Nagasaki, Yü Keng (Yüan-mei), and the prefect of Nagasaki do reveal difficulties between the Chinese and the Japanese police. The police often stopped Chinese on the streets in an arrogant and offensive manner to examine their certificates of registration. The consul was stopped and subjected to rudeness even after he identified himself.[36]

The rudeness of police officers in Meiji Japan was not limited to the Chinese; policemen displayed the arrogance of the samurai toward everyone. The Japanese, however, generally accepted police authority, while the Chinese distrusted the police, considering them prejudiced against the minority. From time to time, the police were surrounded by angry mobs in Chinatown when they tried to arrest a Chinese.[37]

The most serious conflict with the police was in connection with the suppression of opium smoking among the Chinese. Opium had been banned in Japan after the authorities became aware of the opium problem in China. In the commercial treaties with the United States and other Western nations in 1858, the importing of opium was prohibited, and penalties for evading the law clearly stipulated. The treaty of 1871 with China banned opium under the customs regulations, but no stipulation was included concerning the punishment of offenders. This fact made it difficult for the Japanese government to enforce the ban, especially since China had no law in effect against opium smoking. Nevertheless, since many Chinese were addicted to opium before coming to Japan and were thus liable to encourage the

[35] *Tōkyō Yokohama mainichi*, June 26, 1881.
[36] From Consul Yü to Nagasaki prefect, KH 5(1879)/2/21, j3/23, 8/18, KH 6/7/10, 11/1, KH 8/10/14 in "Shinkoku ryōji raikan todome, Meiji 11-16," NKNT.
[37] Usui, "Yokohama kyoryūchi," pp. 891-95.

habit among the Japanese, the government was anxious to suppress the opium habit among the Chinese.[38]

Attempting to reduce opium offenses, the Japanese government negotiated an agreement on penalties with the reluctant Chinese government. An understanding between the Japanese minister in Peking and the Tsungli Yamen was reached in February 1876. Though the Japanese government proposed much severer rules, it was decided that the stipulations in the treaties with the Western nations should be applied to the Chinese residents in Japan. Accordingly, it was prohibited to carry more than three pounds of opium for use on shipboard, with violators to be fined $15 per pound.[39] The details of application of the rules were negotiated in Tokyo between the foreign minister and the Chinese minister, Ho Ju-chang, who arrived in December 1877. Foreign Minister Terashima presented a four-point proposal, one article of which allowed the Japanese police to enter private dwellings to search for and seize all opium on the premises. Offenders would be handed over to the Chinese consul. Ho objected to this provision, stating that the Chinese consul should assume the responsibility for arresting offenders who were specifically charged with violations. He pointed out that Chinese law did not permit police entry at will into private dwellings and that an arbitrary search would be resented and become a source of future trouble. Terashima replied that the search of private dwellings would be limited to special circumstances where immediate action was necessary to prevent the escape of offenders. The Japanese government then notified the prefects in the treaty ports that the four points of the proposal were in force.[40] However, problems arising out of the interpretation of the agreement would soon be apparent.

From March 1886 through September 1888 the Japanese and Chinese governments negotiated the revision of the treaty of 1871. The Chinese remained firm against Japanese demands for specific rules concerning penalties for opium offenders, and the negotiations were largely unproductive. On the question of the right of the Japanese police to enter private dwellings, the Chinese took the position that differences in custom and practice should be taken into consideration. In China, officials could not enter a private house to arrest a criminal;

[38] Satō Saburō, "Kindai Nihon ni okeru ahen no mondai," *Nihon rekishi*, no. 129 (March 1959), pp. 13-17.

[39] *Nihon gaikō bunsho*, vol. 9, pp. 439-60, from Mori to Sameshima, February 17, 1876.

[40] Ibid., vol. 11, pp. 262-67, from Terashima to Itō, September 24, 1879.

their duty was limited to taking appropriate measures to arrest the malefactor when he came out of hiding. In any case, those Chinese who smoked opium in their homes could not spread the habit among the Japanese if the Japanese government took strong preventive measures against the purchase of opium in Japan.[41]

The differences of opinion over opium smoking burst into an open conflict in Nagasaki in 1883. On the evening of September 15, six policemen raided a house in the Chinese community and attempted to arrest an opium smoker. The man denied the right of the police to arrest a Chinese national without the consent of his consul. His argument with the police became a free-for-all when his compatriots tried to release him, and a number of Chinese were injured and one man died. The Chinese residents demanded that their consul protest against the police action as a violation of the treaty and of the administrative regulations of the foreign settlement. The prefect of Nagasaki held that the Chinese did not have the same rights and privileges as other treaty nationals where opium suppression was concerned, and that the police had the right to arrest opium offenders in their homes. His only concession to the Chinese demands was to forbid the police to carry swords for a three-year period.[42]

Coincident with the period of troubles over opium in the 1880's, a violent clash occurred between Chinese sailors and Japanese police. On August 1, 1886, four warships of the Chinese North Pacific Fleet, Admiral Ting Ju-ch'ang commanding, dropped anchor at Nagasaki. The ships were the German-built *Ting-yüan, Chen-yüan, Wei-yüan,* and *Ch'i-yüan,* new acquisitions to the fleet, returning from a cruise to Vladivostok and making a stopover at Nagasaki for propaganda effect. Their appearance alarmed the Japanese, whose naval equipment at the time was much less impressive.[43] On August 13, some two hundred sailors went ashore. That evening, in a brothel, a quarrel broke out between the manager of the brothel and some sailors. One Wang Fa and four other sailors from the *Ting-yüan* damaged the doors and the furniture. When a policeman arrived, the four sailors fled, but Wang Fa attacked the policeman and then ran. Later, he and a large group of sailors came to the police station to harass the police-

---

[41] Ibid., vol. 21, p. 53, from Shioda to Itō, January 31, 1888; p. 71, from Shioda to Ōkuma, May 11, 1888.

[42] *Tōkyō nichinichi,* September 28, 1883, in *Shimbun shūsei,* vol. 5, p. 360; *Chōya shimbun,* August 25, 1886, in ibid., vol. 6, p. 320.

[43] *Tōkyō nichinichi,* March 17, 1887, in Ishida Bunshiro, comp., *Shimbun zasshi ni arawareta Meiji jidai bunka kiroku shūsei* (Tokyo, 1935), pp. 490-93.

man who had tried to arrest him at the brothel. After a brawl, in which both men were wounded, the policeman seized Wang Fa and took him to police headquarters, where he was turned over to the Chinese consul.[44]

The following day was quiet; many sailors landed and strolled the streets, especially in the Chinese quarter. On Sunday, August 15, six hundred sailors landed, and about eight o'clock in the evening large-scale fighting broke out in the Chinese section. According to the consul's report, the sailors were peacefully strolling and shopping on the streets when hundreds of police suddenly appeared and blocked both ends of a street and provoked a fight. Over a thousand Japanese, armed with swords and other weapons, joined the police. Some of them poured water and dropped stones on the sailors from the rooftops. Since the seamen had no weapons with them, they were outmatched and many were injured or killed. The consul blamed the Japanese for initiating the hostilities.[45] According to Japanese accounts, however, the sailors repeatedly insulted the police and, assisted by the Chinese residents, intentionally started the fighting. Around six o'clock, a policeman patrolling Hirobaba was threatened by a sailor waving a knife. Other similar incidents followed. Judging the situation to be explosive, police patrols were increased. About eight o'clock, a Chinese stopped a group of three policemen and struck one man's face, while another Chinese tried to grab his club. At this moment, fifty or more sailors surrounded the three policemen and attacked them with swords, clubs, and stones, killing one and injuring the others. A police squad that arrived on the scene was met by some two hundred armed sailors. By ten o'clock the police had quelled the mêlée. Meanwhile, a policeman riding in a rickshaw was attacked by another group of sailors and was fatally wounded.[46]

All told, two policemen and eight sailors, including an officer, had been killed and many others injured. Both Chinese and Japanese official reports agreed that the sailors were carrying no weapons when they came ashore; they apparently obtained arms in the city, either by purchase or from the Chinese residents. A Japanese staff member of the Nagasaki court, who served as a translator for the joint com-

[44] *Nihon gaikō bunsho,* vol. 20, pp. 529-65, from Foreign Minister Inouye to home minister, minister of justice, and other cabinet members; Nakanishi Akira, *Nagasaki igaku hyakunen shi* (Nagasaki, 1961), pp. 477-78.

[45] *Nihon gaikō bunsho,* vol. 20, p. 531.

[46] *Jiji shimpō,* November 22, 1886, in *Shimbun shūsei,* vol. 6, pp. 363-64; *Nihon gaikō bunsho,* vol. 20, pp. 531-32.

mittee of investigation, recalled that the Chinese in Hirobaba procured some weapons from antique shops in the city and, when the fighting started, handed them out to the sailors. He also noted that most of the casualties were Chinese and that the position of almost all the wounds, fatal or not, indicated that they were inflicted from behind.[47]

During negotiations for a settlement, the Japanese government attempted to establish that the Chinese were responsible because the affair stemmed from the violence committed by the drunken sailors on August 13, and that the police were only performing their normal functions. In a secret telegram to the Japanese minister in Peking, however, the foreign minister admitted that in the events of August 15 "the police acted somewhat beyond strict duty" and that "this is generally known by foreigners." Eventually, the Japanese government accepted the mediation of the German minister in Tokyo and agreed that each side would pay "condolence money" (the term "indemnity" was carefully avoided) to the families of the dead and the permanently disabled of the other side.[48]

The Nagasaki incident was more than a commonplace clash between foreign sailors and local police in an international port. Civilians of both sides participated. Apparently the Japanese residents were much more active than their Chinese counterparts. Four Japanese civilians were sentenced to serve prison terms for killing or disabling Chinese sailors,[49] while no casualties or property damages were attributed to Chinese residents. Japanese hostility was obviously aroused by China's flaunting of its naval superiority. It is also symbolic that the target of Chinese hostility was the Japanese police, who were always considered enemies of the Chinese residents.

Three years later, another incident—this time in Kobe—between Chinese residents and policemen caused a diplomatic dispute. On March 1, 1889, Chien Nien-han, the Chinese consul in Kobe, sent a strongly worded note to the prefect of Hyōgo, Utsumi Tadakatsu, protesting the arrest of a Chinese merchant smoking opium in his own house. The police who made the raid damaged the furniture and

[47] Yamaguchi Rinzaburō, "Meiji 19 nen Shinkoku suihei bōkō jiken temmatsu oboegaki," *Nagasaki dansō*, no. 11 (December 1937), pp. 44-47.
[48] *Nihon gaikō bunsho*, vol. 20, p. 587, from Inouye to Shioda, February 4, 1887; pp. 590-92, Final report of the incident by Foreign Minister Inouye, February 9, 1887; *Ch'ing Kuang-hsü ch'ao Chung-Jih chiao-she shih-liao* (Taipei, 1963 reprint), vol. 10, pp. 7-10.
[49] *Nihon gaikō bunsho*, vol. 20, pp. 596-97, from minister of justice to foreign minister, March 31, 1887.

utensils. The consul based his complaint on an agreement of 1879 between his predecessor and the prefect of Hyōgo, which had stipulated that Chinese houses bearing a door plate with the consul's stamp would be immune to police entry. Utsumi replied that the agreement was applicable only to cases of gambling and offenses against sanitary regulations, and that opium suppression was a different matter. Foreign Minister Ōkuma Shigenobu, supporting Utsumi's report, instructed him to inform the Chinese consul that the Japanese government was entitled to exercise its police power over Chinese residents and that there was no provision in the Sino-Japanese treaty delegating this power to the Chinese government. Consul Chien's second note argued that police entry into a private Chinese home without the consent of the Chinese consul violated the treaty, and that the agreement of 1879 had not been concerned with crime and could not be unilaterally abrogated. Exchanges of notes continued until at least June 1, with each side firmly adhering to its original point of view.[50]

The Sino-Japanese War put an end to diplomatic controversies arising from conflicting interpretation of Chinese extraterritoriality in Japan. The postwar treaty of commerce and navigation made no specific stipulation concerning the rights of Chinese, other than diplomats, to live in Japan. When the revisions of Japan's treaties with Western nations were completed in 1899, foreign settlements and consular jurisdiction were abolished. The Chinese were also allowed to live anywhere in Japan, but of course without extraterritoriality.

After the Sino-Japanese War and toward the end of the Meiji era, the composition of the expatriate Chinese community changed significantly. Many of the merchants and compradors who had left Japan during the war did not return. In general, compradors were no longer used by Western traders; and the Chinese merchants in Japan who traded with central and south China suffered seriously from nationalistic anti-Japanese boycotts which spread throughout the southern coast of China. In the meantime, trade with north China and Manchuria became increasingly important, as Japan's needs for raw materials for industry and markets for industrial products expanded. The trade network for this new frontier was Japanese-organized, and

[50] Ibid., vol. 22, pp. 649-65, from Utsumi to Ōkuma, April 8, April 17, May 13, June 1, June 6, June 7, June 8, 1889; from Ōkuma to Utsumi, April 13, April 26, June 4, 1889.

there was little place left for Chinese traders. No longer did the Chinese merchant communities in Japan enjoy the status of privileged business associates of the Westerners.

The Chinese population in Japan after the Meiji era consisted chiefly of miscellaneous craftsmen and small shopkeepers. Laborers, except for some specified groups, were virtually prohibited from emigrating to Japan, since government ordinances of 1899 required them to obtain government permission to go.[51] A variety of Chinese craftsmen and small businessmen, however, many of them operating restaurants, quietly sought their living in Japan in those areas where no serious competition or conflict with the Japanese population was likely. On the other hand, while the Sino-Japanese War marked the end of a brief period when the Chinese enjoyed the status of privileged foreigners, it was during this period of dramatic transition that a strong sense of nationalism was awakened in them. In the late 1890's and early 1900's, the Chinese in Yokohama and Kobe played important roles in support of Chinese reformers and revolutionaries who set up their headquarters in Japan.

[51] Ueda Toshio, "Nihon ni okeru Chūgokujin no hōritsuteki chii," *Azia kenkyū*, vol. 1, no. 3 (March 1955), pp. 11-16; H. F. MacNair, *The Chinese Abroad* (Shanghai, [1924], 1933), pp. 37-38.

CHAPTER IV

China's Attitudes toward Japan at the Time of the Sino-Japanese War*

SAMUEL C. CHU

The island barbarian Japanese have inscrutable temperaments and petty dispositions. Their hearts are like those of jackals and wolves, and they possess poison like the bees and scorpions. . . . Like the barbarian Yeh-langs of old, who vainly compare themselves with the barbarian king of the greater Yüeh-chih, they, not having any buddhas to worship, dare to title their emperor as the son of heaven in the land of rising sun. It took them 48,000 years before they made contact with China, while in 3,600 years they still have not accepted our celestial calendar . . . illegitimately assuming the reign title of Meiji (Enlightened Rule), they in reality abandon themselves all the more to debauchery and indolence. Falsely calling their new administration a "reformation" they only defile themselves so much the more . . .[1]

Previously Japan impudently swallowed the Ryukyus, following up with plotting an abrupt invasion to take advantage of Taiwan's isolated position. They annexed the land of Taiwan and had further designs on our frontiers. . . . However we always

* This work is part of a larger study on the Sino-Japanese War on which I am currently working. For this piece I am especially indebted to Hao Chang of Ohio State University, C. Martin Wilbur and James Polachek of Columbia University, and Arif Dirlik of Duke University. This and related works have been generously supported by ACLS, SSRC, and Ohio State University. I am also indebted in various ways to the following: Bryant Avery, Paul Cohen, Lloyd Eastman, Chun-tu Hsueh, Masaru Ikei, Akira Iriye, Marius Jansen, Thomas Kennedy, Kwang-ching Liu, Patrick Maddox, Marlene Mayo, Bonnie Oh, Shumpei Okamoto, Tse-chou P'eng, John Rawlinson, Frank Shulman, and others.

[1] This and the succeeding paragraphs are from Yi Shun-ting, "T'ao Jih-pen hsi-wen," as found in his K'u-an ts'ung-shu, Han-mo shih-yü, 3:3b-5a. A punctuated version with minor deletions is found in Chung-Jih chan-cheng (hereafter cited as CJCC; Peking, 1956), vol. 5, pp. 173-74.

bent over backwards to show our broadmindedness and tolerance, in the hopes of living in peace with them.

As for Korea, all the world knows that it is a vassal of China.[2]
And yet Japan took military actions there without reason. Is this
not deliberately provocative? . . . How can we tolerate this willingness to act like "the dog of ancient tyrant *Chieh* barking at
the sage-king *Yao!*" Both the immortals and human kind are
angry, the entire world takes offense . . .[3]

So wrote Yi Shun-ting, a member of Governor-General Liu
K'un-i's entourage, in late November of 1894. Replete with erudite
invective and suffused with haughty exasperation, this broadside was
written in the best tradition of the Chinese literati. It voices the sentiment of the articulate Chinese and represents, colorful language
and all, the general tone of China's views toward Japan at the time
of the Sino-Japanese War of 1894-95.

If Yi had been a bookwormish and purblind member of the
notoriously conservative censorate, his sentiments would have been
understandable. But he was not. Yi's patron Liu K'un-i was an outstanding regional official who, conservative though he may have appeared to the *North China Herald*, nevertheless was most knowledgeable about the foreign "barbarians." Yi himself gave clear
evidence of being well-informed throughout the war. Patriotic and
active, he cannot be regarded as totally ignorant of events unfolding
around him. That is why his reaction is the more instructive, and his
anguish, the anguish of many. In coming up with many schemes to
prolong the war and fight the Japanese to the bitter end, he expressed
a sentiment which, forty years later, was to dominate when war broke
out again between Japan and China at Marco Polo Bridge.

That later confrontation, however, did not occur until a series of
dramatic and traumatic developments had so quickened the pace of
Chinese history that the 1930's seem in retrospect almost an era apart
from the 1890's.[4] In that earlier period China remained substantially
wrapped in her centuries-long feeling of unchallengeable superiority.
The vast majority of its elite and people could not yet reconcile

[2] This phrase was deleted in the version contained in *CJCC*.
[3] I am indebted to my colleague Hao Chang for valuable assistance in translat-
ing these elegant but difficult passages.
[4] In fact, drastic change occurred in public influence on foreign policy within
the decade after Shimonoseki. Akira Iriye, "Public Opinion and Foreign Policy: The
Case of Late Ch'ing China," in Albert Feuerwerker et al., eds., *Approaches to Modern Chinese History* (Berkeley, 1967), pp. 216-38.

themselves to the events of the nineteenth century, when the powers took vast liberties with the Celestial Empire. To most Chinese these changes partake of the qualities of a bad dream, somehow unreal. New developments were much less central in their thinking than the traditional concerns of the Court and the countryside. The lure of the examination hall seduced the elite while the daily rounds of agricultural and commercial toil occupied the masses. The outside world seemed far away.

For men like Yi, however, 1894 was not quite like other bad dreams, for the enemies were not the powerful "ocean devils" but the all too familiar "dwarf pirates." The shock of events was, therefore, doubly shattering. As Yi was writing, Port Arthur fell, one more military debacle following those of Pyongyang and the naval battle of Yalu. Empty victory reports could no longer hide the fact that the Japanese had broken through, and were poised at the gate of China herself. To the educated and the ordinary Chinese alike, the thought was almost unbearable: China's sacred soil was about to be defiled by the feet of the contemptible *wo-nu*, and China was virtually powerless to do anything about it.

The question must have arisen in their minds how this could have happened. The natural reaction was to find scapegoats, and the chief among them was obvious—the powerful and long-entrenched Governor-General Li Hung-chang.[5] There were others also, among them Yüan Shih-k'ai, General Yeh Chih-ch'ao, and the unfortunate Admiral Ting Ju-ch'ang (of whom only Yeh deserved every calumny he received), but these are outside the scope of this chapter. We are concerned here with the Chinese view of Japan and the Japanese. How much did they know about the Meiji Restoration and Japan's subsequent rapid modernization? What was their assessment of Japan's intentions and capabilities when war broke out? How did the series of defeats affect Chinese perceptions? And how did these views of Japan accord, or fail to accord, with the Chinese *Weltanschauung*? The answers to these questions relate not only to the war period of the 1890's, but also tell us a great deal about Chinese attitudes before and after the war.[6]

[5] Li Hung-chang remains an object of attack in China today. See Hu Pin, *Mai-kuo-tsei Li Hung-chang* (Shanghai, 1955).

[6] Because of the scope of this chapter and the nature of the sources, our discussion of Chinese attitudes must perforce be largely concerned with the Chinese elite. There is strong reason to believe, however, that mass attitudes did not depart significantly from those of the articulate elite. See the fascinating cartoonlike depictions of the war in the Shanghai mass organ *Tien-shih-chai hua-pao* for 1894-95.

The Outbreak of the War

From the summer of 1894 on, when vague reports of another internal rumbling (this time the Tonghaks) came from Korea, followed by the sinking of the S.S. *Kowshing* on July 25, and the simultaneous Chinese and Japanese declaration of war on August 1, the number of memorials and edicts related to the war increased greatly. Yet records dating from the time of the apparent imminent breach of the Great Wall by the Japanese Second Army in the winter of 1895, such as the basic source *Shih-lu* (veritable records), continued to contain documents pertaining largely to the mundane and the routine, such as ceremonial acknowledgements of appointments, reports of climate and crop conditions, petty crimes, local happenings, and the like. Even a random reading of the primary documents quickly gives us a very different picture of China than would a study focused exclusively on the war.[7] This provides us with the first departure point in our discussion.

The plain truth of the matter is that Japan was never very important in the minds of the Chinese, not in the days prior to the war, and not even after war had been declared. If there was one extraordinary event which occupied the attention of Chinese officialdom, it was the forthcoming celebration of the sixtieth birthday of the venerable and powerful Empress Dowager Tz'u-hsi, on which enormous amounts of funds were being lavished.[8] The Chinese indifference toward Japan can be attributed to two related factors. First, consistently throughout the nineteenth century, and probably for centuries earlier, the Chinese had always regarded only domestic events as truly important. Events outside China interested only a very small fraction of the Chinese people, a fraction which I daresay may be even smaller than the percentage of the population whom we regard as mentally ill today. To say this is not to suggest that the remarkable few who did concern themselves with *yang-wu* were regarded by their peers as abnormal (although the cases of Kuo Sung-t'ao and Tseng Chi-tse come close to such a characterization), but simply to indicate that the Chinese were conditioned to look almost exclusively inward.[9]

[7] One such narrowly focused study, though a most valuable one, is A-ying (Ch'ien Hsing-ts'un), *Chia-wu Chung-Jih chan-cheng wen-hsüeh chi* (Peking, 1958).

[8] *Wan-Ch'ing Chung-Jih chiao-she shih-liao* (hereafter cited as *CJCSSL*), 16:6a.

[9] This point is also made in Paul Cohen, *Between Tradition and Modernity: Wang T'ao and Reform in Late Ch'ing China* (Cambridge, Mass., 1974), pp. 24-25, 62.

Compared to other lands and peoples, the Japanese occupied in the Chinese mind the curious position of being at once the familiar and the ignored. This leads us to the second reason that Japan was of little interest to the Chinese. Those who addressed themselves to questions of Chinese relationships with other states invariably concerned themselves primarily with England, Russia, and France, practically disregarding the United States, which was on a par with Peru and Spain in the Chinese scheme of things. Japan did not fit completely into the scheme because it was sometimes regarded as belonging to the group of tributary states headed by Korea, Annam, and the Ryukyus. Yet Japan did not have a regular tributary relationship with China, and so did not rate even that ceremonial importance.

In the decades before 1894, the one instance when the articulate Chinese paid attention to Japan was at the time of Japan's Formosan expedition of 1874 and the subsequent dispute over the Ryukyu islands.[10] Chinese sentiments were uniformly adverse toward Japan. The hostile statements made by Chinese officials then are virtually identical with the impassioned writings (some by the same persons) of 1894-95, so much so that our descriptions of the writings of later times can be applied to the earlier period as well. There were, however, two officials whose tempered voices stood out amidst the general chorus of xenophobic tirades, Governor-General Liu K'un-i and Junior Deputy Supervisor of Instructions Ch'en Pao-shen. The latter, writing in 1880, regarded Japan as politically unstable and financially precarious, but counseled against taking strong offensive action because China, then pressed by Russia in Ili, was itself hardly in a better position. Ch'en firmly believed that economic boycotts alone would suffice.[11] Liu, even more concerned about the Russian threat, went further by arguing for a policy of appeasement, even to the extent of sacrificing the Ryukyus in order to gain Japan's good will.[12] But Ch'en and Liu were exceptions. For most of the Chinese officials Japan simply did not count. It would not be too much to say that in the Ryukyus dispute of the 1870's most Chinese officials regarded the Ryukyus more highly than they did Japan.[13]

[10] Hyman Kublin, "The Attitude of China during the Liu-ch'iu Controversy, 1874-1881," *Pacific Historical Review*, vol. 18 (May 1949), pp. 213-31.

[11] *Ch'ing-chi wai-chiao shih-liao* (hereafter cited as *WCSL*), 23:19.

[12] *Liu K'un-i i-chi* (Peking, 1959), pp. 2489-91. Subsequently Liu took a much more hostile view of Japan.

[13] Robert K. Sakai, "The Ryukyu (Liu-ch'iu) Islands as a Fief of Satsuma," and Ta-tuan Ch'en, "Investiture of Liu-ch'iu Kings in the Ch'ing Period," in John K. Fairbank, ed., *The Chinese World Order* (Cambridge, Mass., 1968), pp. 112-64.

For Chinese who did concern themselves with dangers from out-side, war with Japan, while remotely possible if China should choose to initiate hostilities, seemed highly improbable.[14] Far more important were the intentions and potential threats of the European powers. Even as the summer of 1894 approached, when war with Japan over Korea appeared not only likely but even desirable, the larger issue re-mained that such a war might trigger off aggressive actions on the part of Russia, England, or another power toward China.

This frame of mind can best be explained within the context of traditional Chinese views of Japan. Official Chinese records mention Japan as early as the *Hou Han Shu* (History of the Latter Han dynasty), and references to Japan can be found in the histories of the T'ang, the Five Dynasties, and the Sung. The only serious ex-ternal threat to Japan before the modern era was from the Mongol invasion during the time of the Yüan dynasty in China. In the suc-ceeding Ming dynasty relations between China and Japan intensified, first when a number of Ming scholars went to Japan to meet their Japanese counterparts, later as trade between Ashikaga Japan and Ming China expanded, and finally with the attack of the "Japanese pirates" all along the China coast.[15] With the conquest of Ming by the Manchu Ch'ing, refugee scholars like Chu Shun-shui settled permanently in Japan, helping to promote a period of renewed Chi-nese Neo-Confucian influence. Throughout the Ch'ing period scholar-ly contact was maintained. Taken as a whole, early relationships be-tween China and Japan, though not continuously sustained, involved a wide range of contacts, from cultural interchange, to trade, to the one instance of military threat. To the Chinese Japan was a familiar presence. Most Chinese, if they thought about Japan at all, probably assumed that they knew all there was to know about it. Thus China had always harbored an avuncular attitude toward its island neighbor to the east. The Chinese knew about Japan's presumed mythical origins, and how it belatedly borrowed Chinese culture and institu-tions wholesale.[16] They were only too often reminded that China

---

[14] For an example of the views of those few who considered war with Japan, see Chang Chien, *Chang, Chi-tzu chiulu, Cheng-wen lu*, 1:3a-10a.

[15] Yamaguchi Ichirō, *Kindai Chūgoku tai-Nichi kan no kenkyū* (Tokyo, 1971), pp. 14-18. See also articles on this topic by Ishiwara Michihiro and Suzuki Shun.

[16] Sanetō Keishū, as translated by Ch'en Ku-t'ing, *Ming-chih shih-tai Chung-Jih wen-hua ti lien-hsi* (Taipei, 1971), p. 99. This is an appropriate place to refer to the vast body of inquiry into perception stereotypes undertaken by social scientists. Arif Dirlik has compiled a useful bibliography of social science literature on stereo-types. See also Gordon Allport, *The Nature of Prejudice*; William Buchanan and

had given Japan its writing script, governmental framework, religious and philosophical traditions, literature, art, and even pastimes. To the Chinese, the Japanese appeared quaint, amusing, possibly clever, but never to be taken very seriously. The Japanese ability to select elements of Chinese culture and modify them to suit their own temperaments and situations was seen only as evidence of their failure to model themselves upon the Chinese more perfectly. By contrast, the Koreans had been more slavishly faithful to the Chinese model, and were thereby regarded by the Chinese as obviously superior to the Japanese.

Those who did not damn with faint praise the Japanese penchant for absorbing Chinese culture were prone to look upon the Japanese with contempt. This attitude became more evident as wartime events forced Japan upon the consciousness of the Chinese elite. The targets for their contempt were not limited to Japanese military action against China, but were extended to Japanese customs (especially communal bathing, which every Chinese observer noted with either amusement or distaste), the dress and makeup of Japanese women, and in the nineteenth century, their "aping" of Western ways. All of these were objects of ridicule and derision to the Chinese. A vast amount of ignorance enshrouded the Chinese mind concerning Japan, and the little that they did know tended more to confirm their preconceptions than to dispel them.

Small wonder then that the Chinese were supremely confident on the eve of the war. The Chinese knew little of Japan's centuries-old military tradition or the fighting qualities of her soldiers and sailors. What was known about Hideyoshi's campaigns in Korea impressed the Chinese not at all. Instead, accounts of the Japanese invasions of Korea invariably recorded with satisfaction that the Ming forces handily drove the invaders out of the peninsula. Even those rare individuals who did visit Japan and had direct evidence of Japan's modern army and navy were seduced by paper evidence. They saw the army as small, the ships as old and inadequate, and the entire new command as primarily defensive in nature.[17] None of the leading Japanese commanders, not even Yamagata Aritomo himself, was ever

---

Headley Cantrill, *How Nations See Each Other*, and the still useful classic, Walter Lippman, *Public Opinion*.

[17] The Chinese Northern fleet visited Nagasaki in 1886 and Kobe and Yokohama in 1891. No Japanese warships visited Chinese ports until three ships arrived in Foochow in June 1894.

mentioned by name. In the Chinese mind, this neighbor was so insignificant that there was little point in conducting a thorough assessment of its military strength and capabilities.[18]

That same redoubtable Yi Shun-ting we have mentioned earlier pontificated right after the sinking of the S. S. *Kowshing* that Japan was "a mouse and not a tiger . . . her funds all borrowed, her ships made of wood, her troops mere civilians, her accomplishments meager, her national strength hollow, and her people hopelessly divided . . . Japan cannot stand up even against one or two of our provinces."[19] Others, notably the censor Chung Teh-hsiang, made similar assessments about Japan which, to us, sound very much as if they had attributed China's own weaknesses to Japan.[20] As events proved these assertions untenable, other illusions emerged. One of the most curious was the repeated statement that the Japanese would not be able to stand the bitter Korean and Manchurian winters.[21] We can speculate on the reasons for this illusion. It may have been a natural deduction from the Chinese conviction that the Japanese were innately an inferior people. Whatever the reasons, it turned out that Chinese troops, not the Japanese, had a worse time of it because of the lack of adequate winter gear.

Together with this kind of wishful thinking, a note of moral righteousness crept increasingly into Chinese statements about Japan. Superficially they seem to echo the contemptuous attitude prevalent before the war, but as reports of Japanese victories over the Chinese piled up, another element emerged. Contempt was never totally absent, but the stress was now on Japan's moral bankruptcy. Again and again Chinese writers referred to the accepted world order, in which China reigned supreme and all other nations ranged in descending order around it. Here one might argue that the Western powers had already effectively destroyed this world view, but this seeming inconsistency apparently did not bother the Chinese, feeling as they did that white nations were "outside the pale" so to speak, while the Japanese, being a yellow people, "ought to know better."[22]

---

[18] Some Western observers also thought that in a war with Japan, China could more than hold her own. John Rawlinson, *China's Struggle for Naval Development, 1839-1895* (Cambridge, Mass., 1967), p. 169.

[19] Yi, 1:1ab.　　　　　　　　　　　[20] *CJCSSL*, 17, #1404.

[21] Wang I-jung, *Wang Wen-min kung tsou-shu*, 51a.

[22] Even England in the 1840's was termed "rebellious" when she attacked China, but by the 1890's such terms were no longer applied to the European powers, Frank A. Kierman and John K. Fairbank, eds. *Chinese Ways in Warfare* (Cambridge, Mass., 1974), p. 8.

Chinese writers listed all the obedient satellite states, praising especially Korea, in denouncing Japan's blatant challenge to the Asian world order. China was pictured as completely innocent. Tracing Japanese action from the time of the Formosan expedition of 1874 onwards, Chinese writers proved to their own satisfaction that Japan had no justification whatsoever. And by labeling Japan as the wanton aggressor, they implied that right would eventually triumph over might, although few ventured to say just how this would be accomplished.[23]

China's Japan Specialists

At this point one might legitimately ask whether there were some Chinese who contradicted this general picture of emotional overreaction. Were there not some who knew the Japanese well and had formed a more accurate view of their motives and intentions?

The answer is, of course, yes. Fully thirty years before the Sino-Japanese War an obscure official (Kuei Wen-ts'an) had been apprehensive about the Japanese sending students abroad for study. In 1867 Prince Kung himself noted that Japan would be a threat to China whether it became strong itself or remained weak, a pawn of England and France.[24] In fact, the entire Self-strengthening Movement in China, spanning the decades of the 1860's through the 1890's, was promoted by men who were quite aware of, and impressed by, what Japan was accomplishing through a comparable period. As would be expected, the most knowledgeable person was Li Hung-chang, whose writings from 1867 on reveal a clear awareness of Japanese reform efforts and military buildup.[25] Other self-strengthening advocates (men like Ting Jih-ch'ang, Wen-hsiang, Liu Ming-ch'uan, and Kuo Sung-t'ao) all demonstrated early comprehension of Japan's growth and potential rivalry with China.[26] Unfortunately, their knowledge of Japan was exceptional; the vast majority of the Chinese literati neither really knew nor cared about Japan.

More to the point is a group of Chinese who were in Japan officially prior to 1894 and therefore had the opportunity to provide China with accurate information.[27] Within this group a further separation can

[23] A typical example of this line of reasoning is found in A-ying, pp. 495-97.

[24] Wang Erh-min, *Ch'ing-chi ping-kung-yeh ti hsing-ch'i* (Taipei, 1963), pp. 69-70.

[25] Ibid., pp. 70-71; Rawlinson, pp. 52, 90.

[26] Wang Erh-min, pp. 71-72.

[27] Here I excluded the small community of Chinese residents in Japan, many

be made. First, there were the Chinese ministers to Japan, the official representatives of their country in Tokyo. And then there were those who wrote books or reports about Japan. Many of these latter were attached to the Chinese missions.[28]

From 1877, when China sent her first minister to Japan, to the opening of war, there were five Chinese ministers. Ho Ju-chang was the first (1877-81), followed by Li Shu-ch'ang, who had two tours of duty, from 1881 to 1884 and again from 1887 to 1890. In the interval between Li's terms Hsü Ch'eng-tsu held the post. In 1890 Li Shu-ch'ang was succeeded by Li Ching-fang, who two years later was succeeded in turn by Wang Feng-tsao. Wang was therefore China's man in Tokyo when war broke out.[29]

Of these five, Ho and Li Shu-ch'ang stood out, one the first incumbent and the other serving the longest. Hsü's tenure was bracketed by Li's two terms, while the other Li, Ching-fang, was an adopted son of Li Hung-chang and upon being appointed was immediately harassed by his father's rivals. He did little during his tenure.[30] The last minister before the war, Wang Feng-tsao, appeared to be a competent career official, but despite his training and experience, did not live up to his potential. Therefore, at the very time when China needed an astute man to occupy this key post, it had instead a man of little vision. Wang badly misjudged the Japanese, reporting on the eve of the war that they were so beset with internal squabbles that they were not likely to be active externally.[31] To be sure, Wang was not alone in saying this, but the fact remains that he failed to rise above the general assessment, when he was the one person who might have at least warned his government of the diplomatic proclivities and the military capability of the Japanese.

In fairness to Wang and his predecessors, however, we should recall that in the 1880's a Chinese official literally risked his career by taking an assignment abroad. Among his peers such duties were

---

of them compradores for Western firms. These Chinese had virtually no influence on Peking.

[28] On these Chinese Saneto Keishū remains the noted authority. See also Ch'en Lieh-fu, "Chia-wu i-ch'ien ti Chung-Jih pang-chiao," *Hsin Ya-hsi-ya*, vol. 7, no. 3-4 (1934).

[29] Jen Hwa Chow, *China and Japan: The History of Chinese Diplomatic Missions in Japan, 1877-1911* (Singapore, 1975), passim.

[30] Ibid., p. 101. See also Kenneth E. Folsom, *Friends, Guests and Colleagues* (Berkeley, 1968), p. 129.

[31] Mutsu Munemitsu, *Hakushaku Mutsu Munemitsu ikō* (Tokyo, 1929), pp. 296-97.

regarded as demotions at best, and at worst they might even prove fatal to further ambitions. Most Chinese bureaucrats literally had "no stomach" for such assignments. They accepted the need to have representatives abroad (if they did) only in principle. For the handful of unusual persons who either sought those positions or who willingly did their duties when ordered, the Tokyo post ranked far down their list of preferences. London, Berlin, Paris, and St. Petersburg were considered the centers of action. Tokyo by contrast seemed a backwater. Under the circumstances, China was lucky to have the experienced Ho to initiate the position and the energetic Li Shu-ch'ang to man it for the better part of a decade.

A brief glance at the careers and activities of Ho and Li in Tokyo is quite instructive. Ho, born in 1838 and a *chin-shih* degree holder of 1868, was thirty-nine years old when he went to Tokyo in 1877. He had shown early interest in *yang-wu*, and was a "classmate" of several other diplomats (Wu Ta-ch'en, later active in Korea, and Hsü Ching-ch'eng, martyred in 1900) who went on to prominent careers. Almost immediately upon assuming his Japan post, Ho was confronted with the sticky Ryukyu dispute. Sizing up Japan's preoccupation with the Satsuma Rebellion in 1877, Ho strongly urged China to take a firm position, not excluding "brinkmanship," in dealing with the situation.[32] His advice, however, ran counter to that of Li Hung-chang, who consistently avoided outright confrontations, and of others like Tso Tsung-t'ang, who were more worried about Russia in the developing Ili dispute. Thus China adopted a vacillating policy on the Ryukyu issue that fatally weakened her case at the end.

Ho's successor Li Shu-ch'ang was more effective.[33] An early protégée of the great Tseng Kuo-fan and experienced in foreign affairs through previous service with Kuo Sung-t'ao in Europe, Li did his best to represent Chinese interests in the continuing Ryukyu case. In this he was repeatedly rebuffed by the Japanese government, but at least he kept Li Hung-chang fully informed.[34] Thanks to Li Shu-ch'ang's timely warnings, China intervened successfully in Korea in both 1882 and 1884.[35] In his second tour of duty Li Shu-ch'ang provided much useful information to assist China's "forward policy" in Korea, a policy decided upon by Li Hung-chang in Tientsin and

[32] Li Tse-fen, *Chung-Jih kuan-hsi shih* (Taipei, 1970), pp. 261-63.
[33] Arthur W. Hummel, ed., *Eminent Chinese of the Ch'ing Period (1644-1912)* (Washington, D.C., 1943), pp. 483-84.
[34] *Li Wen-chung kung ch'uan-chi, I-han*, p. 321.
[35] Chow, pp. 157-59.

carried out on the spot by Yüan Shih-k'ai.[36] Upon Li Shu-ch'ang's final departure from Tokyo in 1890, he sent a long memorial to the throne warning of Japan's growing strength, arguing that China should on no account be drawn into an armed conflict until such time as the Chinese forces were more adequate for the task.[37] As events were to prove, the Court neither paid heed to this assessment of Japanese strength nor followed his advice about avoiding a showdown.

While Ho and Li obviously could not measure up to such contemporary Japanese luminaries as Ōkubo Toshimichi and Mori Arinori, both of whom went on special assignments to China,[38] they compared not unfavorably with the likes of Yamada Arayoshi, Enomoto Takeaki, or Ōtori Keisuke, all Japanese ministers to China at various times. But in one way the Chinese ministers differed from their Japanese counterparts. Being products of their culture, they spent much time in Japan being lionized by, and consorting with, Japanese intellectuals in cultural activities.[39] The Japanese admired them for their scholarly attainments and belletristic talents. They in turn regarded cultural pursuits and official diplomatic responsibilities as equally important. They spent a good deal of time tracking down editions of Chinese books in Japanese libraries and writing prefaces to books written by Japanese classical scholars.[40] We might venture to say that while Japanese officials went about their domestic politics and external diplomacy (not to mention military preparation) with deadly efficiency and seriousness, the Chinese, true to their scholarly tradition, leavened their official work with literary and artistic interests.[41] After all, in their own eyes, as well as those of their peers, their personal reputations rested as much on their accomplishments as scholars as on their work as diplomats.[42]

Below Ho and Li another group of men served more specifically

---

[36] As shown by a number of studies on Chinese policies in Korea, one of the best being Lin Ming-te, *Yüan Shih-k'ai yü Ch'ao-hsien* (Taipei, 1970).

[37] Chow, pp. 174-75.

[38] For Ōkubo's special mission to China, see Masakazu Iwata, *Ōkubo Toshimichi* (Stanford, 1970), pp. 210-22. For Mori in China, see Ivan Hall, *Mori Arinori* (Cambridge, Mass., 1973).

[39] Chow, pp. 119-20. Also Marius B. Jansen, *The Japanese and Sun Yat-sen* (Cambridge, Mass., 1954), pp. 51-52.

[40] Wang Yung-i, *Tao-hsi-chai jih-chi*, 2:12ff.

[41] Some Japanese also leavened their official functions with cultural pursuits. See Roger F. Hackett, *Yamagata Aritomo in the Rise of Modern Japan, 1838-1922* (Cambridge, Mass., 1971), pp. 346-47.

[42] Chinese accounts of Japan habitually included sections on Chinese literary and cultural works found in Japanese libraries and archives. See, for instance, Fu Yün-lung, *Yu-li Jih-pen t'u-ching*.

as the "intelligence" link between the two countries. The best known among them was Huang Tsun-hsien, who not only wrote the massive *Jih-pen kuo-chih* (History of Japan) but included references to Japan in his poems as early as 1879.[43] A senior assistant to Ho, Huang was intensely patriotic, which ultimately propelled him to embrace a number of reforms as a means of saving China. His fame survives to this day, as attested by several books on him published in China and Taiwan during recent years, and by Noriko Kamachi's new critical study of his life and career. His continuing fame, however, rests more on his accomplishments as a literary figure than as a public official. Even in the latter capacity he is generally praised as much for his patriotic fervor as for his level-headed observations.[44]

Huang's interest in Japan was shared by a number of others. Foremost among them was Yao Wen-tung, to whom Sanetō Keishū, the leading authority on Chinese in Japan, has given ample space in his book *Meiji Nisshi bunka kōshō*. Born in 1852, Yao went to Japan at the age of thirty and stayed a total of six years. Incensed by Japanese action in the Ryukyu case, Yao wrote *Jih-pen ti-li ping-yao* (Important facts on Japanese geography and military) in 1884 with the specific purpose of furthering the course of revenge against Japan. It was his ambition to follow this up with a comprehensive treatise on Japan with the title *Jih-pen kuo-chih*, but for some reason he never did so.[45] It remained for his better-known contemporary Huang to complete this task. Huang's book was finished in 1887 and printed in 1890, but was not widely circulated in China until after the Sino-Japanese War. Yao meanwhile wrote a number of other works on the Ryukyus and on Japan.[46]

The efforts of Huang and Yao were not unique. One of the best accounts of contemporary Japan was written by Fu Yün-lung, who in 1889 published his *Yu-li Jih-pen t'u-ching* (An illustrated account of travels in Japan) as one of a series he wrote on foreign countries,

[43] See Huang Tsun-hsien, *Ju-chin-lu tu-ch'ao*, especially vol. 8. See also A-ying, p. 6. Huang's many "conversations" are printed in Cheng Tzu-yü and Sanetō Keishū, eds. *Huang Tsun-hsien yü Jih-pen yu-jen pi-t'an i-kao*.

[44] One such example of his attitude can be found in the preface to his *Jih-pen kuo-chih*: "I see Japanese scholars can read Chinese books and thereby understand what is happening in China, yet Chinese scholars love to discourse on ancient verities, becoming self-centered and uninterested in external affairs. . . ." (3b-4b).

[45] Sanetō, pp. 69, 82.

[46] Yao later acted on behalf of Governor-General Chang Chih-tung in trying to have Britain take over Taiwan ahead of the Japanese. Leonard Gordon, "The Cession of Taiwan—A Second Look," *Pacific Historical Review*, vol. 45, no. 4 (November 1976), p. 565.

including the United States and Peru. Another knowledgeable person was Yü-keng, long-time consul in Nagasaki starting in 1878. During his service Yü-keng sent regular reports back to China giving full information about maritime and naval movements in and out of Nagasaki harbor. These reports were subsequently published under the title *Yü-keng k'ang-i* (Suggestion of resistance from Yü-keng) in 1897.[47] Three other Chinese who wrote about Japan were Wang Chih-ch'un, whose diary with observations about Japan was published in 1880 as *T'an-yin lu* (Visiting Japan); Ch'en Chia-ling, the author of *Tung-ch'a wen-chien lu* (Records of what I heard and saw in the east), 1887, which was especially good on geographic, political, and social data; and Wang Yung-i, who in 1891 while returning from his post at Berlin kept a detailed log of his travels.[48] In his brief sojourn in Japan, Yung-i was favorably impressed by what he saw, and sent items of military hardware to Li Hung-chang for further study.[49] The very year in which war broke out saw the publication of T'an Tsu-lun's *Wo-tu ching-wu chih* (Scenes and information relating to the enemy capital) and Li Yu-heng's *Ts'e-wo yào-lüeh* (Important plans on coping with the enemy). As expected, the latter work in particular was openly hostile toward Japan.[50]

The books mentioned above are by no means all that were written by Chinese in Japan,[51] but they are sufficient to remind us that there were many Chinese who knew Japan and reported their findings back to their countrymen. Some, like Wang Chih-ch'un, were similar to Minister Ho in betraying a good deal of condescension towards the Japanese.[52] This may be explained in part by the fact that they were seeing the Japan of the late 1870's, before it reached full stride in its modernization efforts. Those who came later, such as Yao and Fu, shared Minister Li Shu-ch'ang's healthy regard for Japan's growing strength. Even then, Ch'en Chia-ling and Wang Yung-i did not think that the Japanese navy was a match for China's.[53] What is clear in all these writings, however, is the generally realistic attitude they displayed, regardless of whether the writer happened to be more or

---

[47] Partially reprinted in *CJCC*, pp. 347-54.

[48] All three men are little known. Wang Chih-ch'un was an early advocate of modernization whose writings were published in 1904 as *Chiao-sheng tsou-i.* Wang Yung-i also had his earlier writings on maritime defense published, under the title *Eh-ya-t'ang chi.* Ch'en Chia-ling was a member of Hsü Ch'eng-tsu's staff.

[49] Wang Yung-i, *Tao-hsi-chai jih-chi,* 2:9a, 25b-27b.

[50] Sanetō, p. 108.   [51] For others, see Sanetō, pp. 100ff.

[52] Chow, pp. 99, 102.

[53] Sanetō, p. 107; Wang Yung-i, *Tao-hsi-chai jih-chi,* 2:13ab.

less favorably disposed toward Japan. All these authors, of course, were intensely aware of, and deeply resented, Japanese pressure upon the Ryukyus and in Korea.[54]

Remarkable though these accounts may have been for their day, we must not lose sight of the fact that they made little impression upon the Chinese back home.[55] Most of China's high officials appear not to have read any of the books. Those who may have done so were not much impressed by Japan. In short, China did not lack for information about Japan, but those who made decisions did not choose to make use of it.

From War to Peace

Asan, Pyongyang, Yalu, Port Arthur—with these disasters following one after the other, the mood of the Chinese turned ugly. The Court continued to thrash about desperately for a viable solution, now in the face of a mounting wave of criticism from many who had not spoken up before. Whether one scans the *shih-lu*, the *Kuang-hsü ch'ao Chung-Jih chiao-she*, or recently published collections of source materials such as *Chung-Jih chan-cheng* or *Chung-Jih-Han chiao-she shih-liao*, one is struck as much by the repetitiousness of the arguments as by the large assortment of persons voicing them. Such officials as Kao Yu-tseng, Wen T'ing-shih, Yu Lien-yüan, Chang Chun-hsin, Ma P'ei-yao, Hung Liang-p'ing, and Chang Ying-huan were especially vociferous in their denunciations and complaints. Many of these men were censors, the traditional repository of Chinese morality and conservatism. Some, however, were not. Regardless of their differing backgrounds, they shared certain common elements, discernible in all their writings.

One such element was bellicosity, which now totally erased the earlier modicum of moderation. Nurtured by long contempt of the island kingdom and stung by China's defeats, the literati now turned characteristically jingoistic. Here it must be mentioned that the Chinese vividly recalled their relative good fortune of a few years back when they stood up to the Russians in Ili and the French in Taiwan—

---

[54] Many who wrote on Japan did so as part of intelligence-gathering activities. Wang Chih-ch'un was actually sent by Governor-General Shen Pao-chen for that specific purpose. Sanetō, p. 102.

[55] Contrast this with the thorough intelligence Japan gathered on China under Yamagata's direction. Marius B. Jansen, "Japanese Views on China during the Meiji Period," in Feuerwerker et al., pp. 167-68, and K. H. Kim, *Japanese Perspectives on China's Early Modernization* (Ann Arbor, 1974), p. 14.

actions which contrasted painfully with giving in elsewhere and at other times, and their attendant failures. Confronted by an enemy they had always despised, the Chinese let all the years of frustrations spill out.

Many wanted a counterattack against Japan itself. Our chief protagonist, Yi, in a six-point proposal made in May 1895, called for China's Southern Fleet to neutralize the Japanese navy, and even suggested an attack on the Japanese wartime headquarters of Hiroshima.[56] Others had already suggested the involvement of the Southern Fleet, with some proposing the employment of Western naval officers to run Chinese ships. Still others suggested the use of Japanese-speaking Chinese as spies.[57] Equal attention was paid to beefing up the Chinese army. The Hanlin scholar Chou Ch'eng-kuang, for instance, urged the retraining of the Green Standard troops,[58] while Yang Chen, a censor, stated that the Huai Army, composed mostly of southern Chinese, was not adequate and asked for the use of more northern Chinese instead. Still others saw the largely uninvolved forces of southern China as untapped resources to mount an attack on Japan. As one anonymous memorialist put it, volunteers from Fukien and Kwangtung provinces would form "dare-to-die" (*kan-ssu jen*) contingents and together with Formosan aborigines would attack the Ryukyus. From there they would go on to attack Nagasaki, Shimonoseki, and Hiroshima. Writing after the fall of Port Arthur and in the face of advancing Japanese troops, this memorialist reassured his imperial reader that it was still not too late for China to turn the tide.[59] Others were more cautious. Yu Lien-yüan, a member of the Imperial Supervisory Office, admitted that it was not possible to press on to Tokyo, contenting himself with a more moderate proposal to divert additional funds for war, including money earmarked for Empress Dowager Tz'u-hsi's birthday celebration.[60] Another who called for strikes against Japan conceded that Nagasaki and Uraga could not be touched without the active participation of the British navy.[61] One thing is certain—none of these memorialists seem to have been aware of how decrepit and unserviceable the Chinese southern forces were. Betraying little

[56] Yi, 34a-39a. This piece is also reprinted in A-ying and *CJCC*.
[57] Yang Ch'eng, *Ch'ing-ya-t'ang shih-wen kao*, 1:12a-14b.
[58] *CJCSSL*, 17, #1405.   [59] A-ying, pp. 479-81.
[60] The empress dowager was extremely reluctant to call off the celebration. *CJCSSL*, 15, #1777.
[61] Ibid., 15, #1224.

technical knowledge of military affairs,[62] these writings strike us as nothing but sheer bravado.

A final paroxysm of rage and defiance broke out among the Chinese literati when the Court sent peace emissaries to Japan. Memorial after memorial was sent, now coming from the provinces as well as from within the central government. Most of them took the view that China had more to lose by making peace than by continuing the war. Such arguments were not directed only against Japan, but the references to the Japanese, while betraying some measure of realism, certainly contained large doses of disdain.

No one exemplified the provincial official's feelings better than Li Ping-heng, governor of Shantung at that time. Patriotic and conservative, Li had consistently argued for a strong policy. On April 19, 1895, he memorialized:

> . . . According to what I have heard of the peace terms, the Japanese would receive all that they presently occupy. Even territories east of the Liao River and the island of Taiwan would be lost to them. In addition an indemnity of 100 million taels are to be paid. I regard these as rumors and not to be trusted. Even if the Japanese should make such demands, Your Majesty surely would not grant these terms. Yet since I have heard them, I cannot help but feel deep worry and anger, and feel compelled to express my thoughts respectfully to Your Majesty.
>
> Japan is an island kingdom, comparable to no more than one or two Chinese provinces. I have heard that recently her foreign loan indebtedness has increased rapidly, putting her in serious financial straits. Surely she is in no condition to make plans for expansion in distant lands. The forces she sent to China came great distances under difficulties. With casualties mounting, her strength can only dwindle. This can be shown by her abandoning Yung-ch'eng and Weihaiwei shortly after capturing them. Also after amassing some of her best contingents at Newchuang and Yingk'ou, there has been little threat from her east of Hai-ch'eng. In the latter part of the Second Month, when she went to attack the Pescadores, there were few enemy vessels around Port Arthur. In view of these facts, it can be seen that they have only limited amount of crack troops. The appearance of her force

---

[62] There were isolated exceptions. The censor Wang P'eng-yün, for one, demonstrated surprising familiarity with technical knowledge.

being on the ascendant is due entirely to the fact that she possesses ships that can shift her forces rapidly on the high seas. Also she has gone her wanton ways because China, to begin with, has had no commanders enduring and brave enough to stand up to the enemies.

However, from last autumn till now we have lost only a few prefectures and districts in Fengtien. As for the vast regions in Manchuria to the east of the Liao River, it is quite uncertain whether they can acquire them even if they work hard to do so. How then can we simply hand over to Japan several provinces which she has no assurance of being able to obtain even after trying hard? . . .

Although your servant is old and exhausted, I am quite willing to lead an army to avenge the accumulated defeats. I would have no regrets even if I should perish. When the enemy is exhausted and we bring them under control, then we can negotiate peace at our own pace. Not only would we not hurt our prestige and incur insults, but thereby we would dampen the avaricious designs of other nations.[63]

This combination of realism and bravado can also be seen in other memorials. Not a few of the memorialists rightly pointed out that China had enormous reserves of land, wealth, and manpower, and that if she could commit herself to a prolonged struggle, adamantly refusing to sue for peace and engaging Japan in a test of patience and endurance, ultimately she would triumph. There were serious suggestions of moving the capital to the interior, near the ancient capital of Ch'ang-an (near present-day Sian).[64] These suggestions were not without merit, and they were actually realized some forty years later. What the Chinese writers of the 1890's failed to take into account, however, was China's utter lack of unity at the time. Thus, embodying hopes built on false premises, their ringing calls to arms seem like shadow boxing, hoping to cow the opponent into submission by brave gestures.[65]

By this time a few Chinese did indicate awareness of China's limitations. Li P'ei-yüan, the deputy prefect of Fengtien province in

---

[63] *Li Chung-chieh kung tsou-i,* 7:24a-27a; also found in *CJCC,* vol. 4, pp. 8-11.
[64] Ma P'ei-yao, *Ma Chung-cheng tsou-i,* 4:9b-13b.
[65] Recent books on Sino-Japanese relations continue to argue that China could have withstood the Japanese at the time. See Li Tse-fen, pp. 320-24.

Manchuria, spoke up about the differences between Chinese and Japanese forces:

> . . . The weaknesses of our troops and the strengths of the enemy contrast too greatly. The old maxim in military arts is "know thyself and know thy opponent, then victory is assured." Generally when we encounter an enemy, we can count on winning only if we hold the advantage in either technique, strength or operation. . . . Today our troops possess all the losing factors and concede all the advantages to the enemy. No wonder we are losing! Witness the fact that our weapons are inferior to theirs. We indulge in comfort while they are inured to hardship; our troops bivouac in civilian quarters while the enemy, well-sheltered and well-clad, camp in the open. We operate on our own territory and yet do not know the topography, but they all carry maps individually and move over obscure paths and waterways as if they were old familiar roads. . . .
>
> Strangely enough, our forces, when confronted by the advancing enemy, would either run away while pretending they would fight, or use the excuse of enemies arriving to indulge first in raping and looting. That is the reason the people do not talk about the plague of the enemy but rather the scourge of our own troops. There is no better way to lose our people's support. The Japanese . . . permit the people free movement to calm them, hire them for work and pay them their worth. In such cities as Feng-huang and Hsü-yen they attract the merchants by assisting them with funds so that they can resume their business. People have actually been running away in the presence of our troops and returning when the enemy arrives. That, in sum, is how they win the hearts of our people. . . .[66]
>
> [The enemy] supply their own women to keep the loyalty of their troops, give great rewards to induce them to fight to the death, provide them with wines to bolster their courage, while at the same time threatening them with capital punishment to prevent their retreating. The Japanese have a treacherous nature and are prone to resort to sinister scheming, and therefore are really not the kind of soldiers easy to keep in line. Yet our troops

---

[66] Here we should add that Japanese troop behavior throughout the war was generally exemplary as indicated. However, one major exception occurred at the time of the taking of Port Arthur, when Japanese troops went on a binge of killing and looting.

do everything to antagonize our civilian population, while the enemy act at all times to win their support. This is very much of a cause for worry.[67]

Li then went on to say that had the Chinese made preparations at the time of suppressing the Taipings (the early 1860's) to build up its strength and compete with the Japanese, China might then have been able to prevail. He implied that the situation as it stood was hopeless.

The Court now moved at long last to a resolution of the war. The barrage of criticism notwithstanding, the key officials held firm to their resolve to negotiate a settlement. All the Grand Councillors except the redoubtable Weng T'ung-ho opted for the course of discretion. Li Hung-chang, the archscapegoat, was trotted out to undertake the thankless job of signing an armistice with Japan.[68] Peace was finally achieved at Shimonoseki on April 17, 1895.

Conclusion

In conclusion, we might compare specific facets of the Japanese attitude toward China with that of China toward Japan.[69] Marius Jansen, in an illuminating article, has called attention to the extreme security consciousness of the Japanese, their sense of being utterly vulnerable to the powers. The Japanese were also unsure about their own self-image, deeply aware of their cultural debt to China. Then too, a strong strain of romance and adventurism colored Japanese feelings about China.[70] None of these elements seems to have applied to the Chinese. No doubt due in part to its greater size and bulk, China never felt as vulnerable to the West as did Japan. Its long history and mature culture had provided a sense of self-assurance that at times bordered on the megalomaniac. As for romance and adventurism, these aspects seem especially lacking in the Chinese emotional

[67] CJCSSL, 30, #2421.

[68] It should be added that, unlike the strong reaction on the part of the Japanese leaders to the attempted assassination of Li Hung-chang at the Shimonoseki peace negotiations, the Chinese documents give no indication that the Chinese leaders were made any more anti-Japanese by this episode. Apparently China's attitude toward Japan had been shaped long before this isolated incident occurred.

[69] It should be noted that certain reactions of wartime Japan, caused by a series of victories, obviously had no counterpart in China. See Donald Keene, "Sino-Japanese War of 1894-95 and Its Cultural Effects on Japan," in Donald Shively, ed., Tradition and Modernization in Japanese Culture (Princeton, 1971), pp. 121-75.

[70] Jansen, "Japanese Views of China during the Meiji Period," in Feuerwerker et al., pp. 163-84.

makeup. There was little glory to be won in fighting the *wo-nu*, and the traditional stance of ignoring external affairs had conditioned the Chinese to distrust the rare individual who yearned to "conquer the world." Only in one aspect can we find a parallel between the two peoples: a sense of duty and mission. Until only a few short years before, the Chinese had always assumed that it was their mission to civilize Japan and other parts of the world, an assumption which the Japanese apparently shared. Now, practically overnight, the Japanese were claiming a civilizing (in this case modernizing) mission over China.[71] China, naturally enough, found this extremely difficult to accept.[72]

The Sino-Japanese relationship had undergone centuries of development prior to the last decade of the nineteenth century, and the Chinese had had ample opportunity to find out about Japan. Contacts throughout, however, were confined primarily to the interaction of scholars and literati types, and the attitudes formed by the Chinese toward Japan were very much colored by this fact. Only toward the end of the nineteenth century did there develop a small but flourishing Chinese community in Japan, and they gained a much more intimate and accurate knowledge of the country. People in this community did influence the members of the Chinese mission in Tokyo, but the attitudes of the Chinese decision-makers do not seem to have been altered much thereby. As a result, the Chinese persistently misjudged Japanese intentions and capabilities. While the two nations were at peace, such misconceptions and ignorance on China's part were unfortunate but not critical. In wartime they became fatal for China.

After Shimonoseki the Chinese became much more ambivalent about Japan. On the one hand, there was continuing resentment toward the Japanese for their victory. On the other, Japan was clearly seen as a model that China might well emulate.[73] The former attitude persisted into the twentieth century, especially since Japanese policies and actions toward China tended to strengthen Chinese resentment of Japan. Thus, while one can accuse the Chinese of suffering from a lingering case of "superiority complex," one can argue with equal justification that the Chinese perception of Japanese hostility

---

[71] Kenneth B. Pyle, *The New Generation in Meiji Japan* (Stanford, 1969), p. 173.

[72] Even Wang T'ao, the most worldly-wise of the Chinese literati at that time, found the Japanese claim unacceptable. Cohen, pp. 121-28.

[73] This ambivalence aside, serious Chinese scholarship on Japan continued to lag, at least into the 1920's and probably thereafter as well. See Hu Han-min's preface in Tai Chi-t'ao, *Jih-pen lun*.

was not totally groundless. Small wonder that much of the Chinese attitude toward Japan at the time of the Sino-Japanese War of 1894-95 lasted clear through to the end of the second conflict between them in 1945. One might speculate as to whether China's negative feelings toward Japan have totally disappeared even in the 1970's.

CHAPTER V

THE REFORM MOVEMENT OF 1898 AND THE MEIJI RESTORATION AS CH'ING-I MOVEMENTS

JOHN E. SCHRECKER

IT IS generally known that Japan was an important influence on the Reform Movement of 1898. Historians have made clear how the success of the Meiji Restoration provided the reformers with a model for an effective program of national prosperity and strength which included heavy borrowing from the West. Recent work on the Reform Movement indicates that there was an additional perspective from which the reformers viewed Japan and, in particular, the transition from the Tokugawa to the new Meiji government. They understood it as an example of a successful *ch'ing-i* movement, a distinctly East Asian form of national renovation.

Explicating this perception is worthwhile because it adds another dimension to the relationship between the Reform Movement and the Meiji Restoration. At the same time it suggests the possibilities inherent in the comparative history of China and Japan in the nineteenth and twentieth centuries. For, understanding the concept of *ch'ing-i* allows one to see certain similarities between the Reform Movement and the Restoration that move beyond their common assimilation of Western influences. More precisely, the *ch'ing-i* paradigm cuts across the historical categories, derived from Western theory, into which the two events are often forced. At the same time, once their common structure is recognized within the *ch'ing-i* framework, dissimilarities between the two events emerge that underscore certain important differences between China and Japan in the nineteenth century.

Ch'ing-i is a difficult concept to translate. "Movement for renova-

© 1980 by Princeton University Press
The Chinese and the Japanese: Essays in Political and Cultural Interactions
0-691-03126-6/80/096-11$00.55/1 (cloth)
0-691-10086-1/80/096-11$00.55/1 (paperback)
For copying information, see copyright page

tion" seems reasonable, for it cuts across words like conservative and radical which are inappropriate to the Confucian political context of the term. Overall, *ch'ing-i* implies a movement of sincere and scholarly literati working outside the centers of power for a change in policy. It also implies that these scholars form a coherent opposition force locked in a power struggle with the group of officials who dominate the government. *Ch'ing-i* movements in China took place in times of crisis involving political and economic problems at home and, typically, a threat from abroad. From the Confucian point of view, of course, both internal and external problems reflected deeper moral inadequacies on the part of the dominant officials.

The Reform Movement of 1898 was a continuation of the *ch'ing-i* movement that began in the 1870's and became an important element in politics in the 1880's and 1890's.[1] A description of this *ch'ing-i*/ Reform Movement can provide further information on the nature of *ch'ing-i* as a phenomenon, and show how the reformers could view the Meiji Restoration within this framework.

Throughout the period from the 1870's to 1898, the rank and file members of the movement were younger officials, men in their thirties and forties who held middle and lower level positions in the government. Their backgrounds included very sound literary training and they came to office by the regular path of examination, rather than the irregular route of purchase. Only the top leaders of the movement—patrons is a better word—were high officials.

This opposition movement developed partly as a natural response to the failures of the Ch'ing government to solve China's growing internal and external problems. It also developed for sociopolitical reasons. There was far less chance for promotion among lower and middle bureaucrats in the last decades of the nineteenth century than earlier. This was because so many young men had moved ahead quickly during the era of the Taiping Rebellion and the T'ung Chih Restoration and because these men still dominated the high positions in the central and provincial governments. At the same time, there was very low morale among literati on the regular route to office. The increase in examination quotas after the Taiping Rebellion had

[1] See Min Tu-ki, "Musul pyŏnpŏp undong ŭi paegyong e taehayŏ t'ŭkhi ch'ŏngnyup'a wa yangmup'a rŭl chungsim ŭro," *Tongyang sahak yon'gu*, no. 5 (1971), pp. 101-51. See also my *Imperialism and Chinese Nationalism* (Cambridge, Mass., 1971), pp. 55-58; and my "The Reform Movement of 1898 and the *Ch'ing-i*: Reform as Opposition," in Paul Cohen and John Schrecker, ed., *Reform in Nineteenth-Century China* (Cambridge, Mass., 1976), pp. 189-305. What follows on the Reform Movement is drawn from these sources.

enlarged the pool of those seeking jobs, and in addition, the tremendous rise in the sale of office had reduced the number of positions available.

The policies of the *ch'ing-i* become comprehensible in the light of China's problems and their own outlook. I should note that by providing a political perspective on the *ch'ing-i*/Reform opposition, I am far from intending to denigrate its sincerity. In fact, the plight in which China found itself, and the *ch'ing-i* sense that they had the answers to the nation's problems, made their desire for influence and their inability to get it all the more frustrating and all the more understandable.

In its overall approach, the *ch'ing-i* emphasized the primacy of domestic politics. They believed that the way to solve China's problems of internal decline and foreign aggression was to create a *shih-feng*, a great national revival and, in particular, the revival of a dedicated public spirit among officials and gentry. Often they spoke about uniting the whole people of China; and, as a Confucian ideal, they meant it. In practice, however, their chief concern was to increase the influence of their own group of middle and lower bureaucrats. More broadly, they were interested in increasing the power of the lower elite, the nonofficial gentry as a whole.

As might be expected, the basic target of the *ch'ing-i* opposition was those in power. After the war with France this meant particularly the Empress Dowager and the high officials. The *ch'ingi-i* views of its opponents was not necessarily accurate and clearly had strong political motivations, but understanding it is essential to understanding the spirit of the movement. From the *ch'ing-i* point of view, the Ch'ing establishment was corrupt, pragmatic, even profligate. It certainly was not fit to lead the national revival the country required. K'ang Yu-wei expressed this attitude when he wrote in 1895:

> Meanwhile the construction of the palaces and parks went on, and the graft and corruption of the officials continued unchecked. Sun Yü-wen and Li Lien-ying dominated the government, while the officials not only kept their mouths shut but suppressed the expression of public opinion. The lower officials had to offer bribes, while the high officials, as soon as they left the court, indulged themselves in drinking and banqueting in the company of prostitutes and actors. . . . Under these conditions not only was political reform out of the question, but even the old form of

[98]

government and its discipline were trampled upon. These conditions presaged China's defeat in *chia-wu* [by Japan].[2]

In foreign affairs the *ch'ing-i* was militant and patriotic and generally constituted the war party. This was true both in the *ch'ing-i* movement proper, when the goal was to expel the foreigners, and in the Reform Movement, when this aim was somewhat transmuted into the desire for full sovereignty and equality for China.

The *ch'ing-i* attitude toward borrowing from the West changed over time. Some adherents remained adamantly against it. But by the late 1880's many of them, including the leaders, had undergone a reversal of opinion. The Reform Movement represents the culmination of this process. The shift occurred partly because Westernization was understood to be the road to national wealth and strength and thus, ultimately the key to resisting imperialism. The interest in things Western also had a political side, however. For new political and educational institutions and other social structures provided new ways for an opposition to influence the government and even to take it over.

Despite the interest in the West which developed within the opposition, the *ch'ing-i* and Reform Movement were generally opposed to the *yang-wu* (Western studies) Movement. This was not because the latter wanted to borrow from the West. Rather, it was because, from the point of view of the *ch'ing-i*, the *yang-wu* people emphasized the wrong things: foreign rather than domestic affairs, technique rather than morality. Furthermore, the opposition felt that the *yang-wu* approach was too mild and compromising in its response to imperialism. Finally, the *ch'ing-i* opposed the *yang-wu* because Li Hung-chang and other leading figures in the latter group were the chief political opponents of the *ch'ing-i*.

As in past *ch'ing-i* movements, the overall political strategy of the nineteenth-century opposition was to use the emperor, to bolster him and encourage him to act to solve China's problems. From 1889 on, therefore, when the Kuang-hsü Emperor officially took control of the government, the *ch'ing-i* supported him. The *ch'ing-i* people hoped, by uniting with the emperor, to circumvent the high officials. He, in turn, found them congenial, as he was looking for new talent to use as allies against the empress and the senior officials whom she

[2] K'ang Yu-wei, *Chronological Autobiography*, tr. Lo Jung-pang, in Lo Jung-pang, ed., *K'ang Yu-wei: A Biography and a Symposium* (Tucson, 1967), p. 50.

controlled. The reformers were acutely aware of the importance of the emperor and emphasized that one reason that the *ch'ing-i* movement of the late Ming had failed was because the emperors were ineffective and weak. The Hundred Days of 1898 was a logical outcome of the *ch'ing-i* approach.

Another political trademark of the *ch'ing-i* was the use of the *yen-lu* and an insistence that the *yen-lu* be kept open. *Yen-lu* literally means paths of communication to the throne. Keeping the *yen-lu* open meant a willingness on the part of the throne to receive general memorials on the overall situation. (Normally, officials were only supposed to memorialize on specific matters relating to their administrative spheres.) It also implied imperial willingness to receive memorials from those comparatively low in the government, either directly or transmitted by higher authorities. In 1898 the reformers particularly emphasized the need to open the *yen-lu* as a means of weakening the political monopoly of the high officials and of discovering fresh talent. There were repeated decrees on the matter and, by September, the *yen-lu* were theoretically open to everyone. This emphasis on the *yen-lu* clearly suited the needs of the *ch'ing-i* as a movement of outsiders. But also, by "uniting above and below," as they put it, opening the *yen-lu* contributed to the creation of the *shih-feng*.

Another striking feature of *ch'ing-i* politics was its constant urging of the throne to find young talent and to encourage it by promoting capable men without strict regard to the rules of seniority. Clearly this fit both perspectives of the movement. Here is a typical memorial, written by the reformer Hsü Chih-ching in June 1898:

Your Majesty has fixed the fundamental directives for reform but their implementation is entrusted entirely to the hands of conservatives. Now if we do not reform we cannot strengthen ourselves, but if we do not use new people we will not be able to reform. At the beginning of the Meiji Restoration the emperor specifically promoted low officials and provincial samurai. . . . They were used without regard to rank and all used their talent to the utmost.

I have heard that the sources of Western wealth and strength are deep and complex and cannot be mastered without thorough study. Today our high officials—beginning with the heads of the Boards in Peking and the governors in the provinces—have all been selected on the basis of seniority. . . . In normal times appointing people by seniority blocks competition for office. But if this method is used in a difficult period it will fail to meet the situation. To carry out extraordinary policies, you must have extraordinary talent.[3]

A final distinctive trademark of the *ch'ing-i* was a very emotional and tough tone toward their opponents. For *ch'ing-i* politics were the politics of moral confrontation. Here is Yang Shen-hsiu in June:

The conservatives say that the new laws should be stopped. Those who are enlightened say that old practices should be swept aside. . . . The two groups are like fire and water, they hate each other as enemies. I say that you cannot allow such divided principles, there can be no neutrality. Without a fixed national policy, there is no way of showing the officials and people the proper direction; without making rewards and punishments clear there is no way for the government to carry out its plans. . . . Now, you have issued repeated decrees to implement the new policies. But the high officials treat these decrees with indifference as if they hadn't heard anything. Sometimes they shelve them and don't proclaim your will. Sometimes they proclaim your will but don't carry it out and sometimes they carry it out but with no zeal. This is all because the national policy has not been set and because rewards and punishments are not clear. . . .

It has been six months since the loss of Kiaochow. It was not cut off by a powerful enemy but by the conservatives who mutinied against our own government. And, basically that happened because the national policy was not set and rewards and punishments were not clear. . . . From ancient times, whenever there has been a time when new policies were being implemented, rewards and punishments have been widely used. . . . This was the case in Japan when the Meiji Emperor abolished the Baku-han system.[4]

As these quotes suggest, the reformers themselves saw the Meiji Restoration not only as a model of successful borrowing from the West, but also as a successful *ch'ing-i* movement.

From a comparative point of view their perception seems justified. Japan's feudal structure during the Bakumatsu period created a funda-

[3] Chien Po-tsan et al., eds., *Wu-hsü pien-fa* (Shanghai, 1953), vol. 2, pp. 335ff.
[4] *Wu-hsü pien-fa tang-an shih-liao*, comp. National Bureau of Archives, Office of Ming and Ch'ing Archives (Peking, 1958), pp. 1ff.

mentally different setting for the *ch'ing-i* phenomenon. Nevertheless, the Restoration as a whole can be understood within the pattern. This should not be surprising, of course, in view of the long influence of China on Japanese political life and, in particular, the dominance of Confucianism in the Tokugawa period.

The social base of the Bakumatsu opposition movement was analogous to that of the *ch'ing-i* group in China. There were some high-ranking patrons, daimyo, court nobles, and others, but most of the important figures were *hirazamurai*. Like the middle and lower officials in China, the *hirazamurai* were clearly part of the elite of the nation. However, they were generally excluded from the important decision-making positions.[5]

The reasons for their opposition, like those of the *ch'ing-i* in China, were a combination of commitment and frustration. One motivating force was an appreciation of Japan's problems. As in China, these ranged from foreign threats to the financial plight of the various governmental units. Another thing that moved the opposition was the contradiction between Confucian norms of office through talent and the hereditary basis of employment in Japan. *Hirazamurai* were likely to be deeply versed in the Confucian and indigenous Japanese ethos of service and loyalty and to be disturbed by their exclusion from influential positions in time of crisis. In some han their exclusion may not have sprung solely from their social origins, but come exactly from the same cause as in China. It has been suggested that one reason for the particular activism of Chōshū and Satsuma was that they had a superfluity of samurai qualified for office.

Finally, the opposition of the *hirazamurai* also sprang from the gradual impoverishment of the group in the course of the Tokugawa. Since this and the other concerns of the *hirazamurai* were also felt by samurai lower down on the scale, the constituency of the Bakumatsu opposition, like that of the reformers, who often represented the gentry as a whole, could include all samurai.

Besides rank, as in China, the chief determinant of membership in the opposition appears to have been age. The leaders of the Restoration were, on the whole, young for the places they assumed in politics.

The overall spirit and outlook of the Japanese opposition were also similar to the *ch'ing-i* group in China. The loyalists and exponents of *sonnō-jōi* who established the dynamics of the Bakumatsu period

[5] The most useful summary of the Restoration has been W. G. Beasley, *The Meiji Restoration* (Stanford, 1972).

saw the same distinctions between themselves and the Tokugawa as the reformers saw between themselves and the Ch'ing establishment. In addition, within the activist han one can also see mini-*ch'ing-i* movements where the same structure emerges in the struggle between the opposition and the local *mombatsu.*

In the eyes of the opposition, the Tokugawa was interested in moderate reform rather than national renovation. At the same time, in foreign policy, the Bakufu, like the Ch'ing, seemed committed to accommodation and self-aggrandisement rather than to a vigorous program of expulsion. As in China, this fervent opposition to imperialism, coupled with a desire for influence at home, led to a dynamic where *jōi* turned naturally into a program of broad change borrowing much from the West.

The specifics of the *ch'ing-i* approach also appear clearly in Japan. The opposition used the emperor as their vehicle for outflanking the power of the Tokugawa. At the same time, they worked to make the emperor the focus of the national revival, the pinnacle of the drive to "unite above and below." They also emphasized the promotion of "men of talent," though seniority was less the issue, of course, than hereditary rank. As one writer put it, "There are times of turbulence and times of peace. . . . In times of turbulence, irrespective of nobility or baseness of rank, one promotes those who are useful and will help to win tomorrow's battle and strengthen the domain."[6]

Finally, the opposition displayed the same passion as their Chinese counterparts in attacking their opponents. It is not surprising, for example, that Yoshida Shōin, the quintessential figure of the Bakumatsu period, was, perhaps, the most admired leader of the Restoration in reformist circles in China. "To wear silk brocades, eat dainty food, hug beautiful women, and fondle darling children," he wrote in the same spirit as K'ang Yu-wei, "are the only things hereditary officials care about. To revere the emperor and expel the barbarian is no concern of theirs."[7]

Despite these similarities in the sociopolitical and ideological structure of the Bakumatsu movement for renovation and the opposition movement in China, there are some important dissimilarities between the two even within the *ch'ing-i* framework. Most importantly, the balance of forces in the two countries was different, and the opposition was larger and became effective more quickly in Japan than in China.

[6] Quoted in Beasley, p. 63.   [7] Quoted in Beasley, p. 150.

One reason for this is simply the well-known fact that, because of the differing histories of China and Japan, a militant hostility to foreign incursions and influence was far more pervasive within the Japanese elite than within the Chinese. As a result, the militant *ch'ing-i* position was closer to the mainstream view in Japan than in China. Even the Bakufu and its followers represented, at heart, a fervent opposition to outside control that went far beyond the *yang-wu* position in China.

Tied to this, it also seems that the opposition in Japan had a sharper and more compelling ideological drive. This was because Confucian elements in their outlook were bolstered by the quasi-religious spirit of Shintō and the rigor of Bushidō. Even Confucianism itself was stronger in a sense, perhaps because it represented an imported ideology. The reformers in China were aware of the need to develop a more solid spiritual base for their activities than was available in the contemporary schools of Confucianism. It was for this reason that K'ang Yu-wei turned to the semireligious *chin-wen* Confucianism. This was a rather artificial and unsatisfactory solution however, and lost more support for the reformers than it gained.

Another reason for the difference in the balance of forces is that the elite in China faced far greater threats from below than did the samurai. The reformers were deeply aware and frequently wrote of peasant unrest and the danger it presented to national stability.[8] There were peasant uprisings in the late Tokugawa, but by no means on the same scale and importance as in China. Hence the dissatisfied elite in Japan could support major change with less fear that it might cause a breakdown that would bring the whole system toppling around them.

One conclusion emerging from this comparative study of the Meiji Restoration and 1898 is that the effective renovationist and anti-imperialist forces in both countries came from opposition groups with a deep sense that successful action required strong moral links with the past. This has been more understood by historians of Japanese history than of Chinese. In fact, the whole connection between the *ch'ing-i* and Reform movements has come to light only recently. Until now they have been seen as antithetical: the *ch'ing-i* as a conservative, xenophobic force and the reformers as a progressive faction, open to strong Western influence. Once they are seen as part of the

[8] For example, in the general memorials on reform collected in *Wu-hsü pien-fa tang-an shih-liao*, the problem of peasant unrest is a common theme.

same process, however, it helps to explain not only 1898, but later history as well. For example, one increasingly has a sense that communism in China is somehow both very radical and very traditional. This may be related to the fact that radicalism in twentieth-century China had its roots in a *ch'ing-i* movement.

A broader conclusion which emerges from the comparison is that the problematique of the study of the Meiji Restoration and 1898 is, perhaps, too influenced by Western history and Western historiography. Roughly the same debate goes on in the study of both events. On the one hand there is a "social" interpretation that emphasizes broad interclass conflict. In studying Japan this interpretation stresses the role of the lower samurai and the discontents of the peasantry and merchant class. In China it speaks of a rising bourgeoisie in conflict with the bureaucratic state. The alternative view has a tendency to deny the importance of social conflict altogether. In the study of the Meiji Restoration the emphasis is on ideological issues and conflicts among the elements of the feudal system: han, court, and shogunate. In China, the characteristic feature of this position has been its concentration almost entirely on intellectual issues.

The "social" interpretations have clearly proven unsatisfactory as they stand. The Meiji Restoration was not led by lower samurai, and the merchants and peasants, for all the difficulties they caused the ruling elite, were not a serious political threat in Tokugawa times, nor did they play much of a role in the Restoration. Attempts to link the 1898 reformers to a rising bourgeoisie have not proven successful. Even the Revolution of 1911 emerges as a gentry-army operation.

Nonetheless, the alternative, as we have seen, should not be to ignore the importance of social conflict. Rather, it seems important to recognize that there was bitter conflict, which, however, involved different levels within the elite, not different classes in the Western sense. Furthermore, because of the nature of these elites and their Confucian outlook this conflict could not be separated from ideological issues. It should not be surprising that intraelite struggles were a strong factor in Chinese and Japanese history in the nineteenth century; in Confucianism, the political realm is of fundamental importance and, hence, conflict within the elite involves high stakes. It is, in fact, of importance not only to the elites themselves, but to the whole society.

This is partly because of the significance of governance in Confucian theory. The victorious side in a consequential political struggle expects to play a critical role in shaping society. More importantly, since the essence of *ch'ing-i*, from a theoretical point of view, is to expand the polity, such a movement is very open-ended in its socio-political possibilities. In a Confucian setting, the notion of "uniting above and below," the idea that there ought to be broader inputs into government, leads very naturally, and with a dynamism of its own, to legitimizing the expansion of the polity to ever-wider segments of the population. It is hardly remarkable, therefore, that these two *ch'ing-i* movements led to extremely rapid changes in both societies.

CHAPTER VI

Konoe Atsumaro

MARIUS B. JANSEN

AT 9 A.M. on Saturday, April 1, 1899, Shimbashi station was crowded with well-wishers to bid farewell to a distinguished traveler. Konoe Atsumaro, head of the House of Peers and of the Peers School, and founder and head of the recently formed Tōa Dōbunkai, was leaving on a journey around the world. The greats of Meiji political life were there: Prime Minister Yamagata, Interior Minister Saigō, Imperial Household Minister Tanaka, Justice Minister Kiyoura, plus another four or five hundred leading figures from public and private life. The students of the Peers School were lined up inside the station. Prince Konoe arrived with his wife Sadako and son Fumimaro. When the train reached Yokohama still others were there to say goodbye. Prince Tokugawa, Count Tsugaru, Marquis Maeda—in all about a hundred more. By eleven o'clock the toasts had been raised and Konoe had thanked his friends for their send-off. His wife and son now stayed behind. Another forty or fifty friends accompanied him on the launch that headed for the steamer. Then at last Konoe was alone with his two traveling companions in Room 8 on a small NYK steamer of four thousand tons, able to write his farewell poem.

> Will not they say I have no heart
> To so desert the flowers of my native place?

The pace of welcome on his return to Tokyo on November 25 left Konoe no time for even this much poetry. Meiji Japan made abundant provision for class and status. Konoe Atsumaro, forty-fourth in line from Fujiwara no Kamatari and head of one of the five regent families, had better claim to their prerogatives than anyone except Mutsuhito himself.[1]

[1] Konoe's diary, which covers the years February 1895 to March 1903, was pub-

The emperor valued Konoe. The two exchanged gifts regularly, and the emperor had held a farewell reception for him. For each the respect due the other was a dimension of his own position. In 1898, when Ōkuma Shigenobu asked Konoe to serve in his short-lived Kenseitō cabinet, the emperor had added his misgivings to Konoe's firmly negative inclinations; a lineage so noble should not risk the indignity of political office, for failure would affect not only Konoe himself, but would cast dishonor on all of his distinguished forebears. Better to remain aloof from politics; better still to tour the globe and report on the state of world affairs. The emperor charged Konoe to study the strengths of royalty and aristocracy abroad: in Russia he was to examine the education of nobles; in Germany, the practice of diplomacy; and in each European monarchy the relations between throne and people. The Imperial Household Ministry provided the funds, and Konoe did some hard bargaining with Imperial Household Minister Tanaka Kōken before he got the sum up to 30,000 yen, the amount he felt commensurate with Japan's new international stature.[2]

Konoe traveled, and was received, like a prince. Everywhere along his path he was the guest of monarchy, and Japanese missions toiled to prepare his schedule. In the United States he contented himself with a few major cities and seats of learning; despite the urging of Nitobe Inazō, whom he met in California and who sent him books and letters on his way, he contented himself with Harvard and Columbia and made no allowance for more democratic Haverford. In Europe the education he saw was closer to his goal, while in China he urged his viceroy hosts to send their youths to Japan for study. Chang Chih-tung had already entrusted a favorite grandson's education to Konoe's care, and while in China Konoe agreed on the spot to admit to the Gakushūin a son of the *tao-t'ai* Ts'ai Chün.[3]

Wherever its numbers sufficed, the Japanese community could be

---

lished in five volumes as *Konoe Atsumaro nikki* (Tokyo, 1968-69) (with a supplemental volume of his writings). Hereafter *Nikki* and *Supplement*. For the Shimbashi departure, *Nikki*, vol. 2, p. 306.

[2] The best biographical accounts are Kudō Takashige, *Konoe Atsumaro Kō* (Tokyo, 1938), in good measure a repeat of a privately distributed work issued by the Konoe Kazan kai, *Konoe Kazan Kō* (Tokyo, 1924). Also excellent, and concise, is the biography in the Dōbunkai publication, *Tai Shi kaikoroku* (Tokyo, 1932), vol. 2, pp. 884-911. Background of the trip in Kudō, *Konoe*, pp. 225-35. There had also been earlier offers of the Education Ministry and the German legation to Konoe.

[3] *Nikki*, vol. 2, p. 442. While in Europe Konoe received word that Chang's grandson was doing much better in Japanese and able to understand some. Ibid., p. 350.

expected to make much of Konoe. Where Japan Societies existed, Konoe was an honored guest. In London, Deputy Chief of Mission Matsui Keishirō accompanied him to a special eighth anniversary meeting of the Japan Society and served as his interpreter for the remarks he was asked to make. Konoe told his hearers that although it pleased him to hear foreigners express astonishment at the progress Japan had made in thirty years, it also pained him to realize how much of that progress was surface rather than basic. "We have made progress in material things. We have trains, wireless and of course a postal system, we have a legal system and a parliament . . . from the outside it looks as if we have been able to learn a great deal. It seems Japanese have always been known as skillful imitators. But often the imitation is limited to what is surface and visible . . . it is more difficult to imitate things of the spirit. When Englishmen are overseas, wherever they go they act as if they were in England. There can be no question of comparing Japanese strength with that of England, but it seems to me that this characteristic of the English is one of your most striking features. I should like the Japanese to master your imperturbable nature at the same time they take over the outward form of things . . ."[4]

There is little need to doubt Konoe's assurance to his diary that his remarks were well received, and that a meeting that began with "banzais to the Queen and to the Emperor" ended equally amicably. In fact, however, Konoe's professions of concern with spiritual content for the Western vessels that Japan was shaping were somewhat misleading. He himself, certainly, had the content, or thought he did, and his chief concern was with the vessels in which it could best be contained and distributed to his countrymen.

Aristocrats, Officials, and People

Konoe's exalted lineage helped him develop a political position that put him beyond the reach of government influence and left him free to recruit popular support for a strong continental policy. The aristocrat who despised officials could mobilize commoners to urge steps to "preserve China" and "contain Russia."

Konoe studied in Germany from 1885 to 1890, his twenty-third to twenty-eighth years. There he mastered German and traveled widely. After periods at a number of universities he received the degree of Doctor of Jurisprudence from Leipzig, with a thesis,

[4] Ibid., pp. 323-24.

"Ministerial Responsibility in the Japanese Constitution," that he had published there in 1890. It is an unremarkable work, combining a brief résumé of Japanese political history with an analysis of the Meiji constitution. Its most important feature was a point on which Konoe took exception to Itō Hirobumi's *Commentaries* that had been published in Tokyo the previous year. "Count Itō, the former president of the Council of State, is in error in stating that ministers are responsible only for advice, and that they are not accountable for the acts of the monarch," he wrote. A German constitutional theorist, Max Seydel, was cited as confirmation for the sentence that followed: "True, ministers are not punished for the dereliction of monarchs, nor do they oversee the monarch's actions as private person, but it is unthinkable that they should not be held responsible where the monarch's deeds as ruler are concerned, since all the monarch's official acts take on true meaning only when they coincide with the will of the ministers responsible for them."[5] The Meiji leaders' tendency to take refuge behind the throne was thus as reprehensible from Konoe's aristocratic perspective as it would become from Ozaki Yukio's more democratic standpoint.

Joseph Pittau has pointed out that the German theorists who helped Itō in the formulation of the Meiji constitution thought of the Meiji leaders and their descendants as a working aristocracy that would be well qualified to govern the country under a functioning monarch.[6] For Konoe, however, a true aristocracy had yet to be built. From his perspective, the aristocrats named to the peerage in 1884 were still parvenus. His diary is studded with names of somewhat greater substance—Tokugawa, Maeda, and Tsugaru, while a Yamagata or an Itō counted for little. "Invited by Count Itō and his wife for the wedding of their child," his diary notes on March 16, 1898; "Of course declined."[7]

Konoe saw it as his duty as head of the Peers School to create a proper aristocracy out of the materials at hand; his goal, one suspects, was to produce types motivated toward public service in the way he thought he was himself. In 1894 he published an article, "On Peerage" (Kazokuron), which called for the development of a true nobil-

[5] Reprinted in *Supplement*, pp. 3-36. Title, *Die Ministerverantwortlichkeit nach der japanischen Verfassung*. Quotation from p. 25.

[6] Joseph Pittau, *Political Thought in Early Meiji Japan, 1868-1889* (Cambridge, Mass., 1967), pp. 156-57.

[7] Sakai Yoshikichi, "Konoe Atsumaro to Meiji san-jū nendai no taigai kōha," *Kokka gakkai zasshi*, vol. 83, nos. 3-4, p. 195; *Nikki*, vol. 2, p. 26.

ity, one of quality and substance. It should not be a mere ornament of the state, but had the duty so to order itself that it would inspire the trust of throne and people alike. One might sum it up in Confucian terms: "let the nobility be the nobility." Konoe did not recognize these qualities in the aristocracy of his day. He considered it his calling to inculcate them in the nobility of the future.

To this end he worked seriously at his duties at the Peers School, to which he was appointed early in 1895. He urged that the school remain under the supervision of the Imperial Household Ministry, to separate it from ordinary educational institutions responsible to the Education Ministry. He wanted the faculty and level of instruction to be comparable to those of the Imperial University, and special salary and office perquisites guaranteeing Peers graduates a status similar to that of Imperial University products. He wanted his alumni well represented in the Foreign Ministry as well as throughout the Army and Navy. He sent representatives to study other schools abroad, he cited the importance of his program as a reason for declining cabinet posts in 1898, and he did not leave on his 1899 trip—itself charged, as will be recalled, with the study of similar schools in other lands—until provisions had been made for an interim head who would step aside upon his return.[8]

In view of Konoe's foreign experience and concern for the role of the peerage, it was natural that Itō should have asked him to enter the House of Peers upon his return from Germany in 1890, then to act as interim head, and then to head that body. But Konoe considered himself above the government and not of it; in fact he saw the Meiji oligarchy as symbol of everything he was against. He established a kind of working arrangement with the Ōkuma Kenseikai group, although he was aggrieved to find himself considered affiliated with it by some. One suspects its chief attraction for him was its role in opposition. When Yamagata came to Konoe in November 1898 to ask him to serve as education minister after the fall of Ōkuma's cabinet, he was rewarded with a stern lecture on what was wrong with Meiji politics. Konoe expressed his strong disapproval of any suggestion of cooperation with Itagaki and the Jiyūtō. Both the political parties were collections of self-interested and self-serving politicians, he warned: "Japanese political parties have borrowed the name of political party, but that's all." If you looked more closely they were

[8] I follow Sakai's excellent study for Konoe's approach to the problem of education for the aristocracy. See also Kudō, *Konoe*, p. 26.

groups of factions; there was a Hoshi party, a Hayashi party, a Masuda party, a Shimada party, an Inukai party. What they lacked, and needed, was a program and belief, or *shugi*, some agreement on the path the country should take. Konoe did not stop there, as Yamagata may have expected him to. "So far" he went on, "I haven't felt the slightest dependence on political parties or on your *hanbatsu*. I don't see that there would be anything to gain from joining with the *hanbatsu* now. Why should I put any effort into something with so little prospect? I don't like to be rude, but both the political parties and the *hanbatsu* are going to break up before very long. When that happens, I'll exert myself in the confusion that follows. If I fail then, that will be my end in politics. But I don't feel like fighting to the death now, and I'm going to put it off a little longer." Yamagata and Tanaka Kōken, Konoe noted, were "dumbfounded" by this blast.[9] No doubt they were not quite used to being spoken to in that way.

Sakai Yoshikichi points out that Konoe's charge against "officials" like the *hanbatsu* was that, through self-importance and self-serving tactics, they had come to stand between emperor and people and thus prevented the achievement of that unity of *ikkun banmin*, ruler and subjects, which he felt was the proper goal of Japanese political life.[10] Konoe's insistence on ministerial responsibility could be represented as somehow "Western" and even "English," but its real thrust was much more "Japanese" and traditional. His scornful attitude toward practical politics and functioning statesmen linked Konoe with the whole spectrum of Meiji opposition, from Tōyama Mitsuru and the right, to "academic" critics of government such as university professors, including the famous "seven jingoes" who gathered at Konoe's residence to organize their campaign against what they saw as the government's appeasement of Russia in Manchuria before the Russo-Japanese War. In his ability to bridge factions, and in his readiness to use the government without really supporting it, Konoe anticipated some of the promise and threat of his young son Fumimaro.[11]

The Progress of an Asia Firster

Konoe's views on Japanese policy in Asia were, as Sakai points out, a projection outward of his desire for a purified and harmoniously hierarchical Meiji state structure. His goal was an ideal world that

[9] *Nikki*, vol. 2, pp. 187-92; November 6, 1898.
[10] Sakai, pp. 200-201.
[11] Referred to by Sadako, Konoe's wife, as "Bunbon" in letters during the 1899 trip. See *Nikki*, vol. 2, p. 439.

had no real place or need for "politics" in the sense of power struggles between competing interest groups. At home the emperor was to be a repository of moral virtues, focus of the affection of a loyal people, and served by a conscientious aristocracy and capable ministry. So, too, in foreign policy: Japan's stance toward its neighbors should be one of moral ascendancy, since it was developing the desirable characteristics of modernity without the moral dereliction of Western imperialism and racism. A properly oriented posture would, in turn, attract the trust and friendship of the upper classes in China.

It was quite in character for Konoe to propose that part of the Chinese indemnity negotiated at Shimonoseki should be set aside for lower public education in Japan. One tenth of it, he calculated, would work out to 4.30 yen per student, or 2,000 yen per school. Such an allocation could have as its purpose the promotion among all Japanese of qualities of loyalty, courage, truth, and integrity, which the new Japan would need in ever greater measure.[12]

Konoe recognized that the victory over China strengthened Japan's position in international affairs. It seemed to him to require new attitudes and a readiness to assume new responsibilities. While he was deferential to his hosts in his talk to the London Japan Society, he was a good deal more confident of his message when he was urging changes upon his hosts in China. The mood of his countrymen was even stronger, however, and this produced a short article from Konoe that may well be compared to his son's famous statement against a status quo settlement after the end of war in 1918.

In the January 1898 issue of *Taiyō* Konoe published a short piece entitled "We must ally with those of the same race, and we must study the China problem." He began with observations on the new Japanese confidence and sense of superiority to China. More and more, the Japanese were coming to congratulate themselves and despise the Chinese. It was true enough that Japan had progressed beyond China in the arts of civilization, he conceded, but to go to extremes was wrong, and harmful to Japan's China policy. "It seems to me," he observed, "that East Asia will inevitably become the setting for a racial struggle in the future. However foreign policies may change for the moment, it is only for the moment. We are fated to have a struggle between the white and yellow races, and in that struggle Chinese and Japanese will both be regarded as the sworn enemies of the whites. Any projection for the future has to keep this disturbing

[12] *Supplement*, p. 100.

point in mind." Over the years, the arrogance of the whites had been shown by their imperialistic activities all over the globe. Wherever they went, they treated the lands they found as though they were uninhabited frontier country. In the case of white aggression against the yellow race, to be sure, there were some significant differences. Asia had not proved to be an Africa that could be carved up at will. In particular, the Japanese victory over China had introduced a new element of respect and caution in white approaches. Nevertheless, the ultimate hostility remained, now revealed in talk of a "yellow peril."

Konoe concluded that while Japan might make tactical arrangements with the white powers, it could never let down its guard and trust them completely. Consequently, it behooved the Japanese to cultivate the Chinese. The Chinese, too, were coming to recognize the West for what it was; they were able to see now that they had been taken in by the counterfeit friendship of the three powers that came to meddle in the war settlement, and they were beginning to think better of Japan. What Japan had to do was to cultivate China, to study China, and to know China. The Chinese could be brought to trust the Japanese and to rely on them. The Japanese had to prepare themselves to face the century ahead. For too long, too many Japanese had oriented themselves entirely toward the West; this dangerous imbalance could not be allowed to continue.[13]

Konoe's view of a predatory, racist West would probably have been shared by most Japanese of that era. It underlay also the urgency with which idealistic Japanese adventurers tried to "revive" China so that it would be able to function in the future struggle.[14] Coming from Konoe, so thoroughly experienced in Europe and so highly placed in the Meiji elite, this call carried authority. From Germany his friends wrote to him that his warnings were attracting attention and providing arguments for Wilhelmine propagandists of "yellow peril"; as a result Konoe did not repeat his warnings in print.[15] But his article soon found a translator for the Shanghai journal *Su pao*.[16]

Konoe's next move was to bolster the study of China. This he did through the establishment of the Dōbunkai (Common Culture Asso-

[13] Ibid., pp. 62-63. Note also p. 65 for an enthusiastic talk with Gotō Shimpei in 1900 on the need to establish Japan's foreign policy for the next hundred years; it includes agreement on the desirability of turning the confusions of domestic politics into unity on continental policy (*kokuron o soto ni tenjite* . . .).

[14] See, among others, the discussions of the Miyazaki brothers about what their life's work should be. Miyazaki Torazō (Tōten), *Sanjū sannen no yume* (Tokyo, 1967), pp. 36-39.

[15] Sakai, p. 212.   [16] *Supplement*, p. 423; issue of May 31, 1898.

ciation) in June 1898. In November it merged with the Tōakai (East Asia Association) to become the Tōa Dōbunkai. The organization was in some sense a Foreign Ministry front, approved by the Kenseikai cabinet and funded by the Yamagata government that followed it. It was launched with 40,000 yen from secret Foreign Ministry funds. The purpose was cultural diplomacy, but it served the needs of a number of government agencies equally well. It set out to establish offices in the principal cities of China and Korea, send Japanese students to familiarize themselves with all parts of both countries, publish vernacular periodicals in these countries, fund and attract Chinese and Korean students to study Japanese, and to bring some of them to Japan. For individual projects and areas financial support came from Navy, Army, and business sources. The Taiwan Government General helped with work in Fukien.[17]

The diary Konoe kept during his trip is studded with the documentation sent to keep him informed of the development of Dōbunkai programs. One can find the number of language students in the several parts of China, the efforts to secure approval of the Nanking branch by Liu K'un-i, and the names of the Japanese dispatched to those areas. Cooperation and coordination with other Japanese agencies were a matter of course. The Nishi Honganji Buddhist community worked in China, the Higashi Honganji in Korea. Dispensaries and hospitals established by these religious bodies could have army doctors assigned to them. Students and travelers could submit detailed reports on conditions and enterprises, as for example the Iron Works set up by Chang Chih-tung at Hankow.[18] These documents show Konoe as an active rather than merely honorary head of the association, just as other letters to him make clear the detail in which he expected to be kept informed about the Peers School.

Konoe's route took him from the United States to London, Paris, Brussels, Amsterdam, Berlin, Leipzig, Vienna, Moscow, Odessa, Bucharest, Istanbul, and Rome; and from there to Colombo, Singapore, Saigon, Hong Kong, Macao, Canton, Shanghai, Nanking, Wuhan, and home. He was received by heads of state in recognition of his own status and of the new international importance of his country. With foreign ministers he discussed the affairs of East Asia, listening, though without much conviction, to their assurances of pacific and non-acquisitive purposes in China.

---

[17] *Nikki*, vol. 2, p. 362. For Mitsui money at Nanking, ibid., p. 436.
[18] Ibid., p. 450.

By the time he reached China he was an authority on world affairs, the representative of a "successful" modernizer, and an exponent of a new and more cordial relationship between China and Japan. Like so many of his countrymen, Konoe found cause for alarm in what he saw of Western power abroad. As a young student bound for Germany in 1885 he had seen the French flag flying over Chinese territory in the Pescadores. His biographers quote him as having written then, "The land of our neighboring countries is gradually being consumed by the Westerners; are we to watch this conflagration on the other shore calmly?"[19] Nothing Konoe knew or saw in 1899 was likely to reassure him, from the international imperialist competition to the disrespect shown for Chinese on his travels. Along the China coast he noted (October 8), "Today a Chinese deck passenger died. He was thrown overboard immediately."[20] And when an unlucky steward spilled something on a member of Konoe's party aboard a mail boat off Canton, the captain, seeing this, immediately dropped his fork and pursued the unlucky fellow to the deck, where he caught up with him and thrashed him soundly. "Really a crude fellow," Konoe wrote of the captain.[21]

Protection, Avoidance, and Advice

By the time he reached China, Konoe was ready with advice that, as he put it repeatedly, "East Asian problems have to be settled by East Asians. China's political power has declined, but the problem lies in its politics and not with the Chinese people. Once there is some leadership, the preservation of East Asia will follow; it will not be difficult."[22]

Konoe's contribution to Japan's China policy provides an interesting example of the way a member of Japan's elite could work effectively through public and private channels. As a member of the top elite he was able to affect government decisions to shelter K'ang Yu-wei and Liang Ch'i-ch'ao after the failure of the Hundred Days in 1898. Concerned to exert influence on the conservative viceroys who were, he thought, holding China together, he did not want to let K'ang become too obviously dependent upon Japanese support, and he supervised the funding that got K'ang out of Japan. Then, as a private individual, he could assure the viceroys that Japan's sheltering of

---

[19] Kudō, *Konoe*, p. 18.   [20] *Nikki*, vol. 2, p. 424.
[21] Ibid., p. 430.
[22] Quoted in Dōbunkai, *Tai Shi kaikoroku*, vol. 2, p. 888, and elsewhere.

K'ang was no more than what international law obliged countries to provide for political refugees.

Japanese support for the flight of K'ang and Liang from China has often been described. Itō Hirobumi was on tour in China, and quick to urge the Japanese legation in Peking to do its best. Hirayama Shū and Miyazaki Torazō, both on government stipend, were on hand in Shanghai and Hong Kong to shepherd the fugitives to Japan. Konoe's diary refers to both Miyazaki and Hirayama as "Dōbunkai members" during his 1899 trip; in 1898 he was fully informed and an active participant in what took place. A diary notation for October 1898 finds Konoe discussing the provision of Foreign Ministry secret funds (2,000 yen) by Inukai for investigations (undertaken by Hirayama and Miyazaki) of conditions along the China coast. He also notes the problem of the refugees' reception in Japan; for Liang he sees no difficulty, but K'ang is too visible; there is no possible benefit in having his failure associated with Japan. Therefore K'ang should receive shelter only temporarily, and then move on.[23]

K'ang arrived at Shimbashi station, Konoe noted, on October 25. From the account of Miyazaki Torazō, who accompanied him, we learn of Miyazaki's futile efforts to get him to talk to people of the revolutionary party. A principal obstacle, Miyazaki felt, was K'ang's conviction that, he could do better in the Japanese political world if he kept his distance from revolutionary extremists. With access to people in Japan's highest circles, K'ang thought he might be able to get official Japanese help for the emperor, whose reforms had been crushed by the conservatives in Peking.[24]

In the event, Ōkuma's replacement by Yamagata made his good will of little importance, but K'ang's access to the Japanese elite was proved by his contact with Konoe. A grateful message from K'ang with appropriate sentiments about neighboring countries reached Konoe on November 2, and on November 12 Konoe received K'ang at night. Instead of promising help, however, Konoe pointed out that the reformers had been much too precipitate. K'ang urged the importance of direct intervention by Japan on his emperor's behalf, only to have Konoe counter with general statements about Sino-Japanese cooperation. "I said: 'The affairs of East Asia are becoming more serious every day. Today the problems of East Asia are not those of

[23] *Nikki*, vol. 2, pp. 168-69.
[24] For K'ang's arrival, ibid., p. 195. Miyazaki's talks with K'ang, *Sanjū-sannen no yume*, p. 135.

East Asia alone. They concern the entire world. The powers of Europe are struggling in East Asia, each for its own advantage. East Asians should be able to settle their problems alone. America's "Monroe Doctrine" is built on that assumption. Your country and mine should develop a "Monroe Doctrine" for East Asia. It's hard to do that today. But that should be our ultimate goal. What do you think?' K'ang: 'Indeed it is as your excellency says . . .' "[25] K'ang tried again to turn the talk to the possibility of Japanese assistance. There was no hope of rebuilding China without the restoration of the emperor; even Yüan Shih-k'ai did not support the Empress Dowager in his heart; Japanese help would bring undying gratitude from Chinese. It was not that simple, Konoe responded; the attitude of the powers had to be considered, and the best he could do was to offer to put K'ang in touch with some people with a special interest in such matters. The prospect of help from Japan was thus clearly slim. On November 27 Konoe met with Liang Ch'i-ch'ao for a similar talk.[26]

Early in 1899 Konoe made it known to the Chinese reformers that in view of his plans to visit China it might be desirable to have K'ang leave Japan for a time, perhaps to visit the United States.[27] He followed this up in talks with Foreign Ministry officials and former Prime Minister Ōkuma. Konoe then talked with Liang about the desirability of K'ang's seeing the rest of the world, and on February 13 he made the same point to K'ang Yu-wei himself.[28] After another visit by Konoe to the Foreign Ministry on March 13, 1,300 yen in Foreign Ministry funds were passed to him on March 15 to be made available to K'ang, who was to leave on the 22nd for Vancouver. Konoe was kept fully informed about K'ang's travels during his own trip abroad. From Vancouver the Japanese counsel reported that he had handed K'ang another 3,000 yen ($1,473.75 Canadian). Later in May Konoe received word that K'ang had left Vancouver for New York and Great Britain, and in November, while Konoe was still in China, came word that K'ang, who had returned to visit his sick mother in Macao, had been denied landing privileges at Yokohama by Japanese authorities and relegated to Kobe; K'ang was reported unhappy and displeased at the lower status he had now been assigned.[29]

The Dōbunkai could thus serve the government's purposes as well

[25] For close transcript of talk, *Nikki*, vol. 2, pp. 195-97.
[26] Ibid., p. 208.   [27] Ibid., p. 238.
[28] Ibid., p. 247.   [29] Ibid., pp. 317, 332, 459.

as Konoe's. Nothing was to be allowed to imperil Konoe's reception in China. That reception came to include meetings with Liu K'un-i at Nanking and Chang Chih-tung at Hankow. These meetings are described by Konoe in great detail, and his pleasure at the ritual of the approach to the yamen, the honor guard, passing through the successive gates, and the courtesy shown him by the dynasty's most prominent servants shows in the accounts he wrote.

Konoe's meeting with Liu was easily the more successful. Liu began with expressions of happiness at the increasing cordiality between China and Japan; Konoe assured him this was indeed the case, that friendship must surely increase in the future, that China's welfare was of concern to all Japanese, whether in public or private life, and that Japan's attitudes differed fundamentally from those of the rapacious Western powers. Liu agreed warmly, and sounded the theme of Sino-Japanese alliance. He went on to reminisce about the Liu-ch'iu argument of a few years earlier. Some, he said, had wanted to stand against the Japanese even if it meant letting the Russians have Ili, which was in question at the same time. He himself had thought it a great error to harm relations with a near neighbor over such insignificant islands, and he was glad the matter had ended peacefully. In response to Konoe's exposition of the aims of the Dōbunkai, Liu expressed his full agreement to the establishment of a Nanking branch; later he donated a plaque in his own hand. The talk was short, out of deference to the viceroy's health, but, Konoe felt, satisfactory. Curiously, while they had referred to the argument about Liu-ch'iu, neither seems to have brought up the more recent unpleasantness.[30]

Chang Chih-tung proved a much tougher conversationalist to handle. The talk began with questions about a military review Konoe had seen, and progressed to the desirability of sending Chinese students to Japan and attracting Japanese teachers familiar with the Chinese educational system to China. Then Chang went on the attack. It was good, he said, that the Japanese government had expelled K'ang Yu-wei, for the man was a traitorous rascal. Konoe demurred; the government had not done this, but some Japanese private individuals had advised K'ang to move on. The Japanese government had to abide by the principles of international law in its treatment of political refugees. Chang suggested that the same private individuals

[30] Ibid., pp. 442-45; October 28, 1898.

ought to tell Liang Ch'i-ch'ao to get out of Japan too. This would be a great help to relationships between the two countries. Konoe did not think so. Liang was much younger and slighter; he was in any case devoting himself to scholarship; when consulted, Konoe hadn't seen any need to ask Liang to leave, nor, in fact, could he have made him leave if the man had not wanted to. Konoe had, however, shortly before leaving Japan, seen to it that Liang was warned against writing in the *Ch'ing-i pao*, and that warning had been heeded. Chang remained indignant. The journal in question was a national disgrace, and the men were traitors, K'ang, T'an Ssu-tung, Liang, the lot of them; and their talk of helping the Kuang-hsü emperor was only a cover for treason. Chinese students were beginning to visit Japan in greater numbers, and they could not be allowed to risk reading poison like this. The talk went on to south China revolutionaries; what did Chang think about Sun Yat-sen? A cheap crook, was the response, and not worth discussing. Chang was thus unbending, and before very long the talk came to an end. "I was very disappointed," Konoe noted in his diary.[31]

As was to be expected, Konoe was careful with the Chinese he met on his trip. In Hong Kong and Canton it was agreed that, despite the offers of Miyazaki Torazō and others there who reported to him on the activities of the revolutionaries, he would not meet with partisans of any kind lest he prejudice his neutrality.[32]

The Japanese community in Shanghai presented Konoe with details of its difficulties in implementing the terms of the Shimonoseki treaty, and generally behaved exactly as an interested group of overseas merchants could have been expected to do. In a speech to some of them, Konoe expressed his belief in the need to get Japanese "from the better classes" (chūryū ijō no hito) to come to China, and stressed the importance of having Japanese abroad educate those at home in order to have a more effective and better founded policy and program.[33]

The trip had been arranged to include visits to Tientsin and Peking, but problems of time and schedule resulted in a decision to postpone them. Konoe did not visit these two cities until the fall of 1900.

Konoe's approach to the practical problem facing Japan in China

[31] Ibid., pp. 454-57.
[32] For Hirayama, ibid., p. 364; for Miyazaki, pp. 426, 434, 436, where he is referred to as "member."
[33] Ibid., p. 441.

was essentially that of a cautious realist. He was conscious of Japan's newfound importance and power, but also aware that Japan was in no position to challenge the imperialist league. Japan should participate in the activities of the powers enough to make sure it did not find itself disadvantaged in relative terms, but it should simultaneously maintain its distance from them enough to be able to pose as a different, more friendly, and somehow beneficial presence to the Chinese. He was full of fears about Japan's participation in the Boxer suppression, for instance, very worried about a spreading guerrilla conflict, and anxious to keep Japan's participation to a minimum. He was vastly relieved when the intervention achieved its purpose, and eager to withdraw Japanese forces thereafter.

The Russian moves in Manchuria following the outbreak of the Boxer Rebellion filled Konoe with fear. At this point he utilized his several roles to bring pressure on the government to avoid compromise. He worked hard to persuade Itō and Yamagata to refuse to deal with the Russians on the basis of a division of influence in Korea. In order to increase the pressure, he collaborated with party politicians, right-wingers like Tōyama Mitsuru, and others to form the Tai-Ro Kokumin Dōmeikai. He met privately with various individuals to rally support for his hard line. When the government contracted the Anglo-Japanese Alliance in 1902, Konoe's league was dissolved; the job was done. He did not long survive that date, and died in 1904, still only 41.

Konoe's life offers an interesting study of a leading figure in the growth of Japan's twentieth-century relationship with Asia. Japan's affiliation with the West, suggested by Fukuzawa's famous "datsu-A ron," did its work in the decade from 1885 to 1895, but with the victory over China and the intensification of European imperialist designs there in the years that followed, there was place and need for a new position. The "preservation of China" (Shina hozen ron) policy and the kind of cultural diplomacy represented by the Dōbunkai were practical and reasonable instruments of this concern. Japan's course was not yet set, nor was its power adequate to affect the course of events single-handedly. For members of the Japanese elite such as Konoe, everything had to be done to bring together the Japanese upper classes and their counterparts in China. Other Japanese with less stake in the Meiji structure—the China adventurers—responded to the new opportunities by cooperating with Chinese revolutionaries; but Konoe's approach, with its Confucian tones of education and morality, was closer to the main line of the Meiji establishment.

Unfortunately, Konoe's vision of an East Asian order had no place for politics or political sensitivity, in the same way as his ideal Japanese state structure lacked tolerance for domestic politics. Just as the education and betterment he wanted for the Japanese masses would make them less amenable to the leadership of their aristocratic elite (unless perhaps that elite had remained selfless and incorruptible, something elites seldom are), a political revival in China would have found the Chinese elite unwilling to defer to Japan simply because it was the prior modernizer.

As a result, Konoe's aristocratic ideals, however distinct from the *bushidō* of the samurai leaders he considered his inferiors, were doomed to a similar disappointment. Moreover, while he saw himself in competition with the Meiji genrō, it is difficult to see that he was basically in conflict with them on Japan's role in Asia. Little of what he had to say could be divorced from the course of power politics. If the Chinese elite refused to listen, or if, as was the case, it lost its place in the turmoil of later Chinese politics, then other steps could be expected.

Konoe wrote that the Chinese were beginning to see that they had been "taken in" by the Triple Intervention, which took privileges away from Japan only to give them to others. He did not live to discover that twentieth-century Chinese nationalism would be equally adamant against the extension of privileges to Japan, and that with the withering of European imperialism Japan would emerge as the principal imperialist danger.

Konoe's conviction of the dangers of Western racism was undoubtedly affected by his own German experience.[34] In all likelihood his son absorbed this viewpoint from his father to distill it in his famous essay against an Anglo-Saxon status quo in 1918. But the

[34] Augmented, no doubt, by subsequent experience. See the diary entry of Dr. Baelz, the respected physician who ministered to the Meiji elite, in June 1900: "Things are in a bad, a very bad way with the German diplomatic representation here. After the two preceding envoys had done their best to make a parade of their dislike of the Japanese, the new chargé d'affaires is behaving worse, if possible. The Russian minister's wife tells me that Count Wedel said to her, 'No Japanese shall get so much as a cup of tea here!'—a remark which has of course been buzzed all over Tokyo among the foreign community and will speedily come to the ears of the Japanese. . . ." See *Awakening Japan: The Diary of a German Doctor, Erwin Baelz* (Bloomington, Ind., 1974), p. 129.

"white peril," with the rapacious imperialisms of the West, was already on the wane by then. The ultimate irony is that it was Konoe's son, a man who came to power calling for a new politics free of the clash of interest groups, who led Japan into its final war with China under slogans of a "New Order" and an Asia freed from Western domination.

CHAPTER VII

CHINESE LEADERS AND JAPANESE AID
IN THE EARLY REPUBLIC

ERNEST P. YOUNG

AMERICAN STUDENTS of twentieth-century Chinese politics have still not recovered from the shock of Marius Jansen's *The Japanese and Sun Yat-sen*. With its publication in 1954, what had often been dismissed as Japanese propaganda or the cynicism of old China hands hostile to Chinese nationalism became unavoidable fact. Sun Yat-sen, revolutionary pioneer and father of the Republic, had frequently compromised his integrity as a nationalist by seeking foreign, especially Japanese, help for his movement. And he was willing to sign away chunks of Chinese sovereignty, prospectively, to win foreign favor. Subsequent research has, if anything, added to the impression of a willingness to depend on Japanese and other foreign support, both private and governmental.[1]

Marius Jansen's language was not accusatory, and a larger context of understanding was provided. But the damage to Sun's historical reputation was severe. In the light of the developing clash between Japanese continental expansion and Chinese nationalism, the prominence of Japanese among Sun's foreign helpers has seemed particularly untoward. Increased knowledge of his acceptance of compromising

---

[1] Harold Z. Schiffrin, *Sun Yat-sen and the Origins of the Chinese Revolution* (Berkeley, 1968); Albert A. Altman and Harold Z. Schiffrin, "Sun Yat-sen and the Japanese, 1914-16," *Modern Asian Studies*, vol. 6, no. 4 (1972), pp. 385-400; Key Ray Chong, "The Abortive American-Chinese Project for Chinese Revolution, 1908-1911," *Pacific Historical Review*, vol. 41 (1972), pp. 54-70; J. Kim Munholland, "The French Connection that Failed: France and Sun Yat-sen, 1900-1908," *Journal of Asian Studies*, vol. 32, no. 4 (November 1972), pp. 177-95; Edward Friedman, *Background toward Revolution: The Chinese Revolutionary Party* (Berkeley, 1974); C. Martin Wilbur, *Sun Yat-sen: Frustrated Patriot* (New York, 1976).

conditions and circumstances in return for Japanese aid has not been the only cause of diminishing esteem for Sun in Western writing on China. But it may be the most powerful element in the general disparagement of the man, and it produces a stunned perplexity among students first learning about Sun's career.

Shock at these revelations has been heightened by our standards for judging patriotism. We expect the leaders of national movements to exhibit unsullied autonomy and self-reliance. (For example, external ties have often been cited to disqualify Communists.) Sun's behavior is so disturbing because it seems weirdly idiosyncratic and contradictory for a national founding father.

Was Sun so unusual? Revelations about secret U.S. funding for Third World national leaders and social democrats in the 1950's and 1960's raise the question globally. Our new knowledge of the CIA's client list suggests that Sun Yat-sen's response to the Japanese was not simply an individual quirk or peculiar blindness. A look at the behavior of other Chinese leaders of Sun's time also shows the generality of the phenomenon.

In this chapter, I intend to examine the responses of a range of Chinese political leaders to the possibility of Japanese assistance in the first few years of the Chinese Republic. My interest is not so much in public statements on Japanese policy as in confidential contacts and secret negotiations, and the attitudes thereby demonstrated. Contact there was, whether sought out or not by the Chinese leaders, since Japanese representatives assiduously cultivated Chinese across the political spectrum. There seemed to be no position on that spectrum which automatically rejected Japanese aid under any circumstances. Nor was the reaction uniform. A discussion of some of the responses may lead us to some observations about the combination of circumstances and attitudes that inclined a political leader to strike deals with Japanese authorities.

The T'ung-meng Hui Group in the Early Republic

The various young Chinese activists who came together in 1905 to establish a national republican revolutionary organization, the T'ung-meng hui, never forged a cohesive, disciplined organization with a clear common line. Among the issues that divided them was the proper posture toward Japan, the host country for much of their organizing activity. Although cooperation with Japan was one of the basic planks in the organization's platform, support for it was not unanimous. In the second issue of the new party organ, the Hunanese revolutionary Ch'en T'ien-hua presented the skeptical view:

"Alliance" and "protection" should not be spoken in the same breath. Protection occurs when one is without real power and receives shelter from someone else, as in the case of Korea [which had just been made a Japanese protectorate]. An alliance occurs when power is possessed equally and succour is mutually provided, as in the case of Japan and England. An alliance arises because of common interests, not from shared writing and race [*t'ung-wen t'ung-chung*, or in Japanese, *dobun dōshu*]. . . . One could say that China has common interests with Japan, but if real power is not equal, there can be an alliance only in name; in reality, a protectorate. Hence wanting an alliance with Japan at this point is to want to become a Korea.[2]

The position represented by this cogent argument was occasionally revived within the group of veteran revolutionaries. And the expectation that Japan would provide crucial support to the revolutionary movement faded for a time. By the 1911 Revolution, Sun was again looking more to Britain as well as America. Although Japanese provided some loans through Sun, Japanese policy during the Revolution was on the whole not helpful to the republicans.[3] But as the entente between the British-supported Yüan Shih-k'ai and the revolutionaries soured in the winter of 1912-13, and as the Japanese grew more restive following the British lead in China, Japanese aid was once more the most attractive option for the opposition.

The general outline of Sun Yat-sen's "indiscretions" with representatives of private and governmental Japanese power over the next three years, until the fall of Yüan Shih-k'ai, is now well known. Publicly preaching pan-Asianism and confidentially offering economic inducements, Sun tried in the spring of 1913 to win Japanese support for his emerging confrontation with Yüan. In April, through the Japanese consul general in Shanghai, Sun offered Japan an alliance in the event of a southern and KMT victory over him. The new Chinese government would adopt the Japanese currency system for its own and the expansion of trade would be planned. If the com-

---

[2] "Ch'en Hsing-t'ai hsien-sheng chüeh-ming-shu," *Min Pao*, no. 2 (May 1906), p. 6.
[3] Masaru Ikei, "Japan's Response to the Chinese Revolution of 1911," *Journal of Asian Studies*, vol. 25, no. 2 (February 1966), pp. 213-27.

ing civil war produced a divided country, then Japan should separately recognize the south, as the United States had recognized Panama.[4] Apparently Sun had wanted to go to Japan to negotiate an alliance, but was dissuaded by his revolutionary colleagues.[5]

Japanese assistance to the anti-Yüan revolutionaries in the summer of 1913 came chiefly from the Japanese army and navy in China, against the wishes of the Foreign Ministry and without the concerted approval of the Tokyo government. It probably owed less to Sun's promises than to dislike of Yüan and general impatience with Foreign Ministry caution. But it was enough to keep Sun's appetite whetted after the 1913 revolt against Yüan failed. With diminished resources and a shrunken following, Sun's offers to Japanese officials in 1914 and 1915 of a special position in China in the event of his accession to power became increasingly extravagant. They included some of the most offensive features of the Twenty-One Demands.[6]

By 1916, Sun no longer had to entice Japanese authorities into aiding the enemies of Yüan Shih-k'ai, since it had become formal government policy to do so. He was given at least 1,400,000 yen between February and April.[7] Disbursements were made to his representatives in Tsingtao (Chü Cheng), Hankow (T'ien T'ung), Shanghai (Ch'en Ch'i-mei), and perhaps Kwangtung (Chu Chih-hsin) to finance the bribery of military forces and to organize and equip uprisings.[8] Sun had at least three April meetings in Tokyo with Tanaka Giichi, vice-chief of the General Staff, before proceeding to Shanghai in May.[9] Sun's group made its largest effort in Shantung, where the obviousness of its dependence on direct assistance and protection from the Japanese army created a scandal.[10] With Yüan's death and the disintegration of his structure of rule, Japanese authorities lost their interest in Sun, who had not managed to establish a major political position in his own country.

[4] *Nihon gaikō bunsho*, 1913, vol. 2, pp. 340-41.

[5] "Letter to Huang Hsing from Ch'en Ch'i-mei," *Chinese Studies in History*, vol. 7, no. 3 (Spring 1974), pp. 9-10.

[6] Marius B. Jansen, *The Japanese and Sun Yat-sen* (Cambridge, Mass., 1954), pp. 188-93.

[7] Altman and Schiffrin, p. 393.

[8] Ibid., pp. 396-97; Aoki Norizumi to chief of the General Staff, #16 (17 March 1916), "En Seigai teisei keikaku ikken. Bessatsu. HanEn dōran oyobi kakuchi jōkyō," (hereafter cited as "HanEn dōran"), vol. 5, 1.6.1.75, Foreign Ministry Archives, Tokyo: Consul general Segawa in Hankow to Ishii Kikujirō, foreign minister, #26 (9 May 1916), ibid., vol. 14.

[9] "Son Bun no dōsei," 9 and 26 April 1916, ibid., vols. 8 and 11.

[10] For a description of this episode, see Friedman, pp. 190-205.

Further revelations about Sun's deals with the Japanese in this period no longer have the power to surprise us. But what of his revolutionary colleagues? Was Sun unique in his solicitation of Japanese help and his willingness to offer inducements? He was not. One need not have been a pan-Asian enthusiast or an old friend of Miyazaki Torazō to find Japanese support attractive.

Huang Hsing, somewhat reluctantly preparing with Sun in the spring of 1913 for the showdown with Yüan, asked that the Japanese government organize the powers to "hint" to Yüan that he should retire.[11] In May 1913 the Japanese consul in Nanking reported a set of propositions from Wang Chih-hsiang that rivaled Sun Yat-sen's. Wang had been the revolutionary candidate for military governor of Chihli province in 1912 and more recently was the facilitator of an anti-Yüan alliance between the former high Ch'ing official Ts'en Ch'un-hsüan and Sun Yat-sen's cohorts. He told the Japanese representative that in return for Japanese help the revolutionaries would reaffirm their old principle of adherence to Japan—"a country of the same writing and race"—in preference to European and American ties. He offered the prospect of the joint management with Japan of railways, mines, and other enterprises in five Chinese provinces where the revolutionaries thought themselves strongest. To effect this collaboration, he floated the notion of a Sino-Japanese bank as creator of currency.[12] Ts'en Ch'un-hsüan himself asked the Japanese for between one and three million yen as the Second Revolution got under way in July.[13]

The battles of the Second Revolution began in Kiangsi, where Li Lieh-chün led resistance to an incursion of Yüan's troops. Li was assisted before and during the fighting by at least thirteen commissioned and noncommissioned officers of the Japanese army (some of whom were on reserve status). The Japanese garrison at Hankow provided an interpreter.[14] The Japanese consul in Nanking counted eleven Japanese still serving with the revolutionaries in that city as it surrendered to the northern army in early September.[15] Japanese diplomatic and military communications, immune from Peking's interference, provided the revolutionaries with a secure channel for messages. And as the revolutionary effort collapsed, the Japanese navy and Japanese commercial lines safely ferried the failed revolutionaries

11 *Nihon gaikō bunsho*, 1913, vol. 2, pp. 341-43.
12 Ibid., p. 352.   13 Ibid., pp. 369-70.
14 Ibid., pp. 366, 370-71.   15 Ibid., p. 460.

to Japan, starting with Huang Hsing at the end of July, and including Po Wen-wei, T'an Jen-feng, Chiang I-wu, Sun Yat-sen, Chang Chi, Ma Chün-wu, Hu Han-min, Ts'en Ch'un-hsüan, and Li Lieh-chün. The Japanese foreign minister objected throughout, but the ferry service was continued.[16]

So the revolutionaries found themselves in the same Japanese boat —almost literally—in their effort to defeat Yüan in the summer of 1913. They had not prepared well politically for a second recourse to arms. They substituted for careful preparation an indiscriminate seeking of alliances, including whatever the Japanese were willing to provide.

Subsequently, however, differences among them emerged regarding Japan. Sun, as noted, forged ahead on the same track, regardless. Many of the others had second thoughts, and with the shock of Japan's Twenty-One Demands, Huang Hsing, Po Wen-wei, Li Lieh-chün, and others said in the course of a long public statement: "We all know that the internal affairs of one's nation should only be solved by the people themselves; to rely on another country inevitably puts one's own nation in danger."[17] Those revolutionaries who split with Sun over this and other issues were not with him in 1916 as he engaged in his most intimate collaboration with Japanese power. They were either rather remote from the whole episode (like Huang Hsing) or had joined with other political groups (like Li Lieh-chün).

Liang Ch'i-ch'ao

Another major political grouping in the early Republic centered on Liang Ch'i-ch'ao, whose responses to the possibilities of Japanese assistance make an interesting contrast to Sun's. Liang was an admirer of the Meiji reforms, escaped the Empress Dowager's wrath in 1898 through Japanese protection, was for most of fourteen years an exiled guest in Japan, and had a political outlook closer to the conservative norm of Japan's political elite than did Sun Yat-sen. Despite these facts about Liang, he is not generally thought to have been notably pro-Japanese. Rather, he was known to be obsessively sensitive to the dangers of foreign, including Japanese, intervention. But, after all, he was not slow to seek out Japanese help when the moment seemed right and the need great.

[16] Ibid., pp. 380-418.
[17] Chün-tu Hsüeh, *Huang Hsing and the Chinese Revolution* (Stanford, 1961), p. 175.

When the Wuchang uprising on October 10 inaugurated what was to be the 1911 Revolution, Liang was already brewing his own scheme for bringing about dramatic changes in the Peking government. Though caught short by events, he nonetheless sailed for Manchuria in early November to see what he could salvage of his plans. He had intended to proceed to Peking after two weeks in Mukden but never got beyond the Japanese-dominated parts of southern Manchuria before returning to Kobe with nothing at all to show for his efforts. Wherever he went, he was assiduously attended by representatives of Japanese officialdom.[18] In Mukden, he consulted on November 11 with the Japanese consul general and asked for Japanese protection on his journey to Peking.[19] The Japanese government at this time was extremely interested in providing security on the Manchurian portion of the Peking-Mukden line.[20] Liang had envisaged the need of a one-to-two-hundred soldier escort for his entrance into Peking, but the manner in which the Japanese might provide him with support was not determined, since the journey was aborted.[21]

Once reconciled with the new republican order, Liang again returned to China. For almost three years he either worked for Yüan Shih-k'ai's government or at least accepted its broad policies. When Japan replaced Germany in Shantung and enlarged upon its position in the fall of 1914, Liang vigorously criticized Yüan's government for not resisting. But the issue of direct relations between Liang's group and the Japanese did not arise until Liang broke with Yüan over the monarchical movement.

The speculation that Japanese authorities, or their agents, orchestrated the Yunnan uprising against Yüan's authority in December 1915 is not supported by any concrete evidence of which I am aware.[22] On the contrary, although Japanese diplomats and other agents in China keenly sought out information regarding opposition to Yüan's monarchy, they seem to have learned of the specific prospect of a movement in Yunnan from the newspapers only three days before its public launching. And they were heavily dependent on British consular reports from Yunnan during the first three weeks of the rebellion.[23] When Liang Ch'i-ch'ao, a principal in the affair, spoke with

---

[18] Ting Wen-chiang, ed., *Liang Jen-kung hsien-sheng nien-p'u ch'ang-pien ch'u-kao* (hereafter cited as *Liang nien-p'u*; Taipei, 1958), pp. 343-45.

[19] *Nihon gaikō bunsho*, vols. 44-45, p. 157.

[20] Ikei, p. 217.   [21] *Liang nien-p'u*, p. 343.

[22] For one effort at such speculation, see Kwanha Yim, "Yüan Shih-k'ai and the Japanese," *Journal of Asian Studies*, vol. 24, no. 1 (November 1964), pp. 68-69.

[23] *Nihon gaikō bunsho*, 1915, vol. 2, pp. 202-62; R. M. MacLean to John Jordan,

Japanese diplomatic and military agents in Shanghai in late December 1915 and January 1916, it is apparent from the contemporary Japanese and Chinese documents that he was embarking on a new relationship, without any backlog of arrangements or commitments.

Although Liang secretly arrived in Shanghai from Tientsin on December 18, 1915, his first recorded conversation with a Japanese official seems to have been on December 30, after the Yunnan movement was publicly announced. In a confidential conversation with the Japanese consul general in Shanghai, he thanked Japan for her warnings to Yüan about the dangers of his monarchical enterprise—warnings delivered on October 23 and December 15, 1915. Yüan's diplomacy, he said, consisted of consorting with those from afar (read England) and attacking those nearby (read Japan). He criticized Yüan for not understanding Japan's position and influence.[24] This approach was only a warm-up. No request for aid was made, and the Japanese consul-general deduced that the purpose of the visit was to seek Japan's sympathy.

In the latter part of January 1916 Liang's relations with the Japanese began to become more important. When on January 21 he wrote to Ts'ai O, the dominant military figure in the Yunnan uprising and Liang's co-conspirator, he could report that Ts'en Ch'un-hsüan was probably going to Japan on behalf of the movement, that the Japanese government had rebuffed an emissary from Yüan Shih-k'ai (the canceled visit of Chou Tzu-ch'i), and that General Aoki Norizumi, well-known old China hand, would be arriving very shortly in Shanghai to consult. Liang expressed the view that it would be possible to discuss with the Japanese the supply of provisions and ammunition. He himself contemplated a short visit to Japan before proceeding to Yunnan (as it turned out, he did not take either trip).[25]

Aoki Norizumi seems to have been appointed to Shanghai by the General Staff only after the Yunnan outbreak.[26] He actually arrived in Shanghai on January 21, 1916, and spoke with Liang on January 23. Aoki's report of the conversation describes Liang sounding him

---

minister in Peking (probably 28 December 1915), Foreign Office Archives, Public Record Office, London (hereafter, FO), 228/2753; Jordan to Herbert Goffe, consul in Kunming (2 January 1916), FO 228/2753; Goffe, Kunming, to Jordan (21 January 1916), FO 228/2753.

[24] *Nihon gaikō bunsho*, 1915, vol. 2, pp. 257-58.

[25] *Liang nien-p'u*, pp. 466-68.

[26] Aoki Norizumi to Terauchi Masatake (29 December 1915), Papers of Terauchi Masatake, item 12.2, Kensei Shiryōshitsu, Diet Library, Tokyo.

out on the attitude of the Japanese government and the likelihood of aid. Liang stressed to Aoki the need for secrecy and hoped that Ts'en Ch'un-hsüan's visit to Japan could be kept confidential.[27] In Liang's description of the occasion for Ts'ai O, he noted that Aoki recognized the strength of those involved in the Yunnan uprising. He also reported Aoki's assurance that the Japanese inclination toward seizing rights from China had been repudiated by informed citizens in favor of forging an alliance with the Chinese people.[28] By relaying these assurances, Liang was preparing the ground for a major commitment to reliance on Japanese assistance.

On the other hand, Liang was not rushing heedlessly into the Japanese embrace, despite the acknowledged financial difficulties being experienced by the Yunnan movement and the urgent need for weapons. In early February, the Japanese consul general in Shanghai noted the relative caution of the "constitutionalists" (that is, those in Liang's political camp) in approaching Aoki, compared to other anti-Yüan groups.[29] Liang, in a late February cable to Ts'en Ch'un-hsüan in Japan (apparently intercepted and decoded by the Japanese army), opposed an agreement for an alliance with Japan. He held that such a decision should be made only after a new government was established. Further, he argued, the job of pressing Yüan Shih-k'ai to withdraw should not be delegated to the Japanese, since this would produce adverse byproducts.[30] The contrast with Sun Yat-sen is notable.

The reserve of Liang's stance toward Japanese ties gradually eroded. Trips to the United States, Japan, and Yunnan were all forgone in preference for proceeding in March to Kwangsi, where the military chief was about to commit his province to the anti-Yüan movement. Liang sought and obtained Japanese protection for the journey, via Hong Kong and Haiphong.[31] En route, on March 12, Liang asked that Japan send one or two gunboats to Canton under the pretext of protecting Japanese nationals, in order to give the anti-Yüan movement moral support. He offered an unspecified "consider-

[27] Major General Aoki to chief of the General Staff (25 January 1916), "HanEn dōran," vol. 3.

[28] Liang Ch'i-ch'ao, Tun-pi chi (Taipei, 1961), pp. 25-26.

[29] Consul general Ariyoshi in Shanghai to Ishii (8 February 1916), "HanEn dōran," vol. 3.

[30] Liang Ch'i-ch'ao to Ts'en Ch'un-hsüan (27 February 1916), ibid.

[31] Liang nien-p'u, pp. 472-80. Aoki to vice-chief of the General Staff (27 February 1916); Ariyoshi, Shanghai, to Ishii (4 March 1916); and Consul general Imai in Hong Kong to Ishii, #45 (4 March 1916?): "HanEn dōran," vol. 3; Imai, Hong Kong, to Ishii, #87 (28 March 1916), ibid., vol. 6.

able security" for the speedy delivery of arms on credit. Though he still stopped short of asking for direct Japanese pressure on Yüan, he did urge Japanese blockage of any international effort to force a compromise with Yüan.[32] In early May, he asked that Japan recognize as a belligerent party the four southern provinces of Yunnan, Kweichow, Kwangsi, and Kwantung (an option already envisaged in a Japanese cabinet decision of early March but ultimately not taken up).[33] And before the end of May, representatives of his political group requested what Liang in February had forsworn: a direct Japanese governmental admonishment to Yüan that he should resign.[34] I have found no credible evidence that Liang promised the sort of intimate ties that were the common currency of Sun's approaches to the Japanese, but he had gone quite far in relying on Japanese help in his campaign to rid China of Yüan Shih-k'ai.

Some Further Instances

Liang Ch'i-ch'ao acted as a representative of the Yunnan-based movement that produced the National Protection Army (Hu-kuo chün). But the Yunnan movement had a life of its own. One notable feature was the predominance of military men, and among them, the high proportion trained at Japan's Army Officers' Academy (Nihon rikugun shikan gakkō). All three commanders and all three chiefs of staff in the three armies of the movement were graduates of this school. Ten of the commanders of the fourteen echelons (t'i-tuan) into which the three armies were divided were graduates of the same school, as were six of the fourteen chiefs of staff of the different echelons. (Indeed, of the twenty-two graduates in these top positions, fifteen of them were from the same sixth Chinese class at this Japanese military school.)[35] A reasonable expectation from a movement so constituted was a close connection with Japan and her representatives. In fact the connection was forged only gradually, as Japan "proved" her usefulness to the movement.

I have already noted that Japanese officials seem to have been

[32] Imai, Hongkong, to Ishii, #51 (12 March 1916), ibid., vol. 5.

[33] Consul general Akatsuka in Canton to Ishii, #148 (6 May 1916), ibid., vol. 13.

[34] Ariyoshi, Shanghai, to Ishii, #39 (28 May 1916), ibid., vol. 17. Liang's representatives in this instance were Wen Tsung-yao and Chou Shan-p'ei. Actually, such admonishment had already been delivered to Yüan's representatives as early as April 12. Hioki Eki, minister in Peking, to Ishii, #298 (12 April 1916), ibid., vol. 8. For later reiterations, see *Nihon gaikō bunsho*, 1916, vol. 2, pp. 62-63, 65-68.

[35] Consul Hori in Yunnan to Ishii, #5 (6 April 1916), "HanEn dōran," vol. 12.

kept in the dark about the movement until the eve of its first public act. The Japanese government had no official representative in the province, nor when the first emissary managed to get there on January 15, 1916, its own channels of communication. What is more, the first Japanese arrivals were treated with coldness. The British consul reported this reaction and also "the considerable fear of [Japan] and her aims in China" among the Japanese-trained leadership of the movement.[36] These impressions might be dismissed as the results of a successful deception of the British if it were not for their confirmation in Japanese documents. In early February, complained a Japanese diplomat just transferred from Canton, official newspapers in Yunnan frequently wrote about Japan's selfish ambition (*yashin*). Leaders of the movement were reportedly worried that, in return for further concessions by Peking, Japan would aid Yüan Shih-k'ai. The Japanese representatives in Yunnan were suspected of being agents of Yüan or of the hostile military governor in Kwangtung, Lung Chi-kuang. And the diplomat thought bad feelings toward Japan were increasing.[37]

By early March 1916 the climate had changed. The official Japanese representatives cited the beneficial effect on Yunnanese opinion of Japan's rebuff to Yüan's emissary and Japan's cooperation in keeping salt revenues from Yüan. It was also a matter of need: Japanese aid seemed more and more attractive as the fighting was prolonged and the prospect of an early victory dimmed.[38] In mid-March, T'ang Chi-yao, Yunnan's military governor, initiated a request for a Japanese legal adviser and invited the local Japanese military representative to move nearer his yamen in order to exchange views more freely.[39] By the end of the month, there was the prospect of a breakthrough to the sea and the possibility of actually receiving Japanese supplies in quantity.[40] But, overall, the response in Yunnan to proffered Japanese friendship had been slow—checked, apparently, by memories of recent Japanese assaults on Chinese sovereignty and by suspicion of Japan's true intentions.

[36] Goffe, Kunming, to Jordan (31 January 1916), FO 228/2753; Goffe, Kunming, to Jordan, #13 (20 February 1916), FO 228/2736.

[37] *Nihon gaikō bunsho*, 1916, vol. 2, pp. 97-98; Akatsuka, Canton, to Ishii, #46 (21 February 1916), transmitting Fujimura in Yunnan, #14 (14 February 1916), "HanEn dōran," vol. 3.

[38] Major Yamagata, Yunnan, to chief of General Staff (16 February 1916), ibid., vol. 3.

[39] Hori, Kunming, to Ishii, #18 (15 March 1916), ibid., vol. 18.

[40] Hori, Kunming, to Imai, #28 (29 March 1916), ibid.

Like Liang Ch'i-ch'ao, there were other outriders of the anti-Yüan movement who dealt with the Japanese. Ts'en Ch'un-hsüan, who had worked with Sun Yat-sen's group in the Second Revolution in 1916, raised money in Japan on behalf of the Yunnan-based southern movement. He was rewarded with a loan of one million yen on March 22, 1916.[41] Henceforth, from when he left Japan in early April, Ts'en was in close touch with official Japanese in China, who urged on him a closer relationship to Sun Yat-sen's people. Ts'en, in turn, resisted the pressure toward integration with Sun and pressed the Japanese for a speedy delivery of arms.[42] T'ang Shao-i, who had entered the insurance business in Shanghai after his departure from the premiership under Yüan in 1912, frequently spoke to official Japanese in 1916 of his opposition to Yüan. Although he displayed some nervousness regarding the overtness of Japanese support for the anti-Yüan movement, he assured an American officer that he was favorably disposed toward the Japanese and did not believe they had aggressive designs on China.[43] In Peking, Vice President Li Yüan-hung was making secret contacts with Japanese officials on his own behalf from the first part of April 1916.[44]

At the conservative end of the spectrum, Chuang Wen-k'uan, the outspoken censor who admonished Yüan against the monarchy, told the Japanese legation on February 6, 1916 that, regrettably, the present situation was likely to lead to Japanese intervention, but that he preferred Japanese to European or American intervention.[45] Wang Ta-hsieh, vice chairman of the Ts'an-cheng-yüan (Yüan Shih-k'ai's appointed pseudo-legislature that had offered him the throne in December 1915), told General Aoki in January 1916 that he was very anti-Yüan and asked that China be saved from collapse by Japanese action.[46] In early April, he called on Japan to work for the restora-

---

[41] Altman and Schiffrin, p. 394. The transaction was soon noted by a Chinese agent for Yüan Shih-k'ai in Japan, though the sum mentioned was 700,000 yüan. Police report of April 8, 1916, "HanEn dōran," vol. 8.

[42] Navy command, "Shin Shun-ken to no taidan" (11 April 1916), "HanEn dōran," vol. 8; Colonel Itogawa to General Staff, #7 (6 May 1916), ibid., vol. 13.

[43] Aoki, Shanghai, to the chief of the General Staff, #1 (25 January 1916), ibid., vol. 3; Ariyoshi, Shanghai, to Ishii, #22 (7 March 1916), ibid., vol. 5; Ariyoshi, Shanghai to Ishii, #155 (29 May 1916), ibid., vol. 16; *Nihon gaikō bunsho*, 1916, vol. 2, pp. 189-90; Lt. Col. D. S. Robertson, military attaché, Shanghai, to Jordan (21 May 1916), FO 228/2738.

[44] Col. Banzai to vice-chief of General Staff, #30 (15 April 1916), "HanEn dōran," vol. 9.

[45] *Nihon gaikō bunsho*, 1916, vol. 2, pp. 28-31.

[46] Aoki to chief of the General Staff, #1 (25 January 1916), "HanEn dōran," vol. 3.

tion of the Ch'ing court—a political objective to which he cleaved after Yüan's death.[47]

Yüan Shih-k'ai

The relationship of Yüan with the Japanese authorities constitutes the story of the formal diplomatic relations between the two countries during the first years of the Republic. Its main events have been frequently recounted, and I have presented my own interpretations elsewhere.[48] A few incidents may serve my comparative purposes in this chapter.

Although Yüan as a Ch'ing official had a history that included conflict with Japanese intentions in East Asia, serious antagonism during his presidency developed only with the Second Revolution of 1913. Over two months before the fighting, the Chinese Army Ministry sought to purchase arms from Japan, a move which the Japanese legation probably correctly interpreted as an effort to forestall Japanese aid to Yüan's revolutionary enemies and to show good will toward Japan.[49] Yüan's government was assured that, aside from the antics of a few irresponsible rōnin, Japanese influence was being used against any recourse to arms by Yüan's Chinese opponents.[50]

When in the event a portion of the Japanese official presence in China provided support for the movement against him, Yüan became preoccupied with discerning its significance for his future relations with Japan. In a long conversation in September 1913 with George Ernest Morrison, one of his foreign advisers, he complained: "Cannot the Japanese Government restrain the military? Why do the Japanese Government permit their men to take part in the rebellion? The Japanese have entered into large contracts with the rebel leaders and now they will not be able to obtain payment."[51] In the wake of Yüan's capitulation before Japan's ultimatum in the episode of the Twenty-One Demands, Morrison recorded these impressions after a session with Yüan on May 20, 1915: "Japan is the obsession.

---

[47] Chief of staff of the Tsingtao Garrison to vice-chief of General Staff (3 April 1916), ibid., vol. 6; Jordan to Grey, #302 (31 October 1916), FO 228/1957.

[48] For good accounts, see especially Madeleine Chi, *China Diplomacy, 1914-1918* (Cambridge, Mass., 1970), and Usui Katsumi, *Nihon to Chūgoku—Taishō jidai* (Tokyo, 1972). My own version is in *The Presidency of Yüan Shih-k'ai: Liberalism and Dictatorship in Early Republican China* (Ann Arbor, 1976), especially pp. 133-34, 186-92, 238-40.

[49] *Nihon gaikō bunsho*, 1913, vol. 2, p. 349.

[50] Ibid., pp. 349-50.

[51] Memorandum of 18 Septetmber 1913, item 142, G. E. Morrison Papers, Mitchell Library, Sydney.

Japan intriguing. . . . He is thoroughly scared of Japan. Fear of this active neighbour paralyses all his actions. . . . He is hypnotised and paralysed by the fear of Japan like a frog in the presence of a snake."[52]

As the Japanese government turned in 1916 toward making his overthrow a formal policy objective, Yüan's response had two separate parts. One was to suggest that the revolutionaries had sold themselves to Japanese purposes and if victorious would destroy the nation.[53] Many Chinese leaders needed no prompting to be concerned about the degree of Japanese intervention, especially in the case of the revolutionary army in Shantung. Yüan's second and contradictory line of response, apparently entered upon after the rebellion had spread beyond Yunnan and Kweichow, was to entice Japanese support with promises of greater privileges and closer ties. Lin Ming-te has reported the discovery in China's diplomatic archive of an offer by Yüan in early April 1916 of the equivalent of the notorious fifth category of the Twenty-One Demands.[54] A few days later, Ts'ao Ju-lin, Yüan's leading Japan expert, was suggesting a Sino-Japanese alliance, but explicitly rejected the path represented by the "fifth category"—in ignorance of the earlier offer or with the intention of retracting it.[55] As in approaches toward Japan by Yüan's enemies, his own people gradually raised the ante. In mid-May, in return for Japanese support of Yüan's remaining in office, two of his chief economic aides proposed to the Japanese legation the establishment of joint Sino-Japanese banks, business enterprises, telephone networks, and steamship companies. Japanese railway construction could be undertaken in south China to the extent that third countries did not object. If Japan wanted to consolidate its predominant position in China, they argued, there was no better means than using Yüan's influence. For all the decline in his prestige, Yüan's effectiveness could not be matched by any of his opponents.[56] Then as now, if you want

---

[52] Diary (20 May 1915), item 104, in ibid.

[53] Peking cable, received from General Staff (3 March 1916), "HanEn dōran," vol. 3; Hioki to Ishii, #295 (12 April 1916), ibid., vol. 8; commander of the army stationed in China (Tientsin) to the chief of the General Staff, #70 (13 May 1916), ibid., vol. 14.

[54] Lin Ming-teh, "Yüan Shih-k'ai's Monarchical Scheme and Japan," paper delivered at the Conference on China and Japan: Their Modern Interactions, Portsmouth, New Hampshire, June 1976.

[55] Col. Banzai to chief of the General Staff, #24 (11 April 1916), "HanEn dōran," vol. 9.

[56] Nihon gaikō bunsho, 1916, vol. 2, pp. 454-57. Yüan's representatives in this matter were Liang Shih-i and Chou Tzu-ch'i.

someone to sell you his country, you should sign a contract with the person who can best deliver the goods.

Nationalism in a Semi-Colony

This recital of approaches by Chinese leaders to Japanese authorities raises many questions. I shall confine my evaluation of its meaning to a few simple but fundamental points.

Since so many indulged in the pursuit of the "Japanese connection," interpretations of the phenomenon that stress idiosyncracies or weakness of character surely miss the mark. Pan-Asian ideology was a factor, but since even those who did not share this outlook sought Japanese assistance, it cannot stand as a general explanation. The common denominator was need. The directness of any approach to the Japanese and the degree to which a Chinese leader was willing to appeal to Japan's expansionist proclivities in order to get help were related to his current political weakness, the power of his enemies, and the urgency of his situation. Rarely does one get the impression that reliance on Japanese support was a *preferred* route to attaining political goals in China. It was taken only when other routes seemed closed or ineffective. Or, when there was the suggestion of preference, as in the case of Censor Chuang, choice was among the different imperialisms pressing on China, with the Japanese version only the least noxious.

Though virtually all Chinese leaders of the time were ready in extremity to depend on Japanese help, some were more susceptible than others to serving Japanese purposes. On this matter, perhaps the best authorities were the Japanese. In the climactic months of Japanese intervention in Chinese political struggles in 1916, there seemed no doubt in official Japanese minds that Sun Yat-sen and his followers were the most reliable in their favorable attitudes toward Japan. (This judgment did not imply that Sun was the Japanese nominee for leadership in China; in such matters the Japanese government was often realistic and acknowledged Sun's lack of political strength.) For example, the Japanese consul general in Hong Kong remarked in February 1916 that Sun's actions since the conclusion of the Sino-Japanese negotiations of 1915 proved his continuing commitment to a Sino-Japanese alliance. The reference was particularly to the efforts of Sun's group to discourage the anti-Japanese boycott of that year. By contrast, Ts'ai O and Li Lieh-chün were thought to be unfriendly and united in favoring "opposition" to Japan.[57] In Hankow, the Japanese consul general in March reported that Sun's party there, centering on T'ien T'ung, would rely on Japanese aid in achieving its objective. The Republican Party contingent had the same objective of overthrowing Yüan, went the report, but feared foreign interference and entertained suspicion of Japan.[58] Although Liang Ch'i-ch'ao increasingly sought out Japanese help in the first half of 1916, and told a Japanese official that he was "abandoning his previous feelings and would sincerely express his friendship toward Japan,"[59] General Aoki opined in mid-May that Liang "cannot be thought of as one who in the end truly desired the intervention of Japanese power." Nor was T'ang Shao-i considered one who would seriously rely on Japan.[60] Yüan Shih-k'ai was not trusted for one minute.

Despite the wooing of Japan by Chinese politicians, Japanese authorities were not deeply persuaded that they had won converts to their cause. Even Sun Yat-sen could not escape a degree of suspicion: "Of course, as Sun is a Chinese, we cannot rely on him completely."[61] Each side was trying to use the other, and ultimately there could be no trust.

One should not conclude from this tale that Chinese leaders of the period were not nationalistic. They were each of them pursuing strategies designed to bring eventual strength and dignity to China, with the concomitant assertion of independence. But no one had discovered a straight path to this goal. There seemed to be necessary zigzags and circuitous detours, which sometimes proved to be dangerous dead ends. Our ideas of nationalism contain unrealistically high standards of heroism and purity. Perhaps we admire it too much in colonial and semi-colonial countries and as a consequence ask too much of it. At the core of nationalism lies the urge to achieve great power, and the search for power cannot but generate complexities and contradictions. In a semi-colony, such as China was at the time, these complexities and contradictions were particularly anguished and sharp.

[57] Imai, Hongkong, to Ishii, #10 (14 February 1916), "HanEn dōran," vol. 3.

[58] Segawa, Hankow, to Ishii, #111 (20 March 1916), ibid., vol. 5.

[59] Akatsuka, Canton, to Ishii, #148 (6 May 1916), ibid., vol. 13.

[60] Aoki, Shanghai, to vice-chief of the General Staff, #98 (14 May 1916), ibid., vol. 14.

[61] Imai Hong Kong, to Ishii, #10 (14 February 1916), ibid., vol. 3.

CHAPTER VIII

Ts'ao Ju-lin (1876-1966): His Japanese Connections*

—————

MADELEINE CHI

SINO-JAPANESE relations in modern times have been turbulent, punctuated with earth-shaking events. The turmoil began with the war of 1894-95 in which the proud Chinese were defeated by their "dwarf" neighbors. Contrary to expectation, the Chinese responded by emulating the Japanese, and droves of Chinese students crossed the waters to study in Japan, to learn from their "brothers" the secrets of enriching the nation and strengthening the army. Over time these returned students became architects of constitutional government, modernizers of education, law, commerce, and industry, and the new bureaucrats of the late Ch'ing and early Republic. In addition, Japanese teachers in China were far more numerous than other foreign nationals, and Japanese advisers were found in many departments of central and local governments.

This wave of admiration for Japan reached its peak around 1910. Subsequently incidents, demands, demonstrations, boycotts, and finally, battles, eroded the relations between the two neighbors. By World War II, many Chinese viewed the Japanese as aggressors and liars who had harbored evil designs on China from time immemorial; Chinese who had political dealings with the Japanese were termed unpatriotic, if not traitorous.[1] Ts'ao Ju-lin was deeply involved in several major political developments between 1915 and 1940 as an

* The writer wishes to thank the American Philosophical Society and Manhattanville College for their grants which, in part, supported her research in Tokyo in the summer of 1975. Grateful thanks are also due Professor Andrew J. Nathan, Columbia University, and Professor J. Kenneth Olenik, Montclair State College, for having read the draft and made valuable comments.

[1] Cf. Chiang Kai-shek's statement of December 26, 1938, quoted in Harold S. Quigley, *The Far Eastern War, 1937-1941* (Boston, 1942), p. 286.

active participant, deserving culprit, interested onlooker, or unwitting victim. This study will examine the career of Ts'ao Ju-lin from his student days through his golden age of power, to his years of disillusionment and decline. All these phases of his life were shaped by his association with Japan and the Japanese.

Formative Years

Born in Shanghai County in 1876, Ts'ao Ju-lin was raised in a bureaucrat's family. Both his grandfather and father worked for the Kiangnan Arsenal, one of the early enterprises of China's self-strengthening movement. In his youth Ts'ao was instructed in Confucian precepts and taught to memorize the classics. In keeping with the trends of the time, he later left home to study technology at the Wuhan Railway Academy. The curriculum of the school was too weak to please Ts'ao; he therefore decided to study in Japan. Since studying abroad had replaced the classical civil service examination as the avenue to officialdom, his family was willing to make a substantial sacrifice by selling a piece of land to pay for his expenses.

Ts'ao Ju-lin left for Japan in 1899. When he reached Tokyo, he marveled at the achievements of the Meiji Restoration and dreamed that China might follow the Japanese example in building up a viable constitutional monarchy. With this in mind he enrolled in the law school of the Chūō University, then known as the Tokyo Law Academy (Tōkyō Hōgakudō). His student days in Japan were happy ones. For two years he boarded with the family of the late Nakae Chōmin (1847-1901), the well-known liberal who introduced Rousseau's *Social Contract* into Japan. Nakae had died before Ts'ao joined the household, but Ts'ao was befriended by his widow and children, and by liberal Japanese intellectuals who came to edit Nakae's works for publication. Later Chōmin's son, Nakae Ushikichi (1889-1942) became a good friend of Ts'ao, and the young Nakae in turn lived in Ts'ao's Peking house for over twenty years. Although Nakae Ushikichi was even more radical than his father, Ts'ao was never susceptible to radicalism. He made no friends among the Chinese revolutionaries in Tokyo; on the contrary, he moved in conservative circles and formed lifelong friendships with men like Lu Tsung-yü (1875-1941) and Chang Tsung-hsiang (1877-1940's) who were studying in Tokyo at about the same time. Lu graduated from Waseda, and Chang earned a law degree from the Meiji University. They would subsequently become Ts'ao's close political collaborators.

By 1904, when Ts'ao had earned his law degree and was ready to return home, he had stored up many favorable impressions of Japan. These were reinforced by the image of a unified and resolute nation about to launch into war against Russia. In short, Ts'ao appreciated and esteemed Japan.[2]

Returned students in the early twentieth century easily found work with the Chinese government. Ts'ao passed a special examination on modern subjects and was assigned to the Board of Agriculture and Commerce. Soon he and his friends, Lu Tsung-yü and Chang Tsung-hsiang, attracted the attention of Hsü Shih-ch'ang, the civilian leader of the Peiyang Clique dominated by Yüan Shih-k'ai. Hsü recommended these three capable young men to the throne, thus establishing a permanent patron-protégé relationship. As a consequence, Ts'ao, Lu, and Chang spent their political lives in Peiyang circles. With the founding of the Republic, President Yüan Shih-k'ai appointed Ts'ao a member of parliament. Evidently Ts'ao fulfilled Yüan's expectations in combating the unruly Kuomintang. Yüan was generally impressed by Ts'ao's abilities, finding him handsome, amiable, efficient, and a charming negotiator who could handle delicate issues. Therefore Ts'ao was rewarded with a cabinet post, that of vice-minister of foreign affairs, in August 1913. Ts'ao remained in the Ministry of Foreign Affairs until Yüan's death in June 1916.[3]

The catastrophic occurrence during Ts'ao's service in the Ministry of Foreign Affairs was the negotiation of the Twenty-One Demands with Japan from January to May 1915. The demands, divided into five groups, required Chinese consent to Japan's hold on Shantung (Group I), where Japan had acquired German interests in the early days of World War I, and to Japan's paramount position in south Manchuria and Inner Mongolia (Group II), and Fukien (Group IV). In addition, Japan desired to legalize its de facto control of the Hanyehp'ing (Group III), the iron and coal complex in the heart of the Yangtze valley. Lastly, in Group V, Japanese demands included the hiring of Japanese political, financial, and military advisers,

---

[2] Ts'ao Ju-lin, I-sheng chih hui-i (Hong Kong, 1966), passim, see especially pp. 16-17, 26, 30-32, 35, 280-82. Ts'ao composed this autobiography for the purpose of rehabilitating his name, and the work was edited by Li Pei-t'ao, a high official of the Bank of Communications and faithful follower of Ts'ao, interview with Li Pei-t'ao by the author, Hong Kong, July 11, 1972.

Ts'ao's life long friendship with Nakae Ushikichi is also treated in Nakae Ushikichi shokanshū, comp. Suzue Genichi et al. (Tokyo, 1974), pp. 429, 445-46.

[3] Ts'ao, pp. 36, 101, 107-109, 347-49.

and the establishment of a joint police force and of a jointly controlled arsenal.[4]

Shocked by this unprecedented diplomatic confrontation, Yüan Shih-k'ai spurred himself to vigorous action. Although he appointed Lu Cheng-hsiang the chief negotiator, Yüan himself reviewed and commented on every item of the Japanese proposal, and gave directives on day-to-day negotiations. Yüan insisted on item-by-item discussion to buy time; he also encouraged Councillor V. K. Wellington Koo's "newspaper diplomacy," disregarding a Japanese injunction of secrecy. Koo judiciously leaked the news to friendly American and British journalists. All these stratagems merely prolonged the inevitable capitulation, for China simply could not withstand Japan's threat of force. When, on May 6, the Chinese cabinet heard that Japan would soon deliver an ultimatum, it sent Ts'ao Ju-lin to inform Minister Hioki, the chief Japanese negotiator, that China would accept all the demands, including the notorious Group V, which the Chinese believed would transform China into a Japanese protectorate.

On that same day, May 6, internal political pressure and adverse world opinion prompted the Japanese cabinet to drop Group V. When Lu Tsung-yü, then Chinese minister in Tokyo, wired this news to Peking, the Chinese were greatly relieved. However, they had to retract the statement made by Ts'ao to Hioki. On May 7, when the Japanese ultimatum was delivered, Ts'ao went back to Hioki to say that his conversation of the previous day presented his personal view, and that his government would accept only four groups of the demands.[5] While Ts'ao regarded this act as heroic and patriotic, he was vilified by half-informed General Chang Hsün for having compromised with the Japanese. Along with the violent anti-Japanese movements that broke out after the signing of the Twenty-One Demands, a vigorous telegram war was waged against Ts'ao Ju-lin. In reply, Ts'ao issued an impassioned circular telegram. He recounted the tension and hardship he had undergone during the lengthy negotiations, and the ingenuity he and his colleagues had exercised to ward off greater losses. Finally he announced that the acceptance

---

[4] Regarding Japanese policy formulation of the Twenty-One Demands and the consequences for Sino-Japanese relations, see Marius B. Jansen, *Japan and China: From War to Peace, 1894-1972* (Chicago, 1975), pp. 193-94, 202-18.

[5] Wang Yün-sheng, *Liu-shih-nien-lai Chung-kuo yü Jih-pen* (Tientsin, 1932-34), vol. 6, p. 304; Minister Hioki to Foreign Minister Katō, May 7, 1915, published in Japan, Gaimusho, *Nihon gaikō bunsho* (hereafter cited as *Gaikō bunsho*; Tokyo, 1966), 1915, vol. 3, pt. 1, pp. 409-10.

of Group V on May 6 was a cabinet decision, not his own.[6] Since high government officials verified Ts'ao's account, no one questioned his sincerity or accuracy, but from that time Group V stood as a symbol of Japan's design to subjugate China, and May 7 was designated the National Humiliation Day. Three or four years later, because of Ts'ao's involvement in the Twenty-One Demands negotiations and his subsequent political activities, the Chinese public would rank him as the number one traitor.

The Twenty-One Demands affected Ts'ao in other ways too. Ts'ao was made keenly aware of the weakness of Yüan Shih-k'ai's China, and of the futility of Yüan's reliance on Great Britain and the United States. These facts were further borne out by Japan's ability to frustrate Yüan's monarchical plan in 1916, and Yüan died a disappointed man in June of that year. Ts'ao Ju-lin concluded that his superior, generally hailed as the strong man of China, had made a fatal mistake in antagonizing Japan, China's closest neighbor. England and America were like water in a distant ocean, Ts'ao argued, too far away to save one's house on fire. China should cultivate Japan's good will because Japan was near enough to help. Ts'ao did not think of self-reliance. "Rely on Japan" was the theme he preached to Tuan Ch'i-jui, who became prime minister in March 1916.[7]

The irresolute Tuan Ch'i-jui never enjoyed the authority that Yüan Shih-k'ai once had, but Tuan's Anfu Clique was the dominant force in Peking politics for the next four years, 1916 to 1920. However, with Tuan's unsteady hand at the helm, factional strife became more intense, politicians' fights for posts more fierce. Moreover, the national treasury had been exhausted by Yüan's preparation for enthronement and his civil war against the republican forces. Money had to be found, by fair means or foul, to maintain the establishment. Whoever could provide the necessary funds could also receive the choicest government posts. Happily for Ts'ao Ju-lin, the change of cabinet in Japan offered him such an opportunity.

Successful Politician?

In October 1916 Terauchi Masatake replaced Ōkuma Shigenobu as premier. The new cabinet was determined to repair the damage

---

[6] Huang-i, *Chung-kuo tsui-chin ch'ih-ju-chi* (Shanghai, 1915), pp. 229-30. See also Matsumoto Tadao, "Taishō yonen Nishi kōshō ibun," *Gaikō jihō*, no. 650 (January 1, 1932), pp. 244-46.

[7] Ts'ao, pp. 160-61; T'ao Chü-yin, *Peiyang chün-fa t'ung-chih shih-ch'i shih-hua* (Peking, 1957-58), vol. 3, pp. 78-79.

done in China by its predecessor's inept handling of the Twenty-One Demands. Trusted members of the Terauchi government—Finance Minister Shōda Kazue, Home Minister (later Foreign Minister) Gotō Shimpei, and Vice-Chief of Staff Tanaka Giichi—decided on economic expansion and peaceful penetration. Although their goal did not differ substantially from that of the previous administration in that they also wanted to strengthen Japan's position in Manchuria, Mongolia, and Shantung, and secure China's raw materials, their method was novel. Making use of the surplus accumulated during the war, Tokyo decided to make loans to China on generous terms, without strict supervision as to their use, and no stringent security requirements, and thus to buy Chinese good will. Since Terauchi had no love for revolutionaries, Tuan Ch'i-jui's Peking government was chosen as the recipient of Japan's largesse.[8] Nishihara Kamezō (1873-1954), in the capacity of Terauchi's personal envoy, was selected to implement these policies.

Nishihara was most eager to accept this mission. Although up to now his experiences were limited to doing business in and promoting economic cooperation with Korea, where Terauchi had been governor-general, Nishihara's vision was not circumscribed. His political mentor, Kanmuchi Tomotsune, was an Asian expansionist and member of the Anti-Russian League (Tai-rō Dōshikai).[9] Nishihara himself had watched developments in China very closely, and drawn up several blueprints for the economic development not only of China, but for the whole of East Asia. His favorite plans for China included unification of currency, tariff reform, railway construction, development of iron and coal, as well as production of wool and cotton. He also advocated joint Sino-Japanese enterprises as the most suitable instruments for assuring Japanese leadership.[10] Between June 1916 and August 1918, he made six trips to Peking, hoping to lay the foundation of lasting peace and prosperity for East Asia.

[8] For Terauchi's reliance on his Chōshū military clique, see James W. Morley, *The Japanese Thrust into Siberia, 1918* (New York, 1957), pp. 10-11, 17-18. For Shōda Kazue's China policy, see Shōda Tatsuo, *Chūgoku shakkan to Shōda Kazue* (Tokyo, 1972), pp. 84-89. Gotō Shimpei's role is outlined in Shinobu Seisaburō, *Taishō seijishi* (Tokyo, 1951), vol. 2, pp. 335-37. The views of Terauchi and his friends were adopted by the cabinet on January 9, 1917, Suzuki Takeo, comp., *Nishihara shakkan shiryō kenkyū* (Tokyo, 1972), pp. 119-20.

[9] Nishihara's early activities are found in chapters 3 and 4 of Nishihara Kamezō, *Yume no shichi-ju-yo-nen; Nishihara Kamezō jiden*, ed. Kitamura Hironao (Tokyo, 1965).

[10] One of Nishihara's more comprehensive plans is delineated in "Jikyoku ni ōzuru taishi keizaiteki shisetsu no yōkō," July 1916, ibid., pp. 83-86.

When Nishihara embarked on his mission, Terauchi instructed him to contact Colonel (later Lieutenant General) Banzai Rihachirō (1870-1950).[11] Banzai was a well-known figure in Peking. He was the master of the so-called Banzai Mansion, a semi-official intelligence center that had an uninterrupted existence from 1911 to 1927. His organization served as the training ground for future celebrated China hands such as Doihara Kenji and Tada Shun, then his aides.[12] Curiously enough, for a good part of his seventeen years in Peking, Banzai was on the payroll of the Peking government, sometimes with the exalted title of military adviser in the presidential office.[13] He had easy access to the Chinese president as well as to the Japanese chief of staff. Secret discussions in the Chinese cabinet were often reported to Tokyo in his dispatches, a fact apparently unknown to his Chinese employer. Delicate messages between Peking and Tokyo were often entrusted to him.[14] Since he was well informed and well connected, he was sought after by Chinese and Japanese alike; officers, diplomats, politicians, and financiers streamed to the door of his mansion. He knew all the top officials in Peking and counted Ts'ao Ju-lin among his close friends.

Banzai introduced Nishihara to Ts'ao during Nishihara's first visit to China in June 1916. Ts'ao's fluent Japanese and willingness to accept Japanese guidance as that of an elder brother pleased Nishihara. At first sight, the latter instinctively felt that Ts'ao was a worthy counterpart to build up Sino-Japanese economic cooperation.[15] Ts'ao was not averse to the use of grandiose language, but his objective was more limited. After Yüan Shih-k'ai's death, Ts'ao had lost his cabinet post and only held the title of governor of the Bank of Communications. He needed funds to buy his way into Tuan Ch'i-jui's government, which was in dire financial straits. With Tuan's consent, Ts'ao,

---

[11] Ibid., pp. 75-76.

[12] *Hiroku Doihara Kenji—Nichū yūko no shūseki*, ed. Johō Kaio (Tokyo, 1973), pp. 72-75, 527-28.

[13] A Gaimushō document indicates, for example, that Banzai was a military researcher in the Chinese president's office from August 1916 to July 1918 with an annual salary of 1,200 silver dollars, "Shina yōhei honpōjin jinmeihyō," June 1918, found in Tōyō Bunko, Tokyo. Banzai might have received instructions from the Japanese Army General Staff, but none of these documents have been preserved (letter from Morimatsu Toshio, editor of the *War History*, Bōei-chō, Tokyo, August 25, 1975). Instructions to Doihara issued on November 28, 1918 and March 20, 1928, when Doihara was employed by the Chinese, were preserved and published in *Hiroku Doihara*, p. 529.

[14] There are many of these dispatches in the published volumes of *Gaikō bunsho* from 1911 to 1921 (Tokyo, 1961-75).

[15] Nishihara, p. 76.

Nishihara, and Banzai became the central figures in concluding eight secret loan agreements that amounted to 145 million yen. In recognition of this large contribution, Ts'ao was rewarded with lucrative and prestigious positions. At one time, March to November 1918, he was both minister of finance and minister of communications.[16]

These Nishihara Loans, despite their designation for economic development and railway construction, were spent on buttressing Tuan's political and military edifice.[17] Tuan, once a patriotic soldier ready to fight against Japanese imperialism, had come to the realization that his regime could not survive without Japanese assistance.[18] Moreover, since September 1917, a rival government of Sun Yat-sen's revolutionaries and southwestern warlords was set up in Canton. Tuan's decision to destroy the southern government and reunify China by force under his leadership greatly increased his expenditures. For the cost of arms, and of recruiting, training, and maintaining troops, he had to rely on Japan. In addition to loans, Japan offered Tuan a military agreement. Tuan thought it would provide him with an army of three divisions, trained and equipped by the Japanese under the direction of Banzai.[19]

The Japanese perception, however, was different. The military agreement embodied the thinking of Tanaka Giichi, Saitō Kijirō, military attaché in Peking, and the uniquitous Banzai. Although the immediate objective of the agreement was to facilitate Japan's Siberian intervention in the wake of Russia's October Revolution, these men had a long-range plan for military expansion in China parallel to that

[16] In his autobiography (p. 183), Nishihara leaves us with a graphic account of how he insisted that Ts'ao Ju-lin had to be the minister of finance.

[17] There were eight Nishihara Loans: the first Bank of Communications loan (January 20, 1917), second Bank of Communications loan (September 28, 1917), a loan for the improvement of telegraphs (April 30, 1918), preliminary agreement for a loan for the construction of Kirin-Huining Railway (June 18, 1918), a loan for the development of gold mines and national forestries in the provinces of Heilungkiang and Kirin (August 2, 1918), preliminary agreement for a loan for the Tsinan-Shunte and Kaomi-Hsüchow extensions of the Shantung railways (September 28, 1918), preliminary agreement for a loan for railways in Manchuria and Mongolia (September 28, 1918), and the war participation loan (September 28, 1918). English translations of the agreements are found in John V.A. MacMurray, comp., *Treaties and Agreements with and Concerning China, 1894-1919* (New York, 1921), vol. 2, pp. 1345-46, 1387-88, 1424-28, 1430-32, 1434-40, 1446-52.

[18] In May 1915 Tuan Ch'i-jui was the only cabinet member who wanted to fight against Japan rather than sign the Twenty-One Demands, Wang Yün-sheng, vol. 6, pp. 310-11.

[19] Usui Katsumi, *Nihon to Chūgoku—Taishō jidai* (Tokyo, 1972), p. 144; Ts'ao, p. 178; Banzai to Vice-Chief of Staff Tanaka, November 26, 1918, *Gaikō bunsho*, 1918, vol. 2, pt. 2, pp. 956-60.

of Nishihara for economic domination. They wanted a unified arms system for China and Japan, and recognition of Japan's right to train, advise, and supervise Chinese troops.[20] With a few divisions of Chinese troops under Japanese control, mused Banzai, the Peking government would surely incline toward willing cooperation with Japan.[21] But the Chinese response in March 1918 was cool, because the Japanese proposals, for example, concerning the direction of Chinese army and police in Manchuria by the Japanese imperial army, resembled the terms of Group V, an issue too explosive for Peking politicians to touch. Even Banzai's feverish work behind the scenes, such as convincing President Feng Kuo-chang, leader of the Chihli Clique which rivaled Tuan's Anfu Clique, was not enough to bring about Chinese acceptance of these harsh terms. After several months of delay, Japan agreed to change the wording so as not to infringe upon China's sovereign rights, and only with Tanaka's threat to terminate Japanese funds and arms did Tuan authorize the signing of the Sino-Japanese joint defense military agreement in May 1918.[22]

Ts'ao Ju-lin was not deeply involved in these negotiations. However, when the news leaked out that Japan was reviving the Group V demands, Chinese students in Tokyo staged demonstrations. Hundreds of them returned home to arouse their countrymen to resist the latest Japanese aggression. Their efforts were aided by Kuomintang members in Shanghai and warlords in southwestern China. Meetings commemorating May 7, the National Humiliation Day, were organized in Peking and Shanghai; on the flying banners were inscribed the words "traitors Ts'ao Ju-lin, Tuan Ch'i-jui, and Chin Yün-p'eng," the last-named being one of the signers of the military agreement. Some of the student publications even threatened the assassination of these traitors. To date this was the largest student movement in China.[23]

These May 1918 demonstrations, however, were ineffectual. Both the central and provincial governments took repressive measures

[20] Tanaka Giichi, vice-chief of staff, to Saitō Kijirō, military attaché in Peking, May 18, 1918, *Gaikō bunsho*, 1918, vol. 2, pt. 1, p. 355; Nishihara, p. 75.

[21] *Zoku taishi kaikoroku* (Tokyo, 1941-42), vol. 2, pp. 828-29. In his public speeches, however, Banzai advocates the "kingly way" of gently leading the Chinese to the way of development. See Banzai Rihachirō, *Rimpō o kataru: Banzai Shōgun kōen shū* (Tokyo, 1933). For a summary of his publicized views of China see *Hiroku Doihara*, pp. 66-68.

[22] *Tanaka Giichi denki*, ed. Takakura Tetsuichi (Tokyo, 1960), vol. 1, pp. 713-16; Morley, pp. 164-65, 188-89.

[23] T'ao Chü-yin, vol. 4, pp. 124-29; Usui, pp. 131-34; Police Department to Gaimushō, Tokyo, May 4, 1918, *Gaikō bunsho*, 1918, vol. 2, pt. 1, p. 331.

and threatened to terminate grants. In three or four weeks most students holding government scholarships returned to their classrooms, and Peking politics went on their usual way. Five out of eight Nishihara Loans were signed in June and September 1918. Thanks to these funds channeled through Ts'ao Ju-lin, Tuan's Anfu Clique enjoyed the heyday of their power. They also succeeded in having their candidate, Hsü Shih-ch'ang, elected president of the Republic. However, the end of their influence was approaching, because the Terauchi government in Tokyo fell in September 1918, and its successor repudiated Terauchi's policy of reckless lending. With a lack of funds, and setbacks in the civil war, Tuan's domestic troubles multiplied. As far as Ts'ao Ju-lin was concerned, the most damaging event was the May 4, 1919 student demonstration.

It is well known that the May Fourth Movement was a concrete expression of Chinese nationalism, and a spontaneous outburst of patriotic youth, shopkeepers, and merchants against venal officials who had sold out China. The demonstrators also blamed the Paris Peace Conference for sanctioning the sell-out. However, Ts'ao Ju-lin, his Anfu friends, and Banzai viewed these demonstrations in a different light. To them the May Fourth Movement was engineered by two groups of Ts'ao's political enemies.

To begin with, Vice-Minister of Communications Yeh Kung-ch'o leaked the terms of the Shantung railway agreement to the press.[24] Yeh's motivation appeared to be political revenge, for Ts'ao had wrested several power bases from Yeh's Old Communications Clique. The Shantung agreement, signed in September 1918 by Chang Tsung-hsiang, minister in Tokyo, contained the phrase "we are pleased to agree." When the secret text became known in April 1919, the Chinese public was enraged that their officials could be so base as to be pleased to sell their country.[25] This popular indignation was capitalized upon by another group of Ts'ao's political enemies, Liang Ch'i-ch'ao's Progressive Clique whose cabinet members Ts'ao had ousted at the end of 1917.[26] Subsequently Liang toured Europe; he was in Paris in the spring of 1919, and wired home news unfavorable to the Peking government. Liang's followers in Peking, among them Lin Ch'ang-min, made maximum use of his communications. Lin and others,

[24] Ts'ao, pp. 182-83.   [25] Wang Yün-sheng, vol. 7, p. 335.
[26] Li Chien-nung, *Chung-kuo chin-pai-nien cheng-chih shih* (Shanghai, 1947), vol. 2, p. 510; Letter from Fujiwara Masafumi, financial adviser to the Bank of Communications, to Nishihara, August 17, 1917, Nishihara Papers, on microfilm at the Diet Library, Tokyo.

according to Ts'ao, planned a rally in the Central Park, Peking, on May 7, to manipulate innocent students for their political ends.[27] The rally was advanced to May 4, when the news of the peace conference's final decision to award German rights in Shantung to Japan reached China. Thousands of students took part in the march, and denounced Ts'ao, Lu, and Chang as traitors. They then marched on to Ts'ao's house, and set it on fire. Chang Tsung-hsiang, who was on leave in Peking and happened to be visiting Ts'ao, was severely injured by the demonstrators. Undaunted by government arrests, the movement gained momentum, not only in Peking and Tientsin, but throughout the major cities of the country. The three traitors' names were shouted out; their treacherous deeds, highly colored, were recounted on street corners and printed in pamphlets. No one, not even their old patron and president of the Republic, Hsü Shih-ch'ang, could save them from popular wrath. They were forced to resign in June 1919.

Ts'ao, Lu, and Chang never thought that this was the end of their political careers. On the contrary, they looked upon their resignation as a temporary retreat. They blamed their misfortune on inadequate police protection, and on the lack of nerve of Hsü Shih-ch'ang. Hsü's passivity was most incomprehensible to them, since he owed his presidency to the election funds paid out from the Nishihara Loans. In the context of Peking politics, however, these happenings were not altogether unexpected. They just had to cultivate anew both power holders and money providers. They fully expected a comeback, not knowing that their government by manipulation and patronage, and their reliance on foreign aid went against the rising national demand for independence and reform. In this misjudgement, Ts'ao was supported by his Chinese and Japanese friends for two more decades.

For the remainder of his life, Ts'ao Ju-lin lived on the personal fortune amassed during these Nishihara years—investments in mines, match manufacturing, real estate, and banking.[28] He also relied on the faithful following he had gathered during this period. In addition to

[27] Ts'ao, pp. 195-204. Among numerous dispatches the Japanese sent to Tokyo, the one sent by Minister Obata is the most detailed. Obata also shared the view that the demonstrations were staged by politicians, Obata to Foreign Minister Uchida, May 8, 1919, *Gaikō bunsho*, 1919, vol. 2, pt. 2, pp. 1148-60. See also Chow Tse-tsung, *The May Fourth Movement: Intellectual Revolution in Modern China* (Stanford, 1967), pp. 92-94, 102-16.

[28] For details of Ts'ao's investments, see Madeleine Chi, "Bureaucratic Capitalists in Operation: Ts'ao Ju-lin and His New Communications Clique, 1916-1919," *Journal of Asian Studies*, vol. 34, no. 3 (May 1975), pp. 683-86.

his old friends Lu Tsung-yü and Chang Tsung-hsiang, his circle, known at the time as the New Communications Clique, included rising financiers Ch'ien Yung-ming, Chou Tso-min, and Wu Ting-ch'ang. Although these younger men left Peking politics after the debacle of May 1919, they remained Ts'ao's loyal friends. And Ts'ao's ties with Ch'ien Yung-ming were strengthened by the marriage between Ts'ao's nephew and Ch'ien's daughter.

Disillusioned Outsider

During the next few years Ts'ao Ju-lin worked strenuously to regain a cabinet post. At first he remained with Tuan Ch'i-jui, the major beneficiary of the Nishihara Loans. Tuan's Anfu Clique had been bickering with the Chihli Clique over provincial governorships and central government posts for several years. Their quarrel came to a head over the control of Honan province and the dismissal of Tuan's confidant, Hsü Shu-cheng. Armed conflict became inevitable. Controlling the War Participation Army (now named the Frontier Defense Army), trained and armed by the Japanese, the Anfu Clique was so confident of victory that Anfu generals played mahjong on their train ride to the battlefield.[29] But alas, the result was totally unexpected; Tuan's clique suffered a resounding defeat in the brief encounter between July 14 and 18, 1920.

Ts'ao Ju-lin had been an intermediary in the negotiations just before the outbreak of the Anfu-Chihli war. He was not impartial, however. He suggested to President Hsü that Wu P'ei-fu of the Chihli Clique, then a mere division commander, be dismissed to placate his friends in the Anfu Clique.[30] This move turned out to be a costly mistake; as we shall see, Wu P'ei-fu would react vehemently.

Now that the Anfu Clique had lost control of Peking and their Japanese-trained army was reorganized, Ts'ao Ju-lin made advances to the Chihli Clique and their ally the Fengtien Clique which had come to dominate the capital. In late April and early May of 1921, Ts'ao's prospects looked bright. He was promised the Ministry of Communications, and his recent ally Chang Hu the Ministry of

---

[29] Ts'ao, pp. 222-23. Banzai, who trained the War Participation Army, did not want it to be used in a civil war and asked Tokyo to prevent Tuan from using the army. His government prevailed upon him and issued strict orders forbidding the Japanese military to get involved in the Chinese civil war. See Banzai to Uehara, chief of staff, June 3, 1920, top secret, *Gaikō bunsho*, 1920, vol. 2, pt. 1, pp. 459-60; Foreign Minister Uchida's two orders, June 30 and July 9, 1920, ibid., pp. 467, 473.
[30] Obata to Uchida, July 8, 1920, ibid., pp. 470-71.

Agriculture and Commerce.[31] In return Ts'ao agreed to secure Japanese funds in the manner of Nishihara Loans, by signing away Chinese assets, this time a port in Chihli. Moreover, some *zaibatsu* were willing to make new loans to China on condition that the Nishihara Loans be renegotiated and adequately secured.[32]

The press got wind of the plot and once more furious attacks were hurled upon Ts'ao. Neither Ts'ao nor Chang Hu received their desired appointments. After half a year's waiting, Ts'ao received (from Liang Shih-i's cabinet) a sinecure entitled special commissioner for promoting industry, only to be singled out again for attack. The Washington Conference was then in progress. The Twenty-One Demands, the Shantung issue, and the 1918 secret agreements were hotly debated in Peking. Ts'ao's political foes, led by Wu P'ei-fu, seized the opportunity to investigate what they called the misappropriation of the Nishihara Loans.[33]

Wu P'ei-fu had sided with the students at the time of the May Fourth Movement. He issued several circular telegrams denouncing traitors Ts'ao, Lu, Chang, and members of the Anfu Clique. He was hailed as savior of the country. This favorable popular response elated him; henceforth he became more and more patriotic and, therefore, more and more anti-Japanese. After his victory during the first Fengtien-Chihli War (April-May 1922) he came out in full force attacking politicians who had worked with both the Fengtien and Anfu Cliques, and they included Ts'ao.[34] In the summer of 1922 Ts'ao was compelled to flee to the safe sanctuary of the Japanese concession in Tientsin.[35] Ts'ao's case, however, was never brought to court for trial, and by the end of that year he returned to Peking.

Even though this pattern of accusation, flight, and return, like summer storms, happened frequently to Peking politicians, Ts'ao felt disheartened. Since May 1918, he and his friends Lu Tsung-yü and

---

[31] Funatsu Shinichirō, consul general of Tientsin, to Uchida, April 22, 1921, Gaimushō documents microfilmed by the Library of Congress, MT 1.6.1.4, Kakkoku naisei kankei zassen: Shina no bu, Reel 90, pp. 16445-46; Obata to Uchida, April 30, 1921, *Gaikō bunsho*, 1921, vol. 2, p. 620.

[32] "Shina seihen ni kansuru ken," by the Kwantung Army, May 13, 1921, MT 1.6.1.4, Reel 90, p. 16624; Yoshida, acting minister in Peking, to Uchida, May 14, 1921, ibid., pp. 16627-28; T'ao Chü-yin, vol. 4, pp. 31-32. Ts'ao also made several attempts to secure loans from the Japanese government, but his requests were firmly turned down.

[33] Ts'ao, pp. 226-27.

[34] Lai-chiang cho-wu, *Wu P'ei-fu cheng chuan* (Taipei, 1967 reprint), pp. 96-98.

[35] Obata to Uchida, June 19, 1922, MT 1.6.1.4, Reel 91, pp. 17497-98.

Chang Tsung-hsiang had probably been called traitors more often than anyone else alive, and the attacks were unrelenting. After Sun Yat-sen had recaptured his Canton base and stepped up preparations for the Northern Expedition, his followers in both the Kuomintang and the Chinese Communist Party carried out propaganda activities far more effectively than those of the warlords. One of the forums they utilized was the commemoration of National Humiliation Day, May 7. Great speakers like Wang Ching-wei used the occasion to denounce the Japanese and their Chinese collaborators, with much more eloquence than Wu P'ei-fu.[36] Anti-Japanism had become part and parcel of a rising politician's way of life, and attacks on traitors Ts'ao, Lu, and Chang the stock phrases in political oration. Their reputation was so unsavory that they could not make public appearances. Out in the cold, Ts'ao and Lu watched the wheels of political fortune turning, gleaned gossip of bargainings for cabinet posts, and repeated them to their Japanese friends in Tientsin and Peking, among them Funatsu Shinichirō (1873-1947), Yoshida Shigeru (1878-1967), Yoshizawa Kenkichi (1874-1965) and, of course, Banzai.[37]

This sad state of affairs did not improve when Tuan Ch'i-jui came back to power for the last time as the chief executive of the Republic. Tuan was first assisted by the Banzai organization in his escape from the Chihli Clique's surveillance in February 1922.[38] More significantly, he and Doihara Kenji, while serving as advisers to President Ts'ao K'un, incited Feng Yü-hsiang, the president's disloyal subordinate, to carry out a coup against him on October 23, 1924.[39] With

[36] "Kakuchi no jōkyō," May 1924, in MT 1.6.1.4, Reel 94, pp. 20565-68. The Japanese were very much concerned and greatly irritated by Nationalists' anti-Japanese propaganda, especially after they established a government in Nanking and carried out "revolutionary diplomacy" and an anti-Japanese educational policy. See, for example, an article by a diplomat, Ijuin Kanekiyo, "Shina hainichi kyōiku to Manshū jihen," *Gaikō jihō*, no. 650 (January 1, 1932), pp. 329-35. Ijuin argues that Nanking's anti-Japanese policy made the Manchurian incident inevitable (pp. 333-34).

[37] Funatsu worked in the Peking legation from 1914 to 1919, and became consul general of Tientsin (1919-1920), of Shanghai (1921-1923), and of Fengtien (1923-1926). Then he resigned from diplomatic service and was appointed head of the Japanese textile association in China.

Yoshida Shigeru was the consul general of Tientsin from 1922 to 1925, and Ts'ao Ju-lin called on him frequently (MT 1.6.1.4, Reels 91 to 96).

Yoshizawa Kenkichi served in the Peking legation from 1916 to 1919 and was minister in Peking from 1923 to 1924.

[38] Ikei Masaru, "Daiichiji Hōchoku sensō to Nihon," in *Taiman-mō seisaki shi no ichimen* (Tokyo, 1966), p. 178.

[39] Ikei, "Dainiji Hōchoku sensō to Nihon," in ibid., pp. 218-19; *Zoku taishi*

Ts'ao K'un out of the way, Tuan Ch'i-jui was able to resume leadership in November 1924. In these clandestine activities Banzai and Doihara acted counter to Tokyo's official policy of noninterference.

Both Banzai and Tuan retained their friendship for Ts'ao Ju-lin. But Tuan had to reestablish his political influence and win a national reputation, and Banzai believed in working with power holders who could form a viable pro-Japanese government. To these ends Ts'ao had nothing to contribute. Since his name was a major liability in Chinese politics, neither Tuan nor Banzai could realistically include him in their maneuvers.

Ts'ao Ju-lin, however, was not altogether idle. Covertly and indirectly, he worked for the repayment of the Nishihara Loans through the China-Japan Industrial Development Company. This joint Sino-Japanese company had a curious history. Its founding was initiated by Sun Yat-sen and his friends in 1912. Before the company took form, however, important Chinese founders had to live in exile because of their failure in the 1913 revolution. Thereupon Yüan Shih-k'ai's followers expressed great interest, and high officials of the Peking government moved in to replace the revolutionaries as directors and shareholders. Ts'ao Ju-lin joined the company in 1917, when he was minister of communications. The Chinese investors owned half of the shares, while the other half was in the hands of Japanese bankers and industrialists. Although the goal of the company was no less than the development of resources in China, its capital was only five million yen. From the start, it led a faltering existence. It functioned more like a broker taking commissions on loans made by Japanese banks to Chinese enterprises than as an important investor in China's economic development. The Terauchi cabinet attempted to infuse blood into this ailing body and to make it an efficient instrument for Japan's economic expansion by allowing it to administer a Nishihara loan extension. But this help was too little to make any difference. By 1922 the China-Japan Development Company was on the verge of bankruptcy.[40] An energetic man, Takagi Rikurō (1880-c.1960), who

---

kaikoroku, vol. 2, p. 832; Gaimushō, "Shina shokuin hyō," March 1, 1924, MT 1.6.1.4, Reel 94, p. 20227.

[40] Suzuki, p. 129; *Chū-Nichi Jitsugyō Kabushiki Kaisha sanjūnen shi*, comp. Noguchi Yonejirō (Tokyo, 1943), appendix, p. 33; Takagi Rikurō, "Chū-Nichi Jitsugyō Kabushiki Kaisha genjō setsumei," May 14, 1924, Gaimushō documents microfilmed by the Library of Congress, MT 1.7.10.23, Chū-Nichi Jitsugyō Kaisha kankai zassen, Reel 287, pp. 902-14.

had enterprises in Manchuria, was appointed its Japanese director with the hope of restoring it to health. The means Takagi chose was the renegotiation of the Nishihara Loans. For that purpose he assiduously cultivated President Ts'ao K'un in 1923, and presented Tuan Ch'i-jui in 1925 with a scheme of repayment by stages. The scheme was worked out with the help of Ts'ao Ju-lin.[41] These efforts were in vain because these unstable, weak, and penniless Peking regimes had no way of repaying China's enormous debts. In a word, Ts'ao's dealings with the Japanese, once so profitable, were now the source of disappointments. As might be expected, a new government headed by the Nationalists would again revile him; in 1928 Nanking indicted him for his crime of "being renowned for base deeds."[42]

Quasi Elder Statesman

It appears that these reverses led Ts'ao Ju-lin to change the direction of his politics. After 1928 he stopped seeking political posts, and contented himself with the occupation of investor. When Japanese money brought him prestige and power, he used them to acquire valuable assets such as the Liu-ho-kou and Ching-ching mines. Now he collected dividends and served on boards of directors. His former protégés also gave him nominal posts. Ch'ien Yung-ming (1885-1958), Wu Ting-ch'ang (1884-1950), and Chou Tso-min (1884-1956), who had left the muddy waters of Peking politics around 1919, founded their own banks and organized the Joint Savings Society and Joint Treasury. Their organizations dominated the finance of north China as well as that of the Shanghai area. It was due to their financial support that Chiang Kai-shek was able to establish a government in Nanking in 1928.[43] Through Wu Ting-ch'ang, Ts'ao Ju-lin was invited to attend one of Chiang's consultative conferences at Lu-shan, in Kiangsi province.[44] Ts'ao never liked the Kuomintang, but before the specter of rising Japanese militarism, he was willing to put aside

---

[41] Takagi Rikurō, *Nikka koyu-roku* (Tokyo, 1943), p. 65; *Gendai Shina no kiroku*, comp. Hatano Kenichi, September 1925, pp. 55-56.

The Japanese government also made many attempts to recover the Nishihara Loans, but met with no success in its negotiations with either the Peking or the Nanking government. After the establishment of Manchukuo, loans pertaining to Manchuria were transferred to Manchukuo and presumably paid back by that country. See Tōkyō Kenkyū Jō, *Nihon no taishi tōshi* (Tokyo, 1942), p. 693.

[42] *Gendai Shina no kiroku*, July 1928, p. 157.

[43] These men were known collectively as the Chekiang Financial Clique. From 1935 on Wu Ting-ch'ang was a member of the Nanking government, but Ch'ien Yung-ming and Chou Tso-min remained aloof from direct involvement in politics.

[44] Ts'ao, pp. 301-303.

his personal distaste and work with Chiang Kai-shek's entourage for a peaceful solution.[45]

The Manchurian incident stirred up great excitement among the Peiyang politicians who had lost influence with the establishment of the Nanking government. Some saw the 1931 crisis as an opportunity to form an anti-Chiang league and thereby to regain power. Others, like Ts'ao, cooperated with Nanking. Throughout 1932 and early 1933 political activities were intense. Unfortunately, records are not complete enough to reconstruct the whole story. It is clear, however, that Ts'ao, his Japanese friends, and Chinese friends of the Anfu Clique tried to have Tuan Ch'i-jui mediate between Nanking and Tokyo. Yoshida Shigeru, who deplored the domination of the Japanese military and was about to resign from the Gaimushō, secretly visited Ts'ao in January 1933. Yoshida suggested that Tuan and Prince Saionji, the last surviving genrō in Japan, take action to limit the conflict.[46] But Tuan did not enjoy the prestige in China that Saionji did in Japan. Moreover, Chiang Kai-shek suspected Tuan of being pro-Japanese and sent Ch'ien Yung-ming to invite him to settle in south China. Ts'ao Ju-lin helped convince Tuan to leave north China, the seedbed of intrigues. Subsequently Tuan agreed to reside in Shanghai as a pensioner of Nanking, thus removing himself as a possible leader of a puppet government.[47]

Some friends also advised Ts'ao to go south, but he felt unable to move his large family which included his aged mother. He continued to live in Tientsin. After over a decade of political eclipse, suddenly Ts'ao was regarded as an elder statesman in north China, and was frequently interviewed and written about. Journalist Hatano Kenichi described him as a man of rare talent and versatility who could no doubt play a major role in north China politics.[48] In 1933, just before Japan's withdrawal from the League of Nations, Yoshizawa Kenkichi called on Ts'ao and perhaps asked his views about a possible local settlement for Manchuria.[49] Ts'ao was considered for

[45] Interview with Ts'ao's nephew, Washington, D.C., January 7, 1975.

[46] Ts'ao, pp. 293-94; Kuwajima, consul general of Tientsin, to Prime Minister Inukai, January 4, 1932, Gaimushō documents microfilmed by the Library of Congress, PVM 30, Nisshi gaikō kankei zassen, Reel P60, pp. 191-92; Kuwajima to Foreign Minister Uchida, January 24, 1933, PVM 37, Manshū jihen; Chokusetsu kōshō kankei, Reel P62, pp. 137-38.

[47] Ts'ao, pp. 296-97; Taiheiyō senso e no michi, ed. Nihon Kokusai Seiji Gakkai (Tokyo, 1963), vol. 3, pp. 19-20.

[48] Hatano Kenichi, Kindai Shina no seiji to jimbutsu (Tokyo, 1937), pp. 229-30.

[49] Zoku taishi kaikoroku, vol. 2, p. 989; Ts'ao, pp. 279-82.

membership in the Nanking-sponsored Hopei-Chahar Political Council (October-December 1935).[50] Doihara Kenji, the schemer of many a separatist movement, invited Ts'ao to head a provisional government.[51] Ts'ao consistently declined these overtures, be they from Nanking or the Japanese military. He claimed that filial piety required that he stay home and provide peace for his octogenarian mother, since his father's life had been abruptly ended as a result of his political activities.[52] (His father had died in the scorching summer of 1922, when Wu P'ei-fu forced the Ts'aos to flee to Tientsin.) In addition, Ts'ao said that he was pro-Japanese, but never in favor of brutal military aggression.[53] Thus during the twilight of his life, if not in his prime, he assumed the posture of preserving his integrity.

It is interesting to note that even in the late 1930's Ts'ao cited a Confucian code of ethics in defense of his political behavior. This anachronistic conservatism was also revealed in a conversation with Takagi Rikurō in February 1938. Takagi visited Ts'ao at his home in Tientsin and asked Ts'ao to give him names of statesmen who could "deal with the current situation." Ts'ao considered T'ang Shao-yi (1860-1938) the most suitable person because he could rally both southern and northern factions.[54] T'ang had been prime minister in 1912, and was intermittently active in important factional negotiations. He was then seventy-seven years old. But in any event, T'ang was assassinated in Shanghai.[55] Whether he was seriously considered by the Japanese military is hard to tell. What we do know is that Doihara, Banzai's disciple, had difficulty in convincing men of prestige and power to head a separatist government. In the end, in December 1937, he set up a provisional government under Wang K'o-min (1873-1945). Wang was also a Peiyang politician of Ts'ao's vintage and outlook. Ts'ao would not accept any position of significance in this Japanese-sponsored government, only nominal ones such as senior consultant, and director of the Hsin-min Publishing Company, the regime's major printing office. Ts'ao had to agree to have his mines operated by the Meiji and Kaijima mines.[56] These acts of cooperation with an invading army were the minimum that Ts'ao

[50] *Zoku taishi kaikoroku*, vol. 1, p. 396; *Taiheiyō sensō e no michi*, vol. 3, pp. 161-62. Li Yün-han, *Sung Che-yüan yü ch'i-ch'i k'ang-chan* (Taipei, 1973), p. 94.
[51] Ts'ao, pp. 321-23; Nakae, pp. 439-443.
[52] Ts'ao, pp. 227-29; Takagi, p. 169.   [53] Ts'ao, pp. 302-303.
[54] Takagi, pp. 156-58.
[55] "T'ang Shao-yi," *Biographical Dictionary of Republican China*, ed. Howard L. Boorman (New York, 1967-71), vol. 3, p. 236.
[56] Ts'ao, pp. 328, 330, 337-78, 341.

had to perform in order to survive. He was sure that there were no grounds for accusing him of being a traitor. On the contrary, on several occasions he went so far as to risk his own life to save the lives of members of the underground resistance force.[57]

Meanwhile, in unoccupied China, Ch'ien Yung-ming, Wu Ting-ch'ang, and Chou Tso-min worked behind the scenes in search of compromise and peace. They were known as the Japan hands in Nationalist circles, and they preferred Sino-Japanese friendship to enmity, though not at the price of losing China's independence. In 1936, Wu Ting-ch'ang worked hard to maintain the autonomous political council in north China.[58] In August 1937 Ch'ien and Chou cooperated with Funatsu Shinichirō, unsuccessfully, to prevent the conflict in Shanghai.[59] During the war, at least twice (in 1938 and 1940), the Japanese asked Ch'ien Yung-ming as Chiang Kai-shek's most trusted friend to convey peace terms to Chungking. On account of the Japanese negotiators' dubious procedure and harsh terms, Ch'ien does not seem to have acted with enthusiasm.[60] Since these and other peace efforts failed, the armed stalemate dragged on until 1945.

The return of the Nationalists to north China in 1945 brought Ts'ao some slight harassment. For a short time he was put under house arrest by the Nationalist secret police, but was set free when his relations with Ch'ien, Wu, and Chou became known. Chiang Kai-shek even wrote him a letter of apology.[61] The Communists, however, drove him out of the country. In 1950 he decided to live in Japan, where he was warmly welcomed. He was sorry that Banzai had died a few days before his arrival, but other old friends like Yoshizawa Kenkichi gathered around him in joyful parties. For special occasions, such as former finance minister Shōda Kazue's funeral, he was invited to deliver the eulogy. By then his savings were exhausted and his income nearly nil, but his Japanese friends showed great concern. Under the auspices of Yoshida Shigeru, now

[57] Ibid., pp. 371-74.

[58] Suma, consul general of Nanking, to Foreign Minister Arita, October 5, 1936, Gaimushō documents microfilmed by the Library of Congress, PVM 32, Teikoku no taishi gaikō seisaku kankei, Reel P61, pp. 575-79.

[59] *Funatsu Shinichirō*, ed. Zaika Nihon Bōseki Dōgyōkai (Tokyo, 1958), p. 195; *Taiheiyō sensō e no michi*, vol. 4, pp. 18-19, 116-17.

[60] For the 1938 venture, see especially Hidaka, consul general of Shanghai, to Foreign Minister Arita, December 2, 1938, Gaimushō documents microfilmed by the Library of Congress, S 1.6.1.1-7, Shina jihen ni saishi Shina shin-seifu, Reel S560, p. 182. For the 1940 "Ch'ien Yung-ming operation" a graphic account is found in Nishi Yoshiaki, *Higeki no shōnin: Nikka wahei kōsaku hishi* (Tokyo, 1962), pp. 337-95. See also *Chou Fo-hai jih-chi* (Hong Kong, 1955), pp. 144, 147-48, 180-81.

[61] Ts'ao, pp. 387-88.

prime minister, and Takagi Rikurō, still an entrepreneur, a club of ten Japanese industrialists was organized. Each member contributed five thousand yen a month for his upkeep. What touched Ts'ao more than the gift were the words of Itabashi Kisuke, director of the Meiji Mines: "We respect you, Mr. Ts'ao, because you dared to be pro-Japanese without submitting to the demands of the Japanese militarists."[62] Ts'ao was deeply moved by this appreciation as he felt gravely maligned by his own countrymen. He remained in Japan for seven years before traveling to the United States to live with a daughter. He died in Michigan in 1966.

Conclusion

Ts'ao Ju-lin entered public service in a fragmented China. Peking politicians of both the late Ch'ing and early Republic were factional, corrupt, and extremely self-serving. They aimed at personal gain, and their methods were subordinated to this overriding concern. Thus to them government affairs meant, first and foremost, the distribution of posts and profits. In this Ts'ao Ju-lin was not much worse than his peers. He might have been aware of this degenerate situation, but this was the China he knew, and this was the China he could not afford to lose, even to the extent of being propped up by foreign aid.[63] Having genuine admiration for Japan, he did not find Japanese assistance objectionable, especially when it brought him handsome personal rewards. No one can deny that between 1916 and 1925 he bartered away national assets for personal gain—though also for his friends' personal gains—in the negotiations of the Nishihara Loans and subsequent efforts for their repayment to Japan. But not every contact he had with Japan involved a deal for selling China, nor was he alone in concluding questionable agreements with the Japanese. His political enemies, for their own reasons, created the image of Ts'ao Ju-lin as the inveterate and unredeemable traitor.

On the other hand, Ts'ao misread the signs of the times by attributing anti-Japanese popular movements solely to the machinations of his political enemies. Rather it was his political enemies who voiced popular sentiments—that Japanese leadership was unacceptable, and that Japanese such as Nishihara and Takagi contributed

---

[62] Ibid., pp. 421, 424, 427-28.

[63] Ts'ao Ju-lin expressed this fear of radical change in his actions rather than in word. Chin Yün-p'eng, Ts'ao's contemporary who signed the 1918 military agreement, did tell Banzai that democratic processes such as the calling of the people's assembly would destroy the existing political order, Minister Obata to Foreign Minister Uchida, August 7, 1920, *Gaikō bunsho*, 1920, vol. 2, pt. 2, pp. 937-38.

nothing to Chinese economic development. The dubious dealings of these men with China's own corrupt officials created suspicion and hostility, which would grow to bitter enmity with the multiplication of intrigues of Banzai's type.

The Japanese intimately associated with Ts'ao's political activities shared his misjudgment of the national temper. Nishihara thought Ts'ao's and his friends' Peking was the whole of China, and that their acceptance of Japanese leadership amounted to China's acceptance of that role. Banzai calculated that a few divisions of troops under Japanese control could make the Chinese government into a pliable instrument. He appeared to believe that covert activities could take the sting out of Japanese interference in Chinese affairs. His aides such as Doihara Kenji, who learned the art of manipulating Chinese politicians under the Peiyang Republic, grew more daring and resourceful in the 1930's and 1940's. Doihara also made the mistake of ignoring the Chinese public.[64] These factors, coupled with the increasing independence of the Japanese military in China, led to the catastrophe of the long war from 1937 to 1945.

Ts'ao Ju-lin was fortunate enough to have survived the war, both physically and psychologically. In the postwar years he was comforted by the respect and concern shown him by his Japanese friends, though he died regretting that his fellow countrymen manifested no such appreciation. Now with the passage of time passions have cooled: May 7 is no longer commemorated in China as National Humiliation Day, and historiography in Taiwan regarding anti-Japanism is showing signs of achieving balanced treatment. Admiration for Japan, like admiration for America, is no longer dismissed with the label treason.[65] While material presented in this study does not completely exonerate Ts'ao Ju-lin, it does suggest that the epithet "traitor" is not an adequate summation of his lifelong contacts with the Japanese. What is lamentable about Ts'ao's Japanese connections is that they became entangled with his shortsightedness in seeking immediate advantages. Ts'ao, of course, was not alone in this respect. He and his cronies tended to confuse personal advantage with public needs. By doing so they contributed to conditions that plunged China and Japan into decades of mutual hostility.

[64] Cf. *Taiheiyō senso e no michi*, vol. 4, pp. 154-55.

[65] In his biography of Huang Fu, Wu Hsiang-hsiang states that the Chinese have in the past been prejudiced, accusing diplomats who handled negotiations with Japan of being pro-Japanese, even being traitors. See *Min-kuo pai-jen chuan* (Taipei, 1971), vol. 2, pp. 270-71.

CHAPTER IX

AN INTELLECTUAL'S RESPONSE TO WESTERN INTRUSION: NAITŌ KONAN'S VIEW OF REPUBLICAN CHINA

⊏━━━⊐

YUE-HIM TAM

NAITŌ KONAN (Torajirō, 1866-1934)[1] is generally known to Western scholars today through references to his "hypothesis" on China's historical development and to his textual studies,[2] and to many Japanese critics through his championing of "imperialism."[3] This chapter will examine both these aspects of Naitō's work, with particular focus on his ideas on Republican China.[*] Central to both is the

[1] Naitō Konan's collected works, *Naitō Konan zenshū* (hereafter cited as *zenshū*; Tokyo, 1969-   ), were edited by Naitō's eldest son Naitō Kenkichi and his student Kanda Kiichirō.

For Naitō's career and thought, see Mitamura Taisuko. *Naitō Konan* ("*Chūkō shinso,*" vol. 278, Tokyo, 1972); Ogawa Tamaki, ed. *Naitō Konan* ("*Chūōkō-ronsha: Nihon no meichō,*" vol. 41, Tokyo, 1971); and Yue-him Tam, "In Search of the Oriental Past: The Life and Thought of Naitō Konan (1866-1934)," Ph.D. dissertation, Princeton University. 1975.

[2] Naitō was first introduced to the Western world as an authority on Chinese textual studies by such French scholars as Édouard Chavannes, "Naitō Konan: Album de photographies des Mandchourie," *T'oung Pao*, serie II, vol. 9 (1908), p. 602; Paul Pelliot, "Manuscripts Chinois au Japan," *T'oung Pao*, vol. 23 (1924), pp. 15-30; and Henri Maspero, *La Chine Antique* (Paris, 1927).

Brief reference to the Naitō hypothesis was first made by Lien-sheng Yang in a book review, "Naitō Torajirō: *Chūgoku kinseishi* and *Chūgoku shigakushi,*" *Far Eastern Quarterly*, vol. 12, no. 2 (1953), pp. 208-209. Further details of the Naitō hypothesis can be found in Hisayuki Miyakawa, "An Outline of the Naitō Hypothesis and Its Effects on Japanese Studies of China." *Far Eastern Quarterly*, vol. 14, no. 4 (1955), pp. 533-52; and Miyazaki Ichisada, "Naitō Konan: An Original Sinologist," *Philosophical Studies of Japan*, vol. 8 (1968), pp. 93-116.

[3] For examples, Nohara Shirō, "Naitō Konan 'Shina ron' hihan," *Chūgoku hyōron*, vol. 1, no. 4 (1946), reprinted in Nohara's *Ajia no rekishi to shisō* (Tokyo, 1965), pp. 152-61; Takeuchi Yoshimi, "Shina kenkyūsha no michi" (1943), reprinted in his *Nihon to Chūgoku no aida* (Tokyo, 1973), pp. 286-92; and Shumpei Okamoto, "Japanese Response to Chinese Nationalism: Naitō (Ko'nan) Torajirō's Image of China in the 1920's" (mimeographed draft).

[*] The writer wishes to thank Professor Marius B. Jansen, James T. C. Liu,

dominant problem of the times: the weakness of the Asian response to Western intrusion. Any interpretation of Naitō's work will be flawed if it does not take account of the bearing of this problem on his intellectual development.[4]

Like many of his contemporaries, such as Uchimura Kanzō (1861-1930), Okakura Tenshin (1862-1913), Shiratori Kurakichi (1865-1942), Nishida Kitarō (1870-1945), and Tsuda Sōkichi (1873-1963), Naitō's ideas were neither purely intellectual nor strictly practicable, but were instead concerned with the construction of a particular historical role for Japan in the all-engrossing turmoil that Asia had been thrown into by Western expansion. Like many of his contemporaries also, it was not Asia in general that was the center of concern, but that portion which was at one time dominated by Chinese culture and which in the nineteenth and early twentieth centuries still stood out as a coherent cultural whole. Any interpretation of Naitō's view, or for that matter, that of many of the Meiji and Taishō thinkers, must begin with this consideration.

The Naitō Hypothesis

A discussion of Naitō's thought, however, must be preceded by a brief statement of his "hypothesis."[5] Its first formulation may be found in unpublished lecture notes handwritten by Naitō in 1909,[6] and it bears more than a passing resemblance to Hegel's view of universal history.[7]

Following Hegel, Naitō found that the most important change from the T'ang (618-907) to Northern Sung (960-1126) dynasties was the emergence of the Chinese consciousness of the state (*kokumin teki jikaku*). This consciousness, which marked the beginning of

---

Teh-chao Wang, David W. Faure, Harry D. Harootunian, and Douglas G. Spelman for their guidance and comments at various stages.

[4] For Naitō's intellectual development, especially his indebtedness to such leading members of the Seikyōsha as Miyake Setsurei (1860-1945) and Shiga Shigetaka (1863-1927), see Tam, pp. 51-105.

[5] The terrain of this statement of the Naitō hypothesis is covered in close detail with full documentation and treatment in Tam, pp. 261-90.

[6] Naitō's 1909 version was published in 1969 for the first time. The document can be found in Naitō Kenkichi's "Atogaki," in *zenshū*, vol. 10, pp. 527-30.

[7] To Hegel, the three stages in universal history—ancient, medieval, and modern—represented three degrees of consciousness of freedom, ranked according to whether it was one, some, or all, who knew themselves to be free. From the different degrees of consciousness, Hegel called the Germanic nations "modern states," the Greek and Roman empires "medieval," and the Oriental countries "ancient" and "barbaric." See his *Lectures on the Philosophy of History*, tr. J. Silbree (New York, 1956).

China's modern history (*kinseishi*), resulted from China's peculiar relations with foreign countries and its unusual military weakness in the face of the "barbaric" menace. Before the Sung, Naitō argued, China was a united empire, regarded as *t'ien-hsia* (all the land under Heaven). Without the contrast of coexisting states the situation was not conducive to an awareness of the nation (*kokka*), and such consciousness by members of the state did not arise until the Sung period, in the face of the breakup of the empire and the successful establishment by the Khitans of rival states in the regions called Yen and Yün. The changes bore directly upon the political structure, and at the same time pervaded the entire country.

Accompanying this consciousness of the state, Naitō maintained, there was also a major political change which influenced the development of individual, personal thought. In the T'ang and earlier, the state was regarded as the private property (*shiyūbutsu*) of the monarch (*kunshu*), who was a member of an aristocratic clan, which in turn regarded him as its private property. Thus, Naitō argued, there were frequent political struggles in which the monarch was involved. When, after the Sung, the monarch became a supreme power above factional politics, he also became uncontrollable. However, his position was such that he retained the respect of his subjects, even when the dynasty fell, as in the closing years of Southern Sung (1127-1279).

The decline of aristocracy came with a guarantee of de facto freedom and safety for the monarch and, to a considerable degree, for the commoner. Hence scholarly and artistic expressions became less bound by tradition than before, and increasingly individualistic. Even the relation of the state to society changed after the Sung. Previously, the state had been able to reshape society, as when Emperor T'ai-tsung (reign 626-649), of the T'ang, redistributed land in the name of Heaven; but since the Sung, official reforms were no more than the adaptation of the state to social changes that had already taken place. Thus, Wang An-shih's (1021-1086) reforms were no more than the state's attempts to recognize existing social practice. Naitō concluded that with these drastic changes China entered its modern period.

It is not generally known that there is more than one version of the Naitō hypothesis. For a restatement, we can turn to Naitō's popular work, *Shina ron* (On China),[8] published in 1914, and to

[8] Reprinted in *zenshū*, vol. 5, pp. 291-482.

other writings.[9] At this time, Naitō was very much under the influence
of Uchida Ginzō (1872-1919),[10] a colleague at Kyoto Imperial University specializing in Japanese economic history, and therefore paid
more attention to the effects of economic development.

When *Shina ron* was published, the Ch'ing dynasty (1644-1911),
the decline of which Naitō had written about earlier,[11] had been
overthrown by the Revolution of 1911. A republic had been established in China, and in the years immediately following, there had
been much debate on the issue of its political structure under Yüan
Shih-k'ai.[12] Naitō's book was written partly to explain what had
happened and partly to explain the historical implications of the
courses that might be taken: would China become monarchic or remain republican?

This question, to Naitō, was closely intertwined with the issue of
the beginning of the modern era in China's history. He was still
following the political criteria he had drawn up earlier. The modern
era, as before, began in the Sung dynasty. There had been a transformation from aristocratic rule to despotism. To understand the
basis of aristocratic rule, Naitō argued, one had to understand the
Chinese clan system (*kazoku seido*). On the one hand, during the
medieval era (*chūsei*) the Chinese emperor was a member of an
aristocratic clan (*meizoku*), and was therefore restrained by all the
familial relations. On the other hand, the emperor governed the country as a father governed his family. Quoting T'ang's first emperor,
Kao-tsu (reign 618-626), who allegedly wanted to "transform his
family into a state,"[13] Naitō made clear that this was seen and accepted by the aristocracy. But toward the end of the T'ang dynasty,
the emphasis on the clan was destroyed through the rise of local
warlords, who not only disturbed the established social order, but
also gradually began passing their power on to their adopted sons
from other clans. During the Five Dynasties era (907-960), there
were instances, as in the Roman Empire, when the army nominated

[9] For examples, "Gaikatsuteki Tō-Sō jidai kan" (1922), ibid., vol. 8, pp. 111-
19; "Kindai Shina no bunka seikatsu" (1928), ibid., pp. 120-39; and *Shina kinseishi*
(1947), ibid., vol. 10, pp. 335-522.

[10] For a brief account of Uchida's career, see Nishida Naojirō, "Uchida sensei,"
in Uchida, *Nihon keizaishi gaiyō* (1939), pp. 130-34; for Uchida's influence upon
Naitō, see Tam, pp. 265-68.

[11] For instance, *Seichō suibō ron* (1912), *zenshū*, vol. 5, pp. 187-290.

[12] Somura Yasunobu, "Tairiku seisaku in okeru imeji no tenkan," in Shinohara
Hajime and Mitani Taichirō, eds., *Kindai Nihon no seiji shidō—seijika kenkyū*
(Tokyo, 1965), vol. 2, pp. 276-85.

[13] *Shina ron*, in *zenshū*, vol. 5, p. 313.

their own candidates as governors-general. The supremacy of the aristocracy was finally destroyed in the Sung. It was now possible for an outsider to rise to the position of emperor.

The potential restraints on the emperor were destroyed along with the aristocracy. Hence, sharp changes appeared in the structure of government. It used to be that the country was the property of the leading aristocratic family or clan, but now it became the property of the monarch-dictator (*dokusai kunshu*). In place of the aristocracy, a full-fledged bureaucratic system (*shinryō seidō*) was developed. The emperor's position also came to be sanctified, leading toward absolute despotism. One consequence of this despotism was that officials were under the strict control of the emperor, and whatever their power, could be removed or punished at his command.

The rise of despotism, however, led to an increased emphasis on the individual rights of subjects, referred to as "commoners" (*jimmin* or *heimin*) by Naitō. After the Sung, private ownership by commoners was fully recognized by law. The land tax could be paid in cash, thus giving the commoner greater flexibility in allocating his own production. It was during the Sung dynasty, too, that the examination system was properly routinized, and channels were opened for practically anyone to rise into the ranks of the government, should he pass the examination. Now commoners, not aristocrats, competed among themselves in such endeavors as education, scholarship, art, and management of the economy. Hence, the Sung dynasty experienced rapid growth in trade, population, urbanization, modern currency, scholarly and artistic creation, both domestic and international transport facilities, and in basic opportunities to participate in the political process. In short, the Chinese way of life was becoming more and more modern. Naitō saw despotism and modernity developing in a parallel fashion from Sung to Ch'ing.

Many difficulties grew out of this despotism and profoundly affected China's modern development. For instance, Naitō argued that politics were no longer very important in the lives of many intellectuals, who preferred to indulge themselves in scholarship and art. Scholar-officials seldom received respectful treatment from their ruler, who answered them as a slaveowner might answer his slaves. They could offer little resistance to either local uprisings or foreign invasions. The scholar-officials had little power and little responsibility, and consequently, lost interest as well as skill in politics.

The bureaucracy grew more complex, Naitō noted, and while there was mobility in the modern period, it was not so straightforward. Without clear standards of promotion, more cunning was needed in administration, and misconduct in office became inevitable. Huang Liu-hung's *Fu-hui ch'üan-shu* (Complete manual for securing felicity and benefits) (1694) was cited to illustrate the complexity of the craft of being an official in modern China. For their own "felicity and benefits," the scholar-officials needed to employ a large number of personal aides or sub-officials (*hsü-li*) to manage daily administrative business. A class of professional politicians developed, who tended to regard politics as merely a game in which they were either players or onlookers, unconcerned with national interests. Therefore, despite its cultural advancement, China came to be hopelessly corrupt and bankrupt.

With a centralized and venal bureaucracy under despotism, Chinese society ran more or less by its own efforts. Modern China, to Naitō, was a collection of self-managing villages and clans. Divorced from national politics, these rural solidarities, or *hsiang-t'uan*, were vitally related to the lives of the Chinese people. They owned "public fields" (*i-t'ien*, or *i-chuang*) for charitable purposes. Male children of the *hsiang-t'uan* received free education from the public schools (*i-hsüeh*) funded by incomes from the "public fields." The *hsiang-t'uan* constituents managed both private and public economic affairs, helping each other secure harmonious lives. Hence Naitō likened the *hsiang-t'uan* to small autonomous states embodying a certain democratic spirit.

At the top of the hierarchy in the *hsiang-t'uan* were the *fu-lao*, or the leading gentry elements, whose major concerns were the peace and prosperity of their own communities. Consequently, their political and economic outlook was characterized by two conflicting features. On the one hand, they had little interest in patriotism and lacked a national spirit. They tended to be submissive even to foreign rule, if local peace and prosperity could be maintained. Oriented toward self-sufficiency, the *fu-lao* often failed to appreciate national interests. Neither could they realize that the development of a modern economy was necessary and possible. On the other hand, the *fu-lao*, in response to social turmoil, were able to mobilize the *hsiang-t'uan* for self-defense, thus serving the dynasty's purpose by maintaining order, as when Tseng Kuo-fan (1811-1872) organized the Hsiang Army to defeat the Taiping rebels. In short, Naitō saw the *hsiang-t'uan* as "the only animated, dignified institution"[14] in the political history of modern China.

It may be noted once again that Naitō's argument was reminiscent of, and yet opposed to, Hegel. To Hegel, the Orient as a whole stagnated in its early, primitive form, while the Spirit rose in the West —an argument complementary to the popular optimism associated with Westernization in Japan and China in Naitō's days.[15] To Naitō, however, the idea of Oriental stagnation was unthinkable. He proved that Chinese history did in fact progress, but not without peculiar problems of its own.

This interpretation of Chinese history is central to an understanding of what Naitō had in mind as he commented on the current scene. His considerable writing on Republican China can be taken as a case in point.

The Abnormal Republican System

In contrast to many of his contemporaries in Japan, Naitō gave an unusual picture of China after the 1911 Revolution: China was to continue the advancement of civilization on an indigenous Chinese basis (*Shina hon-i no bunka*) under an "abnormal republican system."[16] There would be no hereditary monarch or bulky, strong central government. The national government, although respected and supported by its citizens, would allocate its power as much as possible to the localities, and would not need a strong national armed force. Historically speaking, Republican China was in a critical transitional phase, and a return to monarchy was out of the question. Naitō believed that this was a most natural development, as Republican China seemed to him a period when Chinese culture had aged and matured. For him history had confirmed that culture, not politics or military affairs, always came first in the mature phase of historical development. He wrote: "The ultimate purpose of a state is to

---

[14] Ibid., pp. 297, 369.

[15] Marius B. Jansen, *The Japanese and Sun Yat-sen* (Cambridge, Mass., 1954); Carmen Blacker, *The Japanese Enlightenment: A Study of the Writings of Fukuzawa Yukichi* (Cambridge, Mass., 1964); and Kenneth B. Pyle, *The New Generation in Meiji Japan: Problems of Cultural Identity, 1885-1895* (Stanford, 1969).

[16] As early as November 1911, Naitō ruled out the possibility of establishing a "federal state" (*rempōsei*) in China and insisted on a republican system (*kyōwasei*). See his "Shina jikyoku to shinkyū shisō" (a public lecture delivered in November 1911), *zenshū*, vol. 4, pp. 488-94. Later, he coined the term "henkei shita rempō seido," by which he meant an "abnormal republican system." See ibid., vol. 5, pp. 328-29, 380.

promote culture. It is not surprising at all for an old nation like China, sooner or later, to seek to take cultural development as her primary goal."[17] This strong belief in Chinese cultural development gave Naitō common ground with his Chinese peers such as Liang Ch'i-ch'ao (1873-1929) and Liang Sou [Shu]-ming (1893-1962). In their reaction against World War I and in the May Fourth Movement of 1919, they also had emphasized the Chinese basis (*Chung-kuo pen-wei*) of nation building, although in a different context.[18] Naitō, indeed, saw himself on the side of acceleration, opposing those who were inhibiting natural change. Americans and their Chinese students were singled out as targets of criticism for their superficiality and ignorance of Chinese history:

> Countries like the United States, themselves having no long-standing national history, often measure China by the singular standard of [Western-centered] modern civilization. To them the task of nation building is easy: the aged nation of China can be revitalized by applying modern methods. Many young Chinese, whose knowledge of their own history is superficial, of course, go along with the foreigners. Hence, they ignore history completely, thinking that a new China would be easily created in the hands of the new youths.[19]

In the 1920's, Naitō noted that a host of new trends, including Communism and Socialism, had been enthusiastically imported into China from Japan and the West.[20] Whatever their political beliefs, Chinese youths wanted "a rich country and a strong army." Their attitude was straightforward: to transform, if not destroy, the traditional social and political structure in order to transplant Western-oriented systems. But Naitō found these new programs theoretically unsound in that the disparagement of the customary way of life and China's "nationality" (*Shina no kokusui*) would only create unbearable conflicts in the Chinese mind and family rooted in the *hsiang-t'uan*. The Westernizing programs were also ill thought out, because their designers were not aware of the fatal, chronic obstacles intrinsic in China's modern history. To Naitō, political and economic affairs represented the most primitive human activities; their im-

[17] "Shina ni kaere" (1926), ibid., vol. 8, p. 178.

[18] Liang Ch'i-ch'ao, *Ou yu hsin-ying lu chieh-lu*, in Lin Chih-chun, comp., *Yin-ping shih ho chi*, vol. 5, chuan-chi, no. 23; Liang Sou [Shu]-ming, *Tung-hsi wen-hua chi ch'i che-hsüeh* (Shanghai, 1921).

[19] *Zenshū*, vol. 8, p. 176.   [20] Ibid., pp. 171-81.

portance had diminished in the Chinese way of life since the Sung. Naitō went so far as to say, "Not only China, even my own country, Japan, has been mistaken in undertaking 'a rich country and a strong army' as the only national goals."[21] Modern China should therefore follow the mainstream of Chinese development, emphasize culture rather than politics, economics, or military strength. She should turn her back on the West and "return to China" (*Shina ni kaere*).[22]

The key to the return to China was national renovation—China's most pressing task. Naitō's solution to it will be discussed elsewhere in this essay. But, to maintain its nationality, Naitō argued, China had to keep its central government small and weak.[23] A strong, bulky national government would tend to encourage despotism, and this had proved to be a major source of political ills and economic distress. Under the "abnormal republican system," it was possible to limit the power and size of the government and to develop local autonomy by allocating more power to the *hsiang-t'uan*. Decentralization would be conducive not only to the welfare and happiness of the people, but also to the development of democratic institutions. After all, the *hsiang-t'uan*, as stated previously, remained the "only animated, dignified institution" in modern Chinese society. Strengthening its role would be a popular political act. And Naitō noted that he was not alone in emphasizing decentralization, as the same idea had been thoughtfully extolled by such scholars as Huang Tsung-hsi (1610-1695), Ku Yen-wu (1613-1682), and Wang Fu-chih (1619-1692).[24] Naitō also supported his argument by quoting Lao Tzu, who had hoped that "ruling a big country is like cooking small fish"—in the sense that the one should be carried out with as little trouble as the other—so that the burdens of the people would not be amplified.[25]

It has often been charged by his critics that Naitō was in effect advocating an alliance of warlords in the name of a decentralized republican system. But a close reading of his work reveals a contrasting view. Naitō rejected warlord politics on three counts: first, the warlords' domination of China would eventually lead to despotic monarchy; second, it would take at least thirty to fifty years for any warlord after Yüan Shih-k'ai to unify China; and third, the Chinese

---

[21] Ibid., p. 178.   [22] Ibid.

[23] "Shina no seiji" (1916), ibid., vol. 4, p. 567; and "Shina kokuze no kompongi" (1916), ibid., pp. 528-30.

[24] "Shina shōrai no tōchi" (1916), ibid., p. 539.

[25] "Shina ni kaere," ibid., vol. 8, p. 179.

people would suffer too much under the warlords.[26] Naitō himself remained a harsh critic of Yüan Shih-k'ai's polity and the two conclusions he drew on the collapse of Yüan's monarchy attempt in 1916 were first, that it was a failure of centralization, and second, that it was the failure of an anachronism.[27] Naitō was thus confident that the verdict of history had been pronounced in favor of a decentralized republican system in modern China, although he was not unaware of the "unpleasant" (*fuyukai*) and "inert" (*fukappatsu*) hindrances to the realization of this political system.[28]

While Naitō maintained that decentralization was natural and important to Chinese politics, he believed that China's situation was not hopeless in the face of Western intrusion. Contrary to his contemporaries who placed much faith in Western-educated youths, Naitō discovered a hopeful sign in China's peasantry, the masses of the country. Writing on various occasions in the late 1910's and 1920's,[29] Naitō argued that since the peasantry as a class was quite divorced from the mainstream of traditional influence, they still possessed a "rejuvenating potentiality" that could be used as a basis for building a strong China in the future.

Naitō observed that the potential of the peasantry became increasingly obvious in the republican era. Since the fall of the Ch'ing, he admitted, the peasants' tax burden had increased and their peaceful provincial life had been disturbed under the warlords. However, their greater productivity in the republican era might have compensated for the heavier taxation, making their lives in general better than ever before.[30] He further pointed out that as the European demand for Chinese foodstuffs grew after World War I, Chinese peasants became richer. Stimulated by their new economic status, they became politically aware. They began to organize armed forces for their own protection, thus establishing a foundation of power. Naitō noted that these self-defense forces had successfully resisted invasion by new armies influenced by Communism in the region near Shanghai.[31]

One should not be surprised to see the peasantry grow stronger at this particular stage of Chinese history, Naitō argued. The rise of the peasantry was a natural accompaniment to the growth of local

[26] "Shina shōrai no tōchi," ibid., vol. 4, p. 535; and "Shina jikyoku no shiken" (1916), ibid., pp. 547-52.
[27] "En-shi no shippai yori ebeki kyōkun" (1916), ibid., pp. 588-93.
[28] "Shina gensei ron" (1914), ibid., vol. 5, pp. 466-67.
[29] For examples, "Shina no chūkokusha" (1921), ibid., pp. 142-45; and "Shina no kokusai kanri ron" (1921), ibid., p. 156.
[30] Ibid., p. 143.   [31] Ibid.

autonomy and freedom as Chinese civilization matured. Moreover, as the peasants were determined to preserve their traditional way of life, they opposed Western culture, including Communism. On this point, Naitō probably made the worst prediction in all his writing, and this arose from his confusing the *fu-lao* (local elders) with the peasantry.

But China still needed unity and modernization in the Western sense. The problem was how this might be possible under a decentralized "abnormal republican system" governing a strongly traditional, communal society. What may be referred to as Naitō's imperialism arose as a solution to this problem: for effective national reform, China would have to employ foreigners to manage the affairs of state for a certain period, while it continued to develop culturally and to maintain sovereignty and integrity. But again, let us look first at the intellectual roots of this position.

Shifting of Cultural Centers

A clear statement of the intellectual background to Naitō's position on the role of foreigners, especially the Japanese, in China's national development may be found in the *Shin Shina ron* (New thoughts on China) published in 1924,[32] which, despite its somewhat loose and careless presentation, embodied an aspect of Naitō's Hegelian thinking that he had adopted during the 1890's. This particular theory, the shift in Oriental cultural centers (*Tōyō bunka chūshin no idō*), was given a prominent place in the *Shin Shina ron*[33] and in a number of articles published earlier.[34] During its formation, Naitō claimed to have been inspired by such scholars as Chao I (1727-1814)[35] and Okakura Tenshin,[36] in addition to Miyake Setsurei and Shiga Shigetaka. In brief, Naitō argued that, by the unfolding of the law of historical development, China was no longer the center of Oriental culture and its creative energy was spent. Moreover, echoing Giambattista Vico (1668-1744), but antedating Oswald Spengler (1880-1936) and Arnold Toynbee (1881-1975), Naitō saw the West on the decline.

According to Naitō, the evolution of civilization was not arbitrary;

---

[32] *Shin Shina ron* can be found in ibid., pp. 483-543.

[33] Especially in chapter three, ibid., pp. 508-16.

[34] "Chisei okusetsu" (1894), ibid., vol. 1, pp. 117-25; "Jo ron," in *Kinsei bungaku shiron* (1897), ibid., pp. 19-23; "Sō to-Bei sō jo" (1893), ibid., pp. 335-45; "Jūzō to-Bei sō gen" (1893), ibid., pp. 346-48; and "Nihon no tenshoku to gakusha" (1894), ibid., pp. 126-33.

[35] Ibid., pp. 21, 118-20.   [36] "Shina gakuhen," ibid., p. 357.

nothing was accidental. It was determined by two basic factors: time (*jidai*) and the spirit of the land (*chi-ki*, or *chi-sei*). The evolution of culture was actually an historical process in which human beings "used time as longitude and the land as latitude, jumbling them together and making them function."[37] He also held that culture was under the spell of the law of nature in the same way as human life, progressing through phases of childhood, adulthood, and old age. Each phase had a special character of its own, resembling the stages of organic life. Thus, in its ancient period, a culture possessed a childlike dynamism, seen clearly in its experimentation with new institutions. In the medieval period, political and economic organizations developed into a robust, yet rigid, condition. In the final stage of its development— the modern period in history—a culture matured, from which a naturalistic attitude emerged and decadence in art and literature became all-pervading.

Governed by time and the spirit of the land, the evolution of culture, however complicated it might be, followed definite patterns: the cultural center constantly shifted from one region to another. The recorded vicissitudes of Egypt, India, Persia, Phoenicia, Greece, and Rome were to Naitō merely shifts of cultural centers on a worldwide scale.[38] This theory of cultural evolution was almost a synthesis of Miyake's interpretation of Hegel and Naitō's modification of Shiga's emphasis on natural environment.

In these shifts, Naitō argued, national boundaries were insignificant. Chinese history made it clear that in the Ming dynasty (1368-1644), the Kiangsu-Chekiang area had been the center of Chinese culture, and yet this was an area inhabited by non-Chinese barbarians in the ancient period. At present, the center of culture in China seemed to be in Kwangtung, but once again, this area had also been inhabited by non-Chinese tribesmen in previous times. Hence, the movement of the Oriental cultural center was not necessarily to an area that had been inhabited by the Chinese people.[39]

It was a point taken for granted by Naitō that the modern locus of Oriental culture had already shifted to Japan; hence Chinese and other Asian students went there for education. Since Japan had been exposed to Chinese culture earlier than Kwangtung, this should not be a matter of any surprise. Naitō argued:

It is the result of historical inevitability in the development of

---

[37] "Jo ron," ibid., p. 21; and "Chisei okusetsu," ibid., pp. 118-20.
[38] "Jo ron," ibid., p. 22.   [39] *Shin Shina ron*, p. 509.

Oriental culture. The different nations in Asia, the Chinese, Japanese, Koreans, or Vietnamese, may have important problems of their own. However, in terms of the development of Oriental culture as a whole, these problems are trivial. This is because the development of culture, far from being different for different races, follows a definite direction.[40]

A review of Sino-Japanese cultural relations further confirmed Japan's position, Naitō held. It was true that China was the fount of Oriental culture, which had originated in the Huang-ho (Yellow River) area and expanded southward and then northward, and Japan had come under this influence. The impact of Chinese culture, Naitō argued, was not a sudden development, but a process of transformation of original material that had been present in Japan. In one instance, Naitō likened Japan to an intelligent child learning from the advanced grown-up, China.[41] In another place, he compared the development to the process of making bean-curd, in which Chinese culture was like the brine element, or the *nigari*, which had to be put into the bean juice to make it coagulate.[42] It was clear to Naitō that although Japan had learned from China, it remained an independent entity during this learning process. Their independence stemmed from a certain self-awareness among the Japanese people, according to Naitō. First, there was a political awareness of nationhood reaching back to the time of Prince Shōtoku (574-622), who saw Japan as comparable in greatness to China. Second, there was Japan's cultural awareness which came much later, after the Ōnin War (1466-77) and the absorption of much Chinese culture.[43]

Naitō concluded that learning from China could indeed help to strengthen Japan, but that Chinese elements were continually transformed by the Japanese and assimilated into their own unique culture. The great anthology, *Man'yōshū* (Collection of ten thousand leaves), the *norito* (Shinto ritual prayers), and *semmyō* (ancient imperial proclamations in Japan) were equivalent, if not superior, to the *Shih ching* (Book of odes) and *Shang shu* (Canons of Yao and Shun). In Buddhism, the Hōnen and Nichiren sects were distinctively Japanese. In Confucianism, indigenous *sonnō-jōi* (revere the em-

---

[40] Ibid., p. 508.
[41] "Nihon bunka ro wa nani zoya" (1922), *zenshū*, vol. 9, p. 14.
[42] Ibid.
[43] For political awareness, see "Shōtoku Daishi" (1924), ibid., pp. 52-57; for a contrast between political and cultural awareness, see "Nihon bunka to wa nani zoya," ibid., pp. 14-15.

peror, expel the barbarians) thought was so powerful that it became one of the foundations of the Meiji Restoration. In arts, many sculptures in Nara were clearly distinguishable from those of India, Greece, and China; they embodied a unique Japanese purity and flavor.[44] Therefore, Naitō was confident that Japan's claim to be the new center of Oriental culture did not rest merely on its achievements in the post-Meiji years.

Naitō continued to assert that Japan was mandated to lead a new "universal civilization" (kon'yō bummei).[45] He believed that contemporary Western society was approaching its old age and that Western civilization had begun to stagnate and decline. After flourishing for four hundred years, the West was reaching a stage of dehumanization, as shown by its intensified materialistic tendencies. The most obvious symptom was the declining impact of Christianity. Naitō contended that centuries before, robust Christianity had served as an important moving force in Western cultural development, but now it failed to counteract the materialistic and dehumanizing tendencies, which were clearly opposed to Christian spiritual teaching. Western civilization had been poisoned by wealth, a creation of the last few centuries. Westerners could not actually enjoy freedom, for they were slaves of machines. Mass production had been doing its best to destroy human individuality; mechanization in turn encouraged Westerners to quicken their conquest and destruction of nature and culture. As a result, Westerners knew only tension and were ignorant of the true taste of culture and freedom in their daily lives.

Naitō further noted that the senescence of the West was forecast by a group of European scholars who were increasingly interested in Buddhism and other aspects of Oriental culture as a means of revitalizing their own culture. He wrote in 1893:

> The past century has indeed seen increasing appeal of Buddhism to Europeans. Now Europeans have begun to be aware of their endangered position in the face of a destructive, materialistic civilization, which they themselves have created. Little wonder, then, European scholars have been rushing into Oriental studies, and in fact, many of them have made important contributions to this field of study.[46]

[44] "Nihon no tenshoku to gakusha" (1894), ibid., vol. 1, pp. 126-27.
[45] "Iwayuru Nihon no tenshoku" (1894), ibid., vol. 2, pp. 132-33.
[46] "Sō to-Bei sō jo" (1893), ibid., vol. 1, p. 345.

Unlike their Western counterparts, the Japanese, though materially poor, were able to attain the highest degree of freedom. They lived in comfortable wooden houses instead of fancy, artificial apartments made of reinforced concrete. They refused to kill animals for their fur. From nature they produced the best ceramics and chinaware. The Chinese as well as the Japanese excelled in the appreciation of art and antiques. Orientals were concerned with ecological and environmental protection; they made things simple and disliked complexity in daily life. In short, both Japanese and Chinese represented what ought to be the norms in modern life. Measured against these norms, Western civilization was nothing but backward, capricious, and barbaric.[47]

However, Japan and the West were still strongly organized powers, far greater than China, Naitō warned. They became strong because they were in different developmental stages of their national histories from that of China. The simple truth was that China was old, mature, and had come very close to the end of its history, while the West was only now becoming old, and Japan was young and had just started its modern era during Tokugawa times. The law of history dictated the fates of both China and Japan. Naitō wrote:

> The difference between China and Japan today comes from their different stages in their national lives. Had Japan lived through the age of China, Japan would be another China, and China would be another Japan. The reverse would also be true.[48]

To save China from its historical predicament, therefore, Sino-Japanese cooperation and friendship were essential. Naitō explained in 1924:

> Since the Oriental cultural center has now shifted to Japan . . . the intellectual class of Japan would be glad to cooperate with the neighboring nation to advance their common interests, spiritual and material alike. In short, it is the Japanese object to join hands with the Chinese in carrying a cultural movement along broad and lofty lines, irrespective of their national polity and governmental systems.[49]

To the end, Naitō insisted that foreign management of Chinese af-

---

[47] "Minzoku no bunka to bummei to ni tsuite" (1926), ibid., vol. 8, pp. 140-53.
[48] *Shin Shina ron*, p. 526.   [49] Ibid., pp. 509-10.

fairs of state, beginning with the economic opening of China in the republican era, was historically inevitable.

The Chinese Renovation and Japan

History made it plain that twentieth-century China needed thorough reform. But could China be effectively revitalized by the Chinese themselves? Naitō's answers was negative.[50] Briefly, there were three reasons why indigenous reforms were impossible in China. First, effective reform had to be based on the "fresh potentiality" of the "peasantry," but in this case they lacked nationalistic spirit and the necessary schooling. Second, reform had to be carried out by means of military force, but this would bring foreign intervention to protect existing foreign interests in China, which would lead to a renewed scramble for domination, bearing directly upon China's sovereignty. Third, political reform would not be able to penetrate the level of the *hsiang-t'uan*, and hence no complete reform would be possible. In fact, Naitō went on, the cultural reforms being carried out in China after the May Fourth Movement were doomed to fail, because the reformers forgot to take into consideration China's stage of historical development and the residual strength of Chinese tradition to resist change.

In order to facilitate an effective renovation of the "peasantry," Naitō argued, China needed to go through an "unpleasant" and "inert" historical phase during which foreigners would be employed to manage the affairs of state in place of the Chinese.[51] He claimed to be the first advocate of this idea of altruistic control without domination, known to many as the "policy of international control," as he had begun writing about it as early as 1900.[52] He contended that his proposal was basically different from invasion or conquest in that he would never impose it on the Chinese by force. He insisted that the policy would be effective only if the Chinese took the initiative, although it might be instituted by historical necessity regardless of what Chinese or Japanese wanted.[53]

Naitō made it clear that he would object to any attempt by foreigners, including the Japanese, to transplant alien systems into China. Foreigners would be there to illustrate in person the inner workings of "modern" national institutions; their ultimate goal

[50] Ibid., pp. 517-24.
[51] "Shina no kokusai kanri ron" (1921), *zenshū*, vol. 5, pp. 153-58.
[52] For instance, "Seikoku kaikaku nan" (1900), ibid., vol. 3, pp. 283-304.
[53] "Shina no kokusai kanri ron," pp. 154, 158.

would be to train the young Chinese "peasant."[54] Naitō had already taken pains to explain that as China was approaching the most advanced historical phase, what the foreigners had to offer were in effect "backward" and "primitive" spirit and tactics that the Chinese had known well in their medieval and ancient times.

To Naitō, history had testified to the effective and economical results of employment of foreigners, as exemplified in such establishments as Robert Hart's Maritime Customs Service and Kawashima Naniwa's police school in Peking. In 1916, Naitō went so far as to say: "The policy goes well with military affairs, too. The security power of a battalion entrusted to the hands of a Japanese officer is greater than that of a whole division organized by the Chinese themselves."[55]

Naitō urged foreign management of China in China's interests. The projected foreign management of its national affairs would not, he felt, endanger its sovereignty and independence. He characterized the foreigners employed in China as "caretakers" or "guards" serving a wealthy master:[56]

> The master would certainly not lose his status as master when he employs security guards against robbers and thieves. Similarly, would it not be a noble idea for the Chinese to realize their mission in cultural development while having their civilization well protected by others?[57]

Naitō further stated that today's China was armed with a certain "immunity" against any form of destruction, which was derived from her unique social structure and advanced history.[58] The poison of opium, Naitō noted, had destroyed many nations, but failed to exhaust China. Western powers and Japan had furiously scrambled for territories and power in China during the past decades, and yet China in the 1920's remained almost free from foreign control, although divided and militarily weak. On one occasion Naitō went so far as to say that China did not need any defense; safety was guaranteed by its internal structure and historical forces. One negative consequence, however, was that republican China could no longer protect and keep former tributary states such as Tibet and Outer and Inner Mongolia, since they had different social structures and cultural traditions.[59]

---

[54] Ibid., pp. 144, 156.
[55] *Shin Shina ron*, p. 531.
[56] *Zenshū*, vol. 4, p. 546.
[57] Ibid., p. 545.
[58] "Shina ni kaere," ibid., vol. 8, p. 179.
[59] "Shina jikyoku to shinkyū shisō," ibid., vol. 4, pp. 491, 494.

Of all the foreign countries capable of aiding China in this respect, Naitō naturally considered Japan the best candidate. There was a better relationship between Japanese merchants and the Chinese people than between Western merchants and the Chinese people. Western merchants who went to China represented large business undertakings, and were consequently in contact only with the elite of the merchant class. Japanese businessmen in China were mainly small merchants in contact with ordinary people. The Japanese were practical, and were willing to take every inch that China was prepared to give. Amercians were more aggressive, however, because they were interested only in the large operations familiar in their own country.

What Naitō advocated was clear: first, Japan should take on the economic development of China, to be followed by other reforms in politics and military affairs. These should not be along Western lines. A great leap in industrialization, for instance, was deemed impractical. Naitō explained:

China must in the first place be so reorganized as to become a producing country of crude materials needed for manufacturing. . . . In order to reform the Chinese economic system, which still remains as it was in ancient times, it must be considered an improper and difficult plan to introduce and apply here the industrial system that has developed in circumstances entirely different.[60]

It had long been in Naitō's belief that Japan, more a synthesis of Western and Eastern civilizations, had practically everything to satisfy Chinese needs. He wrote in 1901:

At present what the Chinese want from us are essentially the same things that they had expected from the Europeans and Americans, namely, modern education and new ideas. In particular, they appreciate the secrets in our "Oriental brains." What the Chinese do not want from us are precisely the *rōnin*-styled elements of disturbance.[61]

This notwithstanding, the role Japan actually performed after the establishment of the Republic proved unsatisfactory and disappointing to Naitō. During the chaos of the 1911 Revolution, Japan offered nothing but fluctuating self-centered policies, ranging from military

[60] *Shin Shina ron*, p. 516.
[61] "Shina mondai kankeisha no shinkai" (1901), *zenshū*, vol. 3, p. 259.

[178]

assistance for the Manchus to attempts to create two Chinas in the south and north. Naitō's call for non-interference was ignored.[62]

In the first republican years, Naitō also disapproved of Japan's relations with Yüan Shih-k'ai, on the grounds that Yüan's ability as China's leader was overrated.[63] It is sometimes said that it was around this time that Naitō advocated international military rule of China. As Ikeda Makoto's study makes clear, he actually in effect wished to warn that Yüan's government might lead China straight to a second international military rule, modeled after and in the memory of the first international military rule which was imposed at the end of the Boxer Rebellion in 1900.[64] Naitō warned in his *Shina ron*:

> Blinded by the temporary, reactionary trend of the times, Yüan Shih-k'ai has mistakenly believed that he himself has discovered a new tendency of political development. He does not know he is actually throwing the fate of his country into oblivion. Previously he had cared about the financial independence of his own country when he arranged loans from the Five Powers. . . . But now, in inviting foreign investments in the development of the oil fields and the dredging of the Huai River, Yüan Shih-k'ai has completely ignored China's independence. My present book is intended to analyze China from a Chinese point of view. Seeing today's traumatic situation in Yüan's China, I have already sensed that I no longer need to write any more . . . the second international military rule is around the corner.[65]

True to his theory, Naitō objected to possible undermining of Chinese independence. Foreign military rule of China would thus be unacceptable.

The Twenty-One Demands of 1915 were considered by Naitō as a diplomatic failure, since the move was straightforwardly one-sided,

---

[62] "Shina jikyoku no hatten" (November 11-14, 1911), ibid., vol. 5, pp. 446-49, and "Chūka Minkoku no shōnin ni tsuite" (March 18-20, 1912), ibid., pp. 450-55.

[63] Yüan was viewed as "a man beautiful from all angles," "an opportunist," "a politician without any political belief," "a reactionary," "a sinful man leading the Chinese people into oblivion," and "a public enemy of humanity in the world." Yüan's "success" was due to his clear winning of the allegiance of the *fu-lao*. In addition to *Shina ron*, Naitō's criticism on Yüan can be found in the following: "Shina gensei ron" (1913), ibid., pp. 462-68; and "Kakumei no daini shoran" (1913), ibid., pp. 469-82.

[64] Ikeda Makoto, "Naitō Konan no En Sei-gai ron," in *Ritsumeikan hōgaku*, vol. 44 (1963), pp. 501-504.

[65] *Zenshū*, vol. 5, p. 296.

neglecting Chinese interests entirely.[66] First, Japan had missed the opportunity to present demands in 1914 when Peking most urgently needed financial assistance. Second, the Japanese government failed to show respect to the Chinese, by not discussing the matter with them from the very beginning. Third, the Demands themselves were covetous and unresponsive to Chinese feelings; hence such "folly" as the right to religious activities in China by the Japanese was included. The Twenty-One Demands were to Naitō a collection of greedy, arbitrary, and thoughtless "orders" imposed upon China by the lazy diplomats, bewildered military men, and selfish entrepreneurs of Japan, all of whom were ignorant of Chinese national character. Time and again Naitō insisted that he was not against the idea of gaining benefits for Japan, but that any such gain should be concurrently beneficial to China.

Naitō naturally opposed the use of military force to impose these Demands, arguing that it would not solve any problems. He pointed out that even in 1900, when the situation in China was not so complicated, the eight powers had failed to gain absolute control of China in their dealings with the empty-handed Li Hung-chang, who was virtually held at gunpoint. The use of force to implement the Twenty-One Demands would therefore only invite troubles for Japan. Naitō explained:

> Today, China's lack of strength has been thoroughly exposed. She is weak. . . . It is not that Japan is incapable of sending her troops to Peking; there is no problem about that if the Japanese choose to do so. But military action would necessarily create lawlessness in China. I am afraid that it would be Japan, not China, that would have to be responsible for the consequences.[67]

Naitō further explained that the consequences would probably include an all-out war between the Chinese and Japanese, which should be the first thing that both countries wanted to avoid.[68]

It should be clear that Naitō's theories implied an antagonist: the West, not China. Hence Naitō saw the anti-Japanese movements in China as natural, but unnecessary; they represented only artificial

---

[66] "Nisshi kōshō ron" (July 1915), ibid., vol. 4, pp. 516-22. This was the first article written by Naitō after he had examined the text of the Twenty-One Demands. For his views of the same "negotiation" prior to the publication of the Demands, see his "Tai-Shi kōshō mondai" (March 1, 1915), ibid., pp. 505-10; and "Nisshi kōshō o hyōzu" (May 13, 1915), ibid., pp. 511-15.

[67] "Tai-Shi kōshō mondai, ibid., p. 506.

[68] "Nisshi kōshō ron," ibid., pp. 516, 521-22.

hostility provoked by Westerners.[69] None of the Western-oriented ideologies such as individualism, socialism, and communism had any chance of succeeding in China.[70] Hence Naitō would applaud the use of military power on the continent to protect fellow Asian nations, as he had done before the outbreak of the Russo-Japanese War.[71]

I am convinced of Naitō's intellectual honesty in taking this position against the use of force in China, and also of his sincerity in advocating foreign management of China in China's own interests. These views are consistent with an interpretation of the situation according to his broad theories. His views in the 1930's are more problematic; unfortunately, for this period, little is known.[72] Naitō retired from active academic life in 1926 and remained ailing thereafter. He devoted himself to editing his lecture notes and seldom wrote on current affairs. We are told that he was deeply troubled by "a sense of profound fear" over his country's involvement in the creation of Manchukuo in 1931.[73] Three of his Chinese poems[74] reveal that he was seriously disturbed when he learned that Premier Inukai, whom he had known since he was nine years old, was assassinated by militaristic fanatics on May 15, 1932. The murder was a personal loss as well as a national one,[75] and he condemned the assassins as barbaric "thieves and robbers" of Japan's future in the same poems. In spite of possible dangers, he accepted the Inukai family's request that he compose the memorial epitaph. Following the establishment of the puppet state, Manchukuo, Naitō, in his comments on the principles of "nation" building, expressed appreciation of the "deeds of arms" (*bukun*) of the Kwantung Army, but warned that the Japanese military establishment should terminate its control of the "new country" as soon as possible; the "sovereignty" of this country had to be respected. He also opposed transplantation of Japanese political systems into Manchukuo. In short, Naitō believed in Manchukuo for the Man-

[69] "Kentochigai no hai-Nichi" (1919), ibid., vol. 5, pp. 57-58; "Shina no hai-Nichi-ron" (1919), ibid., pp. 61-69; and *Shin Shina ron*, pp. 489-500.

[70] Ibid., pp. 533-43.

[71] For instance, "Ubyū naru hisen-ron" (1903), *zenshū*, vol. 2, pp. 56-68.

[72] Naitō was no longer able to keep up with current developments in China in this period. It is suggested that even the establishment of Manchukuo was made known to him only through his colleague Yano Jin'ichi. See Mitamura Taisuke, *Naitō Konan*, p. 220.

[73] Ibid., p. 221.

[74] The three Chinese poems were composed on May 18, 1932. They were sent to the Inukai family in care of Kojima Kazuo, Naitō's friend since the Seikyōsha days, who became a protégé of Inukai. See Koichinen-kai, ed., *Kojima Kazuo* (Tokyo, 1949), p. 799.

[75] "Inukai shūshō no kotogotomo" (May 17, 1932), *zenshū*, vol. 6, pp. 249-50.

churians.[76] These are but partial indications of a position, and more must await further research.

Conclusion

To characterize Naitō Konan as an imperialist, therefore, is to miss the point. In his writing, he referred to the use of a "big axe or dynamite" if the need arose during the process of reviving China,[77] but he was against military domination and the dispatch of troops to Peking to press for the Twenty-One Demands. Even in 1894, when he supported the Sino-Japanese War, he objected to any possible military takeover.[78] In 1905, too, when Japanese victory over the Russians was assured in Manchuria, time and again Naitō warned against the enlargement of the war zone.[79] In short, Naitō had much faith in China's future, but it was one in which Japan must be involved in a non-military manner.

If one sees Naitō's discussion of current issues in the context of his general arguments, therefore, one gets the impression that it was not the military expansion of Japan that mattered. The issue of the day was not narrow nationalism, but the survival and development of Oriental civilization, in which both Japan and China had their roots. The important issue was not military domination, but something that would go deeper, reaching first into social organization, and then into individual minds. Or, in other words, it was a question of the spirit that would form the center of culture. In this context, the shifting of the cultural center from China to Japan, and the development of a Japanese spirit, was a convenient framework into which Naitō fit his answers to the common problematical issues of his day, and this framework Naitō found in Hegel, just as his contemporaries found theirs in Spencer or Buddhism or Marxism.

For a more complete understanding of Naitō, it must be recognized that the problems were closely bound up with Western intrusion into China. China had the dual function of reflecting what could have happened to Japan in the face of similar Western intrusion, and acting as the source of a deep-rooted Japanese culture that would form the basis of a national identity in an age of rapid change. The political and

---

[76] "Manshūkoku kensetsu ni tsuite" (1932), ibid., vol. 5, pp. 170-80; and "Manshūkoku kongo no hōshin ni tsuite" (1933), ibid., pp. 181-85.

[77] Ibid., p. 514.

[78] "Iwayuru Nihon no tenshoku," ibid., vol. 2, pp. 127-35.

[79] For instance, "Kōsen chiiki no kakuchō" (January 18, 1905), ibid., vol. 4, pp. 144-45.

military weakness of China was not cause for complacency, however. Rather, it was a constant reminder of the threat of Western interference, from which Japan could draw a sense of mission. It was this feeling of having a mission, founded on the unity of Japanese and Chinese cultures, that finally solved Japan's quest for identity. This mind-set was not unique to Naitō and the Kyoto Sinologists; it was common to many of the major thinkers of Meiji and Taishō Japan.

CHAPTER X

ISHIBASHI TANZAN AND THE TWENTY-ONE DEMANDS

—————

SHUMPEI OKAMOTO

Introduction

In August 1914 the Great War engulfed Europe. Taking full advantage of the situation which compelled the European powers to neglect the Far East temporarily, Japan acted to secure for itself a commanding position in China in anticipation of postwar international rivalry over the region. Toward this objective, in January 1915, the Japanese government thrust upon its Chinese counterpart the far-reaching Twenty-One Demands.

With few exceptions, Japanese public opinion approved and justified the Twenty-One Demands. Even when critical voices were heard, they concentrated their attack on the government's bungling negotiations. The so-called "China experts" of the time shared the general public's approving attitude. Yoshino Sakuzō, for instance, went so far as to write that the Twenty-One Demands were "the minimum" that Japan needed to make for the sake of national survival. Viewing Japan's relations with both the Western powers and China, he judged that the government chose "the most opportune moment" for negotiation. Asserting that the demands were in their entirety "measures extremely appropriate" for the future advancement of Japan in China, Yoshino concluded that the withdrawal of Item Five was "acutely regrettable."

Yoshino's expressive assertion in support of the Twenty-One Demands, however, differed from the less reflective opinions of those who advocated Japan's continental expansion. He was aware of the contradiction between "the ideal policy" and "practical necessities" that haunted Japanese relations with China. The ideal China policy

The Chinese and the Japanese: Essays in Political and Cultural Interactions
0-691-03126-6/80/184-15$00.75/1 (cloth)
0-691-10086-1/80/184-15$00.75/1 (paperback)
For copying information, see copyright page

for Japan, Yoshino believed, ought to contribute to China's sound development as an independent nation. Unfortunately, two factors prevented Japan from carrying out such a policy. One was the powers' imperialistic ambitions in China. The other was doubt over China's inherent capability of political autonomy. As long as the powers continued to compete with one another to expand their spheres of interest, and as long as internal turmoil continued to prevent sound political integration in China, neighboring Japan would be compelled to pursue a minimum protective policy such as the Twenty-One Demands in order to safeguard its position in East Asia. Yoshino's argument for the Twenty-One Demands betrayed a high degree of ambivalence toward the dilemma of "ideal" and "practice." Still, it is undeniable that he was willing to accept as an unavoidable requirement Japanese participation in the imperialist rivalry over China.[1]

In the context of this domestic response to the Twenty-One Demands, Ishibashi Tanzan of *Tōyō keizai shinpō* (The Oriental Economist) stood out as an outstanding exception. He opposed the government's action steadfastly and on principle. Although he was familiar with the Yoshino writings on China policy that appeared in *Chūō kōron* (The Central Review), he did not dwell on the problem with Yoshino's painful equivocation. Instead, Ishibashi stood in total opposition to Japan's imperialistic expansion in China.

Upon hearing the rumor that the Ōkuma cabinet had been pressing the Chinese government for a far-reaching settlement of the Mongolian and Manchurian questions, but without knowing directly the details of the Japanese demands, Ishibashi surmised that the event would have "grave consequences" for Japan. He had been aware of Japanese ambitions to place Manchuria under perpetual occupation, and he also recognized that the recent revolutionary turmoil in China, together with the war in Europe, had emboldened the Japanese to aspire to advance beyond Manchuria and into Mongolia. Supported by such sentiments, the Japanese government had joined the war and occupied Tsingtao. In view of these developments, it was quite reasonable for Ishibashi to conclude that the government had embarked on a "foolish act" in demanding new territorial concessions from China.

Ishibashi argued against such action, deriving his argument from his twofold belief in "morality" and "utilitarianism" in international relations. He maintained that, even in international relations, there

[1] Yoshino Sakuzō, *Chūgoku Chōsen ron* (Tokyo, 1970), pp. 23-29; Mitani Taichirō, *Taishō demokurashii ron* (Tokyo, 1974), pp. 155-229.

were "right" and "wrong" kinds of behaviors. Although "wrong" behavior might seem to represent strength, in the final analysis, it was weak. For in international conduct, justice was the ultimate winner. Injustice was destined to be destroyed by the eventual counterattacks not only of the immediate victim, but also of "worldwide public opinion." This was why, according to Ishibashi, Russia had lost Manchuria, and, more recently, why Germany had lost Tsingtao. Never should Japan become a second Russia or Germany.

Furthermore, Ishibashi asserted that from an economic standpoint, Japanese extension of monopolistic rights and interests in China was unprofitable. Japan might succeeed in expanding its own rights and interests in China, but it would be no actual gain because Japan lacked the necessary resources to make any real use of the newly acquired rights. Ishibashi held an optimistic view that as long as China was left open to the powers' investments, China and Japan would be the greatest beneficiaries. Ishibashi concluded in his thoroughgoing utilitarian manner that in its own interest alone, Japan must wish for China's prosperity. It must abandon its habitually "benevolent"—the wolf to the lamb in Aesop's Fables—attitude toward China, and adopt "a thoroughly self-centered" policy that would ultimately regard China's welfare as being in its own interest.

Ishibashi denounced the 1915 Sino-Japanese treaty as "a sheer disaster." To him the Twenty-One Demands were merely an immediate manifestation of Japan's persistent imperialist policy, which he considered to be the basic cause of Sino-Japanese conflict. Consequently, he advocated an early restoration to China of all the territories, rights, and interests that Japan had acquired. He admonished his fellow countrymen not to despise the Chinese people, but to respect China's independence. Such an attitude toward China was unique at the time, but, he affirmed that his opposition to the Twenty-One Demands was no more than "a practical application of a long-cherished opinion."[2] Ishibashi was not one of the so-called "China experts." How did he come to hold these views that differed so clearly from those of most China experts, including Yoshino Sakuzō? On what personal and intellectual bases did his "long-cherished opinion" stand?

His Environment

Ishibashi was born in 1884 in Tokyo, the son of a Nichiren priest. In the following year he moved to his father's new place of duty

[2] Ishibashi Tanzan, *Ishibashi Tanzan zenshū* (hereafter cited as *zenshū*; Tokyo, 1971), vol. 1, pp. 399-415; vol. 2, pp. 328-31.

in Yamanashi prefecture, where he stayed until his graduation from middle school at the age of eighteen. For the first five years, Ishibashi lived only with his mother, separated from his father, in observance of the Nichiren sect practice that a priest's family not reside at his temple. At age six Ishibashi joined his father in the temple. Having a peculiar philosophy of child rearing, his father entrusted Ishibashi four years later to the care and nurture of a colleague at a distant temple. Thereafter Ishibashi rarely saw his parents, spending most of his boyhood as a Nichiren neophyte. During these impressionable and arduous years, he was nurtured by Nichiren teachings, in which evangelism and spiritual defiance of oppression were stressed. Already in his middle school days, Ishibashi aspired to "some religious or educational vocation."[3]

Ishibashi was, however, not a simplistically credulous Nichiren devotee. In middle school he was twice held back, which ironically allowed him to spend his final two years under the principalship of Ōshima Masatake, a first class student of William S. Clark of Sapporo Agricultural College. In his memoirs Ishibashi wrote that he became "a second generation disciple of Dr. Clark" through Principal Ōshima. Clark's democratic educational philosophy and pioneering spirit became for Ishibashi "the precepts of a teacher of society" which "affected his entire life." His abiding interest in Christianity moved him to read the Bible in English during his college days, and to quote scriptural passages in his later writings.[4]

Desiring to do "something that would directly benefit society," Ishibashi decided after middle school to combine medical and religious careers. Toward that purpose, he tried but failed in two attempts at the entrance examination for the First Higher School. Eventually, in 1903, he entered Waseda University to study philosophy. In 1907 he graduated as the top student in the literature department, and was awarded a one-year scholarship to study religion in the postgraduate program of the university. During his university years Ishibashi was profoundly influenced by Tanaka Ōdō, a professor of philosophy who had studied under John Dewey at the University of Chicago. Ishibashi reminisced that Professor Tanaka "first opened my eyes to appreciate life." "If my thought has any distinguished characteristics," he wrote in his later years, "I owe it principally to Professor Tanaka's teaching." That Tanaka's pragmatism left an indelible impression in his student's mind is shown by the individ-

[3] Ibid., vol. 15, p. 16; vol. 1, pp. 621-36.
[4] Ibid., vol. 15, p. 14; vol. 10, p. 520.

ualism, liberalism, and empiricism that distinctly characterize Ishibashi's thought.[5]

In 1908, Ishibashi joined a newspaper company with the recommendation of Shimamura Hōgetsu, a leader of the Meiji naturalist literature movement and a lecturer in aesthetics at Waseda University. After only eight months as a newspaper reporter, however, Ishibashi entered the army to fulfill military service requirements, which had been deferred so he could attend the university. Ishibashi observed that barracks life was "an epitome of society" and "an educational institution." Army life turned out not to be as brutal as he had expected. He was favorably impressed by discipline and cleanliness. In light of his belief in the organic relationship between individual and society, Ishibashi particularly appreciated the *dokudansenkō* (field initiative) principle of the Army Rules of Field Duties. He concluded that the principle simply expounded that effective group life depended upon the maximum contribution of each individual member. He thought that this was an unusually explicit recognition that "individualism is basic to true group life." Military rules, as Ishibashi interpreted them, did not deprive individuals of their freedom. On the contrary, the rules depended upon individual freedom. Ishibashi's boyhood coincided with the first Sino-Japanese War, which had considerably increased the appeal among youth of a career as a professional soldier. But he himself had never wanted to become one. Frightening combat practices strengthened his anti-war sentiment. The idea, "Never think of war lightly. Whenever you do, imagine yourself or members of your immediate family dashing through flying bullets," became an effective part of his anti-war argument.[6]

Dismissed from the Army, Ishibashi joined, in January 1911, the staff of *Tōyō keizai shinpō*, which provided him with a central stage for an editorial career lasting thirty-five years, ending in his retirement as president in 1946. Initially, however, Ishibashi was not employed as a writer for the economic journal. His first assignment was to edit their social and intellectual criticism monthly, *Tōyō jiron* (The Oriental forum). The young writer submitted a treatise, "On Fukuzawa Yukichi," to the entrance interview of the publishing firm. Unfortunately, its contents are no longer known, but it is clear from his several articles on Fukuzawa that Ishibashi held him in high

---

[5] Ibid., vol. 15, pp. 46-49; Hanzawa Hiroshi, "Tanaka Ōdō," in Asahi Jaanaru, ed., *Nihon no shisōka* (Tokyo, 1975), vol. 2, pp. 263-74.

[6] *Zenshū*, vol. 1, p. 535; vol. 15, pp. 69-85.

esteem. He listed Fukuzawa as foremost of the four men whom he believed had most distinguished themselves in the annals of Japanese thought since the Meiji Restoration. The other three were Itagaki Taisuke, Tsubouchi Shōyō, and Shimamura Hōgetsu.[7] While finding in Fukuzawa's thought "many shortcomings" and "considerable bias," Ishibashi valued him highly for always thinking and acting on the basis of his self-interest. By applying this personal principle of thought and behavior to the affairs of the Japanese nation, Fukuzawa reinterpreted Western civilization in accordance with the specific needs of Japan. Ishibashi believed that Fukuzawa's greatest contribution to modern Japan was to encourage the spirit of "independence and self-respect." The young critic took Fukuzawa as his lifelong model, following his admonition that critics advocate only those ideas which they themselves are confident they can practice.[8] *Tōyō jiron* did not sell well, and was discontinued in October 1912. When the *Tōyō jiron* staff were amalgamated into *Tōyō keizai shinpō*, Ishibashi started a new career as an economics writer.

As has been extensively discussed by Matsuo Takayoshi and others,[9] *Tōyō Keizai shinpō* was founded in 1895 by the economic liberal Machida Chūji, who took the London *Economist* as a model. After the Russo-Japanese War, under the editorship of Uematsu Hisaaki and Miura Tetsutarō, the journal came to stand at the forefront of rapidly changing political and social trends, and began to advocate principles of political liberalism. The young editors were both graduates of Tokyo Senmon Gakkō, the predecessor of Ishibashi's alma mater. They were "anti-clan government" and "anti-bureaucratic domination." In domestic politics, the journal endorsed an alternative to genro politics, the civilian control of the military, the principle of party government, immediate adoption of universal suffrage, and the emancipation of women. In foreign policy, they resisted arms build-up as part of their opposition to imperialistic expansion.

As is shown in the editorial of the March 5, 1910 issue, "Great is China's Future," *Tōyō keizai shinpō* paid serious attention to developments in China. Pointing to various advantages that China enjoyed, such as the superior quality of its people, huge territory, and abundance of natural resources, the journal claimed that once its political

---

[7] Ibid., vol. 2, pp. 499-501.
[8] Ibid., vol. 2, pp. 492-94; vol. 13, p. 513.
[9] For example, Matsuo Takayoshi, *Taishō demokurashii* (Tokyo, 1974), pp. 65-92; Ogura Masatarō, comp., *Tōyō Keizai Shinpō genron rokujūnen* (Tokyo, 1955), pp. 3-46; Ōhara Manpei, *Jiyūshugisha: Ishibashi Tanzan* (Tokyo, 1975), pp. 4-5.

consciousness was fully awakened, China would become "the most powerful nation in history." The editors were optimistic about China's capability for self-reform. *Tōyō keizai shinpō* defined the 1911 Revolution from the outset as a movement with a broad popular basis. Like the Meiji Restoration, it emerged from contact between Eastern and Western civilizations. From historical, political, economic, and military points of view, the journal repeatedly maintained, intervention in the revolution by Japan, or any other foreign power, would only be harmful and useless. Among *Tōyō keizai shinpō* staff writers was Katayama Sen, who was under constant police surveillance as a dangerous person. The journal's anti-government stance sometimes stirred official interference. *Tōyō jiron* was suspended twice, including its very first issue. Ishibashi was particularly close to Miura, who guided him with constant personal encouragement. In November 1912, at the age of twenty-eight, Ishibashi married a school teacher, the Miuras having acted as the go-between.[10]

Having settled in ideal home and career environments, Ishibsahi embarked on teaching himself economics. He begrudged wasting even the time spent on commuting streetcars, which he used to read classical works on economics by such authors as Seligman, Toynbee, Mill, Smith, and Marshall. At the same time he continued wide-ranging studies in political and social thought. He perused one major work after another on liberalism, war, labor problems, and women's emancipation. His favorite writers included Rousseau, Hobhouse, Bebel, Angell, Bergson, and Santayana. His enthusiasm for study, self-confidence in work, and ambition for the future were all vividly evidenced in his diary. On April 10, 1914, five years after disclaiming any interest in a political career, Ishibashi recorded that he had made up his mind to establish a new philosophy in preparation for entering political life.[11]

His Thought

"Liberal" is the adjective most commonly and aptly used today to describe Ishibashi Tanzan. He himself claimed that he was "a liberal thinker" who rejected all "isms" and thought freely in the light of actual life.[12] In the preface to his collected works, Ishibashi reflected, "During the last years of Meiji, I was absorbed

---

[10] Ishibashi Umeko, "Omoide no ki," in Chō Yukio, comp., *Ishibashi Tanzan: Hito to shisō* (Tokyo, 1974), pp. 224-38. Mrs. Ishibashi had once been Mrs. Miura's pupil.
[11] *Zenshū*, vol. 15, p. 349.   [12] Ibid., vol. 13, pp. 577-83.

in denouncing conventionalism and proclaiming the arrival of a new era. My writing of the late Meiji and early Taishō periods also dwelt upon these themes."[13] What did he mean by "conventionalism" and "the arrival of a new era?" How did he identify them? Ishibashi's anti-formalistic thought process during those years may be summed up by his own phrase, "a thoroughgoing introspection."[14]

Ishibashi defined life as the process in which each individual perfects oneself. The self is a constellation of ever-changing desires. Satisfaction of one's constantly evolving desires is the motive force for all human thought and action. That satisfaction is the first and the last goal of life. All the ideas and institutions of ethics, religion, philosophy, economy, and government are contrived by man as measures to facilitate satisfaction of individuals' desires. Morality, society, and the state are created in order to realize each person's desires to their fullest. An individual cannot lead a perfect life in isolation; collective living is primary to all men. Moral standards, social forms, and state institutions emerged as a result of the need to order collective living. Human desires being ever-changing, however, ideas and institutions that once served the fulfillment of individuals' desires become obsolete over time. They must be continuously reformed if they are adequately to satisfy new desires. Individuals together create a state, and so unite themselves for common purposes into a nation. They do so in order to live as individuals, not to exist as a super-entity called "nation." Therefore, should the state interfere with the satisfaction of individuals' changing desires, the state must either be reformed, or suffer destruction. The same goes for morality. Moral standards exist to satisfy individuals' desires; individuals do not live in order that a certain moral standard be sustained.

Thus, by "introspection" Ishibashi meant a constant, practical effort to perceive individuals' changing wants, reexamine existing ideas and institutions relating to those wants, and undertake the reforms necessary to satisfy the new desires. Since his introspection was aimed at the improvement of actual life, he could not assume the attitude of an onlooker or escapist. Since he was concerned with the practical effects of reforms, he could not abide by empty formalism, false abstraction, or propagandism. Ishibashi's introspection originated in self-interest. He stressed that each thought and behavior should stem from concern for oneself. However, this self-interest should not be narrow-minded, anti-social, or blind. Precisely because he advocated the

<hr>

[13] Ibid., vol. 1, pp. 5-6.   [14] Ibid., p. 68.

complete satisfaction of self-interest, ending only with maximum and lasting results, one's goals must be consonant with others' interests. Ishibashi's individualism did not allow one to confine oneself in a small, subjective world in disregard of social surroundings. Based on the notion that individual and society are organically and indivisibly related to one another, Ishibashi's individualism emphasized the need for continuous, practical social reforms. His individualism was rooted in full, progressive social concerns. In summary, Ishibashi openly postulated that self-centered pursuit of happiness was the ultimate goal of life. All ideas and institutions were mere means for achieving that ultimate but moving goal. There could be neither an absolute morality nor a sacred state. Because the requirements for individuals' happiness changed with time and circumstances, means to satisfy them must be constantly revised.[15]

From this basic proposition, Ishibashi went on to reflect upon the significance of the Meiji era and the stages of Japanese modernization. To him the fifty years since the Meiji Restoration were an unfinished process of revolution that had bequeathed both positive and negative legacies to subsequent generations. He believed that Japan's imperialistic development was not the real accomplishment of the Meiji era. Its militaristic, overseas expansion was the result of a temporary policy that Japan was compelled to follow in order to maintain its national independence against Western encroachment. The acquisition of Taiwan, Sakhalin, Korea, and rights and interests in China proper had strengthened the Japanese state, allowing it to be ranked among the major imperialist powers. However, the Japanese people were groaning under ever-increasing military and defense demands.[16] Certainly, Ishibashi maintained, the fruits of this state-centered "enrich-the-country-strengthen-its-military" policy could not be considered the true accomplishments of the Meiji era. Ishibashi obstinately asserted that the glory of the Meiji period should be found in the development of political freedoms based upon "the great democratic doctrine" that the emperor had repeatedly announced in the Charter Oath and such other edicts as had been prepared for the imperial constitution and the establishment of the national diet.[17] Pressing needs for centralization and national defense during the Meiji era caused the rise of bureaucratic despotism and narrow-minded nationalism. As a consequence, the ideal of government by

[15] Ibid., pp. 3-15, 40-48, 58-63, 125-30.
[16] Ibid., pp. 231-32.   [17] Ibid., pp. 231, 482-84.

the will of the people failed to reach full realization. However, the Meiji era was, after all, a transitional period. Demands of the times changed constantly. The great task of the Taishō era, therefore, was to reform the political system and overcome the social consequences which had met the needs of a previous era, but which now had become obsolete and negative legacies. If this were done, Japan would fully realize the positive legacy of the Meiji period: democratic government. It was also Ishibashi's belief that such domestic reforms would be in line with changing world trends in which "overseas expansionism had been rapidly replaced by internal improvement."[18]

In domestic politics, Ishibashi considered the lingering rule of the oligarchs to be the greatest negative legacy of the Meiji era. Whatever the form of government, he argued, "the ultimate controlling power" must reside with the people. Representative government was the best means to exercise "the people's sovereignty."[19] In the turmoil of the Taishō political climate, Ishibashi observed clear evidence of the inability of an obsolete political leadership to meet the people's demands for freedom.[20] He was pleased to see a continuous decline of oligarchic power and the ascendancy of political parties. But the slogan, "Protect constitutional government, smash clan rule," did not satisfy him. Ishibashi did not want political change for its own sake, but thoroughgoing change and the establishment of a "good government," that could respond concretely to the people's aspirations.[21]

In fact, Ishibashi expected little of the existing political parties, with their record of deals and compromises with the ruling clique. He likened early Taishō politics to a familiar theatrical program performed by the same old actors on a slightly different stage. He viewed the second Ōkuma cabinet with the same skepticism; despite some high-sounding proclamations, the latter had not adopted progressive policies in either internal or external affairs. Feeling thus, Ishibashi pushed aside the personal respect he felt for the founder of his alma mater and spared no words in criticizing the Ōkuma government.[22] Citing examples from English political history, he warned that party government could degenerate into tyranny. This danger was particularly acute in Japan, where the severely restricted electoral system allowed only one man out of every 33.5 to vote. Worse yet, that small voting population did not fairly represent the various social

[18] Ibid., pp. 241-43.
[20] Ibid., pp. 309-27.
[22] Ibid., vol. 2, pp. 318-19.

[19] Ibid., pp. 348-53.
[21] Ibid., pp. 305-309.

strata among the people. The electoral system overwhelmingly favored the interests of landlords. So long as this situation continued, Ishibashi argued, no sound development of parliamentary politics could be expected. He therefore strongly advocated the early adoption of universal suffrage, as the only means to establish a third alternative party and eventually a government always responsive to the demands of the people.[23]

In external relations, Ishibashi believed that the most burden-some legacy from the Meiji era was the relentless policy of militaris-tic, overseas expansionism. Stressing that one's real inward feeling must dictate thought and action, Ishibashi openly despised his fellow countrymen's "selfless loyalty" and spirit of "national unity." To him, such national traits revealed how unthinking the Japanese people were; they should be regarded as national defects, not merits. Observing the nationwide lamentation over the death of Emperor Meiji, which was generally described as a spontaneous and sincere expression of loyalty and patriotism, Ishibashi wrote that the people were "tinged with derangement and pandemonium," and asked rhetorically, how could a person "without mind and self" be truly loyal and patriotic?[24] Rather, he lamented that such blind acts would only encourage formalism. He publicly derided many Japanese leaders in and out of government, who, instead of rededicating themselves to the fulfillment of the real national tasks bequeathed by the emperor, busied themselves with plans for a "wooden and stone" shrine to his memory. To express their sorrow over the emperor's death, leaders of Buddhist sects petitioned the government to proclaim a prohibition against "slaughtering animals for several days," while some theater-owners voluntarily suspended their business activities for a few days. Ishibashi termed these deeds of loyalty "superstitious," "ignorant and stupid" acts, and urged people to reflect upon the plight of the poor workers who were losing vital wages because of the "vain acts" of "capitalist enterpreneurs."[25]

Ishibashi also regretted that the so-called "national unity" trait of the Japanese people suppressed the spirit of free discussion, allowing an unthinking majority to silence minorities as heretics or traitors, and thereby depriving the nation of precious opportunities to understand issues better and create a true sense of responsibility. For this reason Ishibashi deplored the fact that no significant anti-war move-

[23] Ibid., vol. I, pp. 345-48.   [24] Ibid., pp. 111-13.
[25] Ibid., pp. 232-36.

ment had arisen at the time of the Sino-Japanese and the Russo-Japanese Wars. Had the wars not been pushed forward by the excitement of "national unity" but rather accompanied by persistent public discussion on the pros and cons of fighting, the Japanese nation would have had a better grasp of the significance and the objectives of the wars.[26] Bemoaning the Japanese people's "national unity" so strongly that he once described it "as horses neighing in unison,"[27] he frankly castigated it as a national weakness. Ishibashi naturally saw the worst manifestation of this trait in Japanese attitudes toward the outside world. Despite the arrival of a new era, people were still gripped by the conventional "narrow-minded nationalism" that had served Japan in the past. Unaware of changing trends, they were still clinging to the creed of "big-Japanism." No political party in Japan was advocating "little Japanism" or "anti-imperialism." With blind devotion, people were upholding the militaristic expansionist policy that Japan had had to follow during the recent transition period as if it had to be their country's eternal course of action. The domestic impact of this by now obsolete creed was encouragement of the rise of "military-politicians," and sanctions for heavy tax burdens.[28]

In an attempt to emancipate the Japanese public from the grip of this conventional attitude, Ishibashi asked a fundamental question: Is there a real need for Japan to expand overseas? Does it really benefit Japan? Ishibashi refuted as groundless all the usual explanations for Japanese overseas expansion, such as shortage of natural resources, overpopulation, and national security.[29] In the midst of nationwide excitement over American discrimination against Japanese immigrants, Ishibashi wrote that Japan did not need emigration to solve the so-called problems of overpopulation and food shortages. He urged that emigration that caused international tension be stopped.[30] Striving to turn people's attention to internal solutions, Ishibashi countered conventional arguments for expansion with proposals for domestic improvement based on industrialization and trade. For example, by extensive use of statistics, he demonstrated the possibility of exploiting and industrializing the underdeveloped islands, Hokkaidō and Sakhalin. To realize the full potential of these islands for residence and economy, Ishibashi demanded that the government should cut the wasteful funding of overseas colonization and emigra-

[26] Ibid., p. 113.
[28] Ibid., pp. 243-44.
[30] Ibid., vol. 1, pp. 354-57.

[27] Ibid., pp. 500-502.
[29] Ibid., vol. 2, pp. 192-218.

tion and invest those monies in the rapid development of the northern territories.[31]

Contrary to militaristic, overseas expansionist arguments, Ishibashi maintained that the best policy to assure Japan's national survival and prosperity was to make full use of the domestic resources the country enjoyed, and grow as a full-fledged industrial nation able to supplement what it lacked by overseas trade. To this aim, Japan, lacking natural material resources, must rely upon its abundant human resources, and should implement extensive beneficial legislation in such fields as education, labor, and health. Thus, Ishibashi's internal improvement proposals inevitably demanded reductions in defense, military, and overseas development expenditures.[32] At the same time, the self-interest of a trading nation such as Japan required that it maintain and promote peaceful international relations. Ishibashi was therefore totally against Japan's territorial aggrandizement, which he regarded as the greatest single cause of increased military expenses and international tension. Applying these basic principles to Japan's relations with China, Ishibashi urged the government seriously to contemplate an early abandonment of Japanese vested rights and interests in Manchuria.[33]

By World War I, the idea that "war profits no one" had become Ishibashi's firm conviction.[34] Upon the outbreak of the war in Europe, therefore, he embarked on a vigorous campaign to prevent Japanese participation. The sole responsibility that Japan should carry out in connection with the European war, he asserted, was by every diplomatic means to prevent the fighting from expanding into the Far East. Should Japan unfortunately fail in that effort, it should cooperate with England in accordance with the Anglo-Japanese Alliance in a joint effort to limit the war zone in East Asia to the very minimum and the fighting in the region to the shortest possible duration. Japan should not go one step beyond this. Attacking the small German forces at Kiaochow Bay, for instance, would be an action beyond Japanese duty. Above all else, Japan should not take advantage of this war to acquire new rights and interests in China. Ishibashi denounced those who welcomed the coming of the war as a godsend for Japanese advancement and who demanded immediate Japanese participation. He claimed that they were traitors who endangered the Japanese state

[31] Ibid., vol. 2, pp. 137-49.   [32] Ibid., pp. 174-85.
[33] Ibid., vol. 1, pp. 244-45.   [34] Ibid., pp. 361-63, 382-95.

and jeopardized the peace and welfare of the people.[35] Even after Japan joined the war, Ishibashi kept up his tenacious criticism of the government's warlike actions. At the same time he published articles calling his readers' attention to the tragedies that the war had brought upon common people while a few schemers had amassed great fortunes. He branded the Japanese dispatch of troops to Shantung as a blunder. From the outset Ishibashi warned against Japanese acquisition of Tsingtao. He believed that this action would invite the enmity of the Chinese people and suspicion from the great powers, and further threaten the foundations of peace in the Far East. Furthermore, holding Tsingtao would not benefit Japan from either an economic or a national security point of view.[36] It was at this juncture that Ishibashi heard the rumor that the Japanese government had thrust the infamous Twenty-One Demands upon the Chinese government.

Conclusion

What made it possible for Ishibashi to overcome the pervasive logic of imperialistic rivalry over China, which in 1915 was accepted even by Yoshino? Ishibashi's fundamental refutation of the Twenty-One Demands was not the result of a profound knowledge of China in particular. Rather, his independent mind thought through the issues from first principles. This manner of thinking led him to conclude that the task before the Japan of his day was to fulfill the true objectives of the unfiinished Meiji revolution. Urging the Japanese people to concentrate on internal reforms and improvements as the solution to national problems and for the betterment of their actual lives, Ishibashi argued against the imperialism that seemed to block his domestic proposals.

It is often stated that chauvinism, fostered by an unreflective pride in an imperial Japan, was at least partially responsible for Japanese aggression toward China. Ishibashi's style of methodical introspection, however, made him poignantly aware of his country's own shortcomings and unfinished tasks, and thus protected him from sharing in the growing arrogance of Japan toward its neighbor. His introspection rendered him sensitive and sympathetic to the Chinese national awakening, and this attitude underlay his later writings on China. Ishibashi's approach was often distinguished from that of others by

[35] Ibid., pp. 358-61.   [36] Ibid., pp. 375-81.

his keen sensitivity to growing Chinese nationalism, on one hand, and his outspoken criticism of Japanese aggression, on the other. His life and thought before 1945 suggest the ways in which those who did not share the official framework of policy toward China might have defined their positions.

CHAPTER XI

UGAKI KAZUSHIGE'S VIEW OF CHINA AND HIS CHINA POLICY, 1915-1930

───

MASARU IKEI
Translated by Ronald P. Toby

UGAKI KAZUSHIGE was an army leader and an important political figure in prewar Japan. Moving with equal ease both backstage and before the footlights of politics in the Taishō and Shōwa periods, he earned the epithet "the mystery man of politics" (*seiji no wakusei*). His activities extended over the broadest range of political and military affairs.

He first attracted national attention as the architect of the military force reductions policy of 1922, during his first term as army minister. In 1925 he organized a Sino-Japanese conspiracy, behind Foreign Minister Shidehara Kijūrō's back, to take advantage of the civil war in China. In 1931 a group of right-wing army officers attempted to stage a coup to place Ugaki in power as prime minister, but the coup failed, partly for lack of cooperation on Ugaki's part. In 1937 he again refused to serve as prime minister, but this time the request was a more formal one, coming through Saionji from the emperor himself.

Despite such compelling evidence of the need to understand Ugaki's prewar career, and despite the existence, in the form of his published diaries for the years 1904-49, of excellent materials through which to examine him, surprisingly little research has yet been done on him.[1] This study is part of an attempt to correct this deficiency.

[1] There are only three book-length studies of Ugaki. Two hardly worth reading are Nukada Hiroshi, *Hiroku Ugaki Kazushige* (Tokyo, 1973), and Watanabe Shigeo, *Ugaki Kazushige no ayunda michi* (Tokyo, 1948). Inoue Kiyoshi has done a good, if biased, study, *Ugaki Kazushige* (Tokyo, 1975). Ugaki's diaries have been published twice. Ugaki edited a flattering one-volume version, *Ugaki nikki* (Tokyo, 1954). After his death his family released the complete, less flattering diary, *Ugaki Issei nikki* (hereafter cited as *Diary*; Tokyo, 1971).

© 1980 by Princeton University Press
The Chinese and the Japanese: Essays in Political and Cultural Interactions
0-691-03126-6/80/199-21$01.05/1 (cloth)
0-691-10086-1/80/199-21$01.05/1 (paperback)
For copying information, see copyright page

Some justification must be given for the chronological boundaries of this work. First, speaking in terms of the flow of diplomacy and politics of the time, the period follows immediately on the settlement of the Twenty-One Demands, and goes to the eve of the Manchurian incident, including within its several major developments in Sino-Japanese relations: the Paris Peace Conference, the Washington Conference, and the assassination of Chang Tso-lin, while throughout the period China was wracked by civil war. Furthermore, Japan's relationship to the East Asian subcontinent was the dominant foreign policy question in Japanese politics at the time. Second, Ugaki's personal career was such that these fifteen years formed a coherent period in his life. From 1915 to 1930 he rarely left his homeland. Occupying a series of posts in the Army Ministry and General Staff, he tended to view the China question relatively dispassionately from the standpoint of military and diplomatic interests. After 1931, however, he retired from active duty and was appointed governor-general of Korea, leaving the center stage of politics. His diary shows that his sense of personal ambition began to have a stronger role in his choices from about this time. And with the rising political power of the Army, he tended to become more committed to its interests in domestic political competition. As a result of this, Ugaki ceased to write extensively of China in his diary, making comparable analysis for the later period more difficult.

The Premises of Ugaki's China View

It is important to note that Ugaki's social and geographical background gave him little in common with the Satsuma-Chōshū group dominant in political and military circles. He was born of peasant parents, and came from Okayama, a fief not active in the wars of the Meiji Restoration. In educational background he was also different, attending the English school in Okayama while working as an elementary school teacher, and later studying in Germany;[2] he did not receive the traditional samurai education in the Chinese classics and language, and in Confucianism, so that he did not feel the same cultural affinity for China that many of his military and political peers did.

These factors, particularly his rise from poor peasant origins and the need to rise against long odds, fostered a powerful personal ambition. His ambition interacted with his age: Ugaki was a second-gen-

[2] Ugaki, and Kamata Sawaichiro, *Shōrai seidan* (Tokyo, 1951), p. 27.

eration leader with no personal memory of the Restoration. His world view was influenced by the Sino-Japanese War, the Triple Intervention, and the Russo-Japanese War. Japan, too, like a poor peasant, had to be ambitious.

The Russo-Japanese War gave Japan a foothold in southern Manchuria, a foothold, it was often said, won by the blood of 100,000 Japanese soldiers, and at a cost of 2 billion yen. From this time onward, "The China question was no longer, for Japan, the question of the fate of modern Asia before the invasion of the modern West. Rather, it was transformed into a geographical and physical question of the continent and of territorial control. And rather than the essentially philosophical and cultural question it had been, as Japan moved from late Meiji into Taishō, the China question was transformed into a political issue dominated by power relationships."[3]

Ugaki spent four years studying in Germany, 1902-1904 and 1906-1908, being recalled in 1904 for service in the Russo-Japanese War. In Germany he spent much time in the study of European diplomatic and political conditions. It was in this period that he developed his pure power-politics view of state survival and international relations. "Power is the only determinant in politics. A state which fails to take advantage of a good opportunity with all the power it can muster commits a crime against itself."[4] He made several stops in China en route to Germany and back, witnessing European dominance at first hand. Rather than feeling sympathy for China's plight, he felt that Japan, too, must join in and not lose out in the competition for a piece of the action. "As a first step," he urged, "Japan's policy-makers must make the people aware of the truth that the Yangtze valley is a limitless treasure trove."[5]

If his two trips along the China coast in 1902 and 1906 gave him the impression that China was weak but ripe for plucking, his trip in the spring of 1918 reinforced that feeling. He was dispatched to conclude the Sino-Japanese military cooperation agreement with the Tuan Ch'i-jui regime for mutual defense against Russia, and this time went inland to Peking, where broader observation was possible.

But through all this Ugaki's views were decidedly army-oriented, seeing "army first, navy second," as the main principle. First, a strong naval policy, he thought, had worldwide implications not only vis-à-vis

[3] Nomura Koichi, "Tairiku mondai no imeeji to jittai," in Hashikawa Bunso and Matsumoto Sannosuke, eds., *Kindai Nihon seiji shisōshi* (Tokyo, 1970), vol. 2, p. 53.
[4] *Diary*, vol. 1, p. 111 (1915).   [5] Ibid., p. 44 (1906).

China and Russia, but even with regard to Britain, America, France, and Germany, while Japan could pursue a large-army policy threatening only China and Russia.[6] His second overt reason for stressing army over navy was what today would be called a cost-effectiveness analysis: "A ship costs 30 millions, and only lasts for ten years. That's awfully expensive national defense."[7] It would make more sense, he argued, to invest in industry.

Finally, Ugaki believed that ideally states should be self-sufficient in essentials. Japan, however, was poor in natural resources and could not hope to achieve this goal if limited to the homeland. Thus, he urged, Japan must expand overseas, both economically and territorially, and that expansion ought naturally to be in the direction offering least resistance, that is, into Korea, China, and Manchuria.[8]

Ugaki's View of China

Let us start by looking at Ugaki's view of the Chinese people, at their "national characteristics." As he saw them, the Chinese were too avaricious as individuals to care for the fate of the state, much less the future of their race;[9] he found them particularly arrogant and self-centered.[10] Every concession to their conceit merely increased their deprecation of Japan, so that Japan would not only have to reform them, but at the same time to impress them with its authority.[11] One way in which Ugaki thought Japan might improve its situation vis-à-vis China was to place China in Japan's debt by serving as mediator between China and the powers.[12] Finally, he found the Chinese weak in the face of strength, so that even if the Chinese resisted change it would only be a transitory resistance, not worth worrying about.[13]

If Ugaki saw the national character of the Chinese in this way, then how did he view their leaders? Their leaders, too, were calculating, moving only after assessing the profit to be had. The new forces in China, of no matter what domestic faction, could not move without taking Japan into account, and their leaders were, in Ugaki's view, aware of this truth.[14] "[The leaders of China] do nothing all day but seek to preserve their position or increase their wealth and luxury. Their armies therefore are purely their personal property, which they use for nothing but the advancement of [their own] desires. Today

[6] Ibid., pp. 108f. (1915).
[7] Ibid., p. 109 (1915).
[8] Ibid., p. 112 (1915).
[9] Ibid., p. 106 (1915).
[10] Ibid., p. 168 (1918).
[11] Ibid., p. 468 (June 13, 1925).
[12] Ibid., p. 469 (1925).
[13] Ibid., p. 178 (1918).
[14] Ibid., p. 315 (August 1920).

in all of China it is fair to say that there is not a single army prepared to oppose foreign enemies or to defend the state."[15]

But if China could not move without accounting to Japan, then what was China to Japan? Ugaki considered four aspects: political, territorial, economic, and cultural. Politically, Ugaki saw China as incapable of independence for the foreseeable future, because its people and leaders lacked the essential talent to resist the strength of the powers. Therefore Japan had to protect China from the powers and, by supporting selected Chinese leaders and causing them to respect Japan's will, to use their power on that basis.[16]

Ugaki's territorial views on China were tied to his expectations for the Japanese population. He foresaw continued population growth, which would require lands for colonization and emigration. For this purpose Japan would certainly need territorial control of no more than south Manchuria and eastern Inner Mongolia. Not only did Japan need this territory as a place where its average annual population increase of 500,000 to 600,000 could be accommodated, but indeed it was China's moral duty to turn over this undeveloped territory to the growing Japanese people! South Manchuria and eastern Inner Mongolia alone are "more than twice the size of Japan and the colonies [Taiwan and Korea] together, and yet have no more than 10 million residents. So if we should put them at not even the same population density as the Empire, but only half that, they have room to hold another 20 millions. If we transfer 500,000 people annually to these lands, we can dispose of our population growth for the next forty years." And at the same density as Japan itself, it would easily take one hundred years. "Thus it is unreasonable for the Empire to seek any territory beyond this for quite far into the future, even the unknowable future a hundred years hence!"[17]

Japan's economic interest in China was, from Ugaki's viewpoint, determined by its lack of natural resources: Japan needed China's raw materials and also needed China as a market for its exportable products. "Whether it be for industrial raw materials or for sales routes for finished products, there is no way for the Empire's industries to survive without access to China."[18] However, there was but marginal advantage to China in dealing with Japan—raw materials a little easier to sell, and finished goods a bit cheaper to buy—and China felt no compelling need to develop closer relations with Japan.

[15] Ibid., p. 160 (1918).
[17] Ibid., pp. 111f. (1915).
[16] Ibid., p. 168 (1918).
[18] Ibid., p. 228 (1919).

"Whether selling raw materials to Japan is more convenient than processing them at home, or whether it is more advantageous for them to import Japanese products than to use those produced elsewhere, or in China itself; whether in some cases it is better to let China produce the goods, while providing them with Japanese technology and machinery, but most particularly by giving them substantial infusions of capital, which they insist they lack for the present term; in any case, it is fundamental that we impress them with the importance of their relations with Japan."[19]

Ugaki listed five points on which Japan needed to be continually aware of China's views:

1. The relative merits of exporting raw materials to Japan or elsewhere;
2. whether China should engage in domestic production [of an item];
3. the merits of domestic production compared with purchasing Japanese products;
4. whether they feel Japan has the excess capacity to contribute to Chinese production in the form of technology and equipment;
5. the reasons why China hesitates to import capital from Japan, and their view of the merits of such imports.[20]

As noted above, Ugaki's view of Chinese culture was different from that of many of his peers in the services, since he was not steeped in the Chinese classics. In 1918 he wrote, "It is the foundation of error to state that since the Chinese are of the same race as we, and write the same characters, it is easier for us to be on good terms with them. Indeed, although they are without doubt of the same race and write the same characters, still in those critical areas of life—eating, sleeping, and residence—which occupy most of their day, they are more like Westerners than like us."[21] But the following year he did admit that the cultural and racial affinities of Japan and China rendered good relations possible.[22]

"It appears inevitable," wrote Ugaki, "that [the Chinese] national character is one which takes no account of gratitude, racial or cultural

[19] Ibid.   [20] Ibid.
[21] Ibid., p. 165 (1918).
[22] Ibid., p. 228 (1919). We should note here that Ugaki, as a political and military figure, was not concerned with producing a consistent view of China over the years, and apparent inconsistencies such as this are not infrequent in his diary from one year to the next.

affinity, or other such sentimental values in the face of a question of profit and loss. Giving full consideration to this, from the Japanese point of view, if we want to join with China in preserving the peace of the Far East, unless we establish a hierarchical relationship between Japan and China [with Japan above, of course], there is no way we can expect satisfactory results."[23]

Ugaki's Position on China Policy

Ugaki saw Japanese national power and foreign policy in the following way. He regarded military power as being of the utmost importance, but he meant was military power viewed in a broad sense, including both armaments and popular support. Japan, he felt, was well situated in both these categories. Secondly, Ugaki saw that Japan's economic power was severely limited by its territorial size and lack of resources. The territorial problem was to be solved by moving into weaker areas such as Korea, Manchuria, Mongolia, and China. He saw three potential forces of resistance to this expansion, Russia, the United States, and China. Or, as he expressed it, "Japan is surrounded by 3× [sic]: America, Russia and China all exist as unknowns."[24] That is, the response of these three exes to any given policy, to Japan's intrusion into the Asian mainland, was always the unknown variable, and Japan had always to pay careful attention to the moves of these three countries in any moves of her own.

The best way to observe the operation of Ugaki's view of China on policy positions is to examine a series of major questions from 1915 to 1930, starting with the Twenty-One Demands. Ugaki did not find the Twenty-One Demands objectionable or improper; rather, he thought them perfectly right and natural. This was because he viewed it as essential for Japan to secure by treaty the gains on political and economic fronts since the Russo-Japanese War. He was also very aware of the role of good timing in the conclusion of such treaties.[25]

Although Ugaki thought the demands themselves were proper, they were not implemented, leading him to reflect on the failure in the following way:

Casting ourselves into the whirlpool of the World War was our first error. The necessary course for the enhancement of Japan's prestige was to have maintained a lofty neutrality, keep control

---

[23] Ibid., p. 168 (1918). [24] Ibid., p. 154 (1918).
[25] Ibid., p. 102 (1915); p. 166 (1918).

of the East Asian situation and, at the appropriate time, appear as the savior of the world, bringing an end to the war. Things like whether we get Tsingtao or not are trivial. We should have had China settle such questions during the course of the war.

The presentation of the China demands should have been timed to follow immediately the fall of Tsingtao. Missing the timing was our second mistake.

Whereas we ought to have sent a prominent person to achieve a swift and grand resolution of the question, our policy failed to proceed from this premise. This was our third error.

Failure to be resolute of will before presenting the Group Five questions, which bear on the sovereignty of the other country, was our fourth error.

That, during the course of the negotiations we missed our chance in moving our troops [at the wrong time] was our fifth error.

The addle-brained action of trying to use the return of Tsingtao as a bargaining chip in the negotiations [over the Demands] when we could have used it much more valuably at a separate time to show to the world how just Japan is, was our sixth error.

That we made concession after concession, and failed to remember the word "resoluteness," so that the negotiations, which started with the goal of securing eternal peace in East Asia, ended by increasing China's scorn and resentment for Japan, and transplanted the seeds of disaster for the near future, was our seventh error.

No matter how generously I try to view our foreign policy since last summer [1914], I cannot but see it as mistakes and failures.[26]

Ugaki thus viewed the Twenty-One Demands not as an erroneously conceived goal, but as a disastrously botched job. Japan ought to have stayed out of the war; failing that, she should have used her gains to better advantage. "Having in our grasp a one-in-a-million opportunity, possessed of absolutely supreme power, the recently opened Sino-Japanese negotiations were moving toward expressing the *fait accompli* in a treaty," he wrote in 1915, "but where is there

[26] Ibid., p. 103 (1915).

a whit of diplomatic skill? Nay, they have done no more than sully the scutcheons of military prowess and trust."[27]

The Russian Revolution in October 1917 was a great shock to Ugaki, as it was to most political figures of his day around the world. But for him it had a special meaning—he saw this as the best opportunity Japan would ever have to advance into northern Manchuria and Siberia,[28] and so wholeheartedly supported the Siberian expedition.

But as he saw the Bolshevik forces take the initiative, he shifted his concern to the question of how these developments would affect Japan's relations with China.[29] Ugaki was particularly worried about a Russo-Chinese detente, and frequently discussed with his colleagues at the General Staff proposals for a Japanese policy response. They ultimately proposed that Japan conclude a military alliance with Tuan Ch'i-jui against the Communist menace, and Ugaki was dispatched to Peking as a member of the negotiating team sent by the government of Prime Minister Terauchi Masatake.

Ugaki left for Peking in March 1918 to conclude the Sino-Japanese anti-Communism pact, and remained in China for two months. The pact was a complete success for Ugaki. The main points of agreement were: (1) stationing of Japanese troops in Manchuria and Mongolia as a buffer against Communism; (2) exchange of military specialists (advisers) to cooperate in strategy planning; (3) mutual supply of arms and material; (4) exchange of military maps. In sum, Japan was able through this pact to control the military power of China and to expand Japanese influence there.[30]

Japan took advantage of the preoccupation of the Western powers with the Great War in Europe to strengthen its position in China with the Twenty-One Demands and the so-called Nishihara Loans to the warlord government centered on Tuan Chi'jui.[31] However,

---

[27] Ibid., p. 102 (1915).

[28] Ibid., p. 544 (October 10, 1926). On Japan's response to the Bolshevik Revolution see James W. Morley, *The Japanese Thrust into Siberia* (New York, 1957); Hosoya Chihiro, *Shiberia shuppai no shiteki kenkyū* (Tokyo, 1955), and *Roshia kakumei to Nihon* (Tokyo, 1972).

[29] *Diary*, vol. 1, p. 240 (January 1920).

[30] Text of pact in *Nihon gaikō nenpyō narabini shugō monjo* (Tokyo, 1964), vol. 1, pp. 441-44. The best work on this pact is Seki Hiroharu, *Gendai higashi Ajia kokusai kankyō no tanjō* (Tokyo, 1966), pp. 195-395.

[31] The best studies of these loans are in Suzuki Takeo, ed., *Nishihara shakken shiryō kenkyū* (Tokyo, 1974). Also see Kitamura Hironao, *Yume no shichijūyonen—Nishihara Kamezō jiden* (Tokyo, 1965), and Shōda Tatsuo, *Chūgoku shakkan to Shōda Kazue* (Tokyo, 1974).

Ugaki noted major changes in the situation in China after World War I which had serious implications for Japan's position. First, while the Soviet Union had withdrawn temporarily in the domestic confusion after the revolution, he was wary of the time when the Bolsheviks would consolidate their power. Second,

> The once-great imperium of Britain has begun to decline, and I regard it today as a country which must bend most of its power toward preservation of the status quo in order to defend her colonies. When seen in this light, Japan ought to avoid challenging Britain's colonial interests in China, Australia, or her colonies. In the current situation, with Russia and Germany in fact powerless, Britain is no longer anxious about India, and, I would argue, we approach a point where Britain's basic motivation for the formation of the Anglo-Japanese alliance will have been extinguished. Yet there remains the possibility of an Anglo-American confrontation, and in such a situation the possession or lack of friendly relations with Japan, as one of the great powers in Asia, will be of great significance to both nations from the standpoint of the balance of power, so that it is not inconceivable that Britain will consider the continuation of the Anglo-Japanese alliance, or the possibility of further approaches to Japan from this standpoint.[32]

Third, he was very much impressed with the United States. While he was frankly surprised that "the greatness of American national power has here been clearly demonstrated for future wars,"[33] he was less clear on the American national character, and called for close attention to this question. He was not sure whether the American people were a truly peaceful nation or really an aggressive nation under the guise of pacifism; the Republican victory in the 1918 Congressional elections gave him cause to believe that the latter was the case.[34] Ugaki was also uncertain whether the American people were capable of living in harmony with people culturally different from themselves. American Asia policy, in Ugaki's estimation, had the twin goals of economic development of Asia under American tutelage and the infusion of American-style democracy and values. But he saw a trend in America toward contempt for the Japanese monarchical

[32] *Diary*, vol. 1, p. 187 (December 1918).
[33] Ibid., p. 185 (1918).   [34] Ibid., p. 225 (1919).

system of government, and a tendency to see Japan as an enemy of democracy and a barrier to the democratization of Asia. Thus he urged the necessity of fostering American understanding of Japan's views, and of preparing contingency policies for situations where Japan failed to obtain such understanding.[35]

Ugaki regarded the newly created League of Nations as an Anglo-American move to preserve the international status quo. "The aim of the League itself is the maintenance of peace, in other words the maintenance of the status quo. But a bit more strongly, it is aimed at the suppression of advancement and competition. Moreover, it restricts the use of spiritual and military power, while allowing unlimited activity to the power of capital in the international arena," he wrote.[36] "Britain and America seek, through the League of Nations, to shut off the military power of other states while nibbling away at them through use of their long suit, capitalism. There doesn't seem to be much difference between military conquest and capitalistic nibbling."[37]

In the wake of the war Ugaki argued that with China embroiled in domestic conflict there was no need to treat it as an independent country, nor to take account of its will or power. However, Japan must be cognizant of the fact that, with Japanese power restricted by the League, China had developed the idea that it need not fear Japan.[38] How should Japan respond to the anti-Japanese movement springing up in China? Ugaki argued that this hostile activity was the result of Anglo-American agitation, so that what was called for was to obtain recognition by these two powers of the importance of the China question for Japan.[39] Further, he suggested the manipulation of those British- or American-operated newspapers in the Far East which had anti-Japanese tendencies.[40] Japan should also utilize the Tibet and the loans issues to turn anti-Japanese sentiments into anti-British and anti-American sentiments,[41] and respond to anti-Japanese violence with force.[42]

He next turned to the new international banking consortium being established under the auspices of the United States, Britain, and France. These powers, he thought, were motivated by the following considerations:

[35] Ibid., p. 270 (1920).
[36] Ibid., p. 197 (April 1-20, 1919).
[37] Ibid., p. 195 (February-March 1919).
[38] Ibid., p. 315 (August 1920); p. 228 (1919).
[39] Ibid., p. 432 (1923).
[40] Ibid., p. 434 (1923).
[41] Ibid., p. 202 (1919).
[42] Ibid., p. 206 (1919).

1. To avoid conflict among any of the powers, and to prevent the Chinese from taking advantage of such rifts.
2. Their worries about the security of investments in China and wish to shore up China by concerted protection.
3. To prevent, by the creation of the consortium, any country, particularly Japan, from gaining uncontested economic superiority in China.[43]

Thus if Japan could succeed in excluding Manchuria from the area of consortium action and maintain its special rights in Shantung, the first two goals would collapse and the third be unattainable. If Japan was firm in its position, he thought, the other three powers would have to abandon the consortium plan. What Japan needed was to make sure that China opened her doors to Japanese capital without obstruction. Ugaki felt that France was not strongly interested in number 3 above, and ought to be manipulated into mediating between Japan, and Britain and America.[44]

The four-power consortium developed just about as Ugaki had predicted. In the negotiations Japan argued for the exclusion of Manchuria and Mongolia from the field of application, and tried to use the offer of the surrender of its wartime gains in Shantung as a counter to buy Anglo-French opening up of their spheres of influence in south China and the Yangtze valley. While Japan strove on the surface to cooperate with the other powers, "behind the scenes [Japan] followed the course of supporting to the last pro-Japanese individuals in China, investing between 5-6 million and 10 million yen a year,"[45] and continued to prosecute a policy of unilateral Japanese financial assistance. America was fiercely opposed to the exclusion of Manchuria and Mongolia from the range of consortium activities, and Secretary of State Robert Lansing seriously considered a three-power consortium excluding Japanese participation. But Britain, France, and China all expressed misgivings at the exclusion of Japan. The result was the success of Japanese attempts to delay the formation of the four-power consortium. Finally, Japan waived its reservations on eastern Inner Mongolia and agreed to a consortium that excluded only south Manchuria from its area of activities, as a special region.

The next problem to arise was that of Tuan Ch'i-jui's army. These

---

[43] On this question, see Usui Katsumi, "1919 nen no Nitchū kankei," *Shirin*, 1960, n. 3, pp. 61-80.
[44] *Diary*, vol. 1, p. 217 (August 1919).
[45] *Hara Kei nikki* (August 13, 1919).

forces had been organized at the time of China's entry into World War I in 1918. They were in fact three crack divisions armed with weapons imported from Japan, financed with Japanese money, and led by Japanese officers. They were under the management of Tuan Ch'i-jui's faction and provided it with a powerful political base; it was only natural that both the powers and the southern factions opposing Tuan would demand the end of Japanese loans for these troops and dissolution of the divisions. In fact, these divisions were the principal component of the Anfu Clique's military strength in the Anfu-Chihli War of July 1920. Ugaki, then president of the War College, wanted to use loans and assistance to these three divisions as tools to manipulate Tuan for the prosecution of Japanese policy aims in China. But with the destruction of the Anfu Clique and the fall of Tuan, and the attendant advance of Chang Tso-lin into China proper, Ugaki shifted his ground and argued for aid to Chang to establish him as Japan's man in north China.[46]

The period of the Washington treaty system marked a new stage in Ugaki's thinking on international relations. When President Warren G. Harding proposed the Washington Conference, Ugaki felt that, although the United States professed to favor general disarmament, it really wanted to reach an agreement on three main issues: the Far East question, naval disarmament, and the Pacific question. Ugaki opposed a conference on these issues because he viewed them, particularly the one dealing with the Far East, as satisfactorily settled. Hara Kei saw the significance of the conference quite differently and insisted that Japanese interests had to be represented at the talks. Hara thought that naval disarmament would help solve Japanese financial difficulties and that international cooperation on the China question would, in the long run, be beneficial to Japan.[47] To Ugaki, the conference was an Anglo-American attempt to suppress and check Japanese power, particularly in China, whose raw materials and market were of vital importance to Japan. But when he was confronted with the reality of Japan's attendance at the conference, he conceded that naval disarmament was unavoidable and did not oppose it. He insisted, however, that the army and military disarma-

---

[46] The best studies of Japan's response to the Anfu-Chihli War are Usui Katsumi, *Nihon to Chūgoku: Taishō jidai* (Tokyo, 1975); and Fujii Shozo, "1920 nen An-Choku senso o meguru Nitchū kankei no ichi kōsatsu," in *Nihon gaikōshi kenkyū: Nitchū kankei no tenkai* (Tokyo, 1961), pp. 119-33.

[47] Mitani Taichirō, *Nihon seitō seiji no keisei* (Tokyo, 1967, pp. 260-65; Masuda Takeshi, "Hara Kei no Chūgoku-kan," *Kōbe hōgaku zasshi*, vol. 18 (1969), pp. 3-4.

ment be considered a strictly domestic question unconnected with international considerations.[48] He expressed a favorable attitude toward the Four Power Treaty, since it meant an end to the almost useless Anglo-Japanese alliance and would thus satisfy the United States. In general he felt that the Nine Power Treaty served no purpose except as a definition of the China question in general terms and a statement of the equal opportunity and open door principles, since the treaty did not provide for any means of enforcement.[49] He thought the issue of naval disarmament was left unsettled because the 10/10/6 ratio among the United States, Great Britain, and Japan was established only for capital ships and, with construction of other types of ships unrestricted, each nation was free to develop whatever naval capacity it desired. He really did not think that a long-term peace would come out of these conditions.

Ugaki regarded the withdrawal of Japanese troops from Siberia as unfortunate, but felt that the Siberian intervention had given the Japanese people a significant knowledge of north Manchuria and Siberia, and had forced Russia to realize the extent of Japanese power and expansionist intentions. Japan had thus proved its ability and courage by the intervention.[50] Ugaki criticized the Japanese government for failing to spread sufficient propaganda about the goals of the expedition and win the support of the people.[51] Naturally enough, he regarded the return of Japan's Shantung interests to China as a failure of Japanese diplomacy.[52]

Ugaki's views on Japanese diplomacy in the period of the Washington treaty system must be understood in the context of Foreign Minister Shidehara's policy of giving priority to economic rather than defense issues. Shidehara believed that his country's main interest lay in Manchuria, where he thought none of the powers would enter into direct conflict with Japan. He felt that Japanese military strength need only be sufficient to provide naval security. Consequently, to him the Washington treaty system seemed adequate for general protection of Japanese interests. Though he was aware of anti-Japanese boycotts and heightening Chinese nationalism, Shidehara preferred not to interfere in China's internal struggles so as not to touch off a nationalistic reaction. If Japanese spheres of influence were threatened by the Chinese in China proper, as was pos-

[48] *Diary*, vol. 1, pp. 349-50 (June-July 1921); p. 367 (January 1922).
[49] Ibid., p. 363 (December 1921).
[50] Ibid., p. 380 (July 23-August 10, 1922).
[51] Ibid., p. 443 (August 1923).   [52] Ibid., p. 333 (January 1921).

sible in the case of the Northern Expedition, he felt that temporarily removing Japanese nationals from the area would provide sufficient protection. Regarding Manchuria, Shidehara advocated a policy of negotiation and cooperation with any power in this area in order to safeguard the Japanese position.[53] As he said at his inaugural press conference in June 1924, "The era of Machiavellian, aggressive state policy is now over, and foreign policy must be conducted in accord with the great principles of peace and justice."[54]

The Katō Kōmei cabinet was formed in June 1924 and included both Shidehara, as newly appointed foreign minister, and Ugaki, holdover army minister from the Kiyoura cabinet—two men, it goes without saying, of diametrically opposed views on international politics.[55] Ugaki had little but scorn for Shidehara's conduct of foreign policy: "A debased foreign policy of concession upon concession"; "Failure diplomacy"; "A foreign policy of nonfeasance and impotence," he called it.[56] He feared that Shidehara would eventually lead Japan to abandon its interests in China. The principle of non-interference was ineffective, Ugaki believed, because it depended upon the cooperation of all powers and because the Chinese government was not stable enough to protect Japanese interests. He also pointed out that Shidehara's willingness to cooperate with any power in Manchuria might allow Communist power to go unchecked and eventually threaten China. Ugaki's solution was to lend Japanese support to Chang Tso-lin, the only leader he considered strong enough to provide stable rule in Manchuria. Only indirect Japanese control, he held, could achieve this stability.[57] For example, he welcomed the sudden coup of Feng Yü-hsiang against Wu P'ei-fu in 1924 during the war between the latter and Chang Tso-lin in China proper. Feng's military advisors were Japanese, and they had financed his coup with one million yen in secret funds. Ugaki seems to have known about these plans of the Japanese military authorities in China, although the civilian government in Tokyo did not.[58] Ugaki, commenting on this situation, wrote, "[Shidehara and the Foreign Ministry's] self-

[53] On Shidehara diplomacy, see Akira Iriye, *After Imperialism* (Cambridge, Mass., 1965).

[54] Cited in Usui Katsumi, "Vuerusaiyu-Washinton taisei to Nihon no shihaiso," in Hashikawa and Matsumoto, p. 127.

[55] For some contrasting statements by Ugaki and Shidehara, see ibid., p. 127f.

[56] Cited in ibid., p. 128.

[57] *Diary*, vol. 1, pp. 496f. (December 26, 1925); pp. 539-43 (September 1926).

[58] Ibid., p. 495 (December 1925); Ikei Masaru, "Dai niji Hō-choku sensō to Nihon," *Hōgaku kenkyū*, vol. 37 (1962), p. 3.

congratulatory attitude, when they knew only the externals of last fall's Fengtien-Chihli War is pitiful, but it is also the height of the absurd. They haven't a clue as to why Chang won and Feng pulled off a coup d'état."[59] During the 1925 Chang Tso-lin conflict with Kuo Sung-ling along the Japanese-owned South Manchurian Railway, Kuo was told by Commander Shirakawa of the Kwantung Army that if he entered the Japanese twenty-mile protective zone around the railroads in pursuit of Chang Tso-lin's troops the Japanese army would take the "necessary precautions" to protect Japanese interests in the area. Shirakawa and Ugaki had been classmates at the army academy, and they held the same views.[60]

Ugaki was no less severe in his criticism of Shidehara's response to the Northern Expedition. Shidehara tried to stick to his nonintervention policy in attempting to settle the Nanking and Hankow incidents of March and April 1927, in which the armies of the Northern Expedition inflicted damage to life, and property of the Japanese residents there.[61] Despite the encouragement of the United States and Britain to use force, Shidehara forswore the use of Japanese troops in favor of forcing Chiang Kai-shek, commander-in-chief of the Northern Expedition, to pay indemnities and offer official apologies to the powers. At the same time Shidehara pursued the policy of encouraging Chiang to suppress Communist elements. But public opinion ridiculed this as "weak-kneed diplomacy," and the opposition Seiyūkai attacked this foreign policy in the Diet, while Ugaki criticized from within the cabinet. On April 27, Ugaki presented his views orally to Prime Minister Wakutsuki Reijirō, and Army Vice-Minister Hata reported the gist of Ugaki's remarks to the Foreign Ministry.[62] Ugaki told Wakatsuki his fundamental opinion: "If the powers sit idly by, then the movement to Communize all of China will spread, and it will be but a matter of time until it leaks over into Chihli, Manchuria, and Mongolia." He proceeded to propose three points of policy for immediate execution:

[59] *Diary*, vol. 1, p. 495 (December 7-14, 1925).

[60] Eguchi Keiichi, "Kaku Shorei jiken to Nihon teikokushugi," in *Nihon teikokushugi shiron* (Tokyo, 1975), pp. 90-124.

[61] The best article on the Nanking incident is Eto Shinkichi, "Nankin jiken to Nichi Bei," in *Higashi Ajia seijishi kenkyū* (Tokyo, 1968), pp. 149-76. On Japan's response to the Northern Expedition, the definitive work is Usui Katsumi, *Nitchū gaikōshi: hokubatsu no jidai* (Tokyo, 1971).

[62] In *Diary*, vol. 1, pp. 568ff., the editors have provided the full text of Hata's report to the Foreign Ministry. The following quotation is from this report.

1. To promote even more than heretofore closer cooperation between Japan and [the other] powers in policy toward China. At the least, [we should] conduct frank exchanges of views [with the powers] about the powers' positions and intentions vis-à-vis China, . . . and promote the formation of a structure of cooperation centered on the [Japanese] empire.

2. In concert with the other powers, to follow a policy of the containment of Communism.

   A. Utilizing the news organs of the powers and ourselves, to launch a propaganda offensive against the position of Russia toward China and against the actions of the Chinese Communist faction to bring them to their senses;

   B. To control by force the strategic points of Shantung, Kiangsu, Chekiang, Fukien and Kwangtung, forming a blockade to keep out, in particular, Russian arms and supplies; and using these as support bases, to plan for the gradual revival of trade and commerce.

3. For the suppression and extermination of the Communist faction in the southern portion of the upper Yangtze valley, to supply, with the consent and cooperation of the powers, arms and material to tractable elements in both the northern and southern cliques, and have them go into the breach against the Communists. Since this demands cooperation and compromise between the two cliques, to give significant aid to that end.[63]

Ugaki concluded that if Japan did not move at once to execute these proposals it would merely be laying the groundwork for substantial sacrifice and regret in the future. At the same time, he urged that although at the moment the anti-foreign movements in China were concentrating their energy on Britain, this could be no cause for Japanese satisfaction, for he was certain that Japan would feel the prick of that pin again sometime soon. He therefore urged assistance to Britain. Ugaki's position on military intervention and cooperation with Britain was at one with the interventionist views of Japanese on the scene in China and with the Seiyūkai position that Shidehara's policy was a national disgrace. Thus Ugaki could say of the collapse of the Wakatsuki cabinet and the withdrawal of Shidehara from the govern-

[63] Ibid., p. 570 (April 8, 1927).

ment, "It may be sad for the party and the faction, but from the point of view of the great goals of the Empire it's a blessing."[64]

But Ugaki was not to be entirely pleased with the self-proclaimed "positive" China policy of Shidehara's successor, Tanaka Giichi, who held the posts of prime minister and foreign minister in the cabinet he formed on April 20, 1927. Tanaka's active foreign policy seemed to him little more than a lot of talk without much substance. The eastern conference accomplished nothing except to advertise Tanaka's new foreign policy and to promote the ambitions of Parliamentary Vice-Foreign Minister Mori Kaku. Since Ugaki felt that using foreign policy issues for domestic political purposes was wrong, he thought that any major foreign policy shifts should be relayed quietly to each diplomat and military officer abroad, not publicized through a meaningless conference.[65] Second, he termed Tanaka's three Shantung area expeditions weak and indecisive because they did not help effect a compromise between Chang Tso-lin and Chiang Kai-shek. About the only matter on which Ugaki agreed with Tanaka was his support of Chang Tso-lin in Manchuria. When Chang was killed by the Kwantung Army, Ugaki was outraged and commented, "There could not be anyone among the Japanese so stupid as to kill Chang."[66] He felt that this incident rendered the Japanese position in Manchuria and China precarious. But as always, he was a military man first, and eventually joined those who pressured Tanaka to stop the investigation urged by the emperor to find the murderer, feeling that the military should not be publicly blamed for such an incident.

After Chang's death, Ugaki expressed his views on the future of Japan's role in the Far East in a memorandum of September 1929 to the Army. He proposed that Japan and China cooperate in eastern Siberia to stop Communist influence. He advocated bringing British and American capital into Manchuria under joint Chinese-Japanese administration, under the principles of the open door and equal opportunity.[67] Further, he proposed that should Japan succeed in its attempt to check Communist influence, it be rewarded by acquiring Kirin Poset Bay and thereby be in a position to oppose northern Communism by expanding Japanese influence. He proposed a Sino-Japanese economic alliance to provide for a productive future. However, he advised that Chinese leaders be kept from uniting Manchuria with

---

[64] Ibid., (April 19, 1927).
[65] Ibid., p. 598 (August 25, 1927); p. 605 (September 6, 1927).
[66] Ibid., p. 664 (June 7, 1928).   [67] Ibid., p. 711 (February [?], 1929).

China proper for at least ten years. In the final analysis he was dissatisfied with both Shidehara's "passive" and Tanaka's so-called "activist" China policies. He commented that Shidehara had to be forced to take even the smallest action; on the other hand, the hasty and disorganized Tanaka had to be kept from committing too many errors.[68]

After Tanaka resigned following Chang's death, Shidehara became foreign minister again in July 1929. Ugaki felt that Shidehara's China policy had changed favorably since the early 1920's. Shidehara now sympathized with Chinese efforts to abolish extraterritoriality, although he felt that thorough legal reform would be necessary. He advised China to eliminate extraterritoriality in gradual stages until it was prepared to defend its policy. Shidehara was determined to preserve Japan's vested interests, particularly in Manchuria and Inner Mongolia. Ugaki was pleased with the apparent transformation of Shidehara diplomacy and wryly observed, "he has finally through experience come around to my point of view."[69]

Conclusion

The decade of the 1920's was marked by several transformations. The Anglo-Japanese alliance, a pillar of Japanese diplomacy, was dissolved. Imperial Russia, which had disintegrated in the turmoil of the October Revolution of 1917, was replaced by a new strong state which was becoming an important factor in international power politics in the Far East. America enjoyed increased prestige after the war, and the position of the United States was further strengthened by the Washington Conference. The postwar rise of Chinese nationalism promised to change permanently the future of China in the Far East. In the 1920's Japan experienced for the first time a decade of leadership under a growing two-party system.

Ugaki proved to be more accurate than most in foreseeing international developments in post-Versailles Asia, predicting the decline of Europe and the collapse of the Anglo-Japanese alliance. He was particularly concerned about the rise of Chinese Communism, and urged development of an anti-Communist Japanese sphere of influence in Manchuria and China, and a joint Sino-Japanese anti-Communist front. Yet he was aware of the need to act in concert with Britain and the United States to some degree in any moves to expand Japan's

[68] Ibid., p. 616 (October 8, 1927).
[69] Ibid., pp. 733f. (September 7, 1929).

influence in China, though he lacked a specific program to attain such cooperation.

Ugaki's main mistake was his complete disregard of postwar Chinese nationalism. He felt that it would be sufficient to use force when needed, to cooperate with pro-Japanese Chinese government leaders, and, most significantly, to avoid threatening American and British interests in China. He dismissed anti-Japanese movements, such as the May Fourth Movement, as unimportant, stemming only from the activities of American and British agitators and a few Chinese capitalists.

Ugaki resigned as army minister in April 1931, retired from the Army, and was appointed governor-general of Korea, taking up that post in July. On July 1, 1931, before leaving Tokyo to begin his duties in Seoul, he wrote in his diary, "Whoever is in charge of the governance of Korea must be sure of his footing before he takes a step, and next have a care for the north and the northeast (Manchuria and Siberia) when setting to work. . . . But the people who have held this post in the past have for the main part done their work with their eyes on the homeland, especially Tokyo."[70]

Ugaki Kazushige, now governor-general of Korea, bent his efforts to the governing of that colony, but he always thought of his task in the context of China policy. Not two months after he took up his post, on September 18, the Manchurian incident broke out. True to the positions he had espoused for nearly two decades, Ugaki advised Tokyo to unify national public opinion, and unite the military and civilian segments of the country to prosecute the affair to good conclusion. Taking as given that Japan would be able to obtain the understanding of the powers and the League, he urged Tokyo to establish a new government in Manchuria, and to separate the area politically from China proper.[71]

For a brief time it appeared that Ugaki's hopes were to be fulfilled, but the Army's appetite for continental expansion knew no bounds. In May 1938 Ugaki entered the second Konoe cabinet as foreign minister, and effectively revoked Konoe's January declaration that he would not deal with Chiang Kai-shek. Konoe tried to pursue a peaceful policy, but his attempt was aborted by the military's success in having the Asia bureau removed from the Foreign Ministry right under Ugaki's nose and established as the independent Kōain

[70] Ibid., vol. 2, p. 801 (July 1, 1931).
[71] Ibid., pp. 812f. (September 26, 1931; October 5, 1931).

(China Development Board), which was to be responsible for China policy. Ugaki resigned in protest, his final exit from the main stage of politics. This was fair retribution, for he had downgraded the Foreign Ministry and given his favor to dual diplomacy. The fact that the ultimate victory of Chinese Communist forces was made easier by Japan's total war against China was but a further historical irony for Ugaki.

The errors of Ugaki's ideas on China were demonstrated in the wake of World War II. Yet even after the war he could write, "The Great East Asian War was not a war of Japanese aggression," but merely a war "based on the imperatives of self-preservation and self-defense, defense of Japan's vested interests, and the [attempt to] recover for the weak peoples of East Asia that which had been stolen from them by the Europeans and Americans."[72]

[72] Ibid., vol. 3, p. 1727 (February 8, 1948).

CHAPTER XII

JAPAN'S ECONOMIC THRUST INTO NORTH CHINA, 1933-1938: FORMATION OF THE NORTH CHINA DEVELOPMENT CORPORATION

TAKAFUSA NAKAMURA
Translated by Robert Angel

IN NOVEMBER 1938 the North China Development Corporation was founded through special legislation, with capital of 350 million yen half of which was invested by the government. A leading figure of the *zaikai*, Gō Seinosuke, chaired the founding committee of eighty-three members that included such important businessmen as Yuki Toyotarō, governor of the Bank of Japan, Ikeda Shigeaki representing Mitsui interests, Ogura Masatsune of Sumitomo, Mitsubishi's Kagami Kenkichi, Kushida Manzō, and the governor of the South Manchuria Railway, Matsuoka Yōsuke. The founding board also included political figures such as the cabinet secretary-general, administrative vice-ministers from various ministries, and members of both houses of the Diet. After his retirement as minister of overseas affairs, Ōtani Sonyū was appointed governor.[1] The atmosphere surrounding the founding of the corporation brought to mind the spirit of "one-nation united" that had accompanied the birth of the South Manchuria Railway (abbreviated Mantetsu) following the Russo-Japanese War.

The development of north China had become a focus of attention since the beginning of the Sino-Japanese War in the summer of 1937. For example, in October 1937 *Chūōkōron* published a special edition entitled "North China Development Corporation," entirely devoted to the articles of individuals such as Ōtani Kozui, Kobayashi Ichizō, Adachi Kenzō, Gō Seinosuke, and others. As will be seen later in

[1] Hokushi Kaihatsu Kabushiki Kaisha, *Kita Shina Kaihatsu Kabushiki Kaisha oyobi kankei kaisha setsuritsu shorui shū* (Peiping, 1942), pp. 7-9, 17.

more detail, the governor of Mantetsu, Matsuoka, and the president of Hsing Chung Kung Ssu, Sogō Shinji, battled each other for the right to control the development of north China. In addition, Japanese domestic capitalists were indicating a strong interest in the penetration of China. Ultimately, it was publicly announced that the whole *zaikai* intended to unite together in the development of north China, but the ambitions of Mantetsu and Hsing Chung Kung Ssu were defeated with the establishment of the North China Development Corporation.[2]

Early Aspirations: June 1933-June 1935

In the Spring of 1933 the Japanese army crossed the Great Wall line and advanced into north China (Hupeh province), after which the Tangku agreement was made. The following four points made up the essentials of the agreement:

1. The Chinese army was to withdraw from the triangular area within the line running along the northern side of the railway connecting Peking, Tientsin, and Tangku, and the Great Wall (hereafter referred to as the War Zone, or the Chi-tung area).

2. The Japanese army was to inspect the conditions of the withdrawal by air.

3. After confirming the Chinese withdrawal the Japanese army was also voluntarily to return "more or less" to north of the Great Wall.

4. Thereafter the security of the War Zone would be handled by the Chinese police organization.[3]

In the end the Great Wall was recognized as the border of "Manchukuo" and the War Zone was turned into a neutral zone, which became the foothold for the invasion of north China. But, on the other hand, the war clouds hanging over north China disappeared for a while. The north China administrative committee was formed with Huang Fu as chairman, and relations between north China and "Manchukuo" moved toward stability.

In 1934 and 1935 problems such as extension of rail lines crossing

---

[2] House of Commons, Research Division, ed., *Hokushi shigen kaihatsu ni kansuru ronbun tekiyō* (Tokyo, 1938); House of Peers, Research Section, *Hokushi kaihatsu ni kansuru shinbun zasshi no ronchō* (Tokyo, 1938).

[3] Nihon Kokusai Seiji Gakkai, ed., *Taiheiyō sensō e no michi* (Tokyo, 1962), vol. 3, pp. 46-50.

the Great Wall, mail connections, customs procedures at the Great Wall, and telephone-telegraph connections were settled in a business-like manner.[4] On the basis of this, even with no change in the principle of nonrecognition of "Manchukuo," it seems that signs of a turn for the better in Sino-Japanese relations were beginning to appear. In the spring of 1935 the mutual elevation of the status of the legations of the two countries to embassies was realized. The Chinese side offered to repay old debts dating back to the Nishihara loans. Later, negotiations to improve diplomatic relations were begun in Tokyo and Nanking.

Internationally too there was evidence of a relaxation of tensions in the Far East. For example, in 1934 the British dispatched an investigative group headed by Lord Bernby to sound out the possibilities for economic development in Manchukuo and to look into capital participation in the construction industries. Manchurian investment by France and Belgium was also often discussed. In 1935 an understanding was reached on the Soviet sale of the Chinese Eastern Railway to Manchukuo. This harmonious atmosphere made it likely that, at least in Tokyo, there were hardly any moves in the direction of new advances into north China. But, at the same time, Mantetsu, the Kwantung Army, and the North China Garrison (hereafter called the Tientsin Army) were in contact with each other, waiting for a new opportunity for further advances.

In the case of Mantetsu, since they had cooperated with the Kwantung Army in the founding of "Manchukuo," there was a chance around 1932 and 1933 that they might be able to monopolize the major Manchukuo industries. At that time the Kwantung Army was trying to set up a "control economy" in Manchuria under the slogan, "No *Zaibatsu* in Manchuria." They divided the industries into three types, with the most important—coal, machinery, oil, and telephone-telegraph—under the principle of "one industry-one company." Manchukuo and Mantetsu became the two largest stockholders in these monopolies, and thereby Mantetsu was able to gain control of key industries.[5] Japanese capital entered Manchuria only in the form of bonds floated by Mantetsu, making it an unattractive area for

---

[4] Ibid., pp. 51-66.

[5] Hara Akira, "1930-nendai no Manshū keizai tōsei seisaku," in Manshūshi Kenkyūkai, ed., *Nihon teikokushugi-ka no Manshū* (Tokyo, 1972), pp. 8-56. According to Hara, funds for all such monopolistic and semi-monopolistic firms established in Manchuria before 1936 came from three sources: 30 percent from the Manchukuo government, 30 percent from the South Manchuria Railway, and 40 percent from others.

investment by domestic capitalists.[6] This resulted in a situation in which Manchuria was not receiving sufficient Japanese capital, and Mantetsu alone was unable to provide sufficient management and technology. There were soon moves from within the army to reform the Manchukuo system, adding more Japanese government officials and changing the monopoly position Mantetsu had been enjoying.

By March of 1933 the army was already making plans to try to force Mantetsu to concentrate its activities on railroads, and to make the other sections of the company into a holding company. Mantetsu had informally given their tentative consent, but when news of these plans leaked out and became a public issue in October, the army withdrew its proposal.[7] Mantetsu's position was once more restored, but there was no way of telling when the plan might be revived (in 1937, with the move of Ayukawa Yoshisuke's Nihon Sangyō to Manchuria —discussed later—it was suddenly realized), and so Mantetsu began to look toward future expansion in north China.

Mantetsu Director Sogō Shinji visited China in March and June of 1934, and as a result a plan was drawn up for the establishment of an investment company that would have as its main function negotiations with the Chinese on the implementation of the following plans:

—formation of a transportation company in north China, putting the activities of the Chinese national railways under trust management;

—establishment of a silver bank and management of financial affairs, control over the export of Anshan iron, and control of sea and land transportation through a transportation company all in the Shanghai area;

—increased trade and the establishment of new banking facilities in southwest China.[8]

After reaching agreement on this plan with the leadership of the Kwantung Army and the North China Garrison in March 1935,

---

[6] Hara notes (ibid., pp. 54, 56) that the slogan, "No *Zaibatsu* in Manchuria," was no longer used after 1934-35, and, therefore, that it must have been unstable rates of exchange and general insecurity, and not the slogan, that caused domestic Japanese capital to hesitate to enter the Manchurian market. In any event, it cannot be denied that the financial establishment at home was looking askance at the South Manchuria Railway.

[7] I am indebted to Mr. Hara for this point.

[8] Sogō Shinji, "Chūkaminkoku keizai jōkyō shisatsu hōkoku" (typescript, for private circulation, 1934).

Mantetsu petitioned the prime minister for approval of a plan to set up a subsidiary company, Hsing Chung Kung Ssu, capitalized at 10 million yen. The purpose of the scheme was to "form a unified organ for economic activities in China that could handle direct management, good offices, intermediation, and even investment in the various industries of the economy of north China."[9] The plan was restricted by the Manchurian bureau to "direct management, good offices, intermediation, and investment in China in the industries related to the export of Manchurian products and the development of Manchuria." Both the foreign minister and the finance minister displayed some hesitancy over this arrangement. But after a little difficulty it was finally approved on August 2, 1935, and in December it was launched with Sogō Shinji as president and the lower posts filled with influential individuals.[10]

In early 1935 revisions were also made in the Mantetsu organization. A sixth bureau was added to the Economic Research Association, with a general affairs section and a basic research section. With the "East Asian economy"—actually China—as their area of interest, they were to carry out research on forms of investment and possible investment targets in China, and to make plans and policies concerning the promotion of trade among Japan, Manchukuo, and China.[11]

Mantetsu's plans for research on the north Chinese economy began after November 1933 under sixteen proposed research themes which included industrial policy in the War Zone and coal mining policy in K'ailuan. After that, in May 1934, ten researchers were dispatched to Tientsin and Tsingtao to begin studies of natural resources. And in October and November they also participated in the Tientsin Army's investigations of natural resources in north China. The main purpose of the investigations was to lay the groundwork for "the promotion and expansion of imperial economic power, and the acceleration of the formation of a Japan-Manchukuo-China economic bloc," to aid Japanese efforts to promote Chinese economic development, and to ensure adequate supplies of strategic resources.[12] This

[9] Hsing Chung Kung Ssu, "Kaisha setsuritsu ni kansuru keii" (Dec. 1935), p. 4.
[10] Ibid.
[11] South Manchuria Railway, General Affairs Division, Materials Section, *Shōwa jūnen Mantetsu chōsa kikan yōran* (1935), pp. 65-268; Industry Division, *kaizai Chōsakai ritsuan chōsa shorui mokuroku* (1937), pp. 12ff. The sixth division was abolished in November 1935, and its business transferred to the Tientsin office and broadened in scope.
[12] South Manchuria Railway, Research Division, *Shina keizai kaihatsu hōsaku narabi chōsa shiryō* (1937), pp. 315-67, 384-99.

series of events and the founding of Hsing Chung Kung Ssu stimulated the formation of the sixth bureau. An East Asian division was added to the general affairs bureau of the Mantetsu main office, to be responsible for "external administration" in Mantetsu's operations in all of East Asia, excluding Japan, Manchuria, and the Soviet Union.[13]

In addition to the above activities the Kwantung Army seems to have been entertaining plans for a thrust into north China ever since the formation of the War Zone. Several manifestations of this can be pointed out. After 1933, smuggling in the War Zone ("Chitung smuggling") began to increase, estimated at 20 million yen in 1933 and 15 million yen in 1934 (estimates of between 60 and 100 million yen also were made). The Kwantung Army can be said to have given its tacit approval of this smuggling.[14] An information and strategy organization was also operating in Tientsin, headed by Colonel Osako Michisada of the Kwantung Army, called the Aoki agency.[15] The Chahar-Tolun area was put under the occupation of Li Shou-hsin's army, an ally of the Kwantung Army.[16] A road for military use was built between Jehol and Peking, running through Tientsin, with regular truck traffic running along it. Further, in Inner Mongolia operations of the "Inner Mongolia Autonomous Region" were pushed along, centering on Te Wang.[17] The Tientsin Army also had a positive attitude toward these plans.

In May 1935, protesting the assassination of the presidents of two newspaper companies friendly to Japan, Tientsin Army chief of staff, Sakai Takashi, demanded the removal of the central Chinese army and the Kuomintang representatives from Hupeh, and the removal of Yu Hsüeh-ching from his post as chairman of Hupeh province. And immediately thereafter, because of skirmishes on the Chahar-Jehol border and the coercion of Japanese soldiers and diplomats, the chief of the military intelligence bureau in Mukden, Doihara Kenji, demanded that the Sung Che-yüan army move south of the Great Wall and that anti-Japanese organizations be abolished. Since these two demands were backed up by the Japanese military presence, the Chinese had no choice but to agree, and the Umezu-Ho Ying-ch'in agreement and the Doihara-Chin Ti-ch'un agreement were concluded.

---

[13] *Mantetsu chōsa kikan yōran*, pp. 21-22.

[14] South Manchuria Railway, Tientsin Office, Research Section, *Kitō chiiki no bōeki gaikyō to kanzei jijō* (Tientsin, 1936).

[15] Kawai Teikichi, *Aru kakumeika no kaisō* (Tokyo, 1973), pp. 196, 201-203.

[16] Matsui Tadao, *Naimō sangokushi* (Tokyo, 1966), pp. 16-18.

[17] Interview with Mr. Okada Yoshimasa.

Actually, prior to this, on May 14, the Kwantung and Tientsin Armies had decided on the severance of the five provinces in the north China area from China, the establishment of a new regime, and promotion of the economic development of the region.[18] The arrow had now left the bow.

Hanging in the Balance: July 1935-June 1937

FORMATION OF NORTH CHINA'S NEW REGIME

After the signing of the Umezu-Ho Ying-ch'in and Doihara-Chin Ti-ch'un agreements, the Japanese side suddenly made public its pressures on north China, working to establish a new political regime, and to speed up economic development. Looking only at the economic side, the Tientsin Army, together with the Kwantung Army, planned to establish an investment company called Hsing Kahsiang, which was to become the "nucleus of north China's industrial development companies . . . that should make their appearance in the near future."[19] This move shocked Mantetsu, in the middle of its plans to establish Hsing Chung Kung Ssu, and they made a protest to the Kwantung Army.[20]

At that time, the economic development plan of the Tientsin Army was roughly as follows:

1. The organization of small-scale development companies, mustering such companies as Mantetsu, the Asia Colonization Company (Tōtaku), the East Asia Developing Company, and Chosen Bank.

2. Designation of transportation (rail, auto, air, shipping, and ports), iron and coal mining as investment targets.

3. Together with plans for an "extension of Manchukuo's power into north China," Mantetsu was to "build a rail line encircling the Peiping line (between Mukden and Peiping) that would threaten the latter's independence and work to expel the influence of foreigners in the area."

4. Six areas "that have already requested Japan's cooperation," were selected for development, including the Lungyen iron mines and the Ch'i Tang coal mines.

---

[18] *Shina keizai kaihatsu hōsaku*, p. 97, quoting from the Tientsin Army's document, "Hokushi shin seiken no hassei ni tomonau keizai kaihatsu shidō-an."
[19] *Osaka Asahi shinbun*, July 4, 1935.
[20] Economic Research Association, "Dai-ikkai Kantōgun sanbō, Keichō kondankai kiroku" (June 1935).

5. Industries requiring development included: iron manufacturing (reopening and expanding the Shih Ching Shan iron works), cotton spinning (either buying up existing spinning mills or through trust management, and with expansion of Japanese industry into Tientsin), monopolization of the north China electrical industry, and construction of a large industrial area in Taku.

6. Concerning trade: abolition of tariff barriers, and increasing the flow of Japanese and Manchukuo goods into north China;

7. Concerning financing: formation of a trustworthy note-issuing bank with a Japanese affiliation, and encouraging a flow of Manchukuo currency into north China.[21]

The Tientsin Army thought that this sort of plan could be implemented all at once, along with a sudden upheaval in the political situation, but conditions in north China were not really favorable, and after the end of July, newspaper articles suggesting that these developments might be realized at any moment disappeared completely. It seems that the members of the economic world of north China banded together to show passive resistance,[22] and after the passing of this wave of temporary enthusiasm the Tientsin Army put together plans for a more sober, large-scale economic investigation.

Prior to this, in July 1935, during the height of the above-mentioned excitement, the Manchukuo government and Mantetsu's Economic Research Association were entrusted by the Tientsin Army through the chief of staff of the Kwantung Army, to dispatch personnel to carry out research in north China—the former to engage in political analysis, and the latter in fiscal and monetary studies. Two research teams were promptly sent, one known as the North China Garrison's "A" nonregular research group, and the other as the "C" group. The details of the "A" group's studies are unclear, but the "C" group was given an agenda and told to complete their report by the end of October. The report was submitted in November and the topics covered were:

1. Financial: How much financing could be done if north China should become independent from central China? To what extent

---

[21] *Shina keizai kaihatsu hōsaku*, pp. 97-102.

[22] Some influential businessmen in north China organized a Hopeh business association in August, but according to *Manshū nichi nichi shinbun* it had more the character of a defensive association against Japanese penetration.

should Japan penetrate the north China financial world? A proposal for financial controls in Tientsin. The likely effect on the central Chinese government should north China become independent, etc.

2. Economic matters: Economic dependence among Japan, Manchukuo, and China, especially north China.

3. Tariffs.

4. Trade.[23]

The request seemed to fall in line with the judgment of the Tientsin Army that the sudden separation of the five provinces of north China was possible. Then, on August 20, after the situation was somewhat more settled, the Economic Research Association received a second request from the Tientsin Army for the dispatch of personnel in order to make a "basic research proposal of items for urgent development." The "B" nonregular research group was dispatched. The study was to cover mining, manufacturing, railroads, ports, and the economy (finance, trade, and agriculture) in the five provinces of north China: Hupeh, Chahar, Suiyuan, Shantung, and Shansi. This study was finally completed in 1936 with 151 people involved and at a cost of 15,860,000 yen. The report was later put together by Mantetsu's Economic Research Association in seventy-two volumes, containing specific technical information on railroads, mining, and other subjects worthy of the name "basic research." It certainly served as an important source of information in both the military's and Mantetsu's plans for an economic invasion of north China.[24]

As these economic studies progressed the political situation was becoming more severe. British Special Envoy Frederick Leith Ross visited Japan in September, proposing a plan whereby Japan and Great Britain would reform China's currency system, and China—with conditions attached—would recognize "Manchukuo." Japan's reaction to the proposal was cool. With the warning that Britain might move independently to help China with the problem of currency reform, Ross left for China. On November 3 it was announced that Britain would act alone, proposing currency reforms designed

[23] South Manchuria Railway, Industry Division, *Keizai Chōsakai ritsuan chōsa shorui mokuroku* (1937), vol. 1, pp. 522-23. The "C" group's studies appear to have been printed, but the author has not seen them.

[24] Ibid., pp. 496-521, plus index. Not all the 72 volumes have survived. Moreover, some reports, such as the Economic Research Association's "Shina chūtongun otsu shokutaku-han chōsa gaiyō" (1937), are not included in the index.

to help the Chinese economy cope with a panic due to the outflow of silver.

The currency reform proposal had six parts, including:

1. Designation of the currency issued by the three central banks as legal tender (*fapi*).

2. Requiring that individuals holding silver coins and gold exchange them for *fapi* at designated institutions; and provision for punishment of those concealing or secretly exporting them.

3. Allowing the three banks unlimited transactions in foreign exchange.

The object of these measures was to move toward a managed currency system with the power to issue currency concentrated in the central government. The British backed the reforms and said that they would support the parity of the *fapi* at one shilling 2½ pence. The Japanese, who were planning for the separation of the five northern provinces, took this centralization of the currency system as a challenge from the Chinese.

In the fall of 1935 the Japanese army worked to win Wu P'ei-fu, Yen Hsi-shan, and Sung Che-yüan to their side, and to establish a new north China political order under Sun Ch'uan-fang. They also instigated disturbances such as the farmers autonomy movement. Reacting to the currency reform that had been publicized at that time, the Japanese army moved strongly against Sung Che-yüan (appointed September 28 as commander of the Pingchih Garrison) and other north China military leaders, forcing a prohibition of the ban on the movement of silver out of the provinces, and further increasing pressures for a declaration of self-government from the five provinces. Since the response of Sung and the others was vague, the army rushed to put Yin Ju-k'eng in as War Zone administrator on November 25, and to force the creation of the Chitung anti-Comintern autonomy committee (the Chitung government) in the Chitung area. Then, under the instruction of Nanking, Sung Che-yüan organized a new Chicha administrative committee and became its chairman. Since Chicha was a branch of the Nationalist government in the two provinces of Hupeh and Chahar, these results were inadequate when considered from the point of view of the original Japanese plan. In the end, since a "new government" had been formed, the Japanese military had no choice but to lay down its arms.

Thus, during December 1935, the Chitung government—north China's second "Manchukuo"—and the Chicha government—squeezed between the central Chinese government and Japan—were formed one after the other. The Japanese army planned to have the former handle "internal leadership," as was done in Manchukuo, and to work within a framework of formal diplomatic negotiations with the latter, since it was very much under the umbrella of the central Chinese government; and there were diplomatic missions from the powers in Peking and Tientsin. However, with the establishment of the "new governments," the foundation for an economic invasion was tentatively laid, and the Japanese militarists probably thought that later, through negotiations combined with force, they could somehow accomplish their purpose.

NORTH CHINA-TOKYO-NANKING

After discussions in Tokyo among the Army, Navy, and Foreign Ministries, on January 13, 1936, the "plan for dealing with north China" was decided upon. Its focus was a proposal for "completion of the autonomy movements" in "north China's five provinces," strengthening the Chicha government for the time being, and bringing together Chicha and Chitung. Concerning economic penetration it is interesting to note that the plan called for "guiding events to truly realize the principles of coexistence and coprosperity, with the real intention of introducing the free penetration of private capital."[25] Tokyo had presumably changed tactics after the failure in Manchuria.

Around March 1936, the Tientsin Army posted in north China drew up a "plan for the leadership of north China's industrial development," and in June this became the "North China Garrison's General Staff's foremost plan for the development of north China."[26] The "principle" of this plan stated that industrial development was to wait for "autonomous development" on the part of the Chinese, but that strategic resources required direct investment from Japan. Efforts to "expel foreign influence and to tighten the dependency relationship between Japan, Manchukuo, and China" were called for. Among the "main points" of the plan was the statement that to promote development the Tientsin Army would encourage not only the Japanese governmental authorities but "especially the activities of the *zaibatsu* leaders."

[25] Inaba Masao et al., eds., *Nit-Chū senso* (Tokyo, 1964), vol. 1, pp. 349-50.
[26] *Shina keizai kaihatsu hōsaku*, pp. 103-20.

Industries were divided into "controlled industries," considered important for national security, "prohibited industries," considered socially harmful and unwise for Japanese to be involved in, and "free industries." Controlled industries included the mining of coal and iron, transportation facilities such as railroads, harbors, automobiles, and aircraft, communications, electrical power, iron manufacturing, paper, and oil. Nearly all heavy industries were included in this category. North China was also a cotton-producing area, and there were many spinning mills in Tientsin, but cotton spinning was excluded. This was because of the confidence of the authorities in the "regulative power of the Japanese Spinning Federation."

Even in the case of free industries participation required the approval of the headquarters of the Tientsin Army. Among the controlled industries, the iron mines of Lungyen were to be developed on a large scale with "special capital," and coal mining also was to be "developed uniformly through the use of special capital." Even the specific methods of development were planned, with railways and harbors to be operated by the government. The Tientsin Army probably wanted to emulate the "shining" example of the Kwantung Army, but one big difference between the two was that the former called for the appearance of the "*zaibatsu* leaders."

Further, they called for the establishment of a semi-public investment company as the organ for the development of the controlled industries. It was to be capitalized at 200 million yen, with the Japanese and north China governments owning more than half of the stock. Six-percent dividends were to be guaranteed for ten years. Target industries were iron ore, iron production, metal mining and metallurgical industries, coal mining, electrical power, radio, electric railways, lighting, salt production, oil, and automotive transportation. As pointed out by Yoda Yoshiie, this became the model for the North China Development Corporation. With proposals at the same time drafted for currency, for supply and demand for capital, a public lighting company, an iron and steel company, and a coal mining company, the plans of the Tientsin Army were tentatively decided upon.

In response to the above proposal a "committee to deal with the current situation" was formed in Tokyo on June 19, composed of bureau directors from the Army, Navy, and Foreign Ministries, chaired by the administrative vice-minister of the Foreign Ministry, and it discussed "all matters relating to north China." Then, at a five-ministers conference attended by the army, navy, foreign, finance, and prime ministers on August 7, the "basis of national policy" that took up the "southern advance" and "northern advance" theories was decided upon. On the same day an "imperial foreign policy" was established at a conference of the same group minus the finance minister. Based on the above two policies, on August 11 the "north China action policy" and the "second plan for dealing with north China" were made, and from this time on the invasion of north China became "policy" even for the national government.[27] The Kwantung and Tientsin Armies had completely brought Tokyo around to their way of thinking one year and three months after beginning to stir up trouble.

Before long, the "north China action policy" had made north China a "special anti-Comintern, pro-Manchukuo zone," and further, it was said that defenses against the Soviet Union would be erected with "strategic resources and by aiding in the completion of transport facilities." Concerning economic problems, the "second plan for dealing with north China" sought the creation of a situation in which Japan and China were inseparable through the expansion of rights and interests that "had as their main purpose the free penetration of private capital." It was also part of the plan to help "maintain friendly attitudes toward Japan" in north China. They intended to realize the development of strategic resources (such as iron, coal, and salt), transportation facilities, and electrical power, "if necessary through the use of special capital," following in general the controlled industry theories of the Tientsin Army.

The second appendix of this document listed the following six industries as being especially promising as strategic resources in north China:

> 1. iron ore (to be developed by Hsing Chung Kung Ssu, aided by Mantetsu);
>
> 2. coking coal (placing the Chinghsing coal mines—owned by Germany—under joint Japan-China management; unification of the small coal fields of Shantung; management guidance; placing the K'ailuan coal fields under joint Japanese-British ownership);
>
> 3. salt (expansion of production of Ch'anglu and Shantung salt fields, and export of salt to Japan);

[27] *Nit-Chū sensō*, vol. 1, pp. 357-73.

4. cotton production increases;

5. liquid fuels (liquification of coal in Shansi);

6. increased wool production.

All of this intensified Japanese expectations of resources from north China and served to make more specific the important points of later policies.

However, this sort of expansionism was not to the taste of Ishiwara Kanji, who was on the General Staff at the time. He thought that in order to cement good relations with China and prepare for the decisive battle with the Soviet Union, Japan should restrict its demands to iron, salt, cotton, and wool. As pointed out by Shimada Toshihiko, the scheme related above can be thought of as the product of a compromise between the plans of the army in the area and the ideas of Ishiwara.[28]

In accordance with the above plans, from the beginning of 1936 the Tientsin Army entered into negotiations with the Chicha government concerning basic economic cooperation, but all attempts ended with lower-level talks. It appears that sometime in September, Commander Tashiro Kanichirō of the Tientsin Army presented to Sung Che-yüan a proposal based on the "second plan for dealing with north China."[29] The proposal called for mutual economic cooperation and benefit; public welfare and good living; and in particular, economic development made possible through Japanese loans and Japanese-Chinese mergers, with the Japanese military mediating to channel Japanese capital and technology into China. Eight demands were made as follows:

1. establishment of regular air routes;

2. creation of a Chinshih railroad (between Tientsin and Shih-chiachuang);

3. development of superior coal mines, with expansion of production at Chinghsing and Chenghung;

4. exploration for and development of iron mines, launching an iron industry, first with expansion of production at Lungyen;

5. harbor construction at Tangku;

[28] *Taiheiyō sensō e no michi*, vol. 3, p. 213.
[29] There is no adequate Japanese documentation on this point. For Chinese sources, see Wu Hsiang-hsiang, ed., *Ti-erh-tz'u Chung-Jih chan-cheng shih* (Taipei, 1973), vol. 1, pp. 240-45, and the following item.

6. development of the electrical industry and water power;

7. increases in production of cotton, salt, and wool to stimulate agricultural villages and improve public welfare, and expansion of exports of these products to Japan; improved flood control and water transportation;

8. unification and improvement of communication facilities.[30]

The Tashiro-Sung discussions resulted in general agreement, "with the Chicha side displaying great enthusiasm and indicating a desire to implement the plan speedily, with the understanding that it would not take the form of a so-called treaty or pact, and that in the future it would conform to internal guidance." The gist of the above proposal was written up, dated September 30, and signed on October 1. This document, which was handled with great secrecy, was known to the world as the Tashiro-Sung Che-yüan agreement.[31] However, Sung apparently failed to report the signing of the document to Nanking. Agitation in the area increased, and finally, disturbed by Nanking's strong attitude, the Japanese presented their position only vaguely.[32]

Meanwhile, after the August Ch'engtu incident, tensions increased between Japan and China. Finally a central government order addressed to Sung Che-yüan on December 5 curtailed his discretionary powers, demanding that negotiations for all joint undertakings be handled by the central authorities, that he comply with all central regulations (the export of salt was prohibited, for example) and that he not exceed the existing plans of the central government.[33]

With the Suiyuan and Sian incidents of November and December, anti-Japanese feelings spread throughout the country. Sung could not move toward secession after all, and on January 20, 1937, he made his position clear with the publication of his "defend central China" statement. Later he did discuss with the Japanese the construction of the Chinshih railroad (between Tientsin and Shihchia-chuang), but after meeting with strong opposition from Nanking, events moved toward the Marco Polo Bridge incident with negotiations in north China showing no progress.[34]

[30] Sung to Chiang, no date; and the Executive Yüan's secret order of December 5, 1936, in Chung-hua-min-kuo wai-chiao wen-ti yen-chiu-hui, ed., *Chung-Jih wai-chiao tzu-liao ts'ung-pien* (Taipei, 1966), vol. 5, pp. 464-67.
[31] Kubota (naval attaché at Tientsin) to various naval offices, Oct. 3, 1936.
[32] Wu, pp. 244, 251.   [33] *Nit-Chū sensō*, vol. 1, pp. 400-403.
[34] For details, see South Manchuria Railway, Tientsin Office, Research Section, *Kitō tokushu bōeki no jitsujō* (1936).

In the meantime Ishiwara's idea of a more prudent attitude toward China gained adherents in Tokyo. Under his leadership, at the beginning of 1937 efforts were begun to try to alter the August decision. Ishiwara was then grappling with the "five-year plan for critical industries" which was to drastically improve Japanese industrial productivity within five years, and his main concern was to avoid problems with any foreign country in order to ensure its success. On April 16, 1937, a new "China action policy" and "north China leadership policy" were decided upon by the army, navy, foreign and finance ministers. This plan called for "imposition of an anti-Comintern pro-Japanese zone" and "exploitation of strategic resources" in north China, but it did not include political activities such as "divide and rule north China" or "disruption of internal affairs."[35] This again indicated a willingness to improve Sino-Japanese relations in light of the failure of tough actions in and after December 1935. The situation in north China worsened, however, and though the delegation representing the *zaikai* (led by Kodama Kenji) probably shared this attitude, they were unable to obtain any results..

THE ACTUAL CIRCUMSTANCES OF THE "INVASION"

One of the extreme manifestations of the "invasion" of north China was the great increase in so-called "Chitung smuggling" after the formation of the Chitung government. Charging only about one-fourth of the regular Chinese tariff rate under the name of an "inspection fee," the Chitung government permitted cheap imports to flow into the Chinese mainland, throwing its economy into confusion.[36] This was a calculated, disruptive measure by the Kwantung Army which at the same time provided a source of income for the new Chitung government. In August, the Chicha government likewise conformed to a low tariff rate. However opportunistic these actions may have been, our focus here is on the activities of Hsing Chung Kung Ssu and Mantetsu involving "controlled industries" and "free penetration" of private capital.

"*Controlled Industries*" Hsing Chung Kung Ssu began operations in 1936 after serious difficulties during its founding. Contrary to its

[35] Hsing Chung Kung Ssu, *Kabushiki kaisha Hsing Chung Kung Ssu jigyō gaiyō* (1938).
[36] Hsing Chung Kung Ssu, ibid., and *Hsing Chung Kung Ssu kankei kaisha gaiyō* (1939); South Manchuria Railway, Research Division, *Kitō denki tōsei hōsaku narabi chōsa shiryō* (1937).

original plan, most of its operations were centered in north China, and it also handled trade with Canton and Fukien and the export of K'ailuan coal to Japan. But it had very little to do with the Shanghai area. Its principal interests in north China were in the electrical industry, salt, iron ore, coal, raw cotton, and transportation.[37]

Increased manufacturing in Tientsin led to rising demand for electrical power in that city. A contract was then made to build a joint electric power plant between Tientsin and Hsing Chung. The Tientsin Electric Power Company was established and capitalized at 8 million yüan with Japan and China dividing the investment. Actually, Hsing Chung temporarily financed Tientsin's portion of the investment by inviting the participation of the Japanese electrical cartel, the "electric power league." Consequently, Hsing Chung and the league equally contributed technical aid and the stock of the company. This is the only example of successful "controls" through the mobilization of "special capital."[38]

As for the planning to increase salt production and exports of Hupeh's coastal Ch'anglu salt to Japan, it was decided that a monopoly be formed in Tokyo. But difficulties arose concerning the purchase of the salt because the Chinese government first had to construct conveyors and washing plants in order to export. Operations finally began in May 1937. Hsing Chung also handled the development of the Lungyen iron ore mines. They had been worked during World War I and an iron works had been built, but after the war production was halted. In competition with Hsing Chung, Mantetsu planned to reopen the mines and the iron works, and also to build a new iron works in Tientsin capable of producing 400,000 tons per year. The Chicha government was also making plans for development on their own and the situation was quite confused. Eventually it was decided that operations would begin with investment divided equally between Japan and China with Hsing Chung in charge. As for coal, Hsing Chung planned to have the German share of the joint German-Chinese Chinghsing coal mines (yearly production of 800,000 tons of bituminous coal) turned over to it. In August a temporary contract was concluded, but later things came to a standstill. It also bought the Paoch'ang mines, inactive for the past ten years, which seemed to

[37] See Hsing Chung Kung Ssu's two publications above.
[38] Ibid. See also South Manchuria Railway, Research Division, *Ryūen tekkō kaihatsu hōsaku* (1937).

be an unknown quantity.[39] In addition, it began building storage houses and factories for cotton and was planning port facilities at Tangku.[40] Surveying all these activities, it appears that some progress in the electric power industry and in the export of Ch'anglu salt was made, but Hsing Chung was just beginning to put together its operations in the other areas.

In the meantime Mantetsu did not simply sit idly by, for "in the opinion of the Manchurian bureau, Hsing Chung appears to be handling the industries of north China, but Mantetsu is aiding them from behind the scenes." An agreement existed between Matsuoka and Sogō that "Mantetsu will make the research proposals for the work that Hsing Chung does, and Mantetsu employees will enter the Hsing Chung organization." In this way, Mantetsu's ambitions on the continent were not in the least diminished.[41]

After 1935, at the request of the Tientsin Army, Mantetsu refined the details of an investment plan for north China. The first one, proposed by the China investment problem subcommittee "emphasized an overall self-development plan for north China." During late 1936 and early 1937 a scheme surfaced for including China as one part of the "five-year industrial plan" for Japan and Manchukuo being pushed at the time by Ishiwara Kanji. For this Mantetsu decided to hold a continental economy conference in the summer of 1937 to come up with a comprehensive program for the regulation of the "five-year plan for Manchurian industry," and to form a preparatory committee for the conference in which the five-year-plan proposal that was to be presented could first be refined. The conference was not held in July 1937 because of the Marco Polo Bridge incident, but in the fall the proposal became the basis of the north China development plan, mentioned below, centering around Mantetsu.

Comparing the plan to the "north China development five-year plan" made by the Tientsin Army in December 1936 helps to clarify the intentions of Mantetsu.[42] With an investment of 326 million yen over five years (154 million of which was to be in cash), the Tientsin Army planned to carry out projects such as rail and road

[39] Hsing Chung Kung Ssu's two publications listed in note 36, and its *Tankō kankei hikitsugi chōsasho sōron* (1938).

[40] Ibid.

[41] South Manchuria Railway, Economic Research Committee, "Shina chūtongun, Mantetsu Keizai Chōsa Iinkai dainiji kondankai hōkoku no ken" (no date)—see the remarks by Okumura Shinji, advisor to the Tientsin Army.

[42] South Manchuria Railway, Research Division, *Tai kita Shina tōshi hōsaku* (1937), pp. 1-3, 99-140.

construction, building of port facilities at Tangku, establishment of air routes, improvements of the iron and coal industries, and construction of hydroelectric power facilities and new iron works. In addition there was to be an industrial investment of 50 million yen in soda, light metals, cement, spinning, paper, pulp, and dyes, the capital for which would be provided by the Chicha government, Hsing Chung, and Japan. Mantetsu's name appeared hardly at all.

In contrast, the Mantetsu plan envisioned investment on the scale of 832 million yen over five years, anticipating control of development of transportation facilities, and investment in iron works, fuels, mining, and coal exporting companies. Further, the Asian Colonization Company planned to invest in China by providing exclusive capital for the construction of the Chinshih railroad. It seems that the situation in the area developed with little awareness of the change in plans by Tokyo.

"Free Industries" Meanwhile, the idea of free penetration of private capital was making a strong impression on the Japanese *zaikai*, with a considerable increase in the number of industries looking forward to "penetration." For example, the largest industry in north China was cotton spinning centered around Tientsin. Chinese-run factories were numerous; however, during the depression after 1933 most of them closed. In 1936 the number of Japanese companies planning to move into Tientsin suddenly increased. Kanebō (Kanegafuchi Spinning Company) brought up Yuyuan and Huahsin Spinning and reorganized them into the Sixth and Seventh Factories of Kungta Spinning, the third company of the Kanebo group with factories in Shanghai and Tsingtao. The Asian Colonization Company also independently bought Yuta Spinning, and together with Itō Chū Trading Company, absorbed Paoch'eng Spinning. Tōyōbō (Tōyō Spinning Company) merged with Huahsin Spinning in T'angshan;[43] and when Kanebō bought up Huahsin Spinning, Kanebo president Tsuda Shingo outbid Tōyōbō's 800-900 thousand yüan with a sudden 1.2 million yüan. It is said that profits were so great that he recovered his total investment the following year.[44] The spinning industry presents the most direct example of economic penetration into north China; this can be understood as the result of the presence of raw materials, abundant and cheap labor, and management experience built up in Shanghai and Tsingtao.

[43] Unegawa Shizuo, *Keizai Shina no Kaihatsu* (Tokyo, 1938), p. 107.
[44] Ishiguro Eiichi, *Taiga: Tsuda Shingo den* (Tokyo, 1960), pp. 177-81.

Chart 1. Number of Spinning Spindles in North China
(1,000 Spindles)

Year ending:		1932	1933	1934	1935	1936
Shantung	Chinese Operated	71	86	103	105	108
	Japanese Operated	356	365	401	480	520
Hopeh	Chinese Operated	303	387	296	297	134
	Japanese Operated	—	—	—	—	168

There is some doubt about the degree of accuracy of these figures; they are presented only to illustrate the trend. Unekawa, Shizuo, *Keizai Shina no kaihatsu* (Tokyo, 1938), p. 106.

The following report is from February 1937 and concerns the situation of other industries included in the category of "free penetration." In the Peking, Tientsin, and Chitung area, "the capitalization of industries either in operation or in the process of setting up operations amounts to 56 million yüan, and those in the process of deciding to begin setting up operations amounts to 24 million yüan, for a total of 80 million yüan. The greater portion of these are in the free penetration category.

(1) Those in operation and those soon to begin operations:

Industry	Investor
A. Chitung-area telephone	Manshū Denshin-Denwa Co.
B. Electric lighting	Manshū Denryoku Co. & Hsing Chung
C. Automobiles	Mantetsu
D. Small loan companies	Tahsing Kung Ssu
E. Chitung financing	Chitung Government
F. Fireproof clay	Osaka Yōgyō Corporation
G. Tobacco production	Osaka Yōgyō Corporation
H. Paper production	Hanshin Zaibatsu
I. Aviation	Manshū Aviation
J. Glass production	Shōkō Glass & Tōtaku
K. Spinning	Kanebō and Tōyōbō
L. Wool	Kanebō

[239]

(2) Those now making their business plans:

Industry	Investor
A. Oil imports & sales	Manshu Sekiyu
B. Pulp	(undetermined)
C. Sulfide dyes	Ishin Chemical, Mitsui, & Mitsubishi
D. Spinning	Fukushima Spinning, Shanghai Spinning, Dai Nihon Spinning
E. Medicine manufacturing	Dai Nippon Drugs
F. Hemp	Tientsin-Miyazaki Trading Co.
G. Coal mining	(undetermined)

In addition to the above companies there is also the North China Association."[45]

This was certainly a large number of firms. Japanese business activity in Tientsin can be said to have shifted to "factory penetration," and a building boom after the Chitung trade stagnated because of Chinese protective measures.[46] But when examined closely, it turns out that most of the industrial groups described above either belonged to the Mantetsu group, or were spinning companies and medium-small size capitalists from Osaka. The big *zaibatsu* such as Mitsui, Mitsubishi, or Sumitomo seemed to be still cautious in their penetration of north China, with only Ishin Chemical reputed to be linked to Teikoku Dyes of the Mitsubishi group.[47]

The Ghost of "One-Nation United": July 1937-June 1938

On July 7, 1937, the roar of gunfire dragged Japan and China into an overall war situation. In August the fighting spread to Shanghai. The Japanese army rapidly engulfed all of north China. Even in central China, Shanghai was captured after a bitter battle. Following this,

[45] South Manchuria Railway, Economic Research Association, "Showā jūninen nigatsu Shina chūtongun, Mantetsu Keizai Chosakai dainiji kondankai hōkoku no ken"—see the remarks by Idogaki.

[46] *Manshū nichi nichi shinbun*, March 23, 1937.

[47] After the fall of 1936, there was such an excess of imports over exports that the Yokohama Specie Bank, the main foreign exchange facility, had to borrow funds overseas up to prescribed limits. Under the circumstances, the only way to pay for imports was through gold shipments.

Nanking was invaded in December. From 1937 to the battle of Hsuchow in May 1938, Japan's military operations in the area proceeded with great speed.

In December 1937, the Provisional government was established in north China, led by Wang K'o-min, and in January 1938 the Reformed government was set up around Liang Hung-chih. At the same time the Konoe cabinet announced that it was planning to put together a new political order that "would not deal with the Chiang government." Under these conditions the development of north China's economy again became a critical focus of attention. It looked as though the "development" that had progressed so slowly because of the drawn-out negotiations with the Chicha government might finally get started.

The Japanese domestic economy, however, was facing a real crisis. At the end of 1936 and beginning of 1937 Japan's international balance of payments deficit increased suddenly and in early 1937 the Bank of Japan began shipping gold to cover the deficit. The government also strengthened foreign exchange controls, and there was no choice but to restrict foreign investment by Japanese firms.[48]

After 1936 a huge national budget was drawn up to support preparation for war. Known as the Baba finance program, this budget planned increases in taxes and military expenditures. But such a course of action carried with it the danger of an immediate increase in the level of imports, which in turn would result in a worsening balance of payments situation. This danger unavoidably dampened their hopes.[49]

Moreover, since the plan for the "expansion of productive capacity" that came out of the Ishiwara Kanji-inspired "five-year plan for critical industries" had by then become a supreme command, it was then impossible to follow the usual procedure of dealing with international balance of payments deficits by moving to a deflationary policy that would decrease equipment investment. There was only one way of escaping the dilemma: the enforcement of direct economic controls. It was only a matter of time before they would become necessary. With the outbreak of the Sino-Japanese War, controls were suddenly strengthened over trade, foreign exchange, and equipment investment.

[48] See Nakamura Takafusa and Hara Akira, *Kokka sōdōin: keizai* (Tokyo, 1970); Nakamura, *Senzenki Nihon keizai seichō no bunseki* (Tokyo, 1971), chaps. 8-9.
[49] Katakura Chū, "Ayukawa Yoshisuke shi to Mangyō no omoide," in Sasaki Yoshihiko, ed., *Ayukawa Yoshisuke sensei tsuitōroku* (Tokyo, 1968), p. 111.

Even in Manchuria, Mantetsu's position was not stable. If there were no changes in the current situation and the idea of expanding production were implemented in Japan and Manchuria as planned, Mantetsu, with its lack of experience in heavy and chemical industries, would play a central role in the development. But both the army and Manchukuo had misgivings about these plans.

Thus, after 1936 the Kwantung Army asked the leaders of the *zaikai*'s new *konzern*, including Ayukawa Yoshisuke, Mori Nobuteru, Matsukata Gorō, and Tsuda Shingo, to make an inspection tour of Manchuria. After listening to their opinions, the leader of the Nissan *konzern*, Ayukawa Yoshisuke, was entrusted with Manchukuo's industrial development. This arrangement was made in the greatest secrecy, but was suddenly made public in October 1937 as the so-called "Nissan transfer to Manchuria," under which the Nissan *konzern* was to move the base of its operations to Manchuria.[50] The decision dealt a shattering blow to the exclusive position of Mantetsu in Manchukuo's industries, and ultimately Mantetsu's only remaining option was to devote all its energy to the penetration of north China.

As mentioned above, the Japanese economy was in serious trouble at the time of the Marco Polo Bridge incident, leaving it economically unable to fight a protracted war with China. Moreover, as the area of north China occupied by Japan expanded, it became necessary for the government rapidly to devise some economic policies. These policies can be roughly divided into measures for the management of the various industries in the occupied areas, monetary policies, and policies to deal with problems of the stabilization of the population's livelihood, all of a temporary nature, and more long-term problems such as industrial development and construction—all of which Japan was forced to cope with at once. Touching on the emergency measures only to the extent necessary for explanation, the problem of long-term "development" will be discussed below.

SHORT-TERM MEASURES AND LONG-TERM PLANS IN THE AREA

As the occupied area expanded, the first problem to surface was that of the currency. At first Chosen Ginkō notes were used instead of military scrip.[51] When the exchange rate between the Chosen Ginkō notes and the *fapi* dropped, they began using notes from the Hopeh Provincial Bank, which issued currency for the Chicha government. In

[50] Kojima Seiichi, *Hokushi keizai dokuhon* (Tokyo, 1937), p. 194.
[51] *Chūgoku Rengō Junbi Ginkō gonen-shi* (1944).

the end, the Chinese Federal Reserve Bank was established as the official currency-issuing institution in the area.[52] This resulted in a life-and-death struggle between the *fapi* and Reserve Bank currency.

The factories, mines, and railways that had been seized as part of the war effort were alloted to Japanese industries for trust management. For example, in the case of spinning factories, the big Japanese companies such as Kanebō, Tōyōbō, and Dai-Nihon-Bō, and various other companies in China such as Naigai Cotton Trading, Toyota Spinning, Shanghai Spinning, and T'unghsing Spinning took over their operations.[53] It was further directed that the emergency trust management of railways was to be given to Mantetsu, and telegraph and telephone operations to Manchurian Telegraph and Telephone (Denden). Lighting, coal mining, and the automotive industry were entrusted to Hsing Chung Kung Ssu, which would have the cooperation of Mantetsu and Kaijima Coal Mining.[54] It was therefore not at all unreasonable that leaders of the various industries led by Mantetsu and Hsing Chung should have very high hopes for special positions and rights in the forthcoming development of Chinese industry.

In the meantime, after the outbreak of the Sino-Japanese War in August, the Tientsin Army was reorganized as the North China Area Army, and like the Kwantung Army, its intelligence bureau was given the responsibility for political leadership.[55] The intelligence bureau drafted the "Instructions of the Economy" on September 22, covering the economy in general, production, prices, and monetary and fiscal matters. The opening paragraph expressed their plan in the following undisguised language:

> Economic development is the first order of business once the military activities of the army die down in north China. Japan may encounter some difficulties concerning the political system and the type of management used in the economic penetration of north China, but the most important task is to begin establishing a solid base there that will serve our nation's long-term interests.

It even served notice on the military forces in the area that economic policies and management during the war "are extremely important

[52] Yen Chung-p'ing et al., eds., *Chung-kuo chin-tai ching-chi-shih t'ung-chi tzu-liao hsüan-chi* (Peking, 1955), pp. 144-45.

[53] See Hsing Chung Kung Ssu's various publications, such as *Tankō kankei jimu hikitsugi chōsa sōron* (1938), *Denki jigyō kankei jimu hikitsugi chōsasho* (1935), and *Hokushi jidōsha jigyō hikitsugi chōsho* (1938).

[54] Based on some Colonial Affairs Ministry documents in the author's possession.

[55] Ibid.

for the development of our immediate postwar economic rights and interests. And so it is to be expected that postwar economic development and the acquisition of concessions will be clearly recognized and not neglected."[56]

Soon after on September 30, the North China Area Army's "basic outline for economic development in north China" and the "proposal for a state policy cooperation for the development of north China (draft)" were drawn up.[57] The former plan "aimed at enfolding north China within the imperial economic sphere, contributing to an increase in imperial productive capacity, improving popular livelihood through industrial development by mobilizing capital in the area, and combining capital and technology from both Japan and Manchukuo."

In summary, the plan divided the various forms of industry into "controlled industries" that would be run in accordance with the industrial programs of both Japan and Manchukuo, and "free industries" entrusted to Chinese and Japanese capital. Controlled industries included the development of important mineral resources and processing industries using these raw materials; major transportation facilities; important electric power generating facilities; and the development of salt mines. Controlled industries were to be under "the comprehensive administrative management of the State Policy Corporation." In the area of agricultural policy, efforts were to be made to improve the varieties of farm products, and to plant forests for flood prevention. Local governing bodies would be set up to "guide the organization of farming villages through cooperative societies."

The second document was a proposal for a North China Development State Policy Corporation that was expected to bring together the majority of the controlled industries in order to "avoid the wasting of capital, to nurture those industries, and to stimulate the development of the north China economy." Industries covered included iron, steel, and related industries, coal mining, coal liquefaction, rail and water transportation, salt and soda manufacturing, and electrical power generation. Specific proposals were spelled out for each industry.

In iron and steel, three iron works were to be built to produce 1,180,000 tons of iron and 100,000 tons of steel, of which one million

[56] See, South Manchuria Railway, Research Division, "Kita Shina sangyō kaihatsu keikaku shiryō," in Yoda Yoshiie, ed., *Nit-Chū sensō-shi shiryō* (Tokyo, 1975), vol. 4.

[57] "Shi ju dai nikki" (documents of the War Ministry), 1937, no. 11, War History Room archives, Tokyo.

tons of iron were to be exported to Japan. Several coal fields were to be developed, producing 25 million tons of coal, of which one million tons were again to be exported. Railways were to be "owned" by the north China government, and their management entrusted to the State Policy Corporation. The Chinshih railway was to be separated from the State Policy Corporation and to be built up rapidly. Port facilities at Tangku were to be constructed, designed to be capable of handling about 15 million tons per year. Electrical power generating plants with a capacity of one million kilowatts were planned. Further, the State Policy Corporation was to be capitalized at 500 million yen, and "in north China a new company, tentatively named 'Hsing Yeh Kung Ssu' was to be established, bringing together Hsing Chung Kung Ssu, other existing industrial enterprises, and Mantetsu. Japanese capital was to be rallied, and to the extent possible, indigenous capital was to be used in the area."

All of this shows that after 1935, plans for the formation of a State Policy Corporation in north China suddenly assumed a more concrete form.

MANTETSU, HSING CHUNG KUNG SSU, ZAIKAI

No sooner had the war began to spread in north China than Mantetsu began to move quickly to bring the area under its control. This is illustrated in the "Summary of the plans for the development of north China's industry (draft)" which was appended to the "Proposals and statements of opinion for the consideration of the future treatment of north China (an unfinished manuscript)" devised by Governor Matsuoka of Mantetsu while advisor to the Kwantung Army.[58] It called for the establishment in the five northern provinces of a joint five-province north China autonomous government that would be "anti-Comintern and pro-Japanese." Railroads were to be nationalized and "operated under the control and aid of Mantetsu." Further, "the planned development of important industries was to be carried out under the direction of Japan," and Mantetsu was to be "appointed to the most important role" in the development of basic industries. To promote the acquisition of capital, an imperial order guaranteed that the principal on Mantetsu bonds would yield five percent. Hsing Chung was to be active throughout all of China and to be made a "supporting organ for Mantetsu in north China." Attached to

[58] Both documents can be found in Nakamura Takafusa and Hara Akira, eds., *Nichi-Man zaisei keizai kenkyūkai shiryō* (Tokyo, 1970), vol. 2, pp. 19-35.

this was the "five-year plan" made up earlier by the preparatory committee for the continental economic conference.[59]

The daring proposals of this extremely frank scheme of August 1937 can be seen as Mantetsu's offensive plan, and as an indication of the extent of its expectations. Naturally, the response of the Japanese *zaikai* to these proposals was less than enthusiastic.

Hsing Chung Kung Ssu also could not remain silent. A proposal for organizational reform of Hsing Chung Kung Ssu put forward in September aimed to "accomplish the mission" of north China's economic development. Hsing Chung was to receive four advisors representing Mantetsu, the Bank of Japan, Mitsui, and Mitsubishi. They were to take over the trust management of railways and coal and iron mines seized by the military, build new railroads, and take an active part in the automotive industry, salt production, salt-using industries, and gold refining. In addition, Hsing Chung was to be the central regulator in important industries requiring coal such as iron, steel, and manufacturing. This proposal can be taken as a manifestation of its desire to present a countermeasure to Mantetsu's activities, but it also derived from self-confidence built upon the foundation of past experiences, such as having actually carried out trust management for the army during the war.

At the same time, hopes and expectations for the free penetration of north China under the control of the Japanese army were increasing within the Japanese *zaikai*. A typical example of this can be found in the proposal for a north China industrial enterprise union presented by the president of Tokyo Electric Lighting, Kobayashi Ichizō. According to Kobayashi's plan, the union would be financed through popular investment. War pensions and allowances would be paid to military personnel and war-effort-related individuals in national bonds, and these would be invested in the union, which would be formed with a capital of 100 million yen. For the industries trying for free penetration of north China, the union would invest half of the capital. By installing only a few directors from the union in the various industries, they would be able to exercise their power freely.[60] This was a clever expression of the aspirations of *zaikai* members who were making plans for free penetration.

Tsuda Shingo of Kanebō made the following statement: "I believe

[59] Ibid., pp. 36-39.
[60] Kobayashi Ichizō, "Hokushi keizai kensetsu suikō-an," in *Chūōkōron*, Dec. 1937, pp. 55-61.

that in the early stages of development we should make free economic activity our basic principle, rejecting monopolistic enterprise, and open north China to all industrialists, proceeding on the principle of survival of the fittest."[61] The north China problem investigative committee of the Osaka Chamber of Commerce similarly maintained that "in developing Chinese industry, those sectors important for national defense should be put under a licensing system through a fixed plan, and in the other industries the principle of controls should be rejected and the free investment of private capital should be promoted."[62] The above opinions were expressed by individuals connected to the Osaka *zaikai*, but the ideas in Tokyo were the same.

At the second meeting of the Bank of Japan's industrial discussion group, the opinion of the *zaikai* representatives was that "we should reject the principle of extreme controls in the management of north China, such as are seen in Manchukuo, and as much as possible respect the inventiveness of industry and naturally recognize their right to a profit. By rejecting the unified controls of one large controlling company, business should proceed within each industry, each with its own dangers and relying on its own enterprise."[63] The *zaikai* publicly opposed both the outsiders (Mantetsu and Hsing Chung Kung Ssu) and the plan for a State Policy Corporation. Its opposition was based in part on an optimistic view of the war situation and in part on an indulgent attitude toward the introduction of foreign capital (especially from Britain and the United States). There was enough power behind these opinions to make it impossible for the government and the military to ignore them.

THE FOUNDING OF THE NORTH CHINA DEVELOPMENT CORPORATION

In August 1937 the Japanese government established a new government office, the planning board, which was to deal with economic planning and controls, and other important policy matters. On November 2, they also set up a committee of the board to formulate policy for the Chinese economy and for coordination and adjustment among the various government offices.[64] After deciding to establish the federal bank, it took up the problem of economic development in north and central China. At that time the Japanese international balance of payments deficit was increasing, and the planning board made efforts to

---

[61] *Tokyo nichi nichi shinbun*, Nov. 26, 1937.
[62] Ibid., Dec. 9, 1937.   [63] Ibid., Dec. 3, 1937.
[64] Cabinet decision of Oct. 26, 1937.

keep 1938 imports at 300 million yen (1937 imports amounted to 370 million yen) and to create a plan for the distribution of goods. It was already difficult to apportion funds for large-scale investment in north China and there was difficulty in importing from abroad. Since this fact was well concealed, hopes for north China's development continued to rise. Thus, on December 16, the board committee decided upon the north China economic development plan, and on December 21, it became a cabinet decision.

The outline of the plan was as follows: First, the purpose of north China's development was to "strengthen weak points in the coordinated economic relationship between Japan and Manchukuo, and further to establish a foundation for a situation of coexistence and coprosperity among Japan, Manchukuo, and China." They also added the condition that "provision should be made to suit the international balance of payments situations of Japan, Manchukuo, and north China, and not to misjudge economic conditions, taking into consideration adjustments in the supply and demand of commodities."

Next came the "establishment of a State Policy Corporation for the purpose of developing and controlling the north China economy," with a clause saying it was to be organized in the spirit of "one-nation united," casually rejecting Mantetsu's and Hsing Chung's monopoly positions. This company was to handle "the management and regulation" of "major freight and transportation industries (including port facilities and railways), important communications and electric power industries, salt production, and salt-using manufacturing." These points illustrate the outline of the plan.

In addition, it is of interest to note that it mentioned the "use" of Chinese capital, the cooperation of Chinese industry, the "cooperative investment" of third countries, and the recognition of "the various existing rights and interests of the world powers." Further, two cabinet statements of understanding were attached. They stated that especially in the areas of transportation and communications they did not recognize the monopoly management of a single company throughout Manchukuo and north China, once again crushing the hopes of Mantetsu. However, in the second statement of understanding, detailed consideration was given to making the most of Mantetsu's and Manshū Denden's personnel, technology, and experience in transforming the transportation and communications industries.[65] (At the same time a plan for the development of the central China economy

[65] Cabinet decision of Dec. 21, 1937.

and later the establishment of a Central China Promotion Corporation was decided upon.)

Later in 1937 a plan for setting up the North China Development Corporation, in which the army's military affairs bureau played an important part, was investigated. This planning authority was given cabinet approval on March 15, with some revisions and clauses of understanding attached to the original proposal. It was established as a special corporation capitalized at 350 million yen, with conditions such as half government investment (of which 150 million yen was investment in kind), recognition of the right of preferred dividends for extra-governmental investment, and guarantee of profits for a ten-year period (for preferred stock, 6 percent).

It is significant, however, that severe restrictions were placed upon the actions of the corporation through the cabinet articles of understanding. First, consent was required for the methods of raising and using capital to be employed, in both the main corporation and the subsidiary corporations. Second, since the 1938 plan for the mobilization of goods could not be changed, it was decided that the commodities and foreign currency necessary for the operation of the corporation would be procured from "within those limits with skillful management of funds, through the cooperation of the various government agencies concerned."

International balance of payments crises severely restricted the activities of the corporation from the beginning, but this was kept secret, and the corporation increased in popularity. On April 30, at the seventy-third session of the Diet, the North China Development Corporation Law was passed, and on the same day the founding committee was appointed. Stock was floated in August. On November 7 the initial general meeting launched the corporation.

Meanwhile, in mid-December 1937, just before the north China economic development plan was decided upon, Governor Matsuoka entered into negotiations with the government over the "second plan." This second plan stated that "north China's railroads and undeveloped coal fields in distant areas connected by them" and "operations of a public nature such as harbors should be handled by the government." Instead, Mantetsu wanted to take them over and to entrust the operations of the ordinary industries to specialists.[66] As seen above, that too was flatly rejected by the government.

Even in May of 1938 Mantetsu had not yet abandoned its dream

[66] *Nikkan kōgyō shinbun*, Dec. 14, 1937.

of a "unified Manchurian-Chinese" transportation system. The Mantetsu board of directors, considering Mantetsu's investment in the North China Transportation Company, a subsidiary of North China Development Corporation, decided that in order to "realize the unified management of Manchurian-Chinese transportation" they would have to invest a larger amount in the company than did the corporation. North China Transportation's governor and vice-governor should be selected through the recommendation of the governor of Mantetsu. There would be an exchange of Japanese personnel between companies, and equipment standards for North China Transportation would be made to match Mantetsu's. Should these conditions not be met, Mantetsu would restrict its investment in North China Development and North China Transportation to equipment alone.[67] This proposed policy met opposition from a director in Tokyo and in the end was not implemented. But Mantetsu was extremely tenacious right up to the end. It seems, however, that it had already been decided that Hsing Chung Kung Ssu had carried out its purposes, and on September 12, 1938, the Japanese government planning committee adopted a dissolution plan that would transfer the operations, debts, and credits of the Hsing Chung Kung Ssu to North China Development and Central China Promotion. Upon settlement in October 1941 it was dissolved.

Meanwhile, it should also be noted that light industries, such as spinning and paper pulp, were excluded from the activities of North China Development Corporation; the demands for "free penetration" centered around the Osaka *zaikai* and the spinning industry finally bore fruit at the time the corporation was established.

Thus, on the surface there was the appearance of splendid cooperation between the army and the Japanese *zaikai* in the formation of North China Development Corporation. But, in fact, the Japanese economy was facing a crisis in its balance of payments, and the corporation began operations at an inauspicious time.

Conclusion

It is beyond the scope of this paper to consider the operations of North China Development Corporation after its founding. But I wish to conclude the essay with just one more point: the question of just

[67] South Manchuria Railway, "Showa 13-nen 5-gatsu 26-nichi juyaku kaigi-an" (1938).

how much of a gap there was between plan and reality in North China Development Corporation.

For the development of north China an ideal plan was proposed whereby the management of all its mining would be undertaken by one all-encompassing company. In practice, it was impossible to mix the personnel and capital of several enterprises, so they planned to divide it up among several companies (the plan for six), namely: Poshan-Liuch'uan, Chunghsing-Tawenk'ou, Chinghsing-Chenghung, Tz'uhsien-Liuhekou, T'aiyüan-P'ingk'ung, Tat'ung-Hsiahuayüan.[68] The respective companies were probably to center around Mitsui, Mitsubishi, Kaijima, Meiji, Ōkura, and Mantetsu.

This plan can be compared with the situation at the end of 1941 represented in Chart 2 (below).[69] Only Kaijima's Chinghsing-Chenghung and Mantetsu's Tat'ung-Hsiahuayüan were established as corporations. The others all ended up as small-scale partnership businesses. Those other than Kaijima and Mantetsu, from Mitsui and Mitsubishi on down, have to be seen as ready to flee. When actual profits were calculated, figures quite at odds with the temporary north China boom probably appeared. The plan for the North China Development Corporation ended like a goose that ruptures its belly trying to drink a flowing river dry.

[68] South Manchuria Railway, Research Bureau, *Hokushi tankō kaihatsu keikaku-an* (July 1940), pp. 7-11.
[69] See next two pages.

Chart 2. Summary of Coal Mining Companies
Involved in North China Development Corporation
(end of December 1940)

Name of Company	Stockholder	Shares Invested (one share = 50 yen)	Location
Tat'ung Coal Mining	Mongolian Federated Autonomous Government	400,000	near Changchiak'ou
	North China Development Corporation	200,000	Yuhung, Paochin, Paitung, and four other places
	Mantetsu	200,000	—
Chinghsing Mining	North China Development Corporation	180,000	Chinghsing, Chenghung
	Kaijima Mining	150,000	—
	North China Admin. Committee (successor to temporary gov't.)	270,000	Small mines along Shantung-Chiaochi railroad
Shantung Mining	Mantetsu	55,000	—
	Totaku, Mitsui Mining, Mitsubishi Mining, Okura Mining, etc.	5,000 to 7,000	—

Mining Area	Investor	Total Investment	Management
Hsing Chung	North China Development Corporation & Mitsui Mining	2,240,000 yen	Trust Management of Military Admin., Hsing Chung Mines
Liuch'uan	North China Development Corporation	600,000 yen	Trust Management of Military Admin., Liuch'uan
Tawenk'ou	North China Development Corporation & Mitsubishi Mining	980,000 yen	Trust Management of Military Admin., Tawenk'ou
Tz'uhsien	North China Development Corporation & Meiji Mining	1,080,000 yen	Trust Management of Military Admin., Tz'uhsien
Chiaotso	North China Development Corporation	1,050,000 yen	Trust Management of Military Admin., Chiaotso
Shansi	North China Development Corporation & Okura Mining	1,460,000 (N.C.D.) 1,000,000 (Okura)	Trust Management of Military Admin., 8 mines in Shansi

Source: North China Development Corporation, *Showa 15-nen Kita Shina Kaihatsu Kabushiki Kaisha kankei kaisha gaiyō* (1940).

CHAPTER XIII

Toward a New Cultural Order: the Hsin-min Hui

———

AKIRA IRIYE

Hsin-min chu-i, or the people's renovation movement, has long been consigned to obscurity, and today it is but a minor footnote in the tragic history of Sino-Japanese relations, 1937-1945. Yet at its inception, the movement and its parental organ, the Hsin-min Hui (the People's Renovation Society, hereafter abbreviated as HMH), had an enormous impact upon Chinese and Japanese officials and intellectuals. A movement which counted, according to Nanking's official estimates, 5,000 leaders and more than 3,643,000 members in 1944 cannot be simply dismissed.[1] Its brief history reveals a desperate attempt by Japanese and Chinese to weave the interests and traditions of the two countries together so as to present an acceptable ideology of Sino-Japanese collaboration. This essay will try to examine that ideology and provide some data on the activities of the HMH in order to fill a gap in our understanding of the war period.

"There has to be established a new cultural order" as a basis for the new order in East Asia, wrote Taniguchi Yoshihiko, a professor of economics at the Kyoto Imperial University in 1940.[2] The new order should not merely be a political and economic system, but should be rooted in religious, moral, philosophical, scientific, literary, ideological, artistic, and educational foundations. Only then could Japan be said to be constructing a truly alternative order to replace the hitherto dominant Western civilization. This was the starting point for Japanese officials and publicists as they began, after the outbreak of the Sino-Japanese War in 1937, to grope for a new formulation of

[1] Lü I-feng, *Hsin-min-hui yü hsin-kuo-min yün-tung* (Nanking, 1944), p. 22.
[2] Taniguchi Yoshihiko, *Tōa sōgōtai no genri* (Tokyo, 1940), p. 49.

international relations. Their statements and writings were filled with references to "new order," "new China," "new birth," "renovation," and "rejuvenation," reflecting their sense of freshness and excitement in what they assumed to be a momentous endeavor to create a new world.

References to the cultural basis of the new order derived from the awareness that Japan needed a fresh ideology to justify its action in China. Politics and culture, as so many writers noted, were no longer separate entities as they had been in the West. They must now be rejoined so as to foster a comprehensive outlook and a systematic movement to sustain the military efforts in China and to obtain the loyal cooperation of all Japanese. More fundamentally, it was of the utmost importance to create an ideology that would appeal to other peoples and serve to universalize Japanese action in China; it had to be viewed not as a selfish policy of aggression but as part of a noble effort to restructure world culture. As Fujisawa Chikao, professor at Daitō Bunka Gakuin who joined the staff of the HMH headquarters in Peiping, stated, Japan was identifying its destiny with the world's, and its policy was in accordance with the universal aspiration of mankind for a new cultural order.[3] The world was at a crossroads, where traditional Western principles and concepts such as commercialism, urbanism, liberalism, individualism, and legalism were giving way to yet undefined new forces. It was Japan's, and, in particular, Japanese intellectuals' task to define these forces clearly and construct a schematic approach to the problems of politics and culture.

Men like Taniguchi and Fujisawa were obscure publicists even then, but their writings were filled with ideas and generalities that were popularized by numerous distinguished scholars by the late 1930's. Their basic ideological framework was the view that capitalist civilization had failed in the West both to sustain perpetual economic growth and development, and to prevent selfish rivalries and competition among industrial countries. Writers ranging from Ozaki Hotsumi and Hirano Yoshitarō on the left to Kamei Kan'ichirō and Inoue Tetsujirō on the right, and including now forgotten men like Norimoto Yoshihiro and Ōtani Kōtarō, were virtually unanimous in asserting that industrial civilization had created in the West self-centered, atomistic societies that were deeply hostile to one another and constantly struggling against each other. Toward non-Western parts of

---

[3] Hsin-min-hui, *Shinminshugi ronshū* (Peiping, 1938), pp. 80-81.

the world, they had been exploitative and imperialistic, seeking to subordinate less developed areas to their capitalistic self-interests. There was no unifying principle except for individual greed, and no stability except for temporary arrangements among states to serve their expediencies.[4]

This type of critique of industrialism and capitalism had been commonplace in the West since the mid-nineteenth century, where writers from Karl Marx to Emil Durkheim had expounded upon the disequilibrating and disturbing side-effects of the rise of modern capitalism. Japanese ideologues, it would seem, added little or nothing at this level of criticism. In the 1930's, however, they persuaded themselves that everything that had been said about the inherent weaknesses of Western capitalism and industrialization had been proved right; the world economic crisis, with its huge unemployment, intense labor strife, and exclusive trade blocs, seemed to demonstrate the bankruptcy of the bourgeois civilization that had permeated the world and provided the basic structure of international relations. The once unquestioned supremacy of the West appeared to have ended. It would be foolish for other countries, least of all Japan, to assume otherwise and continue as if Western civilization were still the normative framework for politics and culture.

Thus reasoned, Japan's action seemed to have come at just the right moment in history. It could be viewed as part of the necessary task of rebuilding; as the world faced a severe economic and cultural crisis, Japan was taking the lead in proposing a clear-cut alternative to the discredited Western system of organizing national and international life. It was here that Japan could and should look to Asian tradition and elevate it to universal doctrine. As stated by Takigawa Seijirō, the legal scholar who became a professor at the Hsin-min Academy in Peiping, the international order to be established was founded on the negation of Western concepts and therefore must be based on the promotion of Asian cultural precepts.[5] According to Kawamura Munetsugu, an advisor to the HMH, Asian tradition espoused certain precepts of morality such as sincerity, integration, and

---

[4] See, among others, Ozaki Hotsumi, *Tōa minzoku ketsugō to gaikoku seiryoku* (Tokyo, 1941); Hirano Yoshitarō, *Dai Ajia shugi no rekishiteki Kiso* (Tokyo, 1945); Kamei Kan'ichirō, *Daitōa minzoku no michi* (Tokyo, 1941); Inoue Tetsujirō, "Shisō-jō yori mitaru Shina jihen," in *Shinminshugi ronshū*; Norimoto Yoshihiro, *Shina bunka zakkō* (Tokyo, 1943); Ōtani Kōtarō, *Shina kokuminsei to keizai seishin* (Tokyo, 1943); Uda Hisashi, *Tai-Shi Bunka Kōsaku sōan* (Tokyo, 1939).
[5] *Shinminshugi ronshū*, pp. 117-30.

organic unity, the exact opposite of the materialism, atomism, and individualism of the West.[6] Peace in Asian philosophy, Fujisawa wrote, was derived from a sense of harmony among men and between heaven and earth, not merely from a legally defined absence of war as in the West. Even Asia's economic development, which all these publicists admitted was necessary if the new order were to succeed, would be carried out without the kind of intense competition and rivalry that had been part of the history of the modern West. Asian countries would subordinate nationalistic egoism to the common interests of the entire region. This was possible because of Asia's tradition of close integration and unity. Asia was one, writers asserted, time and again citing the same passages from Okakura Tenshin, and this cultural unity ensured that economic development would not be accompanied by self-destructive individualism and nationalism.

Lest such anti-Western rhetoric should sound too much like Marxist attacks on bourgeois capitalism, Japanese writers hastened to add that communism was just as materialistic and artificial as liberalism, and that both were alike in their refusal to harmonize politics and culture, heaven and earth. As Fujisawa wrote, communism was only an extreme form of liberalism. Like the Western capitalist democracies, the Soviet Union and its allies in China and elsewhere were trying to perpetuate the rule of ruthless materialism and to incite Asians against one another so as to prevent the latter's inevitable union.

The rediscovery of Asian tradition enabled Japanese publicists to present the aggression in China as a creative step toward the reawakening of Asia. Asia was to be rejuvenated through the renovation of China under Japanese leadership. This seemed logical insofar as the two countries had in common a long cultural tradition. Japan was the repository of all Asian virtues, declared Takigawa, and was in an ideal position to help other Asian countries to preserve their indigenous civilization. China was closest to Japan, however, and so it was natural that these two should cooperate first in the joint endeavor of Asian rejuvenation.

Fortunately for Japanese propagandists, origins of the ideology of rejuvenation could be located in the Chinese classics, in particular *Ta Hsüeh*. Its opening passages referred to the ways of the ideal ruler, one of which was "hsin min," or to rejuvenate people, to awaken them to moral consciousness so that they would begin to lead a new life of virtue. Thus interpreted, the passage could be utilized as a

[6] Kawamura Munetsugu, *Tōhō seishin to Shinminkai* (Peiping, 1938).

principle of national reawakening. It was but a step from here to the gloss, repeated by numerous writers, that the Hsin-min principle was a call for people to forsake their past mistakes (characterized, of course, by liberalism, individualism, communism, etc.) and cooperate together to build a new society.

The Hsin-min Hui, established on December 24, 1937, was the institutional expression of the ideology of rejuvenation. It provided a specific institutional framework in which Japanese and Chinese could cooperate to promote their new ideas. In this sense it was the ideological arm of the Provisional government in Peiping that was inaugurated on December 14. This regime was a product of the Japanese army of occupation (the North China Area Army), and its special services unit under General Kita Seiichi was instrumental in the founding of the HMH. Thus from the beginning the society was clearly identified with the Japanese army as well as civilians in north China. Its central offices in Peiping were filled with Japanese functionaries, who occupied positions of influence in the Hsin-min Academy, the HMH's central executive office (chung-yang chih-tao pu) which was to issue guidelines for the operation of local branches, and in the central training institute (chung-yang hsün-lien so) which was designed to train young Japanese and Chinese as future leaders of the movement. Most of these Japanese were colonial parasitic types who wandered from place to place in occupied areas in search of lucrative appointments. According to Tamura Shinsaku, an *Asahi* correspondent, the HMH's initial leaders consisted mostly of Japanese who had either been in the employ of the Concordia Society in Manchukuo or connected with the Shanghai Tōa Dōbun Shoin.[7] They were an arrogant lot, Tamura writes, who pretended to know more about China than the Chinese themselves did. But this was also a trait characteristic of Japanese writers who stayed in Japan but wrote glowingly of the new movement. To them the HMH appeared intellectually and emotionally satisfying. They could visualize the movement as an instrument for universalizing Japanese imperialism by

---

[7] Tamura Shinsaku, *Miao Pin Kōsaku* (Tokyo, 1954), pp. 74-77; Nashimoto Yūhei, *Chūgoku no nakano Nihonjin* (Tokyo, 1958), vol. 1, p. 67. See also Aoe Shunjirō, *Dainihon gun senbukan* (Tokyo, 1970) for a discussion of the relationship between the HMH and Japanese propaganda officers attached to the North China Area Army. A rather sketchy but important Western report on the founding and activities of the HMH can be found in George E. Taylor, *The Struggle for North China* (New York, 1940). A more detailed study of the origin and the initial structure of the HMH is Hachimaki Keiko, "Chung-hua min-kuo hsin-min-hui no seiritsu to shoki kōsaku jōkyō," in Fujii Shōzō, ed., *1930-nendai Chūgoku no kenkyū* (Tokyo, 1975), pp. 349-94.

endowing it with historic and cultural import. For apologists of Japanese policy, here at last was a development that could point to the coming of a new age of Sino-Japanese cooperation. As one writer put it, the Sino-Japanese War was but a manifestation of Japan's attempt to promote the movement for Asian self-awakening. The Japanese were in China to help the Chinese "return to Asia" and rebuild their country free of either Anglo-American or Soviet influence. The Hsin-min principle was thus a renaissance movement designed to overcome the mistaken flirtation with the modern West and to realize traditional cultural ideals in contemporary China.[8]

These were self-serving ideas, but they were taken with utmost seriousness by the men who preached them. Their immediate need, then, was to find Chinese who would accept the renovationist ideology and cooperate in the Chinese renaissance. The task was not as difficult as it might appear in retrospect, because the Chinese personnel of the Provisional government and the HMH was often interchangeable. High government officials, including its successive heads, Wang K'o-min and Wang I-t'ang, became members, and each of them served as the society's honorary chairman. In addition, the HMH was able to recruit some dedicated Chinese, who loyally collaborated with Japanese officials to make the HMH appear a truly binational society, not a thinly disguised puppet organization.

That the HMH went as far as it did to establish its identity as a binational association was due to a great extent to the enthusiasm and dedication of a single Chinese, Miao Pin, head of the HMH's central executive office from its inception. Miao, born in 1889 in Kiangsu province, had been a prominent Kuomintang official, closely associated with Chiang Kai-shek when the latter founded the Whampoo Military Academy. He was active in the party's political and military affairs during the Northern Expedition, and became a member of the central executive committee in 1928. In 1931, however, he became estranged from Chiang during the constitutional crisis involving the latter's struggle with Hu Han-min, and left party affairs.[9] Not much is known about him until he found himself in the limelight in 1937, when he entered Peiping to help organize the Provisional government. He was one of those Chinese leaders who sought a middle way between resistance to and acquiescence in Japanese domination. He had been educated in Japan, and was widely read in Japanese

[8] Nakaya Takeya, "Tai-Shi bunka kōsaku no shomondai," in *Shinminshugi ronshū*.
[9] Tōa Mondai Chōsakai, *Saishin Shina yōjinden* (Osaka, 1941), p. 185.

history. Believing that the best chance for China's salvation lay in cooperation with Japan, he decided actively to support the founding of the HMH and to become its ideological leader.

Already in January 1938, barely a month after the founding of the HMH, Miao published a booklet entitled *Hsin-min chu-i* (The hsin-min principles) to lay an ideological foundation for the movement. "We must correct the mistakes of Western civilization which have brought about its degeneration," Miao asserted, and in order to do so Asians must turn to their indigenous civilization, in particular to the principle of the royal way (*wang-tao*). This principle had various specific aspects, according to Miao Pin. For instance, it would oppose the West's individualism and class struggles with Asia's traditional family ethic. National government should be conducted as an extension of family life, where all members respected each other and cooperated together to live in harmony. In the international sphere, nations would likewise harmonize their interests and realize the royal way, rather than engage in selfish power politics like Western countries. The hsin-min principles, according to this booklet, stressed a new system of government that was neither Western-style party politics, which had been tainted by capitalist corruption, nor a one-party dictatorship like that of the Soviet Union, Italy, Germany, or the Kuomintang. Instead, only those who were moral members of the family system would be qualified to rule. Thus heads of families would come together to elect a village head, and village heads would elect the head of their district, and so on till one reached the level of provincial leadership. Finally, from among the provincial governors, the head of the state would be chosen.

Industrialization, Miao Pin noted, was an important objective of the new movement. But it would not do to recreate the Western example of industrialism. Rather, machinery should be distributed to villages so as to increase agricultural productivity without destroying the rural community structure. Only such a system of rural development would serve to increase productivity. Miao specifically indicated in this connection that he was opposed to wholesale land redistribution. To the extent that land was to be redistributed, he would favor giving land only to those endowed with "morality." Finally, the booklet concluded by rejecting "narrow nationalism" and calling for a league of Japan, Manchukuo, and China as the foundation of a greater Asian league that would ultimately lead to the creation of a harmonious international community based on the royal way. Chiang

Kai-shek should have joined the movement, Miao wrote, but instead he had chosen to ally himself with the West and with the Communists. It was most fortunate, Miao concluded, that Japan had come to China's aid just at the right moment so that together they could contribute to the "restoration of Eastern culture."[10]

Miao Pin was to continue to harp on these themes until he left the HMH for Nanking in 1940. At the end of 1939 he became vice-president of the society, under the titular head, Wang I-t'ang. During 1938 and 1939, he distinguished himself as the ideological leader of the new movement. He wrote several more booklets and made numerous speeches, all dwelling on the importance of combating narrow nationalism and individualism with the traditional ideology of "harmony between heaven and man," and the spirit of "subordinating one's self to the service of the public."[11] Evidently, the whole theory was intended to justify collaboration with Japan. But this was the only road to national salvation and development, according to Miao, since Japan and China shared common roots and represented traditional virtues. It would not do simply to engage in anti-foreign agitation or to follow "the Westernized ideology of national revolution," Miao reiterated time and again, since by doing so the Chinese were forgetting their tradition and doing the West's bidding. "For the Chinese people their country must become the central influence in the building of the world," and this could only be the case if they worked closely with the Japanese.

Miao Pin was by no means the only Chinese propagandist for the HMH, however. From its inception the society was aided by numerous other Chinese who threw in their lot with the Peiping collaborators and actively participated in the movement. A 296-page collection of lectures by Chinese officers of the HMH, published in October 1938, contained numerous testimonials on the wisdom of Sino-Japanese collaboration. For example, Chang Yen-hsing, vice-president of the HMH, recounted how he had participated in the works of the Manchukuo government, and pointed to Manchukuo as a great example of a society with high cultural standards where people lived in security as they pursued their living. The fall of Hsuchow, Chang said, showed that Chiang Kai-shek was vulnerable and had lost the people's confidence. The Japanese victory should serve to consolidate

---

[10] Miao Pin, *Hsin-min chu-i* (Peiping, 1938).

[11] Hsin-min-hui, *Hsin-min chiang-yen chi* (Peiping, 1938), pp. 5-6; *Miao Pin hsien-sheng hsin-min chu-i chiang-yen chi* (Peiping, 1938), pp. 65ff.

Sino-Japanese ties, he declared. Another speaker said he had just returned from Japan, where he had been greatly impressed with the way
its people had retained the "Eastern spirit" of loyalty, courage, and
diligence, while the Chinese had lost it after the May Fourth Movement. This theme, that modern China after 1919 had become too
Westernized, fitted in very well with the HMH's attacks on Chinese
nationalism directed against Japanese aggression. It was as if Japan
had come to rescue China precisely at the moment when the latter
was losing all its self-identity, having turned its back upon tradition.
As another lecturer noted, now that China and Japan were cooperating in north China, Chinese intellectuals should return to the countryside and help restore traditional virtues and eradicate the pernicious
influence of communism and nationalism.[12]

The editor of the collection of these lectures was a man by the
name of Sung Chieh, who had the title of chairman of the education
department, central executive office, HMH. Apart from Miao Pin,
he was probably the most prolific writer and enthusiastic promoter of
the cause. His ideas were less philosophical than Miao's, and he was
a frank apologist for Japanese militarism and imperialism. In a pamphlet published in January 1938, for instance, he tried to justify
Japanese policy to a skeptical Chinese audience by using a number
of ingenuous arguments. After the Sian incident, Sung wrote, the
Kuomintang had allied itself with the Chinese Communists and
sacrificed the interests of the people. The Kuomintang's alleged
adherence to the principle of popular rights was a farce, and four
hundred million Chinese were just slaves, suffering from heavy taxes
and reactionary dictatorship. The Nationalists had pursued a policy
of befriending Russia, Britain, and America to spurn the sincere overtures of Japan. Fortunately for the Chinese, Sung remarked, the Japanese had now decided to come to their aid, since they themselves had
been unable to carry out necessary political reforms. Seen in this
light, the July 7 incident was similar to the attacks upon the Bastille,
the opening shot of the Chinese people's genuine revolutionary movement against the Kuomintang. Thus the new Provisional government was precisely what the mass of Chinese had wanted. The regime
was not a democracy, which would not work in a big country like
China, but a government based on the royal way. Since the masses
had been suffering so long from civil strife, unemployment, high
taxes, and reckless government spending, many of them had become

---

[12] *Hsin-min chiang-yen chi*, passim.

bandits and soldiers. The only hope lay in promoting their welfare through economic development and industrialization. China was rich in resources, but poor in capital and technology. These the Japanese could supply. China's industrial development called for new political and social organization, precisely what the Japanese had come to offer. Japan and China, moreover, were derived from common roots, they shared the same language and religion, and thus they were natural brothers. It was because the Nationalists and Communists had forgotten this basic truth and turned to America and Europe for help that the "unfortunate incident" of July 1937 had taken place. Now that a new page was turned in the history of their relations, Chinese and Japanese must cooperate together to fight against communism, to prevent the white race from dominating the entire world, and to effect China's industrial progress. If they did so, a second world war could never take place. Anglo-American ambitions as well as Russian machinations would be frustrated.[13]

It was to spread these ideas among Chinese in occupied areas in the northern provinces that efforts were made by the HMH to organize various activities and form numerous groups. In addition to various pamphlets and books, the Peiping headquarters published a number of periodicals, including a daily newspaper, a weekly, a bi-monthly, a monthly magazine, and a journal for youth. The HMH also made use of the radio, broadcasting a ten-minute lecture every morning, special twenty-minute lectures twice or three times a week during the evening, and a various assortment of Hsin-min songs and dramas. Hsin-min libraries and tea-houses were established in various communities, and propaganda films were presented. According to a 1940 report, HMH-sponsored movies were shown on fifty-eight occasions in the Peiping area, and were viewed by a total of 50,675 spectators.[14]

The main objective of the HMH, however, was educational: to train Chinese leaders who would be imbued with the spirit of the renovationist principle. Education was of utmost importance not only because of the need to combat the strong influence of nationalism and communism in the schools, but also because the school situation had been seriously disrupted after July 1937. In Hopeh province, for instance, there had been 28,503 primary schools in 1932, attended by over 1,152,000 pupils and taught by nearly 73,000 teachers. In 1940

---

[13] Sung Chieh, *Hsin-min-hui ta-kang shuo-ming* (Peiping, 1938).
[14] Kōain, *Hoku-Shi ni okeru bunkyō no genjō* (Peiping, 1941), p. 119.

there were only 8,273 schools, 328,800 pupils, and 15,700 teachers. Even in 1932 only 27 percent of the children of school age appeared to be attending school, but eight years later the figure was less than 5 percent. Obviously, something had to be done to restore and revitalize Chinese education if the Japanese occupation of north China was to succeed in its propaganda campaign. Accordingly, the Ministry of Education of the Provisional government promulgated a new educational decree in April 1938, establishing guidelines for the reestablishment of the school system. The stress was to be placed on eradicating pro-Kuomintang, pro-Communist, and anti-Japanese influences. For this purpose, textbooks were to be revised, separate curricula were to be worked out for girls, and teachers were to attend orientation meetings to "correct their mistaken ideas." Lecturers at these sessions were often provided by the HMH. In higher education, the Ministry of Education stressed the training of future leaders who would contribute to the creation of a new Asian order based on "the indigenous virtues of our country." The students were to be educated in the principles of anti-Communism, neighborly cooperation, the traditional family system, and strict discipline, to enable them to combat the evils of materialism and utilitarianism.[15] These were the same principles as those espoused by the HMH, a not very surprising coincidence given the overlap of personnel between "government and society." When, at the end of 1938, the China Development Board (Kōain) was established in Tokyo, its liaison office in Peiping took over the task of guiding Chinese educational policy.

Outside these regular schools and institutions of higher learning, the HMH established its own schools, aimed at educating Chinese of all ages and in all walks of life. Before 1937 such schools were called "people's schools," and were attended by young and old men and women who studied the Three People's Principles as well as practical subjects such as agricultural techniques and accounting. In Hopeh province there were 11,089 such schools in 1933. All these were closed down after the outbreak of the war, but some of them were reopened as Hsin-min schools. In 1939, 579 of them were in operation in Hopeh, and another 31 in the city of Peiping. Instead of the Three People's Principles, the students were taught the basics of reading and writing. In Peiping and various other cities, the Hsin-min schools were operated by the newly created Hsin-min educational associations (Hsin-min chiao-yü-kuan), of which there were 150 as of 1940. There

[15] Ibid., pp. 31-48, 73-75.

were four such associations in Peiping, each of which ran a school, held reading classes, showed movies, and operated a library, a teahouse, a nursery, a clinic, and various other facilities. According to information available on one such Hsin-min educational association in Peiping, it had a staff of twenty-four, and its school was attended by a total of forty students. About a thousand visitors a day came to view its exhibits. These were hardly impressive figures, but even these were considered important in spreading the message about Sino-Japanese cooperation and attracting Chinese interest in the educational and cultural opportunities presented by the new leadership.

In addition to such activities oriented toward ordinary Chinese, the HMH headquarters aimed at training a corps of its Chinese leaders. In 1938, for instance, the central executive office drew up an outline of activities in order to initiate an ideological counteroffensive against both communism and the Kuomintang. The HMH was to engage in an educational campaign to stress the return to Asia's indigenous culture and the idea of Asian unity with Japan as the stabilizing force. The ultimate objective, according to the outline, was the establishment of "a new Asian cultural system based on a novel world view." Whatever such abstract goals meant, the HMH would try to recruit adherents by opening special training sessions. One plan called for a three-month session, to be attended by thirty Chinese youths between the ages of seventeen and twenty-five, who would be introduced to the subtleties of the Hsin-min principles.[16]

A central training institute was opened in Peiping in accordance with these ideas. The institute was headed by Miao Pin. Under him served three Japanese: Itō Chiharu as executive director, Yokoyama Tetsuzō as director of training, and Yamamoto Shunji as secretary. In addition, there were four Japanese military training officers and thirteen Chinese officials, including Sung Chieh and Chu Hua. According to an October 1939 report, a total of eighty-two students were enrolled in the institute's six-month program. The success of the training course, as well as the intellectual caliber of the trainees, may be gauged from the collection of brief essays by some of them which was published upon their graduation. One student wrote on the royal way. Another argued that it was the mission of the Hsin-min youth to construct a new Asian culture, instead of succumbing to the "white terror" or "red terror," both of which were utilizing the Kuomintang to prolong China's resistance to Japan and increase

---

[16] Hsin-min-hui, *Kung-tso shih-liao*, no. 2 (Peiping, 1938), pp. 88-90.

people's suffering. Asia should be restored to its 530 million indigenous inhabitants who were heirs to a unique heritage. The youths of Japan, Manchukuo, and China, another writer asserted, must unite to promote the common welfare of the yellow race. Instead, young people in China had been too lax and indulgent, especially after the May Fourth Movement. Patriotism was important, but Chinese nationalists should realize that China belonged to Asia, and that in order to resurrect the nation they must ally themselves with Japan and rally under the flag of the great union of all yellow peoples. Still another student insisted that the only way to end the unfortunate war between the two countries, which was only benefiting Western countries, was to cooperate with Japan in the name of the Hsin-min principles. As noted in another essay, the war had been provoked by selfish Westerners so that they could fish in troubled waters; in fact, however, the "sacred war" had dealt a severe blow to the West and to its puppets, the Kuomintang and the Communists. Another writer speculated that the July 7 incident had been a Communist conspiracy, and one student added that if Japan were now destroyed, the hope of Manchukuo, China, and Siam for independence would be forever frustrated.[17]

In the meantime, local branches of the HMH were being set up in various communities and villages. Executive offices and training institutes were established at both the tao and hsien levels. (Theoretically, north China under Japanese occupation comprised five provinces: Hopeh, Shantung, Shansi, northern Honan, and northern Kiangsu, each of which was subdivided into tao, and each tao into hsien. The area under the jurisdiction of the Provisional government contained a total of 24 tao and 385 hsien.) Each hsien and each tao presumably had its HMH branch, carrying on educational, propaganda, and other activities under the direction of society officials dispatched from Peiping. To cite one example, in Wangtu hsien, Hopeh, the head of the district, Sun Yung-mo, decided as early as February 1938 to invite members of the central executive office to open a local branch. He felt that this was the best way to put an end to the state of lawlessness following July 7, and to persuade inhabitants to return to their homes to resume daily life. Unfortunately, Sun was kidnapped soon afterwards by rebellious district police, but in April a local HMH branch was set up, resulting in increased patrols by Japanese and Chinese forces, and local security was enhanced. The HMH im-

[17] Hsin-min-hui, *Chung-yang hsün-lien-so ti-erh-chi chi-nien ts'e* (Peiping, 1939).

mediately went to work to provide lectures to the residents, urging them to cooperate with the Japanese army against the evil Communists. It also established a youth training institute, a primary school, a tea-house, a club, a market, a hotel, and a "society for economic reconstruction." In 1939 the local HMH organized a cooperative to provide farming instruction, distribute seed, and extend loans to the community.[18]

The organization of the Wangtu HMH was similar to that in other districts. It was chaired by Chao Ju-yeh, a bureaucrat who had succeeded Sun as head of the hsien. Under him there was a Japanese director, a man who had worked for eight years in Manchuria. The head of the youth training institute was also a Japanese who had worked in Manchuria. These examples illustrate the way such Japanese shifted from one occupied area to another as semi-colonial administrators. But these two were the only Japanese staff members of this HMH, and they were assisted by thirty-one Chinese who held various offices ranging from accountant to driver. Three Chinese worked for the training institute, and four others were teachers at the HMH primary school. The former had been local police officers before 1937, and the latter school teachers. It would seem, therefore, that the HMH provided some sense of continuity as well as job security for local residents who chose to stay in an occupied area. The same was true of those who were appointed to various positions in the cooperative. They were almost invariably young men who had been minor bureaucrats in various localities before the war.

The youth training institutes were always given special emphasis by the HMH's central headquarters in Peiping. It was felt that only through educating and influencing the local youth, the majority of whom would be agrarian, could the society promote its goals and succeed in its objectives. Thus the central training institute established rather rigid directives for the curricula of local institutes. Each local center was to have two-month programs in which a small number of young people (not more than fifty) would be enrolled. They would live together and engage in identical activities. According to a blueprint worked out at Peiping, the trainees were to get up at five in the morning and spend the rest of the day alternating between learning academic subjects and working at agricultural and the dairy industry. Among academic subjects, topics to be discussed included provincial finance, hygienics, the Hsin-min principles, and Sino-Japanese-Man-

---

[18] Hsin-min-hui, *Ho-pei-sheng Wang-tu-hsien shih-ch'ing* (Peiping, 1939), passim.

chukuo relations. These latter topics would stress themes such as the moral foundations of nation-building, the spirit of self-sacrifice, anti-communism, coexistence and coprosperity, and the idea that "the country which best exemplifies the Eastern spirit and yet remains the most creative is Japan."[19] At Wangtu hsien these guidelines were duly observed, and the training institute opened its gates to the first group of thirty men on October 1. The students studied the academic subjects and learned techniques for improving crops and seed. They also cooperated with Japanese forces seeking to rid the community of Communist guerrillas, and served as guards and spies to smoke out subversive influences. When Hankow fell, they took the initiative in holding celebration rallies and calling upon Chiang Kai-shek to resign. For all this work they were rewarded with certificates upon graduation on December 1, and they toured Peiping to commemorate the occasion. These graduates then became members of the Hsin-min youth corps, and might go through additional years of training. A number of them, however, would go on to a tao-level training institute for a six-month session. The hope was that these men would in time emerge as reliable leaders of the movement and offer a viable alternative to both the Kuomintang and Communist leadership.

The Hsin-min school at Wangtu was at first a more modest affair. Designed to fill the educational void created by the war, the local HMH executive office opened a school in May 1938 with just one teacher. There were no textbooks, no desks and chairs, no building, and no teaching aids, and the forty-odd pupils sat on the floor to study the Hsin-min principles and sing Hsin-min songs. Eventually, the school expanded to include 120 pupils by March 1939, ranging from 32 first-graders to 24 fourth-graders, the highest grade at that time. Sixty-nine of these pupils came from farming families, and twenty-nine were children of merchants. A directive from the HMH office in Peiping stated that "local gentry" were fundamentally opposed to the interests of the masses but that they should be made use of in promoting the movement. It may be that most of the pupils at the school came from this class of people. Considering the fact that before the outbreak of the war there had been seventy-eight primary schools with 3,227 pupils in this hsien, the one HMH school with 120 pupils could take care of only a tiny fraction of the school-age population. In October 1938 the provincial government opened a primary school in Wangtu, accommodating the initial first-grade

[19] *Kung-tso shih-liao*, no. 2, pp. 12-42.

population of eighty. These two were the only primary schools as of
1939, and all other children of school age presumably stayed home.
Since even before 1937 less than 30 percent of them could be assumed
to have attended school regularly, the situation after 1939 was
tanamount to educational chaos. It would seem that the HMH should
have done much more to improve the situation. At any rate, here was
a good example of the top-heavy nature of HMH activities. The
organization had a fairly well-defined central structure and a sizable
local personnel, but it was totally inadequate with regard to primary
education.

At Wangtu and elsewhere, however, rural cooperatives seem to
have made greater headway. In order to demonstrate the practical
benefits of the society, the HMH established a hsien cooperative with
branches in the local villages. By 1939 forty-eight villages within the
hsien had such branches, joined by 1,716 members. The cooperative
extended loans to them (totaling 15,000 yüan), and helped them
with improving seed, crops, and agricultural implements. Nine officials, all Chinese, staffed the hsien cooperative office, and also visited
local branches to give guidance to their members. Three of these
leaders, all of them nineteen years old, had had their initial training
at the youth training institute before coming to work for the cooperative, while another was a graduate of the Peiping training institute.
The two institutions were related in that the trainees from the hsien
training institute were periodically required to visit villages to give
lectures to cooperative members. The hope was that these young men
would eventually become leaders of the cooperative, thus contributing to economic improvement as well as political stability in the
region.

It is impossible to ascertain how effective the HMH was in influencing Chinese opinion and turning the Chinese toward cooperation, active or passive, with the Japanese army of occupation. In the
final analysis, of course, all such propaganda would mean far less than
the actual behavior of Japanese in north China. Nevertheless, there
is evidence that aspects of HMH ideology did penetrate the minds
of some Chinese leaders outside north China. During 1938-1940 an
increasing number of them began writing and speaking out on Sino-
Japanese relations, and some of them, who could never be accused of
simply being Japanese puppets, came to echo certain ideas of the
HMH. Chou Hua-jen, for instance, wrote in 1939 that there was a
philosophical foundation to pan-Asianism, going back to the teachings

of Confucius and Mencius. By returning to that tradition, Asia could be liberated from the domination of the West, a condition prerequisite to China's own freedom and independence. The Sino-Japanese War was a most unfortunate interlude, but it had made men realize the crucial truths of Asianism. Only by accepting the principles of greater Asianism, could the two countries come to peace and jointly help restore Asia's greatness.[20] Similarly, T'eng Tu-ch'ing demonstrated that China and Japan had so much in common: just as Japan had borrowed its institutions from China, the new, reconstructed China would learn from Japan's modern achievements, and together they would contribute to the making of a new Asia. The theme that Chinese civilization had laid the basis for Japan's development was picked up by many other authors, who justified the idea of Sino-Japanese cooperation as historically rooted and therefore inevitable. Japan, which had owed such a lot to China, was now offering to help the benefactor. The two could cooperate to build a new China, and on that basis a new Asia would arise. The stress on cultural heritage common to the two countries was designed to show their shared interest in reducing Western influence. This was particularly important, Chang Lü-shan argued, because the Western powers were intent on dividing the colored races of the world so as to perpetuate their domination over them. It was incumbent upon the Chinese, therefore, to thwart the West and cooperate actively with Japan for Asia's liberation.

It is evident that these were mostly ideas contained in the Hsin-min principles. It would be difficult to establish an exact sequence in which HMH-sponsored ideas came first and then influenced Chinese outside north China. After all, Sun Yat-sen had articulated his pan-Asianist theme in 1924, a fact which virtually every writer on Sino-Japanese relations after 1937 stressed. Nevertheless, it seems plausible to argue that the intensive HMH propaganda campaign served to propagate certain concepts among Chinese who were not inclined to follow the lead of either the Kuomintang or the Communists. During 1937-1940, the Hsin-min principles gave them what appeared to be an acceptable ideological framework, sufficiently flexible to enable them to appear both patriotic and desirous of peace. They could justify their stand on the basis of tradition, and could also appeal

---

[20] Kōain, *Shina minkan ni rufu saruru Shina shidō genri* (n.p., 1940), pp. 13-15. Other examples in this paragraph are also taken from this booklet, a collection of Chinese articles on Sino-Japanese relations.

to shared perceptions of Western imperialism and white domination. By harping on these themes, and by reiterating notions of the common destiny of Chinese and Japanese to rebuild a peaceful, liberated, and harmonious Asia, Chinese writers undoubtedly hoped to influence Japanese as well as Chinese policy. As several writers put it, Japan should persist in the true spirit of great Asianism to establish a really coprosperous sphere of equality and peace, instead of subverting the spirit to serve its own selfish ends. Should that happen, Japan would be no less imperialistic than Western powers. Chinese writers thus could make use of the Hsin-min principles to remind the Japanese to be true to their words.

Events in 1940 did seem encouraging from such a point of view. Although, as John Hunter Boyle's detailed study has demonstrated, the inauguration of Wang Ching-wei's Nanking regime was a fiasco if for no other reason than that the Japanese leaders themselves did not take it very seriously, there was at least the possibility that the creation of such a regime might tend to lessen Japan's military hold upon occupied China and restore a sense of stability and orderly life in the area. The HMH's ideal of harmonious cooperation between the two countries, it may have been hoped by Wang's Chinese followers, might now be applied outside north China and become the basis for a new central government of the country. As Wang Ching-wei asserted in January 1940, China and Japan both aimed at eradication of communism and imperialism from Asia. China must turn to Japan for help because the latter was stronger militarily and economically. At the same time, Japan should realize that there could be true cooperation only if China were given the freedom to achieve its full potentials and share the responsibility for their common struggle. As Asia's one advanced nation, Japan must help an undeveloped country like China. But help should not take the form of interference.[21] Such ideas became official doctrine of the Nanking government. Its essentials were little different from the Hsin-min principles. As the propaganda department of the Nanking government put it in one of its earliest publications, "Cooperation on the basis of equality between the Chinese and Japanese peoples must take the form of great Asianism. This is the spirit of the royal way, and it seeks the principles of benevolence, sincerity, and morality." It was to be hoped that the new Asianism would so define Japanese policy that it would actively promote China's struggle for independence.[22]

[21] Ibid., pp. 29-31.   [22] Ibid., p. 32.

In theory, at least, the establishment of the Nanking regime could have led to the extension of Hsin-min doctrine beyond north China. HMH activities, to be sure, were not immediately launched in the Nanking-controlled areas. Wang Ching-wei preferred to regard himself as the direct heir of Sun Yat-sen, and Nanking as the legitimate seat of the Kuomintang. From his point of view there was no need for another politico-ideological organization. Peiping's HMH leaders, on their part, tended to be jealous of their prerogatives and fought against an extension of Nanking's authority to the north. Eventually, however, closer ties developed between the two segments of occupied China. Miao Pin left Peiping to work for Wang Ching-wei's government, and the latter made trips north to address HMH meetings. Contact between the two regions became even closer after December 1941. For three years December 8 would be celebrated throughout occupied China, and appropriate speeches would be made by HMH and Nanking authorities.

In 1943 the HMH established a branch in Nanking, with Wang as honorary chairman and Ying T'ung as vice-chairman. The society came to be seen as an integral part of Wang Ching-wei's Hsin Kuo-min (the new people's) movement. According to a 1944 publication of Nanking's Central News Agency, the HMH was the only organ in north China designed to provide a channel of communication between government and people, and was thus identical in character to the Hsin Kuo-min movement. Both aimed at serving the state through love of Asia, respect for morality, and observance of discipline. The two movements, the pamphlet pointed out, must unite to "reawaken China and carry out the great Asianist principle of the Founder of the Nation."[23] They would mobilize the masses to engage in purification campaigns to rid the country of Communists, anti-Japanese factions, and pernicious drugs (opium). These activities were actually sufficiently extensive that Chungking authorities took note of them in their propaganda statements. In 1944 they credited the HMH with having mobilized innocent masses, and accused the society of deceiving unsuspecting people.[24]

[23] Lü, *Hsin-min-hui*, preface. See also the essays in a collection edited and published by Nanking's propaganda department, *Ta-tung-Ya chan-cheng yen-lun chi* (Nanking, 1942), some of which explicitly equate the Hsin Kuo-min movement with the HMH. According to them, the HMH had now become part of China's heroic struggle for freedom from Western domination.

[24] Li Ch'ao-ying, *Wei-tsu-chih cheng-chih ching-chi kai-k'uang* (Chungking, 1944), pp. 29-38.

The inauguration of the Nanking government also brought about a greater emphasis on Chinese initiatives in the administration of non-Kuomintang and non-Communist areas. As Chinese leaders of the Hsin-min movement gained experience and self-confidence, they tried to take over control of HMH activities from the Japanese. Disputes and mutual recriminations between Chinese and Japanese became more and more frequent until, in 1943, most administrative functions of the HMH were transferred to the Chinese. Japanese officers of the society either resigned or were forced to give up their sinecures, to be replaced by over 5,000 Chinese. Only a small number of Japanese remained as advisors, causing the more disgruntled among them to create a Hsing-hsin Hui (society for the revival of the Hsin-min Hui).[25] But Japanese withdrawal from the HMH was part of the "new China strategy," designed to let the Chinese administer their own affairs while the Japanese concentrated on preserving law and order. This was a reflection of the increasingly desperate war situation in the Pacific, necessitating the diversion of Japanese manpower and resources to the South Seas.[26]

It would be illuminating to know what these 5,000 Chinese leaders of the HMH did after 1943. Unfortunately, there is little specific information. Almost all articles in HMH publications were now written by Chinese, and their rhetoric continued to emphasize the need for building a new nation on the basis of Asian liberation. Upon Japan's defeat, some of the erstwhile HMH leaders undoubtedly were arrested and executed, as was Miao Pin, whose last-minute efforts to bring about a reconciliation between Tokyo and Chungking had ended in failure. Other Chinese officials of the HMH may have gone through self-recanting transformations, as did so many of Japan's wartime pan-Asianists. The activities of both Chinese and Japanese members of the HMH were, in the final analysis, but an obscure interlude in the larger drama of China's struggle for independence. Nevertheless, one should not be too harsh in condemning their ideas as self-serving, servile rhetoric. If an anti-Western, pan-Asianist sentiment was a potent force in China's, as well as Japan's, modern history, affecting Kuomintang no less than collaborationist ideology, then the HMH was perhaps the most dramatic

[25] Far Eastern Bureau, British Ministry of Information, New Delhi, "Chinese Translation Series," no. 34, October 13, 1943.
[26] Defence Agency, ed., *Hoku-Shi no chian-sen* (Tokyo, 1958), vol. 2, pp. 313-17.

exemplification of its promise and its inherent contradictions. This was where the modern history of the two countries touched ideologically, and the nature of that encounter seems to hold important clues to understanding the tragic interactions between China and Japan in this century.

CHAPTER XIV

FACETS OF AN AMBIVALENT RELATIONSHIP: SMUGGLING, PUPPETS, AND ATROCITIES DURING THE WAR, 1937-1945

LLOYD E. EASTMAN

MUCH HAS been written about the surge of Chinese nationalism resulting from the Japanese invasion in the 1930's and 1940's. Often we are left with the impression that China and the Chinese were transformed by a deep and irreconcilable hatred of the aggressor. But Chinese reactions to the Japanese invasion were not of one piece. It is true that some elements in society—most notably the intellectual class—had become strongly nationalistic. In several areas of Chinese life, however, there was an astonishing degree of peaceful interaction with the "enemy." The sentiments of Chinese and Japanese toward each other during the war were in fact highly ambivalent. This was evident, for example, in Wang Ching-wei's collaborationist government in Nanking and in Chiang Kai-shek's frequent dallying in peace negotiations with the Japanese. Ambivalence was also evident in the more mundane, but no less significant, spheres of commercial intercourse, military puppetry, and day-to-day relations between the Japanese army and Chinese civilians.

THE "FRONT" that divided Japanese-occupied from unoccupied China was largely illusory. From Shansi in the north to Kwangtung in the south, it ran for well over 2,000 miles. Patently, neither side could guard every foot, or even every mile of the boundary. The front was therefore highly porous, permitting a more or less steady flow of people and goods from the side of one belligerent to the other. Postal service, for example, was maintained between the two areas virtually without interruption throughout the war.[1] All hotels in Wan-hsien, on the upper course of the Yangtze, had "travel agents" to assist persons in the Nationalist area to reach Japanese-held Hankow. And students, businessmen, and families of Chungking officials were able throughout the war years to reach the interior from the Japanese-held coastal cities. There were no regular schedules for these trips, of course, but the ingenuity required and the inconveniences encountered in passing from one side to the other were never great.[2]

The largest and most significant traffic between the two areas was commercial. Millions of men engaged in trade, and goods as diverse as tungsten and toothpaste, sheeps' wool and vacuum bottles, timber and cigarettes, automobile tires and opium, passed from one side of the front to the other. This trade was usually termed "smuggling." Yet it was frequently carried on openly, and import and export duties were imposed much as in the trade between the United States and Canada. The term smuggling, therefore, obscured the actual character of the exceedingly complex and frequently changing relationship.

During the initial stage of the war, both the Chinese and Japanese proscribed any commercial relations with each other. As early as September 1937, the Japanese declared a total blockade of all Nationalist ports.[3] The next month the Nationalist government—responding to a surge of anti-Japanese feeling, which in the past had frequently resulted in popular boycotts of foreign goods—decreed a complete ban on trade with Japanese persons, with Japanese-held areas, or in Japanese-made products. Despite these official policies, goods in considerable quantities flowed from one area to the other. During this phase of the war, all such trade was illicit and therefore quite properly regarded as smuggling.[4]

By 1939, the Nationalist government, now driven back into the

[1] Interview with Paul K. T. Sih, Urbana, Illinois, May 1976; Gerald F. Winfield, *China: The Land and The People* (New York, 1948), p. 219.

[2] OSS (Office of Strategic Services), doc. C: China 2.3-c, "Trade between Occupied China and Free China," June 16, 1942, p. 2 (Office of War Information, Box 397); William L. Tung, *Revolutionary China: A Personal Account, 1926-1949* (New York, 1973), pp. 222-23; State Dept., doc. 893.00/15019, Atcheson to State, June 20, 1943, encl., p. 1; *Foreign Relations of the United States, 1943*, China (Washington, 1957), pp. 229 and 435 (hereafter cited as *FRUS*).

[3] *Shina kōsenryoku chōsa hōkoku*, prepared by Minami Mantetsudo chōsabu (Tokyo, 1970, reprint of 1940 ed.), p. 277.

[4] T'an Hsi-hung, ed., *K'ang-chan shih-ch'i chih Chung-kuo ching-chi* (Hong Kong, 1968, reprint of 1948 ed.), vol. 2, p. 572.

mountainous and economically primitive provinces of west China, had begun to suffer the consequences of its economic isolation. Demands for consumer goods mounted inexorably, helping to generate danger-ous inflationary pressures. Essentially cut off from sources of supply in the outside world, and with its own productive capacities unequal to the demands, the Chungking authorities sought relief from the only available source: occupied China. In July 1939, therefore, Chung-king lifted the ban on all but 168 (reduced in 1942 to 103) import commodities "irrespective of their places of origin"—a Nationalist euphemism meaning "from Japanese-held areas." Not only did the Nationalist government tolerate this trade; it actively encouraged it. Official and semiofficial government agencies carried on much of it. To stimulate this commercial activity, the government cut import duties to one-third of the prewar rates, promised financial aid to traders, and in 1944 even reduced rail-freight charges by 15 percent on all commercial imports from the occupied areas.[5]

Just as it did all other foreign commerce, Chungking taxed the import and export trade with the occupied areas. Tax evasion was, however, a major and continuing problem during the war years. To combat it, the Smuggling Prevention Bureau, headed by the chief of the military secret service, General Tai Li, employed over 60,000 men.[6]

On the Nationalist side, the trade with the occupied areas was complex, some of it being legal and some being illegal. The Japanese side, officially at least, was free of such complications, for the Japanese authorities throughout the war maintained and reaffirmed their policy of total economic blockade of the Nationalist areas. In fact, however, implementation of this policy was beyond their capabilities. From the very beginning, therefore, the Japanese blockade was pragmat-

---

[5] *China Handbook, 1937-1945*, comp. Chinese Ministry of Information (New York, 1947), p. 421; *FRUS, 1943*, pp. 435-36; *FRUS, 1944*, pp. 138-39; She I, "Tai Yü-nung te i-feng ch'in-pi-hsin," *Ch'un-ch'iu*, vol. 110 (Feb. 1, 1962), p. 5; Chang Kia-ngau, *The Inflationary Spiral: The Experience in China, 1939-1950* (Cambridge, Mass., 1958), p. 327; OSS, doc. C: China 2.1, "A Fortnightly Letter on Economic Conditions in China," issued by the Foreign Dept. Head Office, Bank of China, no. 47 (June 16, 1944), p. 8 (Office of War Information, Box 397). The organization and activities of the Nationalist agency chiefly responsible for trading with the Japanese occupied areas, the Commodity Transport Control Bureau, are discussed in Ch'iao Chia-ts'ai, *T'ieh-hsüeh ching-chung chuan* (Taipei, 1978), pp. 399-401.

[6] Yang Ming-t'ang, *Ts'ung wu-ming ying-hsiung tao yu-ming ying-hsiung: Tai Yü-nung hsien-sheng te fen-tou li-ch'eng* (Taipei, 1976), pp. 57-60; Ch'en Kung-shu, *Lan-i-she nei-mu* (Shanghai, 1942), pp. 14-15; OSS, "A Fortnightly Letter," no. 47, pp. 8-9.

ically selective, focusing primarily on obstructing trade that would contribute to the Nationalists' war effort.[7] Soon after the war began, many Japanese authorities shut their eyes to all forms of the trade or even participated actively in it.

Early in the war, with commercial networks in north and central China thoroughly disrupted by fighting, the leading entrepot for goods destined for the Nationalist areas was Hong Kong. Other major cracks in the blockade at this time were French Indochina, Macao, and the port of Kwangchowan. With the Japanese seizure of Canton in October 1938 and of Nanning in Kwangsi in November 1939, the trade routes in south China became constricted. Activity thereupon shifted to ports in Chekiang and Fukien that had not fallen into Japanese hands. In 1939, for instance, fully 55 percent of the cloth manufactured for export in Shanghai—which was the chief supplier of goods traded to the Nationalist area—were shipped through Ningpo, Wenchow, and Foochow. Lei-chou and Pei-hai (Pakhoi) in Kwangtung were other major ports of entry, accounting for nearly 23 percent of unoccupied China's imported cloth. Only 10 percent of its imported cloth was shipped into the Nationalist area by way of the upper Yangtze route.[8]

Gradually, as the fighting stalemated after late 1939, trading operations became more generalized, being conducted in wholesale proportions from north to south. The volume of trade with the occupied area is, however, impossible to determine with any precision. Estimates varied wildly. In 1940, for example, the Nationalist government estimated it to be worth Ch$400 million (about US$21 million). The United States' Office of Strategic Services the same year reported its value at roughly Ch$2,280 million (about US$120 million).[9] (The explanation for this discrepancy is presumably that the former counted only legitimate transactions, whereas the latter probably included the illegal trade as well.) In 1941, the amount of trade was probably even greater. Each month, an average of 20,000 tons of goods was brought in just from Hong Kong, Macao, and Kwangchowan—approximately twice the tonnage being carried over the Burma Road. At the same time, "large quantities" of cars, trucks, tires, tools, gasoline, etc., were

[7] *Shina kōsenryoku*, p. 350; Israel Epstein, "Japanese Goods in Free China," *Asia* (Sept. 1941), p. 502.
[8] *Shina kōsenryoku*, pp. 333-39. Percentages are calculated from table in ibid., p. 337.
[9] Hubert Freyn, *Free China's New Deal* (New York, 1943), p. 73; and OSS, "Trade between Occupied China and Free China," p. 1.

shipped in from Shanghai and Hong Kong by way of Ningpo and Wenchow. And sizable amounts of less bulky consumer goods, such as textiles, pins, needles, buttons, medicines, enamel dishes, and soap, seeped through the porous borders in north and central China.[10]

Although accurate aggregate data on this trade is unavailable, the impact on the consumer in the Nationalist areas was clearly substantial. Shop shelves in 1940 and 1941 were reportedly crowded with items from the Japanese-held areas. One estimate, which is so high it appears improbable, stated that fully 70 percent of retail goods were from the occupied areas.[11] But Evans F. Carlson, then a Marine Corps major, also reported after a tour of east China that stores from Chekiang to Kweichow were "filled" with Japanese goods. Residents of Chungking and Sian throughout the war purchased toothpaste, soap, and similar things originating in occupied China, because they were of much higher quality than the locally produced brands.[12]

During the later stages of the war, the volume of these imports decreased. In 1943, the value of *legal* imports from occupied China amounted to only US$22.7 million, and declined further to a minuscule US$6 million in 1944. The continued importance of the trade is suggested, however, by the fact that these figures represented, respectively, fully 46.5 percent and 34.6 percent of Nationalist China's total legal imports in those two years—a reflection of the extreme economic isolation of this area late in the war.[13] Moreover, the size of the illegal trade, which in those years had presumably grown, is unknown.

This trade with the occupied areas, both licit and illicit, became virtually institutionalized. At the city of Shang-ch'iu, in northeast Honan on the Lung-Hai Railroad, for example, Chinese shippers in 1940 paid a fee of 4 percent *ad valorem* to the Japanese at the train station. Then the merchandise was brought into the city some five miles away, and at night was transhipped across the Nationalist lines, three to four miles from the city, to the Chinese customs station

[10] OSS, "Trade between Occupied China and Free China," p. 1.

[11] Hugh Deane, "Scarcity Breeds Repression: China's Economic Problem," *Amerasia* 5.6 (Aug. 1941), p. 251.

[12] State Dept., doc. 893.00/14631, encl. 1, Carlson to Hornbeck, Dec. 19, 1940, p. 2; and interviews with former residents of Chungking

[13] Yu-Kwei Cheng, *Foreign Trade and Industrial Development of China* (Washington, D.C., 1956), pp. 148-49. The figures cited are for goods from Japan and Germany. Because the flow of Axis goods from Europe was doubtless small, the German goods had presumably been stored in Chinese coastal cities since the early period of the China war.

at Kaishoutsi. Upon payment of a 10 percent tariff there, the goods were distributed freely to Loyang, Sian, and other Nationalist-held markets in north China.[14]

In south China, to cite another example, Sha-p'ing was a major trading center. Sha-p'ing lay on the south bank of the Pearl River, just thirty-five miles from the city of Canton. A mere village when the war erupted, by 1943 it had grown to a town of over 20,000 inhabitants, most of whom were traders or persons who served the traders: hoteliers, restaurateurs, bankers, or customs officials. The imports that were shipped into Sha-p'ing by boat, or on the backs of coolies from Canton, had typically originated in Shanghai. Cotton goods and cotton yarn, sorely needed in the Nationalist areas, made up approximately half the imports. Other imported products included electrical supplies, paper, carpentry tools and nails, Japanese-made medicines, rubber shoe-soles, chemicals (bleaching powder, ammonium carbonate, caustic soda, and phosphorous). In return, the Chinese sent to the Japanese-held areas food (rice, bean cake, vegetable oils), which eased the Japanese burden of feeding the residents of Canton, and raw materials such as wood and tung oil, hemp, mercury, and copper for Japanese industry.[15] One of the important exports here and elsewhere in south China was tungsten, used in the manufacturing of steel. Nationalist officials discounted this trade, asserting that no more than two to three hundred tons of tungsten were smuggled to the Japanese areas each year; unofficial estimates, however, indicated that the actual amounts exported were much larger.[16]

At Sha-p'ing, the Nationalist government maintained a branch of the Chinese Maritime Customs Service, an office to collect the consumption tax, and a special surtax bureau. Also in Sha-p'ing and at several points along the transportation lines in the area, the Chinese army maintained inspection stations. The ostensible purpose of these outposts was to impede smuggling of unauthorized or untaxed commodities to the Japanese, but the guards connived at the illicit trade, and the smuggling continued. The Japanese, too, condoned the traffic. Three times they raided Sha-p'ing, for it was practically defenseless. Each time, however, the Japanese troops withdrew, and the trade continued almost without interruption.[17]

[14] State Dept., doc. 893.00/14641, encl., Davis to Johnson, Oct. 31, 1940, p. 4.
[15] State Dept., doc. 893.00/15275, Ringwalt to State, Feb. 10, 1944; FRUS, 1944, pp. 138-39.
[16] FRUS, 1943, p. 659; OSS, doc. 52918, "Smuggling between Free and Occupied China," Nov. 30, 1943, attach. 1e, p. 1, and attach. 1i.
[17] State Dept., doc. 893.00/15275, Ringwalt to State, Feb. 10, 1944, pp. 2-3.

Farther north along the coast, in Fukien and Chekiang, large-scale trading continued despite the Japanese occupation of Ningpo and other major ports in the spring of 1941. In 1943, some 300 to 500 large junks were engaged full-time in the trade between the Japanese-held ports (such as Shanghai) and the current centers of ingress to Nationalist territory (such as Futsing and Chuanchow, south of Foochow). These carried approximately 3,000 tons of rice to the Japanese areas each month; "enormous quantities" of timber were exported (one shipment, intercepted by Nationalist forces, carried over 26,000 poles); vegetable tallow, pig bristles, wood oil, and leather were other items of export. Imports to Nationalist territory consisted largely of cotton and silk goods, medicines, and opium.[18]

This trade in Fukien and Chekiang was, on the Japanese side, controlled largely by Chinese acting as agents for the Japanese. They collected a tax on all goods, and also exacted a passport fee from the traders. Bribes to Japanese marines also had to be paid. On the Chinese side, the legitimate trade was taxed by the Customs Service. In 1943, however, the Chinese tariff was increased by the imposition of a 25% *ad valorem* consumption tax, and this pressured much of the otherwise legitimate trade into the smuggling routes. As a result, some of the largest shipments in this area were illegal, accompanied by Nationalist soldiers who were as concerned to protect the cargoes from customs officials as from bandits.[19]

This involvement of military personnel in the trade with the occupied areas was evident all along the front. In Yunnan there was a regular trade, often carried on in army trucks, with the Japanese in Indochina and Burma. Stores in Kunming, as a result, were well stocked with Japanese beer, cigarettes, cotton goods, and even Japanese gasoline (Kunming was also plentifully supplied with non-Japanese imports brought, usually illegally, over the Burma Road). Some of these army units in Yunnan even purchased their rice rations from the Japanese-held area. Indeed, when their monthly rations did not arrive in January 1943, the Chinese commanders complained loudly to the Japanese, who quickly dispatched the rice by special boat.[20] In payment for the rice, the Chinese army sent vegetables it had grown, or—according to unconfirmed but credible reports—Red Cross

---

[18] OSS, doc. 52918, "Smuggling," attach. 1d, pp. 1-3; State Dept., doc. 893.00/15300, encl., Feb. 26, 1944, "General Report on Fukien Province," pp. 5-7.

[19] Same as note 18.

[20] *FRUS, 1943*, p. 28.

supplies of quinine, sulfa, and aspirin, which in the Nationalist areas were in grievously short supply.[21]

After five or six years of desultory warfare, Chinese officers at virtually all levels of command were engaged in the traffic. T'ang En-po, a favorite of Chiang Kai-shek and deputy commander of the First War Zone in Honan-Anhui was allegedly reprimanded by General Tai Li for devoting too much attention to commerce and neglecting his military responsibilities. In Yunnan, "officers of all ranks," including generals, participated in the trade, which "rapidly became more important and certainly more lucrative than their regular occupations." In Honan in 1943, the "great majority" of officers were involved in trading; and, the same year, John Paton Davies reported that in Hunan Chinese commanders had "settled down with their wives and families and gone into trade."[22]

That this kind of commercial involvement enervated the Nationalist army's commitment to their military duties is shown in particular detail in the case of General Yü Han-mou, commander of the Chinese forces in Kwangtung. Yü had a special interest in the operations of the coal mines near Hua-hsien, adjacent to the Japanese-held area. In March 1944, his representative negotiated a verbal agreement in Hong Kong with Japanese army representatives, whereby Yü promised not to attack Canton, and the Japanese promised not to attack Yü's coal mines or other areas under his control. The agreement further provided that Yü would ship coal and tungsten to Canton, and the Japanese would consign cloth, yarn, and other consumption goods to Yü's area. Subsequently, according to the postwar testimony of Japanese officers, Yü fulfilled his side of this bargain when he disobeyed Chiang Kai-shek's orders and refused to attack Canton.[23] Not always did the Nationalist army units conclude such formal agreements with the Japanese, but the results were nevertheless much the same. On one occasion in Hunan, for example, a British sabotage unit was planning to blow up a bridge used for trading between the Japanese and Chinese lines. Hearing of this, the Chinese commander in the area "ordered the British out, suggesting that they go and fight their own war—everything was peaceful and harmonious there and the British wanted to start trouble."[24]

[21] OSS, doc. 52918, "Smuggling," attach. 1L, pp. 1-2.

[22] Ibid.; OSS, doc. 116311, Rice to Atcheson, Jan. 6, 1945; OSS, doc. 43615, "Memorandum of Conversation with Graham Peck," Mar. 12, 1942, p. 2; FRUS, 1943, pp. 27, 435.

[23] "Statements of Japanese Officers, World War II" (in Office of the Chief of Military History), vol. 5, Statement no. 512, pp. 1-2.

[24] FRUS, 1943, p. 28.

Most Westerners reporting on the trade with the Japanese-held areas were highly critical, referring to the entire operation as "smuggling," and at least implying that this smuggling betokened the complete degeneracy and corruption of the Chinese civil administration and army. Such traffic with the enemy was, Israel Epstein observed, "not only morally obtuse but strategically nonsense."[25] Partisans of the Chungking government, however, defended the trade, convinced, as an American reported, that they were "playing Japan for a sucker."[26] Or, as Hubert Freyn asked, "which side gains and which side loses if Japanese army gasoline finds its way, for a consideration, into Chinese hands? or if Japanese cloth is bought to make uniforms for guerrillas or shivering Chinese farmers? or if Shanghai and Hong Kong manufactures are 'smuggled' through the lines in order to fill, in the rear, a gap which local production is unable to close?"[27]

In economic terms, it is probable that the Nationalists generally benefited from the inflow of goods. Without the cloth and other consumer goods brought in from the occupied area, life in the interior would have been harsher and perhaps even intolerable. Moreover, to the extent that these goods partially satisfied consumer demands, the trade had a moderating effect on the spiraling inflation.

Even if the Nationalists derived economic benefits from the trade, however, these benefits must be weighed against the detrimental effects of the trade on the Chinese war effort. Supplying the enemy with food and with raw materials for their industries was surely a pernicious practice. And the massive involvement of the military appears to have thoroughly corrupted the officers stationed where they could participate in the traffic, which provided them with a personal interest in avoiding conflict with the Japanese.[28] And the corruption and self-serving that were engendered by their commercial involvements weakened the already frail moral fiber of the Chinese army.

The Japanese, like the Nationalists, attempted to rationalize this curiously amicable relationship in the midst of war. They, of course, derived needed food and raw materials from the trade. And they exacerbated the inflationary trend in the Nationalist areas by paying markedly higher prices than could legitimate Chinese merchants. In Kwangtung, for instance, agents for the Japanese were paying between

[25] Israel Epstein, *The Unfinished Revolution in China* (Boston, 1947), p. 311.
[26] State Dept., doc. 893.00/15300, "General Report on Fukien Province," Feb. 26, 1944, p. 5.
[27] Freyn, p. 73.
[28] Ch'en Ta, *Lang-chi shih-nien* (Shanghai, 1946), pp. 193-94.

Ch$5,000 and Ch$7,000 for a picul of tungsten, whereas Chungking had fixed a maximum price of only Ch$1,000 per picul.[29] "The consequences of such use of *fapi* [Chinese Nationalist currency]," wrote George Atcheson, the United States Chargé, in 1943, is that "the inflation is doubly aggravated by drain of goods from and increased supply of money in Free China."[30] In addition, the Japanese thought that the trade seduced Chinese businessmen, politicians, and army officers into supporting the puppet regime of Wang Ching-wei, rather than Chungking.[31] Such policy considerations may explain part of the Japanese participation in the trade. John P. Davies probably accurately explained the other part, however, when in 1943 he wrote that "the Japanese are as corrupt as the Chinese. The difference . . . is that corruption has not yet enervated them."[32]

BETWEEN A half-million and a million Chinese performed military service during the war for the Japanese. These, to use the terminology of the Nationalists, were the puppet armies (*wei-chün*); and officials in Chungking, including Chiang Kai-shek, many times declared that these collaborators with the enemy would be punished and could never be forgiven.[33] Yet Chiang may actually have looked with favor on the defection of these troops to the Japanese. After the war, many of the puppet military commanders, together with their troops, not only were not punished as traitors, but were reinstated in the Nationalist army with undiminished rank and honor.

The precise number of puppet troops is impossible to ascertain. Chungking authorities at the end of the war counted a total of 683,569 such troops.[34] Communist authorities, however, informed the United States government in early 1945 that the puppet armies then numbered approximately 900,000—410,000 of which were regular army forces and 490,000 of which were local armed units.[35] Whatever the

[29] OSS, doc. 52918, "Smuggling," attach. ii. See also *FRUS, 1943*, pp. 436.
[30] *FRUS, 1943*, p. 440.
[31] "Statements of Japanese Officers, World War II," vol. 5, Statement no. 516, p. 1. See also *FRUS, 1943*, p. 46. For the suggestion that the Japanese engaged in "smuggling" before the attack on Pearl Harbor primarily as an instrument in their currency warfare with the Nationalists, and after Pearl Harbor primarily to obtain goods, see Ching Sheng, *Chan-shih Chung-kuo ching-chi lun-k'uo* (n.p., 1944), pp. 91-92.
[32] *FRUS, 1943*, p. 28.   [33] *FRUS, 1944*, p. 389.
[34] Ibid. But General Ho Ying-ch'in, one of the Nationalists' top commanders, subsequently asserted that there were nearly one million puppet troops at the end of the war. See Ho Ying-ch'in, "Chi-nien ch'i-ch'i k'ang-chan tsai po chung-kung te hsü-wei hsüan-ch'üan," *Tzu-yu chung*, vol. 3, no. 3 (Sept. 20, 1972), p. 28.
[35] State Dept., doc. 893.00/2-2345, Atcheson to State, encl. 3, p. 1. Other Com-

exact figure, many of them had been members of Nationalist units that had defected—officers, men, and equipment—to the Japanese. The remainder of puppet troops had been recruited within the occupied areas.[36]

During the early part of the war, relatively few Nationalist troops had defected. As the war of attrition progressed and as morale throughout the Nationalist area declined, however, defections increased sharply. According to Israel Epstein, twelve Chinese generals, together with their commands, defected to the Japanese in 1941; in 1942, the number was fifteen; and in 1943, the peak year, forty-two defected.[37] These figures correspond closely to those provided by Communist sources, which reported that between 1941 and 1943, sixty-seven general-grade officers defected, taking with them over 500,000 troops.[38]

Defecting troops were not herded into prisoner-of-war camps. Instead, they were reorganized under one of the several puppet governments, given new insignia, and put into the service of the Japanese war effort. Occasionally they were employed in combat operations, but the Japanese provided them with insufficient arms to make them highly effective combat units.[39] The truth is that the Japanese placed little trust in their Chinese collaborators. They therefore assigned the vast majority of the puppet forces to garrison duty in cities or to policing communication lines and other targets of the guerrillas. According to Communist sources, 90-95 percent of the puppet armies were deployed against Communist forces—a claim that probably accurately reflects the Japanese practice of employing the puppets primarily to maintain security behind the front lines.[40]

Communists, who usually ascribed the most invidious motives to their rivals in Chungking, have explained the puppet phenomenon in terms of the rising tide of anti-Communism in Kuomintang China. After the New Fourth Army Incident in January 1941, they contend,

---

munist estimates variously put the number of puppet troops in 1943 at 620,000 and 780,000. See *Kuo-Kung liang-tang k'ang-chan ch'eng-hsü pi-chiao*, ed. Propaganda Bureau of the 8th Route Army (n.p., 1946, preface dated 1943), p. 1; and Li I-yeh, *Chung-kuo jen-min tse-yang ta-pai Jih-pen ti-kuo-chu-i* (Peking, 1951), p. 66.

[36] *Lost Chance in China: The World War II Despatches of John S. Service*, ed. Joseph W. Esherick (New York, 1974), p. 49; Epstein, *Unfinished Revolution*, p. 317.

[37] Epstein, *Unfinished Revolution*, p. 317.

[38] Li I-yeh, p. 60; *Kuo-Kung liang-tang*, p. 45.

[39] State Dept., doc. 740.0011 Pacific War/3450, Atcheson to State, Aug. 31, 1943, encl. 1, p. 1; *Lost Chance in China*, pp. 49-50.

[40] *Kuo-Kung liang-tang*, p. 1; Li I-yeh, pp. 66, 75.

the central government was less concerned about the Japanese invasion than about the expansion of Communist influence throughout the Japanese-occupied areas. In 1943, for example, the Communist newspaper *Hsin-hua jih-pao* (New China Daily) asserted that the Nationalist authorities now regarded the Japanese as a lesser enemy than the Communists. Nationalist troops had therefore lost their anti-Japanese fervor, and were easily won over by the blandishments of the Japanese and the Wang Ching-wei regime.[41] In 1951, however, a Communist historian Li I-yeh asserted that the puppet forces had not simply been won over by the enemy. He claimed instead that fully 62 percent of the puppets had defected on the direct orders of the Nationalist authorities. It was impolitic, Li asserted, for Chungking armies to attack the Communists overtly. Chiang Kai-shek therefore directed these forces to defect, so that they might carry on anti-Communist operations without the political hindrances that they would inevitably encounter as long as they remained allied with the United States and other anti-Japanese forces.[42]

Such conspiratorial interpretations of the Nationalists' actions provided juicy Communist propaganda. Although the Communists claim to have captured documents proving that Chungking had ordered its troops into the service of the Japanese, these have never, to my knowledge, been made public.[43] And Japanese sources indicate that the vast majority of defecting troops came over to the Japanese side only when they were in danger of being overrun, either by the Japanese or by the Communists.[44]

It must be concluded, therefore, that the Nationalist authorities never, at least on a large scale, ordered their troops to defect. And the motivations of the defectors appear to have been considerably more complex than a simple determination to fight the Communists. For instance, it is undoubtedly significant that none of the prominent puppet commanders—generals such as P'ang Ping-hsün, Sun Tien-ying, and Sun Liang-ch'eng—had been members of Chiang Kai-shek's central army. They had belonged instead to the *tsa-p'ai*, miscellaneous regional armies that were vestiges of the warlord era. These officers had never, in all probability, felt strong ties of loyalty to Chiang Kai-shek. To the contrary, to the extent that they felt loyalty to persons other than themselves, it was probably to their previous commanders,

[41] *Kuo-Kung liang-tang*, pp. 70-72.   [42] Li I-yeh, pp. 60, 66.
[43] *Kuo-Kung liang-tang*, pp. 46-47.
[44] Tetsuya Kataoka, *Resistance and Revolution in China: The Communists and the Second United Front* (Berkeley, 1974), p. 287.

former provincial militarists such as Feng Yü-hsiang and Chang Hsüeh-liang, who had been defeated and dispossessed by Chiang Kai-shek.

Nor were they strongly committed to the Nationalist government or to the goals of the Kuomintang. They were essentially mercenaries. True to their warlord background, they easily switched sides if the price was right or if defeat in battle was likely. In the late 1920's, these regional militarists had pledged themselves to the Nationalist government when the balance of power had shifted to the coalition headed by Chiang Kai-shek. But Chiang now disabused their "loyalties." They were ill-paid and short of supplies. Worse, these *tsa-p'ai* commanders were convinced that Chiang Kai-shek worked to deplete their military, and hence political, capacity by placing their units directly in the path of the superior Japanese war machine, whereas Chiang's better equipped central armies nursed their men and weapons in the rear.[45] Moreover, Japanese agents plied these *tsa-p'ai* commanders with propaganda that the Communists could not be defeated as long as Japanese and loyal Chinese fought against each other; that they could expel British and American imperialism from China only by cooperating in the Greater East Asian Co-prosperity system; and that the Japanese would provide them with better pay, food, and arms than they received from Chiang. The *tsa-p'ai* generals were encouraged, furthermore, to defect not to the Japanese, but to one of the Chinese administrations, most notably that of Wang Ching-wei, who even after his defection from Chungking was one of the most attractive political personalities in the whole of China. Given these conditions, a *tsa-p'ai* commander—even one possessed of a spark of nationalism—could easily rationalize his decision to defect.[46]

Although it is doubtful that the Nationalist leaders had ordered the *tsa-p'ai* commanders to defect, Chunking did perceive a potential advantage to be derived from the puppets after they had defected. For the Communists by 1943 and 1944 had extended their influence throughout much of the occupied areas, including the environs of Shanghai and other valuable coastal cities. After 1943, too, the defeat of Japan could be foreseen. The Nationalist leaders feared, therefore,

[45] State Dept., doc. 740.0011 Pacific War/1-2045, Richard M. Service to Hurley, Jan. 20, 1945, p. 2; State Dept., doc. 893.00/7-644, Ringwalt to Gauss, July 6, 1944, encl. 1, pp. 1-2. A Japanese officer also testified that Chiang discriminated against the provincial armies. See "Statements of Japanese Officers, World War II," vol. 5, Statement no. 516, p. 5.
[46] *Lost Chance in China*, pp. 53-55.

that after the Japanese collapse, the occupied areas would fall like plump fruit into the waiting hands of the Communists unless the puppet troops could first seize that fruit on behalf of Chungking. John P. Davies was doubtless correct, therefore, when he wrote in December 1944 that Chiang Kai-shek "looked with complacency if not approval upon the [puppets'] 'surrender.' "[47]

Relations between Chungking and the puppets were sometimes exceedingly cozy. Puppet commanders entertained Nationalist agents at dinners, and provided protection to Nationalist guerrilla forces when, for example, the guerrillas laid mines in Japanese-held harbors.[48] Chungking could therefore easily enter into negotiations with the puppets, providing guarantees that they would not be punished as traitors after the war if they cooperated by resisting postwar Communist expansion. Indeed, after the United States' landings in the Philippines in late 1944, when the tide of the Pacific war had turned strongly in the Allies' favor, many of the puppets approached the Nationalists with the hope that they could insinuate themselves back into the favor of the winning side. The puppet air force, for instance, tried to persuade Tai Li, head of the Nationalists' secret service, to allow them to defect back. Tai dissuaded them, however, "even though," in the words of Tai's friend and collaborator, Admiral Milton Miles, "we knew that the Japanese would feel the loss if the puppets were actually to change sides." About 500,000 of the puppet armies in late 1944 were, by Tai Li's own count, "friendly puppets."[49]

Following the Japanese surrender on August 15, 1945, this Nationalist strategy paid handsome dividends. In Canton, for example, Admiral Chao Kuei-chang, who had been commander of the Canton Harbor Garrison and vice-minister of the navy under the Wang Ching-wei regime, was designated by Chungking to establish interim control. On the basis of an understanding with Chungking, Chao reorganized the puppet troops in the area into a force called the Vanguards. For two months these Vanguards maintained order and—as an American intelligence unit reported—"kept the Communists from capitalizing on the surrender situation." By mid-October, when Nationalist forces had re-entered Canton, the Vanguards

---

[47] *FRUS, 1944*, p. 726.

[48] Milton E. Miles, *A Different Kind of War* (Garden City, New York, 1967), p. 59.

[49] Ibid., pp. 345, 489.

were incorporated into the Second War Zone Army as regular units of the Nationalist Army.[50]

This example—despite Chungking's formal declaration that all officers in the puppet armies above the rank of major were to be tried as traitors[51]—was typical of the Nationalists' use of the puppets in the period immediately after the war. Indeed, on August 11, three days before the Japanese surrender, Chiang Kai-shek announced to the puppet troops that, by maintaining their present positions and by refusing to be incorporated into any military force—implying, of course, the Communists—without his authorization, they might "atone for their crimes and strive to redeem themselves."[52] Whatever prior arrangements had been made with Chungking, many of the principal puppet officers—P'ang Ping-hsün, Sun Liang-ch'eng, Chang Lan-feng, Wu Hua-wen, Liu Tsu-sheng, and Kao Te-lin—were each awarded commands of units in the central army.[53] Even when the Nationalists did begin arresting puppets—and these, to the consternation of the Chinese public, were relatively few—it was primarily civilian puppets who were punished; military puppets had presumably adequately "redeemed" themselves.[54]

The Japanese, for their part, had readily tolerated the ambivalent "loyalties" of the puppets. They knew that the puppets had constant, even intimate, contacts with the Chungking government, and even acknowledged that many of them were highly patriotic.[55] Yet it was far more beneficial, from their point of view, to employ the Chinese defectors as a gendarmerie than to incarcerate them as prisoners of war. This relieved them of the burden of housing and feeding hundreds of thousands of nonproductive prisoners; it also enabled them to deploy their own troops in ways more useful to the war

[50] OSS, doc. 28796, "The Handling of Former Puppets in Kwangtung Province," pp. 2, 15-16, 22-23.

[51] Ibid., pp. 3-5.

[52] *Ch'u-li Jih-pen t'ou-hsiang wen-chien hui-pien*, ed. General Headquarters of the Chinese Army, China Theater (Nanking, 1946), vol. 1, pp. 17-18.

[53] OSS, doc. 18104, "Developments in China after Japan's Surrender," Sept. 15, 1945, p. 33; *Shou-hsiang pao-kao-shu*, comp. Commander-in-Chief of the Chinese Army (Nanking, 1945), Table 9.

[54] *Hsin-min pao*, Nov. 5 [*sic*], 1945, in *Chinese Press Review (Chungking)*, no. 299 (Nov. 4 [*sic*], 1945), p. 2; *Shih-shih hsin-pao*, Dec. 10, 1945, in *Chinese Press Review (Chungking)*, no. 328 (Dec. 10, 1945), p. 3; *Shih-shih hsin-pao*, Dec. 14, 1945, in *Chinese Press Review (Shanghai)*, Dec. 14, 1945, p. 1.

[55] See, e.g., Masao Kanda, "China after Four Years of Hostilities," *Contemporary Japan*, vol. 10, no. 8 (Aug. 1941), p. 996.

effort than, for example, guarding a line of railway track in central China.

Furthermore, the Japanese during the latter phase of the war were only slightly less desirous than the Nationalists that the Communists not acquire control of a large part of China. Japanese leaders had long had an aversion to the Communists. Now, faced with the prospect of defeat, they believed that the Nationalists would be less vindictive than would the Communists. By 1943 and 1944, therefore, the Japanese not only acquiesced in the puppets' contacts with Chungking, but were probably disinclined to overthrow the Chungking Government even if they might have done so.[56]

The thesis that the Japanese, fearful of the Communists, were no longer striving during the last years of the war to destroy the Nationalist regime is supported by a long train of circumstantial evidence. During the famed Ichigō offensive of April 1944-February 1945, for example, overwhelmingly superior Japanese forces had sliced through the Chinese defenses from Honan to Kwangtung. In late 1944, after the Japanese had taken the Kwangsi cities of Kweilin and Liu-chou, the route to Kunming lay virtually open to the aggressor. And if Kunming fell, Chungking would be cut off from Allied support. The fate of the Nationalist government seemed therefore to hang by a thread, and panic spread. On December 3, however, the Japanese suddenly, inexplicably halted their advance. General Albert Wedemeyer, when informed that the Japanese still had large forces with which to continue the attack, "was at a loss to account for the pause."[57]

Rumors were rife at the time, even at the highest levels of the Chinese government, that the Japanese had discontinued their advance because they were in collusion with Chiang Kai-shek. When Wedemeyer asked Chiang about it, however, "the Generalissimo was absolutely noncommittal. There was no indication, emotional or otherwise, that he either denied or admitted it. His spontaneous reaction was a dry cackle."[58]

That Chiang Kai-shek had actually obtained a formal promise from the Japanese that they would not attack the base areas of Nationalist China now appears improbable. Significantly, Japanese who might

[56] *Lost Chance in China*, p. 52; *FRUS, 1944*, p. 726.

[57] Charles F. Romanus and Riley Sunderland, *Time Runs Out in CBI* (Washington, 1959), p. 176. See also Wedemeyer to War Dept., telegram #CFBX31783, Jan. 22, 1945, in Archives of the Joint Chiefs of Staff, 381 Chinese Theater (12-7-44), Sec. 1, p. 1.

[58] Romanus and Sunderland, *Time Runs Out*, p. 176.

have been privy to such an agreement have, in postwar interviews, denied its existence.[59] Still, Chiang had received ample reassurance, by means of Japanese propaganda and through "various intelligence channels," that the goal of the Ichigō offensive was simply to eliminate the airfields used by the United States Air Force, not to destroy the Chinese armies.[60]

Why were the Japanese so solicitous of the feelings and fate of their supposed enemy in Chungking? The explanation of Lo Lung-chi, a liberal critic of the Nationalist government in late 1944, is at least plausible:

> The Japanese [preferred] the retention of power in China by the present regime because (1) they feared that a new regime would prosecute the war against Japan more effectively and (2) the Japanese were looking to the long future and the post-war period —the Japanese now knew that they would lose the war but they counted on the weakness of Kuomintang leadership to ensure that China would not emerge as a strong nation which could in the foreseeable future play a deciding role in the Far East and oppose the resurgence of Japanese power. Present Kuomintang leadership would also be expected to be more friendly to Japan than a regime under liberal [and Communist] leadership.[61]

The Japanese preference for Nationalist, rather than Communist, rule in postwar China was apparent also in their conduct at the end of the war. On August 10, 1945, the Communists ordered that the Japanese must surrender to "any anti-Japanese armed force," including the Communists.[62] General Okamura Yasuji rejected the order. He did, however, obey General Douglas MacArthur's order of August 15 to surrender only to Chiang Kai-shek's forces.[63] Actually, Okamura had not needed MacArthur's instructions to decide whether

---

[59] "Statements of Japanese Officers, World War II," vol. 5, Statement no. 516, pp. 3-4.

[60] Ibid., p. 4. See also Romanus and Sunderland, *Time Runs Out*, pp. 9, 56; and Charles F. Romanus and Riley Sunderland, *Stilwell's Command Problems* (Washington, 1956), pp. 316, 409-10.

[61] State Dept., doc. 893.00/8-2344, encl. 2, Sprouse to Gauss, Aug. 18, 1944, p. 2. John P. Davies offered a similar interpretation. See John Hunter Boyle, *China and Japan at War, 1937-1945: The Politics of Collaboration* (Stanford, 1972), p. 321.

[62] Li Shou-k'ung, *Chung-kuo hsien-tai-shih* (Taipei, 1954), p. 246; *FRUS, 1945,* pp. 514-15.

[63] Herbert Feis, *The China Tangle: The American Effort in China from Pearl Harbor to the Marshall Mission* (Princeton, N.J., 1953), p. 341.

to aid the Communists or Nationalists in regaining control of the Japanese-occupied territories. For, even without directives from MacArthur or Chiang, he had already ordered his forces to surrender only to the Nationalists. And Okamura's subordinates carried out this order scrupulously. They fought against Communist forces with a dedication seldom evinced even during the war, and thus saved for the Nationalists such key points as Peiping, Tientsin, Shanghai, and Taiyuan.[64]

Chiang Kai-shek was duly appreciative of this Japanese cooperation, evidenced by the treatment that he accorded General Okamura after the war. Okamura was convicted as a major war criminal, and was nominally, at least, imprisoned. Yet Chiang treated this former "enemy" handsomely and used him as an advisor during the post-1945 fighting against the Communists. Just before Chiang resigned his presidency in January 1949, Okamura's war-crimes case was reviewed; he was pronounced innocent; and, with a Communist victory a virtual certainty, he was sent out of China and safely back to Japan. According to a Communist source—but denied by the Nationalists—Chiang Kai-shek in the following year, 1950, employed Okamura in Taiwan as a senior training officer in the Research Institute of Revolutionary Practice.[65]

None of this proves collusion between Chiang Kai-shek and the Japanese during the final stages of the war. At the very least, however, it suggests that relations between Japan and Chungking were not uniformly belligerent. It also suggests that the Japanese probably did as much as they could, within the constraints of a war, to assure that the Nationalists, and not the Communists, governed China when peace was restored.

BUT WHAT ambivalences in the relationship could exist after the brutish, senseless, sadistic treatment—murder, torture, rape, looting, wanton destruction—by Japanese of defenseless Chinese civilians? Most infamous of the Japanese atrocities was the sack of Nanking. In the months since the Marco Polo Bridge Incident on July 7,

[64] *Ch'u-li Jih-pen*, p. 105; Lionel Max Chassin, *The Communist Conquest of China: A History of the Civil War, 1945-1949* (Cambridge, Mass., 1965), p. 57; Theodore H. White and Annalee Jacoby, *Thunder Out of China* (New York, 1946), pp. 283-84.

[65] Graham Peck, *Two Kinds of Time* (Boston, 1950), p. 683; *Selected Works of Mao Tse-tung*, vol. 4 (Peking, 1961), p. 331, note 3. *Ta-kung pao*, Feb. 2, 1949, in *Chinese Press Review (Hong Kong)*, Feb. 1-2, 1949, p. 2; interview with the director of the Kuomintang Historical Commission, Ch'in Hsiao-i, Taipei, June 26, 1978.

1937, reports of the Japanese soldiers' savagery had trickled to the newsrooms of the world. Most journalists and editors had greeted these with disbelief, for they seemed too gruesome to be anything but crude Nationalist propaganda. At Nanking, however, Japanese behavior was put on public display, before Westerners of indisputable credibility, leaving the world aghast and uncomprehending.

Nanking, capital of Nationalist China, fell to the Japanese on December 12-13, 1937. These troops since August had been engaged in the most sustained fighting of the entire China war. Blood had flowed in horrendous quantities: there had been approximately 40,-000 Japanese and considerably more than 250,000 Chinese casualties in the Shanghai fighting alone; 300,000 civilians had been killed as the Japanese advanced from Shanghai to Nanking.[66] Most Chinese, in terror, had fled Nanking as the Japanese approached, although Chiang Kai-shek had vowed that it would be defended to the last man. The discretion of T'ang Sheng-chih, Chinese commander in the city, overcame his valor, however, and he took to his heels on the evening of December 12.[67] Thus, when the Japanese entered Nanking, no further resistance was offered.

Chinese inhabitants remaining in the city looked hopefully to a restoration of order and calm under the Japanese. The retreating Nationalist troops had gone almost berserk with terror in their last hours in the area, even killing to obtain civilian clothes and thus, they thought, to escape the enemy.[68] The Japanese had dropped pamphlets from airplanes assuring the populace that "Japanese troops exert themselves to the utmost to protect good citizens and to enable them to live in peace, enjoying their occupations." And two days before the massacre began, the Japanese commander had promised, "Though harsh and relentless to those who resist, the Japanese troops are kind and generous to noncombatants and to Chinese troops who entertain no enmity to Japan."[69]

The Japanese brought neither kindness nor generosity, but barbarism. Looting was carried out both pettily by individuals, and systematically by organized units of soldiers with trucks. Everything,

---

[66] Hata Ikuhiko, *Nitchū senso shi* (Tokyo, rev. ed. 1972), p. 281; F. F. Liu, *A Military History of Modern China, 1924-1949* (Princeton, N.J., 1956), p. 198; Edgar Snow, *The Battle for Asia* (New York, 1941), p. 57.

[67] H. J. Timperley, ed., *Japanese Terror in China* (New York, 1938), p. 26; Frank Dorn, *The Sino-Japanese War, 1937-41: From Marco Polo Bridge to Pearl Harbor* (New York, 1974), p. 90.

[68] Timperley, p. 26.   [69] Ibid., p. 18.

from wristwatches and pens to grand pianos and automobiles, was wrenched away. Stores, government offices, ornate residences, and grubby shanties were entered repeatedly, until nothing of value remained. Large parts of the city were purposely put to the torch.

Most abhorrent was the Japanese treatment of the people. Informed that large numbers of Nationalist soldiers had thrown away their weapons and uniforms, and determined that no enemy soldier should escape alive, the Japanese systematically searched out Chinese deserters and murdered them. The Japanese decision not to take prisoners was deplorable; the methods of carrying out the decision were truly execrable. For the Japanese might determine who was and who was not a soldier simply by inspecting the men's hands. If there were calluses, the man was adjudged a soldier, and herded into a group destined for execution. On other occasions, a ring around the head, caused by habitual wearing of a cap or hat, was regarded as sufficient evidence of service in the army. Probably thousands of coolies, pedicab drivers, and other innocent civilians thus received the death sentence. Some of these were murdered with machine guns; some were roped together in groups of fifty or more, kerosene poured over their heads, and burned to death; others were used as live targets in bayonet practice; still others were buried alive.[70]

Women were treated no less harshly. "Other armies," John P. Davies has observed, "may have traveled on their stomachs; the Japanese army traveled on its libido."[71] Japanese entered homes or hospitals and seized Chinese women. Protesting husbands were often killed. Some of these women were raped by the sides of the streets in full daylight; others were dragged away for an entire evening of lustful orgy, often being raped by a succession of men; some were never seen again. One woman, six months pregnant, having resisted her assailant, was stabbed with a knife sixteen times in the face and body, including the abdomen. On the campus of Nanking University, a girl as young as nine and a grandmother aged seventy-six were raped.[72] Searle Bates, living in Nanking throughout the Japanese seizure of the city, conservatively reported that, based on verifiable accounts, 8,000 women had been raped in less than a month. The estimate of John H. D. Rabe, chairman of the International Committee for the

[70] See note 75 below.
[71] John Paton Davies, Jr., *Dragon by the Tail: American, British, Japanese, and Russian Encounters with China and One Another* (New York, 1972), p. 201.
[72] Testimony of Searle Bates, *International Military Tribunal of the Far East*, p. 2634.

Nanking Safety Zone, was that at least 20,000 women were raped in the first month after the Japanese entered the city.[73]

This savagery in Nanking raged at a peak of intensity for nearly three weeks, relenting somewhat, but still continuing, for another four weeks. How many were murdered during those seven weeks will never be known exactly. Searle Bates, in testimony at the Tokyo War Crimes Trials, put the figure at a minimum of 42,000. He testified that of the 250,000 civilians, no less than 12,000 had been killed. And within seventy-two hours of the city's capture, over 30,-000 soldiers had been slaughtered, killed in cold blood.[74] The actual number of persons massacred probably went at least several thousand higher, because many of the dead were thrown into the river, were buried in other ways, or simply were not accounted for.[75]

The sack of Nanking stands out in the history of Japanese atrocities because of its scale and intensity, and because it was committed in full view of neutral observers. It was not, however, a unique occurrence, and the historian sickens in reading the repeated and relentless accounts of similar acts of inhumanity. Soon the mind ceases to differentiate among the reports of villages pointlessly burned; of troops

[73] Ibid., pp. 2633-34; Haldore Hanson, "Humane Endeavor": The Story of the China War (New York, 1939), p. 142.

[74] Testimony of Searle Bates, p. 2642. Bates's testimony is similar to Lewis S.C. Smythe, War Damage in the Nanking Area: December 1937 to March 1938 (Nanking, 1938), pp. 7-8 and especially p. 8, note 1.

[75] There is a sizable literature on the sack of Nanking. See Shuhsi Hsü, Documents of the Nanking Safety Zone (Shanghai, 1939), which is an extensive collection of the correspondence sent and received by the International Committee for Nanking Safety Zone. This committee comprised a small group of non-Chinese who were in Nanking throughout the ordeal. See also Timperley, cited above, which is also a collection of contemporary documents; and the International Military Tribunal for the Far East, passim, a guide to which is Paul S. Dull and Michael Takaaki Umemura, The Tokyo Trials: A Functional Index to the Proceedings of the International Military Tribunal for the Far East (Ann Arbor, 1957).

Regarding the number of persons massacred at Nanking, the sources cited in note 74 appear to be relatively reliable. Most other sources, however, suggest a much higher mortality figure. At the war-crimes trial in Nanking, the figure was fixed at 300,000. (See official verdict quoted in Shih Mei-yü, "Shen-p'an chan-fan hui-i-lu," Chuan-chi wen-hsüeh 2.2 [Feb. 1963], p. 38.) Dorn, p. 93, states that "over 200,000 civilians, and possibly as many as 300,000 had been senselessly massacred." Hsu Long-hsuen and Chang Ming-kai, comp., History of the Sino-Japanese War, 1937-1945 (Taipei, 1971), vol. 1, p. 377, gives a figure of 100,000.

Suzuki Akira, Nankin daigyakusatsu no maboroshi (Tokyo, 1973), is a notable revisionist study of the sack of Nanking. Suzuki discounts the mountain of evidence that there was a massive atrocity in Nanking, and asserts that what occurred there was probably of little significance. But he adduces virtually no positive evidence to support his view, his chief argument being based on the well-founded admonition that all estimates of deaths and other atrocities during that period must be treated with extreme caution.

raping women and girls, then bayoneting them, sometimes grotesquely; of men bound with wire and used for bayonet practice. Yet some reports stand out, poignant even in this sea of savagery. A young girl near Hankow in 1938, for example, fled several Japanese soldiers who threatened to rape her, and waded to the middle of a pond, immersed with presumably only her head exposed. Frustrated, the soldiers began shooting at her. The girl's father pleaded with them to stop. Shoving him aside, they continued shooting until they killed her.[76] In Hopeh in 1937, eight soldiers in succession raped a thirteen-year-old girl. She subsequently died.[77] And, in 1941, the Japanese wreaked retribution on the Hopeh village of P'an-chia-yü for cooperating with Communist guerrillas. Surrounding the village at daybreak, they herded all the inhabitants into a courtyard, massacred them, and totally burned the village. Over a thousand men, women, and children died there that day.[78] And one is puzzled that some Japanese soldiers delighted in being photographed by a friend as they were in the act of committing rape. Others dutifully recorded these atrocities in their diaries. One diarist recorded raping nineteen women during a seven-week period; by his own estimate, the women ranged in age from forty-seven to eleven.[79]

How many of the Japanese soldiers were guilty of such outrages? Were most of them thus brutalized and cruel? Or was it—as an official Japanese pamphlet put it early in the war—less than 1 percent, perhaps only 0.1 percent, of the army that was responsible for the atrocities?[80] I do not know the answers to these questions, though I think the figure was surely higher than 1 percent. Assuredly, however, within the total context of the Japanese occupation, atrocities were the exception rather than the rule. In areas where the Japanese had consolidated control, life and labor went on more or less normally. The Japanese were, it is true, often harsh and arrogant toward the conquered Chinese. They evinced a Prussian-type strictness that was exceedingly intolerant of the usually more casual and individualistic Chinese manner. And Chinese felt humiliated by having to bow to the commonest Japanese trooper, or by being slapped for some

[76] State Dept., doc. 893.00/14374, encl., Davies memorandum on "Conditions in Rural Areas near Wuhan," p. 4.

[77] Testimony of a Chinese from Hopei, *International Military Tribunal for the Far East*, p. 4615.

[78] Kuo Shih-chieh, *Jih-k'ou ch'in-Hua pao-hsing lu* (Peking, 1951), pp. 15-20. Another poignant work is Wen Han, comp., *Jih-pen chün-fa ch'in-Hua t'ung-shih* (Kowloon, 1963), which is a collection of reminiscences by Japanese.

[79] Hanson, pp. 144-45.   [80] Timperley, p. 135.

imagined offense. One Chinese peasant simply but expressively re-marked of the Japanese soldiers, *"t'a-men te p'i-ch'i pu-hao"* (they have a bad temper).[81] Usually, however, the bad temper, impatience, and qualities of a martinet resulted only in frictions and unpleasant-ness, rarely (relatively speaking) in atrocities.

Many Japanese, moreover, regarded the Chinese with compassion. If published Japanese battle memoirs may be believed, some of the Japanese soldiers pitied the hungry, frightened civilians they en-countered; observed how much they resembled neighbors back home in Japan; and one, looking upon dead Chinese soldiers, reflected that they "might much better be friends." Some also sensed the enchant-ment of the fabled beauty of West Lake at Hangchow, admired the poetry of Su Man-shu, became close friends with Chinese civilians, and fell in love with and planned to marry Chinese girls.[82] And there was the kindly Major Satō, commander of a Japanese garrison in Honan, who offered candy to the local children if they would shout, "Long live the emperor of Japan, down with Chiang Kai-shek." When the children instead shouted "Long live Chiang Kai-shek, down with the emperor of Japan," Satō, rather than flying into a rage, patiently tried to win them over with persuasion. (This part of the story is easier to tell than the rest. Later, Chinese guerrillas attacked the garrison, and Satō was so severely reprimanded by his superiors for not inflicting sufficiently harsh retribution on the villagers that he, together with several of his men, committed suicide.)[83]

At the top echelons of command, too, some Japanese gave evidence of a humane concern for the Chinese people. Prince Konoe, Japanese premier in 1938, for example, expressed the desire to treat with China on a basis of equality and "neighborly amity," and to assist the Chinese in the task of rebuilding and modernizing their nation.[84] General Matsui Iwane, commander of the troops at the time of the Nanking massacre (who in 1948 was executed for his war crimes), maintained that one of his chief goals in life was "to promote sincere friendship between Japan and China."[85]

[81] Hanson, p. 180.

[82] Ashihei Hino (pseud), *War and Soldier*, tr. Lewis Bush (London, 1940), passim; and Masaru Taniguchi, *The Soldier's Log: 10,000 Miles of Battle*, tr. R. Toombs Fincher and Yoshi Okada (Japan, 1940), passim.

[83] State Dept., doc. 893.00/14374, encl., Davies memorandum on "Conditions in Rural Areas near Wuhan," pp. 9-10.

[84] *The China Year Book, 1939*, ed. H.G.W. Woodhead (Kraus Reprint, 1969), pp. 428-30.

[85] Snow, p. 71. See also Testimony of Hidaka Shinrokuro, *International Military Tribunal for the Far East*, pp. 21446, 21448.

These expressions of goodwill toward the Chinese may have resulted from sheer hypocrisy and cynicism. But they may have been sincere. Haldore Hanson, who knew many Japanese intimately, stated in 1939 that "I am convinced that these men [Japanese officers and soldiers] are deeply sincere in their vision of peace, however misguided their methods. Japanese idealism is no tongue-in-cheek hypocrisy."[86] And Edgar Snow similarly asserted that "I sometimes felt that Japanese . . . were in their own peculiar way quite in earnest" about establishing Sino-Japanese friendship.[87] But for all their idealism, the record of the Japanese military in China forms an ineradicable stain on the history of the Japanese nation.

(In fairness, it must be recorded that Chinese soldiers were not innocent of atrocities against the Japanese. The massacre of some 280 Japanese at Tungchow in August 1937 by Chinese gendarmes, employees of the Japanese, is well documented. And Lin Piao in the same year criticized Communist troops for having "taken a mistaken policy toward Japanese prisoners, such as burying them alive, burning them, or cutting their bellies open.")[88]

Despite the harshness and brutality of the Japanese soldiers, many Chinese—especially, it seems, the peasantry—were by no means hostile to them. In north China, a Japanese pilot crash landed in unoccupied territory. The villagers, rather than arresting or murdering the pilot, stood watching as he repaired his craft and then flew off again.[89] Many Chinese, attracted by reports of high wages in the occupied areas, crossed over to the Japanese side to build roads or dig trenches for the Japanese.[90] And the Japanese soldier Hino Ashihei recalled that "in one place a group of old men, women, and children formed a human fence round their encampment, each holding a flag which they waved as we approached, and lining the road to welcome us. They offered us eggs, chickens, and vegetables and seemed so happy that we felt we were taking part in some triumphal ceremony."[91] Seldom, perhaps, did the peasants greet the Japanese so lavishly, for they usually had piteously little to spare. It was, however, common for villagers to welcome their conquerors with tea, smiles, and offers

---

[86] Hanson, p. 174.   [87] Snow, p. 71.

[88] Hanson, pp. 65-69; *What Happened at Tungchow?*, comp. The Foreign Affairs Association of Japan (rev. ed., Aug. 1937), 21 p.; Kataoka, p. 65.

[89] Donald G. Gillin, "'Peasant Nationalism' in the History of Chinese Communism," *Journal of Asian Studies*, vol. 23, no. 2 (Feb. 1964), p. 280.

[90] Ibid.; Peck, pp. 238, 261.

[91] Hino, p. 439. See also Taniguchi, p. 29.

of assistance. Peasants in Nationalist territory were, as Graham Peck observed, "curiously neutral" toward the war.[92]

This indifference, this lack of concern regarding the fate of their nation, may be partially explained by the peasants' remarkably low level of political consciousness. Even as late as 1948, peasants in a Szechuan village, forty miles from Chungking, had barely heard the name of Chiang Kai-shek, knew nothing of Mao Tse-tung, had never had contact with the Kuomintang, and comprehended only vaguely that a civil war was being waged somewhere.[93] It may be assumed, a fortiori, that during the war these same peasants were at least equally indifferent to the war with Japan. This was not their war, and they only hoped to emerge from it unscathed.

Contributing to the peasants' lack of nationalism was the fact that their encounters with representatives of their own government—the tax collectors, heads of the *pao-chia* system, army conscription agents, and the army—were usually painful and extortionate. Peasant contacts with the Chinese army illustrates this point.

Chinese troops were frequently like a plague upon the common people. They were inadequately supplied by Chungking, cheated by corrupt officers, and often brutalized by deprivation, mistreatment, and the bloodshed of war. When, as was often the case, these troops were billeted in the villages, they freely seized food, fuel, beds and bedding from the inhabitants. When they moved on, they took carts and oxen with them. Frequently the villagers were forced into service as coolies for the army, carrying equipment or digging trenches. Little or no money or food was provided in return for the work. During a campaign in western Hupeh in May 1943, Chinese troops ordered whole towns evacuated on grounds of military necessity—and then plundered them for everything of value. Persons too old to move and who remained in the towns were killed as traitors.[94] As

---

[92] Peck, p. 261. Even in the Communist-held areas, anti-Japanese sentiment may not have been as potent as many scholars today assume. Elinor Lerner writes: "In many areas [controlled by Communists], especially those removed from immediate fighting, the CCP had great trouble arousing the enthusiasm of the peasant for the Anti-Japanese war." "The Chinese Peasantry and Imperialism: A Critique of Chalmers Johnson's *Peasant Nationalism and Communist Power*," *Bulletin of Concerned Asian Scholars*, vol. 6, no. 2 (Apr.-Aug. 1974), p. 51. This is the conclusion also of Kataoka, pp. 281-83, 295-302.

[93] A. Doak Barnett, *China on the Eve of Communist Takeover* (New York, 1963), p. 115.

[94] State Dept., doc. 740.0011 Pacific War/3559, encl., "Report of What I Saw and Heard on the Lake Side District in West Hupeh [a confidential report by a journalist for the *Ta-kung pao*]," pp. 6-7.

a result of such mistreatment, an American reported in 1944, the peasant felt "a terrible hatred" for the soldiers. On several occasions during the war, retreating Chinese soldiers were actually attacked by infuriated civilians, who disarmed them, even killed them, and in some instances buried them alive.[95]

These civilians had occasionally learned by word-of-mouth that peasants in the occupied territory were faring reasonably well under the Japanese.[96] And, tormented beyond restraint by their own kind, they sometimes looked to the Japanese as a source of relief. In Hupeh in 1943, for instance, a Chinese commander complained that "the country folks, . . . stealthily send pigs, beef, rice and wine across the line to the enemy. The country folks are willing to be ruled by the enemy, but do not wish to be free citizens under their own government."[97] And a *Ta-kung pao* ("*L'Impartial*") reporter wrote that many of the civilians near the front "thought that when the enemy arrived they would not cause any disturbance. . . . Wherever they passed, [the Japanese] asked them to supply tea and water only. At the time [the Chinese civilians] all said that the enemy was better than the Chinese troops."[98]

The peasants were sometimes deceived in this expectation. For if the Japanese subsequently withdrew from an area, they abandoned the "soft-policy" and destroyed with a vengeance, killing men, raping women, destroying dikes, and burning entire towns. "The enemy," wrote the *Ta-kung pao* reporter, "was extraordinarily crafty and cunning toward the Chinese people."[99]

On balance, the destruction, brutality, and sadism endured by Chinese civilians at the hands of the Japanese were assuredly on a more terrible scale than the damage and hardships inflicted by the Chinese troops. And the motivation of the latter was different. Chinese soldiers were materially deprived; extortion, confiscation, and pillage were sometimes their only means to keep alive. These were considered part of their "salary" or remuneration for services rendered—the functional equivalent of the officers' squeeze from the enlisted men's salaries. Japanese maltreatment of Chinese civilians is more difficult to explain. Many interpretations of the phenomenon have been pro-

[95] Ibid., p. 3; OSS, doc. 2032, Hal to Donovan, p. 2; OSS, doc. 116311, Rice to Atcheson, Dec. 18, 1944, p. 2.

[96] Peck, p. 261.

[97] State Dept., doc. 740.0011 Pacific War/3559, encl., "Report of What I Saw and Heard," p. 3.

[98] Ibid., p. 9.

[99] Ibid., pp. 3, 9.

posed, yet we are as far from a definitive explanation today as we were in the 1940's. It has been suggested, for example, that the Japanese soldiers' behavior was due to the dehumanizing character of their military training, to the officers' woeful lack of a liberal education, to a national inferiority complex, or to the frustrations resulting from the pertinacious Chinese defense. Another explanation frequently offered is that Japanese conduct is customarily guided by a "situational ethic"—by the behavioral norms provided by other persons in any particular circumstance—rather than by an internalized, absolute ethical code ("guilt ethic") that does not vary from one situation to the next. When Japanese soldiers were transferred to China and placed in a battle situation, they were deprived of the familiar ethical guideposts, whereupon they became literally amoral.[100]

Psychological interpretations, however, provide only part of the answer. For Japanese maltreatment of Chinese civilians was also part of a conscious policy to terrorize the Chinese into submission. In areas that they could not occupy, the Japanese sometimes applied a scorched-earth policy. To combat Chinese guerrilla operations, they often wrought fearful retribution against innocent civilians. Even the mistreatment of Chinese women was partially related to practical considerations, for it was condoned by officers (who themselves were usually followed closely by units of *femmes de combat*) only until prostitutes could be acquired for the enlisted men. Thereafter, raping by Japanese soldiers was less common.

Furthermore, as the Nationalist soldiers' conduct toward Chinese civilians suggests, the Japanese atrocities may be partly explained by a tradition in China and Japan of military maltreatment of civilians. This tradition ought not, however, be ascribed to something uniquely "Asian." The German atrocities in World War II, the raping of Korean girls by American soldiers during the Korean War, and the Mylai Incident during the Vietnam War should remind us that war may bring out the worst in a man, whatever his national or cultural background.

AMBIVALENCES in the Chinese relationship with the Japanese appear to derive substantially from the fact that the spirit of modern nationalism had touched the Chinese people only lightly. Most citizens did not sense that the foreign aggressor, the Japanese, con-

---

[100] Boyle, pp. 341-44; Hanson, pp. 143-46; Edwin O. Reischauer, *The United States and Japan* (New York, 3rd ed., 1965), pp. 139-41.

stituted the danger *ne plus ultra* to their well-being. Nor did they perceive that their welfare was directly related to the well-being of their nation and their government. Although the history of modern China is in large part the story of the growth of nationalism, only a small minority of the Chinese population in the 1930's and 1940's was deeply moved by that sentiment. Educated youth, intellectuals, some of the political leaders, and a part of the urban population had evinced the spirit of nationalism most strongly. Evidence of a lack of national feeling, even in time of war, however, was everywhere apparent. Industrialists at the beginning of the war, for instance, ignored the Nationalist government's appeals to move inland, preferring the amenities of Shanghai and Hong Kong to the rigors and uncertainties of the interior. Financiers allowed their wealth to lie idle in the coastal ports, or sent it to the security of the United States, rather than aid their capital-starved government in Szechuan. High Nationalist officials, generals, and landlords became war profiteers, to the obvious detriment of the war effort. And we have seen how peasants sometimes readily cooperated with the Japanese while turning angrily against the soldiers of the Nationalist government.

The fundamental reason these Chinese did not identify their own well-being with that of the state was, perhaps, that no Chinese government before the Communists had evolved a system of political organization that enlisted the political participation of the people. The Nationalist government was elitist, founded upon military power, and administered by a bureaucracy that was responsible not to the people but only to itself. The bulk of the population was therefore excluded from the government, and the essence of politics was the competition for power, prestige, and wealth by mutually antagonistic military and bureaucratic cliques.

The army commanders who became puppets of the Japanese, therefore, were those who had lost in the political struggle within the Nationalist camp. Peasants who cooperated with the Japanese did so because their main concerns were food and safety for themselves and their families, and because the Japanese frequently loomed as a lesser peril than the Chinese soldiery and tax collectors. In individual cases, the motivations were no doubt more complex than suggested here. And these trends varied at different times during the war and in different places across the huge expanse of China. At base, however, the ambivalences in the Chinese responses to the Japanese appear to have been directly related to the character of the government. Nationalist China was not a modern nation-state; it was ruled by a narrow minority that was too often corrupt and grossly self-serving. The structure and the conduct of the government did not, therefore, encourage citizens to identify with it. Lacking a viable object of supra-personal loyalties, many Chinese worked easily with the aggressor in a way that perplexed foreign observers who were accustomed to a different and closer relationship between a government and its people.

CHAPTER XV

CHOU FO-HAI: THE MAKING OF
A COLLABORATOR

SUSAN H. MARSH

IN THEIR separate studies Gerald Bunker and John Boyle have ably
and exhaustively documented the peace movement headed by Wang
Ching-wei.[1] In this study the focus is on Chou Fo-hai (1897-1948),
the articulate spokesman and "chief of staff" of this peace movement.[2]

Wang Ching-wei was a long-time disciple of Dr. Sun Yat-sen and
an illustrious revolutionary in his own right. He had a history of
rivalry with Chiang Kai-shek for leadership of the Kuomintang
(KMT). Frustration and his romantic craving for martyrdom[3] could
have induced him to leave Chungking in 1938 in pursuit of a different
policy toward Japan. In previous years Wang had been in the habit
of going abroad when politics in China were at an impasse. His leaving Chungking for Hanoi in December 1938 was therefore consistent
with his established pattern of political behavior. On all the earlier
occasions, sojourning abroad was for Wang only the prelude to being
called back to China to take up an important post when political align-
ments changed. By comparison, Chou Fo-hai did not have such advantages, and he clearly did not have Wang's stature and prestige. Although he had met Wang as early as 1924, and was impressed by

---

[1] Gerald E. Bunker, *The Peace Conspiracy: Wang Ching-wei and the China
War, 1937-41* (Cambridge, Mass., 1972); John H. Boyle, *China and Japan at War,
1937-1945: The Politics of Collaboration* (Stanford, 1972).

[2] Tso Pi, "Chi Chou Fo-hai hsien-sheng," appended to Chou Fo-hai, *Wang-i
chi* (Shanghai, 10th ed., 1944), p. 149. Also, see Chu Tzu-chia (Chin Hsiung-pai),
Wang Cheng-ch'üan te k'ai-ch'ang yü shou-ch'ang (Hong Kong, 1959), vol. 2, pp.
17-18.

[3] Howard L. Boorman, "Wang Ching-wei: China's Romantic Radical," *Political
Science Quarterly*, vol. 79, no. 4 (December 1964).

his charisma, he remained outside Wang's immediate circle until 1937.[4] Rather, Chou was Chiang Kai-shek's man.

Also, in 1938, Chou was different from many actual and would-be collaborators, who were caught by events in occupied China and who were thus willy-nilly eased or pressured into collaboration with Japan. Chou deliberately left Chungking for the occupied areas, a move requiring determination and premeditation, yet he was an enigma in that he gave no warning that he was about to defect from the heart of the KMT camp in 1938. On the eve of Japanese surrender, he was the most powerful figure in the Shanghai-Nanking area, in control of a sizable military force, daily administration, and financial and material assets. He was approached by emissaries from Chungking as well as Yenan. No one would have expected him to give himself up easily to Tai Li, to be arrested, imprisoned, and tried for treason as he was. Many a lesser figure, such as Jen Yüan-tao, made preparations for a comfortable exile. Why did Chou not think of self-preservation?

Why did Chou leave Chungking in the first place? What kind of collaboration scheme did he have in mind when he started out? And what did he think would be his lot should he fail? To answer these questions, I propose to delve into three related issues: (1) Chou's lifelong ambition and his assessment of the prospect of realizing it in Chiang Kai-shek's service; (2) historical precedents of collaboration, and contemporary views on collaboration, providing Chou with an idea of what was politically possible; and (3) the peace movement as a form of opposition to Chiang Kai-shek.

Chou and Chiang

Chou Fo-hai was a prolific and facile writer and the author of at least two best sellers: one, the *San-min chu-i chih li-lun te t'i-hsi* (Theoretical system of the Three People's Principles), which we shall discuss later, and the other, *Wang-i chi* (Bygone days), a collection of articles reminiscing about important episodes of his life.[5] Containing refreshing commentaries on contemporary politics, *Wang-i chi*

---

[4] Chou Fo-hai, "Wang Ching-wei hsien-sheng hsing-shih-lu shu," in *Wang-i chi*, p. 2.

[5] These articles were first published in a literary magazine, *Ku-chin pan-yüeh-k'an*, and later collected in the volume entitled *Wang-i chi*. The first edition appeared in January 1943. Eight editions appeared within the first year of publication. The tenth edition appeared in August 1944. Abridged Hong Kong editions appeared in 1955.

reveals a good deal about its author, as Chou was not embarrassed either to brag or to deprecate himself. Reportedly, being open and direct was what endeared him to his friends and associates.

As a youth Chou was impulsive, but extremely clever and perceptive. He told his readers how he passed his first hurdle on the road to success. He was required to write an essay on patriotism during an entrance examination to a modern school. Having read some of Liang Ch'i-ch'ao's writings, Chou set out to imitate Liang's style of larding his argument with emotive sentiments, and he threw in all the new terms he had learned from reading Liang. In a small hsien school in his native Hunan this was unprecedented, and his essay was judged the best. Thus he achieved distinction among his peers.[6] On another occasion, he was worried lest his Japanese prove not fluent enough to pass the oral part of the entrance examination to the First Higher School in Tokyo. He thought that the oral examination might dwell on the war currently being fought in Hunan, and asked a friend who was fluent in Japanese to compose a piece on that subject. Chou then memorized that piece. On the day of the exam, he found that his foresight had paid off. He was able to discuss this topic eloquently in Japanese and won his admission to the First Higher School. At that time the Chinese government automatically awarded scholarships to Chinese students who could qualify for enrollment in one of the five Japanese government schools, the First Higher School being one of them. Thus Chou was able to embark on an elite education, culminating in graduation from the Kyoto Imperial University in 1924.[7]

By Chinese standards, Chou came from a reasonably comfortable background; although his father had died early, the family still had over a hundred *mu* of land. But he could not count on his family's support for studies abroad; a series of lucky breaks enabled him to transcend the limitations of his circumstances. These lucky breaks Chou called "fate" (*ming-yün*).[8] Very early in life he began to consult fortune tellers to the extent that their predictions became almost self-fulfilling prophecies.[9]

[6] Chou Fo-hai, "K'u-hsüeh chi," in *Wang-i chi* (Hong Kong, 1955), pp. 6-7.
[7] Ibid., pp. 22-24.   [8] Ibid., p. 12.
[9] Consultations with fortune tellers and interpretations of omens were often recorded in historical accounts of leaders in China. In part, this practice was based on the philosophy of not overreaching oneself, of knowing the time to advance, to make full use of one's opportunity, and the time to retreat. During 1916-28, the warlords, in their contest for power in China, patronized the art of fortune telling,

Having had most of his higher education in Japan, Chou could not have failed to be impressed by the Meiji Revolution and the accomplishments of Meiji statesmen in a period when Japan's progress toward modernization and national strength was particularly impressive to Chinese intellectuals.[10] Meiji statesmen believed less in ultimate values and ideals, and more in the possibility of manipulating men and political institutions. When Chou consciously dared to modify secular history as much as he felt was humanly possible, and when he acted on behalf of a nominal superior, he was emulating the Meiji leaders.

He confessed that he had harbored political ambition very early, and that such ambition was nurtured by two contemporary events: the Paris Peace Conference and the Russian Bolshevik Revolution. At first he dreamed of becoming a statesman-diplomat on the international stage with power to decide the fate of mankind, like the Big Four at Versailles. Later, he fancied himself a leader of the masses bent on the overthrow of the ruling class, just as Lenin and Trotsky had been.[11] All through his student years in Japan he was the organizer of a Chinese students' debating society, and each week he engaged in public speaking, because he considered this ability an indispensable quality of a national leader. When praised as a good speaker, he fancied himself China's Lenin.[12] He became a Marxist, was one of the twelve delegates to the First Congress of the Chinese Communist Party (CCP) at Shanghai in July 1921, and was elected there the CCP's deputy general secretary, acting for Ch'en Tu-hsiu during the latter's absence. In the fall of 1921 he had to interrupt his party activities to return to Japan to finish his studies at Kyoto.[13]

In 1924, at the invitation of Tai Chi-t'ao, he became secretary of the propaganda department of the KMT at Canton, shortly after the KMT decided to admit Communists. Chou and Tai remained intimate friends until Chou's defection from Chungking in 1938. Tai had been Sun Yat-sen's secretary and one of the earliest Chinese to interpret Marx's works and to explain Chinese conditions in terms of Marxist

---

and anecdotes abounded and were well circulated. This was the kind of atmosphere prevalent in higher circles when Chou began his ambitious career.

[10] After spending a year in the preparatory class at the First Higher School in Tokyo, Chou transferred to the Seventh Higher School in Kagoshima. In his *Wang-i chi* he stressed the fact that Kagoshima was the birthplace and home of Saigō Takamori. Chou Fo-hai, "Fu-sang chi-ying su tang-nien," in *Wang-i chi*, 10th ed., p. 23.

[11] Ibid., pp. 28-29.   [12] Ibid.

[13] Ibid., p. 39.

economic theory; later he became an anti-Communist interpreter of the Three People's Principles. Tai and Chou had parallel intellectual interests, as Chou soon resigned from the CCP and became a theorist of Sun Yat-sen's Three People's Principles. It was through Tai, also an intimate friend of Chiang Kai-shek's, that Chou began teaching in the political department of the Whampoa Military Academy. His launching into a bureaucratic career with the Kuomintang coincided with his increasing aversion to Borodin's control of the Communists in Canton. While he formally abandoned his commitment to the Communist enterprise, he never gave up Marxism as a tool of analysis. He was, however, like Ch'en Kung-po, suspected by the KMT of being a Communist, and attacked by the Communists as a renegade. Unable to tolerate Borodin, he left Canton to teach at the Wuchang Commercial College.

After the arrival of the National Revolutionary Army (NRA) in Wuhan, Chou again became involved in politics. He was appointed by Chiang Kai-shek as secretary of the Wuhan headquarters of the NRA headed by Teng Yen-ta. Concurrently, he was also appointed general secretary of the Central Military and Political Academy and head of its political department. In the academy he had to work with Yün Tai-ying, a most able and astute Communist, and he encountered much difficulty caused by KMT-CCP competition for power. In January 1927 Chiang Kai-shek paid a brief visit to Wuhan. Late one evening Chou went to call on Chiang and told him about the complicated situation at the academy. Chiang encouraged this vigilance.[14] We can presume that from that time on Chou steered close to Chiang. Nevertheless, his position within the KMT was not secure, for he was arrested in Shanghai during the purge of 1927. Rescued through the intervention of friends, he was later vindicated as a loyal KMT member when Chiang recruited him to work at Nanking. Ch'en Kung-po and Chou Fo-hai, both early CCP leaders turned KMT members, experienced extreme abuse from the Comintern- and Borodin-dominated Communists. They never again trusted the Communists and in 1945 preferred to brave the punishment of the KMT government than accept an offer from the Communists. By then, of course, their revulsion against the CCP had hardened after years of anti-Communist activity in the peace movement, and they remained

[14] Chou Fo-hai, "Sheng-shuai yüeh-chin hua ts'ang-sang," in *Wang-i chi*, Hong Kong ed., p. 33.

impervious to the Communists' reportedly repeated overtures for liaison.

From 1929 to 1932, Ch'en Kung-po, as the spokesman of the Reorganization Clique of the KMT headed by Wang Ching-wei, criticized the manipulations of the dominant faction headed by Chiang. Chou Fo-hai, on the other hand, owed his rise in the KMT hierarchy to his association with this dominant faction. It was decided that delegates to the Third KMT Congress be appointed by the party's high echelons. Ch'en was critical of the measure and as a result was expelled from the KMT, while Chou was appointed a delegate "representing KMT members in the Philippines." At the Fourth KMT Congress, when it was decided to retain all the members of the Central Executive Committees and Central Supervisory Committees of the previous congresses, new members were added with Chou Fo-hai heading the list. He had received the largest number of votes cast by the delegates, and was dubbed *Chuang-yüan chung-wei*, signifying his status as the first among the newly risen leaders of the KMT.[15]

In those years Chou was serving alternately and sometimes concurrently as editor of the *Hsin sheng-ming yüeh-k'an* (New Life Monthly), a Chiang publication; as director of the political department of the Central Military Academy at Nanking; and as a member of Chiang's entourage to draft documents. With the publication of his *San-min chu-i chih li-lun te t'i-hsi* in 1928 Chou established himself as the most authoritative scholar of the doctrine of Sun Yat-sen. Under his pen, the Three People's Principles became highly systematic and internally consistent. Forty thousand copies of this work were sold in the first three months.[16] It was not only a comprehensive explanation of Sun's doctrine, but was also a program for the KMT to follow in the future and a guide to its step-by-step implementation. It was adopted by the Central Military Academy and many universities and middle schools under KMT jurisdiction as a textbook for party doctrine (*tang-i*), a regular part of the school curriculum. Chou's becoming an authority on Sun's doctrine coincided with the emergence of the cult of Sun Yat-sen, promulgated by Chiang's faction perhaps to confer on Chiang the necessary aura of legitimacy as Sun's revolutionary heir. Chou became an important cadre of the

15 Ibid., pp. 51, 68-69.
16 The first edition appeared in April 1928 and the ninth in May 1929, Shanghai.

CC faction inside the KMT and a top cadre of the secret Blue Shirt organization because of his connections with Whampoa and Central Military Academy graduates. His friendship with Ch'en Li-fu, the most important leader of the CC faction perhaps started when they both were part of Chiang's entourage on a 1928 visit to Peking. On that occasion they became congenial fellow tourists in their lively exploration of Peking and Tientsin. Their disposition and their penchant for action differentiated them from the more staid characters of Chiang's group, such as Ch'en Pu-lei.[17]

In 1931, when Chiang Kai-shek was about to step down from Nanking in one of his many maneuvers to prove his indispensability, he assigned Ku Chu-t'ung to the governorship of Kiangsu province in preparation for his comeback. Ku, realizing his limitations as a military man, requested the services of Chou Fo-hai from Chiang. Consequently, for six years Chou was a member of the Kiangsu provincial government and head of its department of education, succeeding in making the area a stronghold of the KMT on the cultural and educational front. Chou's tenure in Kiangsu demonstrated his administrative ability, and he was considered the more remarkable because of the fact that he was not even a native of Kiangsu.[18]

Thus Chou came to posts near the apex of supreme power in China, or at least closest to the most powerful person in China, and enjoyed a rapid rise in the KMT and government hierarchies.[19] He was quite aware of the value of factionalism in promoting his own interests; and he understood that organizational means were crucial to the individual's advancement. He was flattered that many senior military men and politicians befriended him and sought his company. This may have been because of his proven ability and brilliance. On the other hand, he could not be quite sure that this was really the reason. Perhaps these military men and politicians only wanted to insure their access to Chiang Kai-shek by cultivating him. On many an occasion Chou expressed his gratification of his new status, influence, and affluence; but he also disparaged the part he played by calling it *p'ao-lung-t'ao te chiao-she* (the role of a valet attending to the needs of

---

[17] Chou Fo-hai, "Ssu-yu Pei-p'ing tsa-kan," *Wang-i chi*, 10th ed., p. 92.

[18] Chou Fo-hai, "Sheng-shuai yüeh-chin hua ts'ang-sang," pp. 69-70. Also, see I Chun-tso, *Hui-meng san-shih-nien* (Singapore, 1954), pp. 108-10.

[19] In a sense Chou was not different from the many Japan-, Europe- and U.S.-returned students going into politics and bureaucratic careers. The times required their services and expertise, and most of them rose quite rapidly. Professor Noriko Kamachi has pointed out to the author the similarities between Chou Fo-hai and Ts'ao Ju-lin.

a star actor of the troupe), indicating a certain measure of discontent.[20] A contemporary associate of Chou's has observed that most of the high commanders of the NRA were on good terms with Chou because he was learned and witty. Chou's fondness for seeking pleasure in wine and women, ability to converse, and glowing sense of humor suited the taste of these military men; and because Chou was in charge of general political work for Chiang, he saw these men often.[21]

As a self-styled "valet," Chou was an astute understudy of Chiang's style of operation. One particular instance especially impressed the observant Chou. When Yen Hsi-shan and Feng Yü-hsiang declared their independence of Nanking in 1930, Chiang proceeded on two fronts to quell the rebellion. Militarily, his advance northward was temporarily halted at Liu-ho; politically, Chiang's emissaries Chang Ch'ün and Wu T'ieh-ch'eng were diligently at work at Mukden to persuade the "Young Marshal," Chang Hsüeh-liang, to lead his forces to Shanhaikuan to threaten Yen's rear. Chou made this observation: "Old Yen was reluctant to spend money while this side [Chiang's men] was dispensing gold like dirt." Later, the Young Marshal did lead his forces to Shanhaikuan and the Yen-Feng front collapsed. "Of course, this outcome was not entirely due to having spent a lot of money; but money spent was one of the crucial elements in deciding it," Chou concluded.[22] In later years Chou, like Chiang, was not interested in accumulating private wealth, nor did he live ostentatiously; but he did consciously use money to tip the balance in political negotiations or to buy people's allegiance. Like Chiang, Chou periodically presented sums of money to people deprived of power like T'ang Sheng-chih;[23] even Ch'en Tu-hsiu, in the days after his release from prsion in 1937, was dependent upon Chou's subsidy through the I-wen Yen-chiu She.[24] After arriving in occupied Shanghai, Chou began even more systematically recruiting and retaining people with regular stipends so as to make himself the hub of activities of the peace movement.[25]

Did Chou like Chiang as a superior? While he never said anything

---

[20] Chou Fo-hai, "Sheng-shuai yüeh-chin hua ts'ang-sang," pp. 50, 74.

[21] I Chun-tso, p. 108.

[22] Chou Fo-hai, "Sheng-shuai yüeh-chin hua ts'ang-sang," p. 62.

[23] Chou Fo-hai, *Chou Fo-hai jih-chi* (Hong Kong, 1955), p. 158.

[24] Howard L. Boorman, ed., *Biographical Dictionary of Republican China* (New York, 1967-71), vol. 1, p. 247.

[25] Chu Tzu-chia, vol. 1, pp. 38-39.

disparaging about Chiang in public, his intimate knowledge of Chiang's style of operation must have been a factor in deciding his course of action in leaving him. Chou indirectly and yet unmistakably registered his perception of Chiang's ruthlessness when he said in 1941 that if peace between China and Japan should become a reality, Chiang might lean heavily on Chou for a year or two, but afterwards, Chiang surely would have him assassinated.[26] This type of apprehension, based on his knowledge of Chiang, the man, was not conducive to an ambitious person like Chou remaining with Chiang if he had a reasonably good alternative. In comparing Chiang with Wang Ching-wei, Chou found Wang the more congenial, warm, and appreciative. Chou, even in the days when he had every reason to believe that the peace movement was doomed, still maintained that he could never desert Wang because Wang had regarded him as a *kuo-shih* (learned and respected first minister of state),[27] whereas he had been only an aide in Chiang's personal office. In his years of service with Chiang, Chou often had to guess what Chiang would do next at critical moments. He never had the distinction of being consulted as to the policy and program to be adopted or the strategy to be pursued. Chou felt that he was merely told to draft this or that document with this or that slant. With Wang, Chou felt that he had his leader's complete confidence to manage things as he saw fit.[28]

The constellation of talents around Chiang in 1937-38 was such that Chou saw no likelihood of his becoming his number one minister. Chang Ch'ün and a host of the Cheng-hsüeh-hsi people were staffing the major bureaucratic posts and were Chiang's trusted emissaries. These people were well versed in the politics of the warlord era and were therefore skilled in negotiation between factions. Men such as T. V. Soong, H. H. Kung and Sun Fo preempted many other important posts because of their family connections with Chiang. Substantive provincial posts, on the other hand, were usually assigned to Chiang's trusted generals. On the staff side, there were Ch'en Pu-lei, Ch'en Li-fu, Ch'en Kuo-fu, Shao Li-tzu, and others to share the work, and Chou was merely one of them, and a junior one at that. If we take into account the endings of those who worked long and

---

[26] Chou Fo-hai, *Chou Fo-hai jih-chi*, pp. 105, 115.

[27] Ibid., p. 149.

[28] Despite his having been exposed to Western philosophical ideas and Marxist analyses, Chou still appreciated the classical adage "shih wei chih-chi-che yung" (the gentleman-scholar serves the one who appreciates him). His acquiescence in this view could have been an impetus for his political choice as well as a justification for his shifting to a new superior.

closely in Chiang's personal office, we might suspect that a certain malaise was being nurtured there. Ch'en Pu-lei committed suicide in 1948, as did Tai Chi-t'ao, Chiang's long-time intimate friend. Ch'en Li-fu, who spent more than two decades of his adult life working single-mindedly to promote Chiang's career, found it prudent to leave Chiang after 1948 and seek a life of exile in the United States. Had Chou remained in Chungking with Chiang, would he have fared any better? Or, if he had been given substantive posts, would he have done better than, say, Wu Kuo-chen, whose parting of the ways with Chiang was bitter and irreversible?

It seems, as far as satisfying Chou's ambition was concerned, that service with Chiang, for a number of reasons, was a dead-end street.[29] Any alternative that would permit Chou to exercise his ability to the fullest extent looked attractive to him. Opportunity came in the form of working under Wang, the titular leader, with himself playing the Meiji statesman, to create a new situation. When the Nanking government was established in occupied China in March 1940 with Wang as the head, Chou Fo-hai held the following posts: vice president of the Executive Yüan, minister of finance, minister of police, vice chairman of the Military Affairs Commission, and general director of the Central Reserve Bank. In addition, he personally controlled the secret service and was the chief negotiator with Japan on behalf of Wang. In his diary a few weeks before, he boasted, "The entire government will come into existence under my pen in the next ten minutes."[30] That kind of pleasure could never have been his had he remained in Chungking with Chiang.

Historical Precedents and Contemporary Views

There were certain historical precedents for outwardly treasonous acts. One example was set by Chang Chih-tung and Liu K'un-i in 1900 at the time of the Boxers Uprising.[31] They favored, in essence, a tem-

---

[29] Chou Fo-hai, *Chou Fo-hai jih-chi*, pp. 149, 158-59.

[30] Ibid., p. 18.

[31] Chu Tzu-chia, vol. 5, p. 98. In 1900, Chang was governor of Liang-Hu, and Liu, governor of Liang-Chiang. After their failure to warn the Empress Dowager of the danger of her policy of antagonizing foreigners, Chang and Liu decided to take the matter in their own hands. First they interpreted the Boxers' uprising as a "rebellion" against the legitimate authority of the Empress Dowager; any edict from Peking ordering them to support the Boxers was regarded as the work of people who had usurped the imperial authority. They jointly informed the consular body in Shanghai that they as governors would guarantee the safety of foreign lives and property in the Yangtze region if the foreign powers promised not to land troops there. The proposal was accepted by the powers and the arrangement was imitated

porary separation of the provinces under their control from central authorities, and this was in fact outright treason. The important point, however, was that Chang and Liu preserved the empire by forestalling large-scale foreign military intervention, and subsequently enabled the Empress Dowager, by punishing the Boxers and their supporters, to remain in power. Chang and Liu were considered meritorious and rewarded accordingly. Therefore, for those who knew recent Chinese history, the criterion of loyalty was not the technical issue of obeying the legal government, but whether actions fostered the good of the nation. Chinese politicians and intellectuals loved allusions. In 1937-38, if fighting the Japanese on the battle front was not a feasible policy and was to be avoided, then pursuing a policy of peace should not be condemned outright. In leaving Chungking, Chou and Wang emphasized that even a person of Wang's position had no chance of voicing his opinion there, much less of starting an open debate. Thus their initial move was explained as an escape from one-faction rule in Chungking so as to have freedom to speak and to work for peace in pursuit of a more correct policy.[32]

Meanwhile, in the occupied areas, Japanese savagery had caused the legal authorities of the various localities to flee, and there was chaos and much unnecessary suffering. Not infrequently, it was to counter the abuses of the Japanese soldiers, rōnin, and Chinese rough-necks that a number of local elders, who otherwise would have remained in retirement, ventured to make direct contact with the Japanese authorities, hoping to act as intermediaries between the Japanese military and the Chinese population in the immediate post bellum situation. In this role they could claim precedents in Chinese history. The gentry, while not employed in the central bureaucracy, rendered service as local leaders in times of civil strife or in the interim between different central authorities, to maintain peace and order. Their reference group was not the new intellectuals of nationalist inspiration. Traditionally there was no stigma as traitor or appeaser in performing this role to protect local welfare. Most of the peace maintenance committees that were set up in small towns and hsien cities were formed by local elders in the spirit of public service to cushion the blow of the invading forces. Upon the inauguration of more

by viceroys and governors elsewhere. See Arthur W. Hummel, ed., *Eminent Chinese of the Ch'ing Period* (Washington, D.C., 1943), vol. 1, pp. 30f., 524f.
[32] Chu Tzu-chia, vol. 1, pp. 16, 54-55.

formal governing bodies under the conquerors most of these leaders faded out of the scene.[33]

With the conquest of more Chinese territory by the Japanese, the peace maintenance committees multiplied as the lowest level administrative organs. In time, formal administration was restored, with a system of Japanese military control corresponding to the hsien and municipal levels of Chinese administration. In north China, the revived local administrations as well as the East Hopei anti-Communist autonomous government were incorporated in January 1938 into the Provisional government of China, which was established in Peiping with Japanese military sponsorship. In the Shanghai-Nanking area, the first sizable group of collaborators headed the so-called Ta-tao municipal government, which proceeded to have jurisdiction over Shanghai, excepting the International Settlement and the French Concession, as the Chinese army retreated from the area in November 1937. In March 1938, a Reformed government was set up in Nanking, sponsored by the Japanese military and headed by Liang Hung-chih, a retired Peiyang bureaucrat and a gifted poet of considerable renown. This government in theory incorporated the Ta-tao municipal government.

Japan had been trying to enlist more prestigious personalities, including the retired warlord Wu P'ei-fu, to head these puppet regimes. Wu's terms for collaboration were too severe to be acceptable to the Japanese, and his premature death in December 1939 ended the matter. The public of the occupied areas, whose attention was focused on Wu during the months of negotiation, did not censure him for having talked with the Japanese. The idea of working out an arrangement with the occupying power was not abhorrent or degrading. Rather, the conditions of collaboration were crucial and of great interest. When Wu died without committing himself, he was portrayed as loyal, patriotic, and uncorruptible. Having negotiated with the Japanese did not tarnish his reputation at all. The only way the Nationalist government could have put an end to such Chinese responses to Japanese overtures was through assassination. For instance, when

[33] Chinese Communist accounts, particularly in dramas, almost invariably link these "peace maintenance committee" members with exploitation of the peasantry in the local areas, and thus make them into a class enemy as well as traitors to the national interest, with the exception of Communist underground workers or agents posing as traitors. This portrayal has an element of truth. However, it fails to account for most of the arrangements for transition from the military phase to the "normal" phase in areas under de facto Japanese occupation.

T'ang Shao-i, a former premier of the Peiyang era, was suspected of negotiating with the Japanese, he was assassinated, as was Ch'en Lu, an accomplished diplomat of World War I vintage.

From Chungking's official viewpoint, collaboration with the Japanese in occupied areas was treason. But in the everyday world of people under occupation, the working out of a modus vivendi was the most urgent matter of the moment. Certainly a large amorphous Chinese population could not live side by side with an occupation force without some kind of arrangement, and it was certainly to the benefit of the local people to have the best men available to arrive at the terms. Respected community leaders remaining in the area were subject to that kind of pressure. Most of the personnel of collaborative regimes before that of Wang Ching-wei and Chou Fo-hai were former Peiyang politicians and bureaucrats who had never espoused the KMT ideology. Only a scant ten years earlier they had been in charge of Chinese government and politics. To people in occupied areas, they were certainly less reprehensible to deal with than the foreign conquerors known for their cruelty and arbitrariness.

There had been repeated turnovers on the Chinese political scene since the demise of the Manchu dynasty. Each new administration brought in its own ruling groups and put into retirement politicians and bureaucrats of the former regimes. In cities such as Shanghai and Tientsin there were many retired politicians and bureaucrats whose training and abilities would have made them useful under any regime, but whose ideological orientations made them unsuitable. Many of them had been trained in Japan and had known Japanese connections, and for many of them a pro-Japanese administration was tolerable, if not preferred.

In his analysis of the Chinese political scene, Chou Fo-hai recognized the complementary roles of the revolutionary and the career bureaucrat; while the ideology of the KMT spread northward as a result of the Northern Expedition (1926-28), the influence of the northern bureaucrats expanded southward to Nanking. This was inevitable, he observed, since no policy or program, no matter how well conceived, could be carried out unless there were good administrators.[34] Revolutionaries were usually too busy to acquire training and expertise in administration. Hence, bureaucrats of former regimes were inevitably utilized even in revolutionary governments. For

---

[34] Chou Fo-hai, "Ssu-yu Pei-p'ing tsa-kan," pp. 95-96. Also, Chou Fo-hai, "Sheng-shuai yüeh-chin hua ts'ang-sang," p. 32.

Chou, those who had not been recruited to the KMT enterprise and those who had been left out of the resistance effort constituted an untapped pool of human resources. Therefore, although initially Wang and Chou had expected a number of major military figures to follow them from Chungking, when this failed to materialize, Chou remained undaunted because he expected to be able to draw on talents idling in the occupied areas. The first step he took upon reaching Shanghai was to contact and recruit trained personnel, and to retain them with monthly stipends even before the organization of a new government at Nanking was accomplished.

Those who had preceded Chou in collaborating with Japan were not without their own ideologies. The ideology of the Provisional government in north China was clearly retrogressive and reprehensible to both Wang and Chou. The ideology of the Reformed government, on the other hand, had to counter the fact that the Nanking-Shanghai area had been a KMT stronghold before it was abandoned. It therefore proceeded to erode the legitimacy of the KMT and its government in the Yangtze area by propagating a new interpretation of the doctrine of Sun Yat-sen. Emphasizing Sun's effort in 1924-25 to convene a national assembly, Reformed government spokesmen claimed that Sun had given no explicit instruction on one-party rule; the KMT one-party dictatorship was a stumbling block to the development of nationalism and representative government. Citing Sun's concept of pan-Asianism, they advocated negotiation with Japan in order to avoid the scourge of war. "People of the same Yellow race should not have internal quarrels."[35] While they traced the cause of the Sino-Japanese conflict to Japan's need to protect its own safety in the face of the Western powers' encroachment on neighboring territory, they condemned the Chinese Nationalist government for its lack of wisdom in negotiating with its eastern neighbor and for its lack of preparation for national defense when it failed to keep peace. "At peace time it was engaged in suppressing public opinion, at war, it had no way to lead the masses"—a condemnation that unfortunately rang true to many ears and ran parallel to propaganda put out by the Chinese Communists. Furthermore, the Red menace was considered the source of all troubles. They cited the KMT's alliance with the Chinese Communists as endangering the security of all Asian peoples, and therefore they held that Japan's action was anti-Com-

[35] This and the subsequent abstract of the ideology of the reformed government are based on Wu Ch'eng-yu, *Wei-hsin cheng-kang yüan-lun* (Nanking, 1939).

munist in intention, and its invasion of China defensive in nature.[36] These ideas were close to the viewpoint of Wang and Chou and of those who were pessimistic about the outcome of organized resistance, except that neither Wang nor Chou could condone the Reformed government's unorthodox manipulation of Sun's doctrine. Both Chou and Wang had a stake in the proper interpretation and implementation of this doctrine, Wang as Sun's most trusted disciple, and Chou as an authority on the subject. Cooperation with Japan therefore must be on the basis of Sun's teaching, but not as it was interpreted by the Reformed government. To have an orthodox KMT and a KMT-sponsored government was the sine qua non of collaboration. If collaboration with Japan were necessary, Wang and Chou believed, they could do the job better and in a proper manner.

Japan profited from the fact that the Nationalist government had not only virtually neglected to reorganize and evacuate industries and skilled workers of the coastal areas to the hinterland, but had also failed to immobilize Shanghai, Nanking, and other strategic cities as potential enemy war bases before they were abandoned. Japan was able to capture their resources and industrial plants, as well as employ the abundant Chinese labor supply of the coastal provinces. Occupying forces took over all Chinese government property and all means of large-scale production, and monopolized the distributive services. They imposed manufactured goods on the Chinese market in return for Chinese Nationalist government banknotes for foreign exchange. Treating China as an internal market, the Japanese brought in and took out vast quantities of commodity and capital goods without passing through customs at all. This state of affairs, characterized as *i-chan yang-chan* (to use the war to support the war), worried many Chinese leaders for fear that severe depletion of Chinese resources would result. In addition, the Japanese government exerted strong pressure on British officialdom, and by April 27, 1938, succeeded in negotiating an agreement with the British ambassador in Tokyo. This agreement allowed the Reformed government at Nanking to take over and deposit in Yokohama Specie Bank all future Chinese customs receipts after deducting funds for servicing China's foreign loans. Thus, the proceeds of China's customs went to Japan. In the years before the war, some 40 to 50 percent of the Nationalist government's revenue came from customs receipts in

[36] Ibid.

[318]

Shanghai alone.[37] Chou could not have failed to see the importance and possibility of laying his hands on this huge source of revenue. In fact, after he reached Shanghai in 1939 he was able to get the Japanese to release part of this deposit from the Yokohama Specie Bank to finance his peace movement. Chou regarded this as the first instance of returning Chinese resources to Chinese hands.[38] It was no accident that subsequently he chose to be minister of finance and general director of the Central Reserve Bank. Chou had been trained in political economy at Kyoto, but he had had no part in financial and fiscal matters in Chiang Kai-shek's service.

Chinese cities under Japanese occupation, because of all their industrial, commercial, and distributive facilities, enjoyed a measure of prosperity unmatched by cities in Free China. People like Chou Fo-hai were convinced not only of the necessity of preventing the flow of Chinese resources to Japan, or their depletion by other means, but also that the higher-level industrial capacity and prosperity of the coastal areas provided a better material base on which to build a new Chinese administration. In this belief, Chou consciously compared the prospect of the peace movement about to be launched with that of the Northern Expedition. On the eve of the Northern Expedition the insiders of the KMT knew well that in terms of sheer military strength, the National Revolutionary Army was no match for the forces of Wu P'ei-fu and Sun Ch'uan-fang; yet the effort was made, and it altered the power constellation in China. If a regional KMT government situated in a corner of south China could in three years by sheer willpower develop into a national government of China, why should not a peace movement with all the resources of the Yangtze area shape the destiny of China likewise?[39]

According to Wang, the Japanese conditions for peace as transmitted by the German ambassador, Oskar Trautmann, at the end of 1937 were acceptable to Chiang, and the mediation would bear fruit were it not for Chiang's concern over his own position. It was generally believed that only through resistance to the Japanese peace terms could Chiang command the allegiance of the different political

[37] William Crane Johnstone, Jr., *The Shanghai Problem* (Stanford, 1937), pp. 174-75, and footnote 8 on p. 175: "It is also alleged that much illegal revenue is gained in the Shanghai area."
[38] Chu Tzu-chia, vol. 1, p. 28. Also, see Chou Fo-hai, *Chou Fo-hai jih-chi*, pp. 59, 88.
[39] Chou Fo-hai's preface to the Japanese edition, appended to *Wang-i chi*, 10th ed., pp. 3-4.

groups in China. If Chiang were for peace, the different KMT factions as well as the CCP would openly challenge his leadership. For Chiang, it was not wise to stop an external war to fight a civil war. But, queried Wang: "What would be the use of domestic unity if the entire nation should suffer disastrous annihilation?"[40] Chou Fo-hai, on the other hand, had estimated that the military strength of the Nationalist government, though woefully inadequate to fight the Japanese, was strong enough to exterminate the Communists and to suppress domestic dissidents, and to permit Chiang to remain in power and maintain peace and order. Chou had opposed China's plunging into military conflict with Japan on the strength of mere hopes that a protracted war would eventually bring about Japan's financial and military collapse, and that further complications in the international situation would bring helpful allies to China's side.

Chou was initially sent by Chiang Kai-shek to confer with Wang Ching-wei and to coordinate their views on national policy. Chou easily agreed with Wang and regarded peace at a price as preferable to continuation of war; the latter course would only bring Communist forces to the fore in a China too devastated to rebuild.[41] In their moving away from Chungking, Chou preceded Wang to Kunming, to Hong Kong, and to Shanghai.[42] In a way he was leading Wang on, getting Wang step by step committed to a course of action designed by him.[43]

With the participation of the resourceful and articulate Chou Fo-hai, the peace movement, which started out by seeking an opportunity to expound a new policy, took a drastic turn.[44] The so-called Chou Fo-hai line prevailed: that was, in order not to dissipate the strength of the peace movement and its potentiality, a government should be organized in occupied China to rally all would-be peace workers. Should Chungking fail to negotiate for peace, the new regime would bargain independently with Japan. Chou had already made an estimate of the material and human resources available in occupied areas for

[40] Wang Ching-wei, "An Example," written on March 27, 1939, reproduced in full in Chu Tzu-chia, vol. 5, pp. 56-62.

[41] Ibid., vol. 1, pp. 17, 41.

[42] Chou Fo-hai in fact preceded Wang to Kunming. See Ch'en Pu-lei, *Ch'en Pu-lei hui-i lu* (Taipei, 1967), p. 138.

[43] Chou Fo-hai, *Chou Fo-hai jih-chi*, pp. 61, 55-56.

[44] While Wang sojourned in Hanoi, an attempt on his life was made under the overall direction of Cheng Chieh-min, a Chungking agent. Wang escaped unharmed, but his longtime protégé and confidant Tseng Chung-min was fatally wounded. This episode very much enraged Wang and had a lot to do with his decision to go to the Japanese occupied areas.

such a venture. Meeting with Japanese agents in early April 1939 in Shanghai, he proposed that Japan sponsor the establishment of a rival Chinese government in Nanking under Wang's leadership for the purpose of bringing the Sino-Japanese conflict to an end. Chou had argued strongly for this course of action at a conference presided over by Wang in Shanghai and won Wang's approval. In taking this tack, Chou and Wang were venting their frustration at the lack of international concern for China's plight, a frustration shared by many prominent Chinese leaders. The Brussels Conference called by the League of Nations had failed to settle the Sino-Japanese war. Hence, the concept of collective security was completely discredited. In spite of President Roosevelt's quarantine speech, no substantial aid had been extended to China by the United States. The Neutrality Act was useful to Japan but barely helpful to China. On the other hand, China and Japan had enjoyed a tradition of direct negotiation since the Mukden Incident in September 1931. Dependence on a third power to mediate between China and Japan so far had produced little result. In other words, it would be better to continue negotiations between the two countries once Wang Ching-wei was premier. Finally, but most basically, Chou and Wang believed that Japan was anti-Russian and anti-Comintern in orientation, and as such, would not provoke the United States and Great Britain; therefore, it was futile for China to hope that the two Western powers would come to its aid against Japan in the present conflict. In their opinion, to have a Chinese government led by Wang in the occupied areas was to realize a partial peace; this partial peace could be used as leverage to induce a total peace.[45]

Chou was counting on all the human and material resources available in the occupied areas as well as the ambiguity of the issue of war or peace among a segment of the Chinese population. In launching the Chou Fo-hai line Chou made himself indispensable to the realization of his scheme. On a separate occasion, in total frankness, he admitted that to get ahead in high places one must make oneself indispensable.[46]

The Peace Movement as Political Opposition

The schism inside the KMT in the immediate prewar years and the rivalry between Chiang Kai-shek and other KMT factions were

[45] Chou Fo-hai, *Chou Fo-hai jih-chi*, pp. 10-11.
[46] Chou Fo-hai, "Chi-lo ssu," in *Wang-i chi*, 10th ed., p. 131.

vivid elements in the political awareness of people like Chou Fo-hai, and they figured prominently in Chou's estimate of how his defection from Chungking might be regarded. Chou had personally weathered the Nanking-Wuhan split in 1927. In that episode, after months of antagonism, the governments at Wuhan and Nanking had resolved their major differences through negotiations; no sanctions were imposed by any legitimate authority, for there was no such undisputed authority.

Again, in 1930, Wang Ching-wei had sided with Yen Hsi-shan and Feng Yü-hsiang in attempting to establish a rival government at Peking. When this move proved unsuccessful, Yen and Feng did not face any censure, and their influence in their own provinces remained undiminished. Wang Ching-wei then went to Canton, and in 1931 participated in the independence movement of Kwangtung and Kwangsi against Nanking. Although Wang repeatedly failed, he was never punished. The only sanction amounted to "permanent expulsion" from the KMT for some of Wang's close associates at the height of the crises. Wang himself was unscathed. Soon, the "permanently expelled" members were received back into the fold when national emergencies called for a renewed effort at unity, and Wang was called back to head the Executive Yüan.

Throughout 1927-37, although Chou and Wang were in opposite factions, it became obvious to Chou that Chiang had no more claim to legitimacy than Wang. Chiang could never accuse Wang of treason simply because Wang opposed him. Nor could he put Wang under house arrest as he did to Hu Han-min, an act which backfired. Wang's essentially political argument and civilian stance rendered Chiang's primarily military power ineffective or inapplicable; stopping Wang was impossible, short of outright assassination. There was always a sizable body of opinion within the KMT, backed by regional military groups, that would sympathize with Chiang's opponents. Having perceived all these things, Chou perhaps thought light of the consequence of siding with Chiang's opposition.

In 1937-38, Chou was the person in Chiang Kai-shek's private office who transmitted messages from Kao Tsung-wu to Chiang.[47] Kao was an official of the Chinese government; his unauthorized secret negotiations with Japan were obviously treason. Yet when told of this, Chiang's comment was merely "*Huang-t'ang! huang-t'ang!*"[48] Chiang

[47] Chu Tzu-chia, vol. 5, p. 9.
[48] Ibid. *Huang-t'ang* can be interpreted as "nonsense."

[322]

apparently condoned Kao's unorthodox activities, for they provoked no immediate censure. It thus seems that at that time Chiang was tolerant of efforts to find a way to reach Japan, not anticipating, of course, that this eventually would lead to the foundation of a government challenging his own authority. Perhaps grown used to Japan's interventionist policies in the prewar years, even Chiang thought lightly of negotiating with the Japanese after resistance had been declared to be the government's policy.

As major collaborators, Chou and Wang obviously did not think that their actions in 1938-40 betrayed Chinese interests. Their general attitude toward collaboration was best illustrated by Ch'en Pi-chün's (Madame Wang Ching-wei's) "protest" at her postwar trial. Her adamant gesture fully indicated her sense of being trapped by "improper procedures." She vehemently stated that had Wang been alive, the whole question of the Nanking government would have been settled by "political" means.[49] In fact she never accepted the prosecution and trial as legal. Although in 1945 Chou was much more aware than Ch'en Pi-chün and many others that China's new international status and the watchfulness of the much-strengthened Communist Party had limited Chungking's freedom in the disposition of the collaborators, in 1939 he would never have anticipated that arrest, trial, and the death sentence were to be his lot for having sided with Wang Ching-wei. Exile or retirement might be his fate, or at worst, assassination—certainly not open trial. This, of course, was due to the fact that up to the time of their defection in 1938 there had not been a tradition of legality in the KMT, nor had the Nationalist government under Chiang's domination a sufficiently strong sense of legitimacy to pass judgment on other factions; the collaborators did not expect to be actually judged by ex post facto laws. Thus, in a sense, despite the gravity of the war-peace issue, in 1938 Chou thought of his action, in part at least, in the light of past opposition to Chiang. What then was his chance for success?

Both Chou and Wang had a stake in the propagation of Sun's *San-min chu-i*. Wang wanted his orthodox KMT to carry out the unfinished work of Sun; Chou thought that forms of government could undergo changes and that even the KMT could undergo reorganization, but that the principles of Sun Yat-sen should be upheld at all costs.[50] In addition to insisting on the use of the same tricolor national

---

[49] Ibid., vol. 4, pp. 89-90.
[50] Chou Fo-hai, *Chou Fo-hai jih-chi*, pp. 60-61.

flag, Wang called the Sixth KMT National Congress at Shanghai as the first step leading to the formation of a central government. Delegates to the Congress were either appointed by Wang himself or recommended and guaranteed by Wang's trusted lieutenants.[51] This procedure had precedents in KMT history, and there was really no constitutional ground to consider this revived KMT in occupied areas any less representative than the KMT in Free China.

The peace movement was not thought to be traitorous by its adherents because it was also part of their aims to modify Japanese behavior and policy toward China. At his postwar trial, Ch'en Kungpo lamented the fact that Japan's middle-level officers were insubordinate and without any political sense.[52] Chou had voiced the same opinion.[53] However, in the beginning it was precisely on this middle level of the Japanese military that Chou's group had pinned their hopes in the negotiations. They displayed some knowledge of decision-making processes in Japan when they looked to Colonel Kagesa and associates for action. Kagesa's influence was much greater than might have been expected from his level in the hierarchy, but it was actually at the level of colonel that policy innovation originated. Their error was in taking one segment of these middle-level officers, those in favor of terminating the China conflict, to be representative of all the middle-level officers. In trying to deal with the Japanese, Chou exhibited no small amount of intellectual arrogance in his assessment of his own influence. In his diary he indicated how he had received the calls of Japanese journalists, writers, and politicians, and how he had tried to enlighten them as to the proper view to take with regard to the China question.[54] His *San-min chu-i chih li-lun te t'i-hsi* was translated into Japanese by Inukai Ken, enhancing Chou's self-confidence in dealing with Japanese intellectuals. In fact, ever since his student days, and especially after his defection from Chungking in 1938, Chou had made sure that his major writings were translated and published in Japan.[55] He expected to have a large readership there and to influence public opinion, particularly that of the younger generation, so that the Japanese public would develop a genuine sense of cooperation with China.[56]

[51] Chu Tzu-chia, vol. 1, pp. 39-40.

[52] Ch'en Kung-po, *Ch'en-ni Kung-po tzu-pai shu—pa-nien-lai te hui-i* (Shanghai, 1946), p. 29.

[53] Chou Fo-hai, *Chou Fo-hai jih-chi*, pp. 87-92.

[54] Ibid., pp. 162-63, 167.   [55] Published in Tokyo, 1939.

[56] Ch'en Wen-yüan's preface to Chou Fo-hai, *Wang-i chi* (Hong Kong, 1955), p. 1.

Although circumstances forced him to accept men such as Liang
Hung-chih and other collaborators of greater seniority into the
Nanking government, Chou and his associates at no time considered
themselves run-of-the-mill collaborators; rather, they saw themselves
as principled architects of a new world in Asia. Hoping that China
and Japan could be united in the web of a compelling ideology of
anti-Communism, Chou perhaps aimed to establish in the occupied
areas a political power similar to the post-World War II satellite
governments; in that setup, the Chinese would be guaranteed internal
autonomy while Japan assumed the military task of neutralizing
Chungking's forces. In this scenario, Chou could gradually consolidate
a political regime and create a sense of legitimacy by the very fact
that he and his people were there manning the positions.

Conclusion

The major argument advanced by the accused at the postwar trial
was that when they defected in 1938 from Chungking, they went to
the occupied areas empty-handed. What they succeeded in building
up in the following years was wrested from the hands of the enemy.
Hence, they claimed that they were in fact restoring Chinese resources
to Chinese hands. Ch'en Pi-chün, for instance, asked: "When large
chunks of Chinese territory were abandoned by the Nationalist government to the Japanese, where was the nation that Mr. Wang could
have to sell [to betray] to the Japanese?"[57] The treason trial became a
Pandora's box, spotlighting many theoretical questions such as, what
constituted legitimate authority—de facto rule or a priori claim? What
was nationalism? And what were the criteria for patriotism and loyalty? By then, the Communists ruled over portions of many provinces
as a result of their resistance effort against the Japanese, and had
claimed legitimate power and allegiance.

In one of the many prefaces to the many editions of his *Wang-i chi*,
Chou listed in 1944 the accomplishments of the peace movement as
follows: "Who [in the depressing days of 1938] could have dreamed
that the Nationalist government could return to Nanking, the blue-
sky-white-sun flag could unfurl on the side of the Tzu-chin Mountain? Who could have dreamed that extraterritoriality is now
abolished and foreign concessions returned to China? We have obtained from Japan [the promise] that when peace becomes a reality,
Japan will immediately withdraw all her soldiers from Chinese soil,

[57] Chu Tzu-chia, vol. 4, p. 90.

to the extent that she would not even insist on her right to station troops in north China as stipulated in the Boxer Protocol."[58] At his trial, Chou stated that in the first half of the Wang regime he had collaborated with Japan to benefit China, and in the last half of the regime, he had collaborated with Chungking at the expense of Japan.[59] He had made elaborate arrangements in the Nanking-Shanghai area to protect Chinese lives and property in the event of an Allied offensive, or in the face of Japanese wanton destruction in case of defeat. Unfortunately for Chou, these arrangements were not put to the test, as Japan surrendered prior to Allied landing on the China coast. In the last stage of the war, Chou had collected enough raw materials, including cotton, newsprint, and gold, to finance the anticipated counteroffensive of the Chungking forces against the Japanese. The unused assets were later turned over to Chungking authorities after VJ Day. The amount was of staggering size, and is listed in one of Chu Tzu-chia's volumes on the Wang regime. Chu allegedly obtained the information firsthand from Ch'ien Ta-k'uei, who had been deputy director of the Central Reserve Bank, when they were fellow inmates in jail awaiting trial.[60] This information is confirmed by another KMT publication. In a volume commemorating Tai Li, there is a complete list of the assets Tai Li was able to "confiscate" by his skillful manipulation of Chou Fo-hai.[61] In this sense, Chou's claim to have benefited China was essentially correct. In the final analysis, Chou's contribution consisted in his organizing ability and in his systematic recruitment of trained individuals to strategic positions in occupied China, thereby promoting a semblance of peace and order and the maintenance of a minimal degree of dignity for the Chinese under Japanese domination.[62] The fact that, when the regime dissolved itself after VJ Day, there was not a single notable case of violence against it by people under its rule was an indication that as a government it was viable and had fulfilled certain useful internal functions. Thus, it might be correct to say that Chou Fo-hai and his associates, by engineering and maintaining a Chinese

[58] Chou Fo-hai's preface to the Japanese edition, *Wang-i chi*, 10th ed., p. 4.
[59] Chu Tzu-chia, vol. 4, p. 106.
[60] Ibid., vol. 4, p. 117; vol. 1, pp. 117-20.
[61] *Tai Yü-nung hsien-sheng nien-p'u* (Taipei, 1966), pp. 138, 156, 170, 189, 201.
[62] Even sources hostile to the Wang regime admit that it dared to argue with Japanese authorities regarding Chinese sovereignty and legal rights. See Ta-sheng pien-wei-hui, *Wei-tsu-chih mi-mi* (Shanghai, 1945), p. 48; Kung Te-po, *Wang Chao-ming hsiang-ti mai-kuo mi-shih* (Taipei, 1963), pp. 109f.

government under the Japanese military, provided for peaceful resistance to Japan in contrast to Chungking's armed resistance.

The personal tragedy of Chou and his fellow collaborators was that they had learned their trade and universe of operations in the prewar KMT when things were in flux, and yet they were to be judged by postwar standards. The prewar conduct of the political man was learned through warlord politics, which were deficient in a sense of legality. After the war, the Allied victory lent the Chungking government the aura of strength needed to press for a monopoly of legitimacy after eight years' war against Japan. In asserting this newly won power in the face of the Chinese Communist challenge, Chungking lost much of its flexibility in dealing with the collaborators.

That Chou was ambitious is beyond doubt. One could even make a case for him as a confidence man, creating a situation in which he could put his ability to full use. Being a good understudy of Chiang Kai-shek, he learned a good many of Chiang's manipulative skills. However, long schooled in factional politics, he could not transcend them; despite the lofty ideals and sentiments, the worthy schemes and programs outlined in his *San-min chu-i chih li-lun te t'i-hsi*, his domination of the Nanking-Shanghai area never led him to break out of the confines of prewar KMT practice, namely, divide and control, with one man as the hub of all authority.

When the confident and decisive Chou refused to entertain the idea of utilizing his military and administrative positions in the Yangtze area to bolster his own personal safety in 1945, he marked the true end of the warlord period. By this time, however, he was ill and exhausted, although he still managed to carry a demanding work load. The fortune tellers had predicted that he would hold supreme power for only about five years.[63] In August-September 1945 it seemed to him that the five years were up, and that it was time to succumb to what fate had in store for him. He took his chances on Tai Li's promise to testify on his behalf and on Chiang's appreciation of his contributions toward keeping the Yangtze area intact for the Nationalist government during the last two years of the war. Chou was tried; his death sentence was commuted to life imprisonment by Chiang Kai-shek. He died in prison in 1948.

[63] Chou Fo-hai, *Chou Fo-hai jih-chi*, pp. 79-80.

CHAPTER XVI

JAPANESE PERSPECTIVES ON ASIA: FROM DISSOCIATION TO COPROSPERITY

———

BUNSŌ HASHIKAWA

Datsu-A-ron and Its Critics

There is no way of knowing what kind of reception the editorial "Datsu-A-ron" (Dissociation from Asia) received when it was first published in the March 16, 1885 issue of *Jiji shinpō* (News of the Times). Written by that newspaper's editor, Fukuzawa Yukichi (1834-1901), this essay presented the thesis that Japan should dissociate itself from Asia and strive for a status equal to European nations. Other editorials by Fukuzawa appearing around that time were similar in content: "Maxims about interdependence are unreliable,"[1] "Wipe out China and make peace with Europe,"[2] and "Poland of the Orient."[3] While there is no particular reason to distinguish among them, only the "Datsu-A-ron" achieved fame, probably because it was later interpreted as a prophecy of the Sino-Japanese War. The statement by historian Hattori Shisō (1901-1956), for example, that "The Sino-Japanese War amounted to the faithful execution of Fukuzawa's manifesto,"[4] testifies to the impact of the editorial.

The text consisted of only about five manuscript pages, and in places, its message is very succinct. Its evocative initial paragraph compares the enthusiastic adoption of Western "civilization" then in fashion to a measles epidemic.

Western civilization spreads like measles. The epidemic now raging in Tokyo began at Nagasaki in Kyūshū and then fanned

---

[1] *Jiji shinpō*, September 4, 1884. [2] Ibid., September 24 and 25, 1884.
[3] Ibid., October 15 and 16, 1884.
[4] Hattori Shisō, "Tōyō ni okeru Nihon no chii," in *Hattori Shisō chosakushū* (Tokyo, 1955), vol. 6, p. 270.

[328]

out as if carried by the advancing warmth of spring. Even if we were to abhor the damage done by this epidemic, and seek to prevent it, would there be anything we could do? I assure you, we could do nothing. Even against a destructive contagion, there is really no effective antidote which will blunt its force. How much more so in the case of civilization, which combines harm with great benefit. Not only can we not prevent the spread of civilization, but as men of wisdom we should endeavor to promote its spread so that the people may enjoy its beneficial effects.

Japan, which found in the infiltration of Western civilization an irresistible force, proceeded to

tear down its old government and erect a new one, adopting contemporary Western civilization in all things, official and private, across the entire land. Japan is alone in having freed itself from old ways, and it must now move beyond all Asian countries by taking "dissociation from Asia" [*datsu-A*] as the keynote of a new doctrine.

Yet Fukuzawa sensed a problem, centering on Japan's two traditional neighbors.

Although Japan lies close to the eastern edge of Asia, the spirit of its people has transcended Asian conservatism and moved towards Western civilization. What is most unfortunate about this location is its neighboring states, China and Korea. . . .

When we compare Japan, China and Korea we find that China and Korea are more similar to each other than either is to Japan . . . their affection for convention and antiquated custom has remained unchanged throughout hundreds and thousands of years. . . . From our perspective, in an age when civilization advances steadily eastward, it appears inevitable that they will lose their independence. . . . I feel certain that in only a few years, these nations will lie in ruin, their territory divided amongst the civilized nations of the world.

His basis for this ominous prediction was that,

as civilization and enlightenment move against them like a measles epidemic, the Chinese and Koreans resist its natural diffusion. Sealing themselves in a closet in order to avoid contagion, they succeed only in blocking air circulation and suffocating to death.

Even worse,

> The old adage *hosha shinshi* [interdependence] means that neighboring countries should cooperate, but China and Korea to-day are unable to help Japan at all. Not only that. Because of our geographical proximity, civilized Westerners may think all three nations are the same, and exact demands from Japan based on their evaluation of China and Korea. . . . This is something like a group of houses in a village, whose inhabitants have a reputation for stupidity, cruelty and lawlessness. Even if the members of one family in that group were very proper in their relationships inside and out, their virtues would be concealed by the ugliness of the rest.

No matter how hard Japan might strive toward civilization and enlightenment, Fukuzawa observed, if its neighbors did not share similar aspirations, not only would they be of no help, but there was even more reason to fear that their inaction would work to Japan's disadvantage. It seemed to Fukuzawa that Korea and Ch'ing China were looking coldly down their noses at Japan's enlightenment, smugly defending the ancient bastions of "Confucianism." He concluded,

> In pursuing its goals, Japan cannot afford to wait for the enlightenment of its neighbors, in hopes of working with them for the betterment of all Asia. It should break formation and move forward along with the civilized countries of the West. Rather than offering China and Korea special treatment just because they are neighbors, we should deal with them just as Western nations do. If we associate with disreputable friends, we shall have to share their bad name. In my heart, I spurn their companionship.

"Datsu-A-ron" was written against the background of Fukuzawa's own sense of frustration over attempts to modernize Korea, a cause to which he had contributed unstintingly by dispatching some of his students in connection with the Kōshin incident. His biography, *Fukuzawa Yukichi-den*, says,

> Kim Ok-kyun and Pak Yong-ho acted from the outset on [Fukuzawa's] advice. He used to say, "I am like a playwright

[330]

who merely composes the script. I take great pleasure in watching it performed on the stage, but I take little interest in who the actors are. Nor do I hope for any personal fame." But he was not just a playwright for the scenario acted by Pak and Kim. He selected the actors, taught them, set the stage, and directed the action.[5]

These shadowy activities and his subsequent agitation over their failure led Fukuzawa to write the editorial "Prepare an Imperial Expedition!"[6] published on January 8, 1885. In this powerful essay, Fukuzawa called for the establishment of an imperial headquarters in Shimonoseki. He wrote, "When the world first hears of this [Imperial Expedition], it will be called preposterous, impossible to carry out." But if the emperor had been able to prolong his stay in Kyoto for several days during the Seinan War of 1877, would it not be possible for him now to come to Shimonoseki? "If it is possible during times of domestic strife, how much more appropriate it would be now for a military action in which the nation's survival is at stake."

This was somewhat inconsistent with Fukuzawa's normal editorial tone. But, as noted above, "Datsu-A-ron" was far from being his only expression of views concerning China and Korea, and they all bear witness to his frustration and intense contempt for these two nations.

In 1884, the year before "Datsu-A-ron" appeared, the article "Kō-A-saku" (Policy for enlightening Asia)[7] was written by Sugita Teiichi (1851-1920), a member of the Liberal Party and later speaker of the House of Representatives, whose orientation was quite different from Fukuzawa's. Sugita observed,

The yellow race is about to be devoured by the white. We used to be told that the white race loves freedom and values equality. It is very curious that they then proceed to subvert freedom and deprive others of equality. They may boast that they are the guardians of liberty, but I am more inclined to conclude that they are actually its destroyers. While the countries of Asia are inseparably bound to a common destiny, our thoughts are thousands of miles apart; we lack mutual empathy as members of

[5] *Fukuzawa Yukichi-den* (Tokyo, 1932), vol. 3, pp. 340-41.
[6] *Jiji shinpō*, January 13, 1885.
[7] Saiga Hakuai, *Sugita Kakuzan-ō* (Tokyo, 1928), pp. 543ff.

a common race, and any spirit of mutual aid, despite the fact that we face the same difficulties. Under such circumstances, it is only by virtue of the balance of power among our enemies, the European nations, that we Asians are able to maintain a semblance of life. How can we allow ourselves to fall into such a convoluted state? Could anything be more ignominious? . . .

While we are far from wise, my colleagues and I have been calling for recognition of Japanese civil rights. Now we must go even further, and appeal for freedom throughout Asia under the banner of universal justice, dispelling the illusions that have caused the seven hundred million people of Asia to temporize and act with servility for hundreds of years. We must cast off the shame of past insults at the hands of the white race, and take steps to usher in a new age of freedom and enlightenment.

Sugita's ideas were based on a concept of Sino-Japanese alliance[8] first espoused at the beginning of the Meiji period by such heroes of the Restoration as Iwakura Tomomi (1825-1883) and Ōkubo Toshimichi (1830-1878). To resist the ever-encroaching pressure of the Western powers, Sugita proposed an alliance of all Asian countries, especially Japan and China.

Spurred on by the outbreak of the Sino-French War of 1884-85, Sugita hurried to Shanghai, there to set up the Tōyō Gakkan (Oriental Academy), which later became the Nisshin Bōeki Kenkyūjo (Institute for Sino-Japanese Trade) under Arao Sei (1859-1896). The name was subsequently changed again to Tō-A Dōbunkai (East Asian Common Culture Association). Sugita's *Keisei shinron* (New theory of state-craft), published in February 1880, is said to have influenced the work of the famous statesman and reformer K'ang Yu-wei (1858-1927) and that of K'ang's compatriot, the poet and reformer Huan Tsun-hsien (1848-1905).[9] The woman revolutionary Ch'iu Chin (1867-1907) also read Sugita's book at the suggestion of her relative and Tōyō Gakkan student, Hung Hua-chuan, and was deeply moved by it. Ch'iu was executed in 1907 at the age of forty, for complicity in the assassination of a provincial official.

Sugita himself, however, found his first visit to China in 1884 a disappointment. Returning to Japan, he wrote in "Yūshin yokan" (Impressions of travel in China),[10]

[8] *Iwakura-kō jikki* (Tokyo, 1927), vol. 2, pp. 543ff.
[9] Saiga, pp. 586ff.   [10] Ibid., pp. 582ff.

While observing the customs, institutions, and mentality of the people there, I realized that there is a difference of night and day between what one reads in literature and what the reality is. . . . Western powers in China squabble over their interests, each trying to assert hegemony over the country. As close as we are to this scene, my colleagues and I wonder whether Japan will be served up as the main dish in the coming feast, or whether it should join the guests at the table. Surely it would be better to sit at the table than to be part of the menu.

He then adds that the time is ripe:

Chinese soldiers have opened fire on our troops, burned down the Japanese legation in Seoul and committed atrocities against our people. Timing is important, and this is one chance in a thousand. If we let it pass, we may never again have such an opportunity.

Sugita's opinion had come to match that of Fukuzawa.

In 1886, Arao Sei opened a pharmacy in Hankow, part of a chain called Rakuzendō. There he was joined by Munekata Kotarō (1864-1923), Ura Keiichi (1860-1889) and others of similar inclination, to form a China study group.[11] They received a great deal of support from Kishida Ginkō (1833-1905), manager of the Rakuzendō head-quarters in Shanghai; later this group became the Nisshin Bōeki Kenkyūjo which Arao and his associates set up in 1889. Arao's views on China are summed up in his *Tai-Shin benmō* (Refuting Japan's China logic) published in March 1895, in which he argued vigorously against expropriating a piece of Chinese territory following the Sino-Japanese War. Although a bit out of chronological sequence, his message is germane to the present discussion.

If Japan were to demand the cession of a large piece of Chinese territory, the powers would carry out their greedy designs to carve up the rest. The day we take over a province, or even a county, all of China will be dismembered and hung before the fangs of the wolf and the claws of the leopard. China is already divided, with red-headed, blue-eyed foreigners now running rampant through its heartland. Seizing a province or an island at this time is not at all in Japan's interests. There is no sense in

[11] Inoue Masaji, *Kyojin Arao Sei* (Tokyo, 1910), p. 30.

acting alone. We cannot single-handedly bring about the liberation and prosperity of East Asia.

Until such time as the Japanese people embrace the Imperial Benevolence and become convinced of the urgent need to help the Chinese in their time of difficulty, occupation of Chinese territory should not be considered. If we were to succumb now to the elation of victory, taking advantage of our enemy's discomfiture and plundering its territory and people to our own aggrandizement, we would only sow the seeds of future calamity, an event we would deeply regret.[12]

Viscount Tani Kanjō also urged that Chinese territory not be infringed upon.

France's Alsace-Lorraine is insignificant compared to the land Japan has just seized from China. It is where the ancestors of the present Manchu emperors first rose to power and where the tombs of their forebears lie. Without Port Arthur and Weihaiwei, there is no Peking. What we have done is like holding a knife to someone's throat to keep him from talking. How can peace be preserved in such a fashion?[13]

Most Japanese at the time were so intoxicated with the heady wine of victory that they paid little heed to the advice of knowledgeable men such as these. When the Triple Intervention of France, Germany, and Russia forced Japan to relinquish rights to the Liaotung peninsula, however, swirling voices called for determination and perseverance in a mood of revenge.

Returning to the 1884-85 setting, let us examine more thoroughly the contemporary Japanese attitudes on the Korean question. The most intriguing personalities in that connection are Ōi Kentarō (1843-1922), Tarui Tōkichi (1850-1922), and Nakae Chōmin (1847-1901).

Ōi Kentarō and other radical members of the Liberal Party were arrested in Osaka on November 23, 1885, almost one year after the abortive Kōshin coup d'état. The Osaka incident was stimulated by a series of desperate uprisings—the Kabasan, Chichibu, and Iida incidents, which occurred around the time the Liberal Party was disbanded. It was also spurred on by the supposition that the East Asian situation was worsening for Japan as a result of France's vic-

---

[12] Ibid., pp. 204ff.
[13] Hirao Michio, *Shishaku Tani Kanjō-den* (Tokyo, 1935), pp. 702ff.

tory in the Sino-French War and the failure of the coup in Korea. The conspirators became more convinced than ever that forceful action could be used to bring about reform in Korea at the same time as it fed the fires of patriotic sentiment at home. Ōi's plan entailed moves which would

> . . . embroil Korea, Japan and China in a complicated tangle, transform the course of public affairs and stir up the emotions of the people, thereby causing such confusion that the government would be forced to heed public opinion. In that case, reform would be easily within reach. In external affairs, we must do the right thing by helping to secure the independence of Korea. Domestically, we will wipe out political corruption and initiate a politics of constitutionalism. The policies we implement will achieve both goals.[14]

When the plot was unearthed by the police, the activists were arraigned on a number of charges. Ōi said at the time,

> To remain silent while our country acquiesced in the Korean situation would have been inconsistent with the principles of freedom and equality that we espouse, so we decided to intervene on our own initiative. . . . In a normal war, combatants stand against the enemy to do battle, while in this case, we sought not to conquer their country but to strengthen it. That is, although we are Japanese, we tried to put ourselves in the place of the Koreans and work for a more powerful Korea. We did not confront the Korean nation as the enemy; it would be more fitting to say that we pitted ourselves against a certain group within Korea. In our direct action, we did not engage the entire nation, nor did we act against the Korean people.[15]

This passage is typical of the views of Liberal Party radicals.

It was also in 1885 that Tarui Tōkichi wrote down his views on a united Asia.[16] The original manuscript was lost when he was held on charges of complicity in the Osaka incident, but much later it was rewritten and published in August 1893 as the "Daitō gappōron" (Discourse on the great East federation) in the journal *Jiyū byōdō keirin* (Freedom and equality) edited by Nakae Chōmin. The original,

---

[14] Itagaki Taisuke, ed., *Jiyūtōshi* (Tokyo, 1958), vol. 3, p. 133.
[15] Hirano Yoshitarō, ed., *Bajō Ōi Kentarō-den* (Tokyo, 1938), p. 150.
[16] Tanaka Sōgorō, *Tōyō Shakaitō-kō* (Tokyo, 1970), p. 162.

however, had been written at about the same time as Fukuzawa penned the "Datsu-A-ron."

Tarui's essay proposed that Japan and Korea unite on an equal basis to form the country of Daitō (great East). The conception was uniquely Tarui's. By pursuing the course he outlined, he hoped that Japan and Korea could work together in common defense against the encroachments of the Western powers, and that Korea could be set on the road to modernization. With regard to China, he hoped that

> After Japan and Korea unite, we can help China, Tartar, Mongolia and Tibet to regain their independence and join the grand federation. . . . Japan and Korea should unite first, to be joined next by China. In this way we shall all be able to defend ourselves from mistreatment by foreigners.[17]

Since China had not yet proposed such a union, Japan and Korea would first demonstrate its concrete advantages by joining together, and China would later be invited in. If it had not been for the prevailing atmosphere of pressure from the Western powers and the weakness of Korean nationalism, it is unlikely that such a radical program would have been conceived.

This brings us directly to the views of the leader of the Freedom and Popular Rights movement, Nakae Chōmin. Two years after Fukuzawa's "Datsu-A-ron," Nakae wrote "Three drunks discuss government."[18] This essay provides a fairly complete picture of the opinions of a man who once told Sugita Teiichi,

> If things work out in the direction you are heading, Sugita, you will wind up as king of some province in China. I don't like kings at all. For my part, I will show you how the power of the pen can bring civilization to four-hundred million Chinese in the twinkling of an eye.[19]

Nakae must not have been joking, for he soon left for China where he participated in the founding of the Tōyō Gakkan. In addition to publishing Tarui's essay, as mentioned above, Nakae was elected to the Diet in the first general election held in 1890. He resigned his seat after only one year, and went to Hokkaidō to become editor-in-chief of the *North-Gate Report* (*Hokumon shinpō*). Quitting that

[17] Tarui Tōkichi, *Daitō gappōron* (Tokyo, 1894), p. 133.
[18] *Meiji bunka zenshū seiji hen* (Tokyo, 1929), pp. 371-408. Also included in the Iwanami Bunko series as *San-suijin keirin mondō*.
[19] Saiga, p. 565.

job as well, he became involved in a number of enterprises, finally joining Konoe Atsumaro's National People's Alliance (Kokumin Dōmeikai) late in life. Hence it is difficult to characterize in a word just what were his views on Asia. At any rate, the three drunks of the story—Western Gentleman, a democrat who idealizes peace; Eastern Hero, who is given to aggression; and Nankai Sensei, who sits quietly in between, sipping sake—clearly anticipated the various attitudes toward Asia subsequently developed by the Japanese.

Schematically, four types of attitudes toward China may be delineated:

(1) The Japan-China Alliance Thesis—Western pressure is seen as forcing Japan and China to work together, making an alliance expedient.

(2) The Renovation of China Thesis—Since China is powerless as an ally, steps must be taken to renovate and strengthen it.

(3) Dissociation from Asia Thesis—Since the onset of the age of imperialism has created an emergency that precludes waiting for the restrengthening of China, any notion of concerted action should be discarded.

(4) The Invasion or "Protect China" Thesis—The need for Japan to conform to the ways of the advanced imperialist powers dictates that part of China be seized, necessitating a war with that nation.

In reality, of course, the period of the Sino-Japanese War cannot be understood in such simple, unilinear terms. While it is possible to label such views as alliance, renovation, or invasion theses, they seldom occurred in pure form. Furthermore, there were often contradictions between surface appearances and inner realities. It is still apparent, however, that around the time of the Sino-Japanese War, these various impulses combined to define the complexities and subtleties of Japanese attitudes toward China. It was not unusual for the same personality to combine extreme reverence for Chinese culture on an emotional plane, with a radical form of the "protect China," or invasion thesis, in the realm of politics. Attitudes did not appear nearly as systematically as the above list might suggest, and at times, variations of the theses fluctuated diachronically in the thought of a single individual. Fukuzawa's "Datsu-A-ron" definitely falls into category three, while Tarui's "Great East Federation" is a special case of category one. Ōi Kentarō's ideas were very complex, combining aspects of each of the first three categories. Nakae Chōmin displayed a strange blend of one and four, changing emphasis later in life from the former to the latter; his conflicting orientations seem somehow apparent in the "absolutely contradictory self-identity" (Nishida Kitarō) that underlay the silence of "Nankai Sensei" in "Three drunks discuss government."

Apropos of Chōmin's position, which may be perplexing, I would like to refer to the history of the Gen'yōsha (Dark Ocean Society), founded in 1881. The Gen'yōsha is generally regarded as the well-spring of the Japanese radical right, but at the time of its inception it tended toward the Freedom and Popular Rights movement which opposed the government. Later, the society did become clearly nationalist. It first gained public attention when one member, Kuru-shima Tsuneki (1858-1889), tried to assassinate Foreign Minister Ōkuma Shigenobu (1838-1922) with a bomb on October 18, 1889. The only foreign action sponsored by the group had to do with Korea, as might be expected—the matter of the Ten'yūkō (Knights of Divine Protection). It is said that this group entered the Korean peninsula prior to the Sino-Japanese War, uniting and scheming with the Korean religious cult, the Tonghak (Eastern Learning), which later staged an uprising.[20] There is no clear evidence that this collaboration took place, however. This association, made up of Suzuki Tengan, Ōhara Yoshinori, Takeda Hanshi, and Yoshikura Ōsei, and led by Uchida Ryōhei (1874-1937), gave rise to the type of Japanese expatriate later called "Tairiku rōnin." This sort of individual played an active role in Japan's invasion of the continent, generally displaying a mentality similar to that of Nakae Chōmin. All of the above-mentioned categories were somehow mixed together in this rōnin approach.

What, then, were the attitudes of Japanese nonintellectuals at the time? It seems that they can be characterized as a mixture of two extremes: abundant curiosity and goodwill toward China, on the one hand; and contempt and prejudice on the other. The following excerpt, from the recollections of Ubukata Toshirō, illustrates the former.

In our house, we had two six-panel screens that my father was very fond of. On them were painted pictures of several tall, refined men with long, pleated gowns and crowns on their heads. There were also a number of charming children playing with small turtles and other objects. When I asked my mother about the pictures, she told me they were Chinese people amusing

[20] Kiyofuji Kōshichirō, Ten'yūkyō (Tokyo, 1903).

themselves with their children. Certainly one could search forever without encountering refined people like these in the country place where we lived. To me, those pictures represented the Chinese.

We also had several small green dishes which were used only at the time of the Blue Warrior Festival (*kōshin-machi*). To my child's eyes, they were indeed gorgeous to behold. My father said they were Nanking plates, and that such beautiful things could not be made outside of China. My father was also fond of calligraphy, and he was just as lavish with his praise of the Chinese-made ink stones used in that art.[21]

Another example is provided by Kyūshū-born businessman and author Tominaga Yoshio (1886-1962). In his *Hasu no mi* (The lotus seed), Tominaga wrote,

When we were children, even after the Sino-Japanese War, we would always refer to someone from China as "acha-san," which implies affection and respect. Even if the person were a door-to-door salesman peddling kimono material, we would doff our hats and bow.[22]

Tominaga and Ubukata were from totally different parts of Japan, Nagasaki in the west, and Gunma in the east. But their common goodwill and affection toward the Chinese could be understood by any Japanese. Another example is the *Ōkōchi monjo* (The Ōkōchi papers) which includes dialogues between Ko Ju-chang, the first Chinese ministerial envoy to Japan, and Ōkōchi Teruka, former lord of the Takasaki domain in Kōzuke province.[23]

Alongside such amity and affection, there were certainly other Japanese who were arrogant and contemptuous toward China. Fukuzawa's feelings of scorn, as noted above, provide one example. There was particularly intense hostility toward the common Chinese people who flowed into Yokohama, Kobe, and other ports then only recently opened to world trade and commerce.

Imperialism and Revolution

The period from the Sino-Japanese War to the end of the Russo-Japanese War may be broadly characterized as an age of relative peace

[21] Ubukata Toshirō, *Meiji-Taishō kenbun shi* (Tokyo, 1926), p. 32.
[22] Tominaga Yoshio, *Hasu no mi* (Tokyo, 1964), p. 111.
[23] Sanetō Keishū, ed., *Ōkōchi monjo* (Tokyo, 1964).

with China. It did not bring about any marked revision in the Japanese image of China. There was admiration for the Meiji Restoration among Chinese youths after the Sino-Japanese War, and the number of Chinese students who came to study in Japan increased sharply. Thus it remained a period of peace for the two nations, at least until the rise of a Chinese revolutionary movement. From this perspective, it appears that friction between Japan and China did not amount to much.

Three important factors must be recognized as contributing to this situation. One was the rising resentment toward Russia touched off by the loss of the Liaotung peninsula through the Triple Intervention. Writing at the time of this diplomatic reversal, Tokutomi Sohō (1863-1957) said, "I can safely say that reversion of the Liaotung peninsula exerted a dominant influence on the course of my life. I was a different person from the moment I heard of it."[24] This type of sentiment spurred Japan to become a major imperialist power, but initially it was aimed at Russia and did not arouse Chinese hostility.

Another factor was Western fear of the "yellow peril." Kaiser Wilhelm II (1859-1941) began propagandizing about the "peril" around 1895 and the notion gained currency throughout the world in the period following the Sino-Japanese War. In his *Jūkyūseiki sōron* (Reflections on the nineteenth century),[25] Takayama Chogyū (1871-1902) said that the Western nations were making use of this idea: "It seems that the last nation-states of the Turanian race, China, Japan and Korea, are now being subjected to an encirclement attack by the Aryan race." In that connection, Takayama vehemently criticized Japan for alienating China, its fellow Asian nation, and for the irrationality of attempting to seize Chinese territory. Many voices in Japan at the time were calling for friendship with China in order to prepare for a struggle against the Caucasians.

The third factor had to do with Japanese ideas of what was happening in China per se, and in that there were two distinct groups: those who sought to protect the Ch'ing dynasty, and those who aided revolutionary movements trying to overthrow the Ch'ing. The latter group was further divided into two segments, with some, like Uchida Ryōhei,[26] who saw aid to China as a means to gain special rights for Japan, on one side, and on the other, the pure revolutionary

[24] Tokutomi Sohō, *Sohō jiden* (Tokyo, 1935), p. 310.
[25] *Chogyū zenshū* (Tokyo, 1905), vol. 8, pp. 604ff.
[26] See, for example, Kokuryū Kurabu, ed., *Kokushi Uchida Ryōhei-den* (Tokyo, 1967), pp. 173ff.

group including Miyazaki Tōten (1870-1922),[27] who harbored no such designs.

These factors conspired to form the basis of Japanese national psychology after 1895. Between the Twenty-One Demands of 1915 and China's May Fourth Movement in 1919, a dramatic change took place. An opinion paper presented by the *genrō*, Matsukata Masayoshi (1835-1924), to Prime Minister Terauchi Masatake (1852-1919) in October 1915 said:

Our policy toward China is without doctrine or guiding principle. What is constructed with the left hand is torn down with the right. What we support at one time, we summarily reject at another. The inconsistency of our policy is the cause of disorder, such that many of the so-called disturbances and incidents that have taken place in China in recent years have not been fomented by the Chinese people themselves. Rather they seem to have resulted from plots devised by Japanese.

It appears, in short, that the intentions of the Japanese Empire in China lack not only legitimacy, but unity. Japan or Japanese citizens have been involved in almost every incident in China from the autumn 1911 Wuchang revolt to the recent troubles with the Tsung She Tang in Manchuria. The inevitable result is quarrel and conflict among Japanese themselves. Such conflict not only takes place between the Japanese government and its people, but goes on within the government itself. One ministry takes this policy toward China, the other takes that. In Tokyo, government offices are still unified under the cabinet but in the various regions of China, there is fierce competition and infighting among them. I cannot but be concerned that if this situation continues, the Empire will be unable to realize hegemony in East Asia.[28]

That paper was written just as victory in the Russo-Japanese War had brought a sudden expansion of Japan's rights and interests, and World War I had generated a spate of schemes for demarcating spheres of influence in the Far East. These activities, as Matsukata noted, were not derived from any consistent image of China.

In his book, *Seikai hiwa* (Inside stories of the political world),

---

[27] Miyazaki Tōten, *Sanjūsannen no yume* (Tokyo, 1943). Miyazaki's personality pervades this work, that of a man dedicated to the interests of the underdog.
[28] Quoted in Iwabuchi Tatsuo, *Tai-Shi gaikōshi-ron* (Tokyo, 1946), pp. 54ff.

Nagashima Ryūji wrote that "Japanese people do not even attempt to understand China. They give up before they start, saying that 'China is a country which just cannot be understood,' and 'Naturally we don't understand.' "[29] In *Aru gunjin no jiden* (Autobiography of a soldier), Sasaki Tōichi (1886-1951), who was teaching at the War College, said, "At the very beginning of classes for first-year students, I would give a test on the names of Chinese individuals and places. Part of the test consisted of writing in the names of provinces on a blank map. Not one student ever answered all of them correctly."[30]

Vignettes such as these indicate confusion in the Japanese image of China. But why should the Japanese have had a confused image —or rather, perhaps, no image at all—of China during the Taishō period? Simply put, the great convulsions and tumult that China was going through as it entered its revolutionary era were incomprehensible in Japan. The reasons can be outlined as follows:

1. Japanese of the older generation in the Taishō period received a very thorough training in the Chinese literary tradition, and their emotional ties to classical China were strong. Accordingly, they tended to harbor deep antipathy toward a China that was now in the throes of revolution. They did not even engage in the sort of criticism Fukuzawa leveled at Confucianism. For example, the Chinese "literary renaissance" of 1916 with its epochal criticism of Confuciansim was just passed off as the misdirected ardor of youth.

2. Also, among what was basically the same generation there was a tendency for images of China to focus not on the teachings of Confucius and Mencius, but rather on the supposed rule over society exercised by local communal organizations (*hsiang-tang*) and their patriarchal elders. According to this view, China lacked the ability to govern itself through the agency of a modern state.

3. Among the younger generation during the Taishō period were some who were more interested in contemporary happenings than they were in classical China. They held a sympathetic image of a new country where second and third revolutions followed the initial one in 1911. As what might be called the Taishō democracy generation, their understanding of China shared the limitations of that movement. In other words, this generation never adequately came to know the new China.

[29] Nagashima Ryūji, *Seikai hiwa* (Tokyo, 1928), p. 23.
[30] Sasaki Tōichi, *Aru gunjin no jiden* (Tokyo, 1963), p. 129.

The first group of the older generation included most of the political leaders and opinion makers of the period. Men like Ōki Tōkichi (1871-1926), Egi Kazuyuki (1853-1932), Ogawa Heikichi (1869-1942), and Hiranuma Kiichirō (1867-1952),[31] for example, were leaders of the Daitō Bunka Kyōkai (Great East Cultural Association) founded in 1924.[32] Among the activities of this group was a lobbying effort on behalf of the Proposal to Encourage Chinese Learning, and it was pursuant to the passage of this proposal into law that the Diet ratified a supplementary budget establishing the Daitō Bunka Gakuin (Great East Cultural Academy). The members of this association, along with those of the Kokuhonsha (National Foundations Society) and the Seitenkai (Blue Heaven Association), were representative of the political establishment in the latter part of the Taishō period, and they all may be said to have belonged to the first group listed above.

The keynote of their intellectual orientation was defense of the *kokutai* (national essence), with a concomitant hostility toward democracy, pacificism, socialism, and the labor movement. Most of them delighted in Chinese studies, objets d'art, and poetry, but their love for things Chinese had nothing to do with contemporary China. When former prime minister Kiyoura Keigo (1850-1942) visited the continent in 1926, for example, he visited Taishan and the tomb of Confucius, in a gesture of Japan's friendship for China. In Peking, however, Chou Tso-jen, writing in his *Tan hu chi*,[33] pointed out the absurdity, under the circumstances, of Kiyoura's adoration of Confucianism, and the inadequacy of pieties about "same script, same race" and interdependence.

Naitō Konan (1866-1934) and Inaba Kunzan (1876-1940) immediately come to mind as representative of the second group. Naitō was a famous China scholar, author of *Shina ron* (Thesis on China, 1914) and *Shin Shina ron* (New thesis on China, 1924). In his view, Chinese society was built around local communal organizations and clans, and ruled by their elders. Winning over the patriarchal elders, Naitō contended, "is the secret to success in China, regardless of the virtues of their legal system, or the moral character of their leaders."[34] He also maintained that China was destined to become a

---

[31] Itō Takashi, *Shōwa shoki seiji-shi kenkyū* (Tokyo, 1969), p. 392.
[32] Ibid., p. 394.
[33] Chou Tso-jen, *Tan hu chi* (Hong Kong, 1929), p. 543.
[34] Naitō Konan, *Shina-ron* (Tokyo, 1938), p. 9. This volume also includes *Shin Shina-ron*.

republic rather than continue as a monarchy, but his analysis was strangely warped. He believed that the patriarchs, as the key element in Chinese society,

> . . . attach little importance to notions of patriotism and independence vis-à-vis foreign nations. As long as their village is secure, their clan prospers, and they can enjoy their day-to-day life, they will meekly obey whatever power rules over them.

Naitō also stated that the Chinese situation was unique in that "even if its national defenses were totally abandoned, the amount of territory that could be invaded by a foreign power is limited and there would be no threat to national independence."

Naitō acknowledged the superiority of Chinese tradition and culture: in *Shin Shina ron* he wrote, "The people of Japan and Europe are gravely mistaken if they think themselves more advanced than China." On the other hand, he said,

> To me, it seems that it would make little difference if the present Chinese state were to perish, for the brilliance of Chinese culture would spread throughout the world, and the glory of the Chinese people would thrive so long as there is a heaven and an earth.[35]

This is indeed paradoxical. Naitō argued for the unparalleled universality of the Chinese cultural tradition while believing there would be no problem at all were the Chinese state to collapse. On one hand he claimed that the uniqueness of Chinese society guaranteed its cultural magnificence; on the other he viewed the autonomy of the Chinese state and people as trivial. Naitō's views are generally treated not as having constituted carte blanche support for Japan's imperialist policies, but to have been based on the objective scholarship of a top-flight Sinologist. It is, however, quite clear that he took a very particular set of circumstances in China—social dominance by communal organizations and clans—and reified it as a definite and immovable reality. His view of China never escaped the bonds of that conception.

The emphasis on communal and kinship ties appears even more strongly in the writings of Inaba Kunzan, such as *Tai-Shi ikkagen* (My views on China, 1921) in which he advocates the necessity of international control over China.[36]

[35] Ibid.
[36] Inaba Kunzan, *Tai-Shi ikkagen* (Tokyo, 1921).

The thinker most representative of the third group is Yoshino Sakuzō (1877-1933). In his essay on the May Fourth Movement, entitled "Pekin gakuseidan no kōdō manba surunakare" (Don't deride the actions of the Peking student groups), published in *Chūō Kōron*, June 1919, this adherent of *minponshugi* (government based on the people) wrote,

> We must try to restrain the China policy of Japan's military and financial cliques and communicate the peaceful desires of the Japanese people to our friends in China. It is for these ends that we have worked for many years to liberate our beloved Japan from the bureaucrats and militarists. Are the aims of the Chinese student movement any different from ours?[37]

Having thus given vent to his feelings of sympathy for contemporary China, he concluded that "those devoted young people, the new citizens" have the future of the country in their hands. Compared to most of his contemporaries, who favored a policy of chastising China for its impudence, Yoshino's foresight regarding China was extraordinary. One publication of the time maliciously likened the May Fourth Movement to the outburst of a "hysterical woman."

On the other hand, Yoshino had endorsed the Twenty-One Demands as "an extremely well-timed solution,"[38] and the contradictions involved in these two statements can only be seen as symptomatic of more basic contradictions and weaknesses in the underlying foundations of his thought. These limitations are generally viewed as inhering in Yoshino's advocacy of the governing principle of *minponshugi* itself, but what Yoshino had in mind amounted to a dual conception of raison d'état. That is, on the one hand, he had built his defense of *minponshugi* around an exposé of Japan's so-called reason of state, seeing it as merely a rationale for pursuit of particular interests on the part of the militarists, bureaucrats, and financiers. On the other hand, he could not dispute that it was the principle of raison d'état that undergirded the international order of the time and marked the universalization of the democratic values espoused by the European countries. Hence, that principle represented both Japan as a militarist aggressor and Japan as a peaceful member of the comity of nations.

Similar in thinking to Yoshino was Tsuchida Kyōson (1891-1935),

[37] Yoshino Sakuzō, *Chūgoku Chōsen-ron* (Tokyo, 1970), pp. 206ff.
[38] Ibid., p. 25.

who must be given credit for his advocacy of friendship with China. He was keenly attracted to the new Chinese culture movement, with its strong element of pragmatic thought, partly because of his earlier attraction to the pragmatism of Tanaka Ōdō (1867-1932). Ueki Toshirō has called Tsuchida the "Spiritual Ambassador to China."[39]

Toward the East Asian Coprosperity Sphere

The father of the Chinese Revolution, Sun Yat-sen (1866-1925), visited Japan in 1924, the year before his death, and in Kobe delivered his famous speech on "Pan-Asianism."[40] There he said in part, "The Japanese people should seriously consider whether Japan, vis-à-vis world culture, will become a dog in the service of the Western way of despotism, or a stalwart defender of the Eastern way of righteous government." By that time, Japan had already opted, though at times hesitantly, for the Western way of despotism.

In July 1926, more than a year after Sun's death, the new leader of the Kuomintang, Chiang Kai-shek (1887-1975), announced the Northern Expedition. Wuhan fell to Kuomintang forces in the same year; Nanking and Shanghai were occupied in 1927. It was also in November of 1927 that Mao Tse-tung (1893-1976) set up his headquarters in Ching Kang Shan. In July, Japan held its Conference on East Asia, with the purpose of setting out the fundamentals of a China strategy. The continental policy determined at that time was disseminated throughout the world as the "Tanaka Memorial to the Emperor," purportedly written by Tanaka Giichi (1863-1929) who was prime minister from 1927 to 1929. The memorial was later taken up at the League of Nations as evidence of Japanese aggression in the Manchurian incident of 1931.

The memorial was made famous by its dictum, "He who conquers Manchuria and Mongolia will conquer China." There is a marked similarity between the content of the memorial and the explanation given by Ishibashi Tanzan (1884-1973) of Tanaka's thought at the time. Ishibashi wrote, "He [Tanaka] was not thinking about the annexation of Manchuria and Mongolia, but hoped that an independent state could be created there."[41] Furthermore, there is a surprising

---

[39] For a discussion of Tsuchida Kyōson see the works of Ueki Toshirō, particularly "Seishinteki Chūgoku taishi Tsuchida Kyōson," *Seikei ronsō*, February 1972.

[40] For the text of Sun Yat-sen's speech, "Pan-Asianism," see *Kuo-fu ch'üan-chi* (Tokyo, 1960), pp. 1022ff.

[41] Ishibashi Tanzan, *Mantetsu shachō no Man-Mō keizai kaihō-ron*, in *Ishibashi Tanzan zenshū* (Tokyo, 1971), vol. 6, p. 231.

degree of correspondence between the contents of this mysterious document and Japan's actual behavior. In my opinion, the document is a forgery, not actually written by Tanaka at all. I must admit, however, that it is very accurate as prophecy. It is difficult to resist viewing the appearance of such an accurate forecast in 1926 as a manifestation of the "unseen hand of fate."[42]

From this time on, between the assassination of Chang Tso-lin (1873-1928) in June 1928 and the Manchurian incident of September 1931, Japan was very successful. Caught in the throes of the Great Depression, no other nation was able to offer more than token interference. Not even China itself could mount determined resistance, because of the disarray of its government following unification, and thus Japan had its own way in Manchuria. The new country formed there was presented to the world as a "paradise of the Kingly Way" and a "harmonious union of five peoples."

After recognition of the Japanese-controlled state of Manchukuo in September 1932, there followed Japan's withdrawal from the League of Nations in March 1933, the cease-fire accords at Tangku in May 1933, and the Ho-Umezu and Chin-Doihara agreements of June 1933. As Japanese aggression against its territory gained momentum, China's own will to resist rose. After the Marco Polo Bridge incident in July 1937, the Japanese people had little alternative but to concur blindly in the events that followed. Throughout the following four years of war with China, it seems that only very few people recognized in their hearts the significance of those hostilities. One searches in vain for signs of a nation totally united for battle as in the cases of the Sino-Japanese and Russo-Japanese Wars. Rather, the mood of soldiers and their families as troops left for the front was closer to melancholy and depression.

In the September 1937 issue of *Chūō Kōron*, Yanaihara Tadao (1893-1961), a Christian and Tokyo Imperial University professor, criticized Japanese aggression in China in an article called "Kokka no risō" (Ideals of the state).[43] Other authors critical of militarism, albeit from differing viewpoints, were economist Kawai Eijirō (1891-1944), journalist and later prime minister Ishibashi Tanzan, critic Kiyosawa Kiyoshi (1890-1945), China expatriate Nakae Ushikichi (son of Nakae Chōmin), lawyer and humanist Masaki Hiroshi (1896-

---

[42] Hashikawa Bunsō, "Tanaka jōsōbun no shūhen," in Hashikawa, ed., *Jungyaku no shisō* (Tokyo, 1973).

[43] Included in *Yanaihara Tadao zenshū* (Tokyo, 1963), vol. 18.

1975), journalist Kiryū Yūyū, military expert and critic Mizuno Hironori (1875-1945), and politicians Ozaki Yukio (1858-1954) and Hamada Kunimatsu (1868-1939).[44] But to a greater or lesser extent their writings were eclipsed by government oppression, and it was largely the flood of arguments for chastising an "unruly China" that rode the crest of the times into the popular mind. During the Taishō period, reports on the nationalist revolution generally had been suppressed, and the government's reward for such efforts was a population that now was easy prey for opinion manipulation by government and military leaders.

Hence the period of war with China was almost totally devoid of creative thought. At the beginning of the war, the American journalist and historian Edgar Snow (1905-1972) met some Japanese soldiers on a train in north China, and asked their opinion of the conflict. None of the answers went beyond pro forma statements, offering an instructive contrast to the fiery determination of the young students from Mukden who escaped to Peking when Manchuria fell to Japanese forces.[45]

Once Japan had taken Nanking, and then Wuhan and Canton in turn, it found itself in a military stalemate. A solution was sought through the peace moves of Wang Ching-wei (1885-1944), while at the same time it became necessary to devise a new set of ideals for that purpose. From this effort came the call for a "New Order in East Asia" and the conception of an "East Asian Community." These proposals can be viewed as the only intellectually creative efforts to emerge during the Japan-China war, a period which I have characterized elsewhere as intellectually barren.[46]

These two concepts were broadly extolled in both government and intellectual circles from the autumn of 1938 into the following year. The discussants were among the elite of the intelligentsia of the time—including journalist and China expert Ozaki Hotsumi, philosopher and critic Miki Kiyoshi, journalist and critic Ryū Shintarō,

---

[44] For a detailed description of these views, see Hashikawa Bunsō, "Teikōsha no seiji shisō," in Hashikawa Bunsō and Matsumoto Sannosuke, eds., *Kindai Nihon seiji shisōshi* (Tokyo, 1970), vol. 2, pp. 399-413. Translated into English under the title, "Antiwar Values—the Resistance in Japan," by Robert J. J. Wargo, in *Japan Interpreter*, vol. 9, no. 1 (Spring 1974), pp. 86-97.

[45] See Edgar Snow, *The Battle for Asia* (New York, 1941), translated into Japanese as *Ajia no tatakai* (Tokyo, 1956), for a description of the struggle by Chinese students in the war against Japan.

[46] Hashikawa Bunsō, "Tō-A shinchitsujo no shinwa," in Hashikawa and Matsumoto, vol. 2.

political scientist Rōyama Masamichi, political and economic critics Taira Teizō and Sugihara Masami, economic critic Yamazaki Seijun, economist Kada Tetsuji, philosopher Funayama Shin'ichi, and agricultural historian Aikawa Haruki—and they published their views in the most respected journals, including *Chūōkōron*, *Kaizō*, and *Nihon Hyōron*. In content, however, their fulminations amounted to little more than the self-gratification of intellectuals fleeing from the brutal realities of war. Ozaki Hotsumi admitted at the time that "we must ourselves recognize how petty this theory of an East Asian Community really is."[47] Suzue Gen'ichi, author of the *Son Bun den* (Biography of Sun Wen [Sun Yat-sen]), and his mentor, Nakae Ushikichi, were also critical of the concept.[48]

Be that as it may, the East Asian Community thesis was proffered as the theoretical foundation for the "Construction of a New Order in East Asia," and in that sense it purported to overcome and surpass the earlier framework provided by conceptions like the "Japan-China Alliance" thesis and the "Datsu-A-ron." To some extent this re-examination can be attributed to the unexpected strength of Chinese nationalism, but it did not fundamentally alter the unfortunate fact that even as Japan was actually invading China, it was seemingly impossible to carry out a truly adequate process of self-criticism. It is only to be expected, then, that the Shōwa Kenkyū Kai (Shōwa Research Society)—the group which spawned the East Asia Community idea—should conclude after the war, "How were those research activities and their results reflected in the actual conduct of politics? . . . One may conclude, it seems, that they exerted no influence at all."[49]

The Chinese reaction to the ideas of "A New Order in East Asia," and its theoretical foundation, the "East Asian Community," was stormy. In the first volume of *Tai-Nichi genronshū* (Collection of articles on Japan),[50] Chiang Kai-shek wrote, "This policy was merely a catch-all designation for Japan's plan to overturn the international order in East Asia, enslave China, establish hegemony over the entire Pacific region, and conquer the world." Others who very adroitly pointed out the fraudulence of the "East Asian Community" thesis included Communist leaders Kuo Mo-jo and Ch'en Shao-yu,

---

[47] For Ozaki's view of the China Incident see my introduction to *Ozaki Hotsumi senshū* (Tokyo, 1977), vol. 1.

[48] For a description of Nakae Ushikichi and Suzue Gen'ichi's thought and activities see *Nakae Ushikichi shokan-shū* (Tokyo, 1964).

[49] See Shōwa Dōjin Kai, ed., *Shōwa kenkyū kai* (Tokyo, 1968).

[50] Generalissimo Chiang Kai-shek (in Japanese), *Tai-Nichi genronshū* (Shanghai, 1946).

Kuomintang ideologue T'ao Hsi-sheng, and anti-Chiang figures such as Feng Yü-hsiang and Ch'en Pu-lei.[51]

Nevertheless, it must be emphasized that dimly perceivable in the "East Asian Community" concept is an effort to break away from the scornful attitude toward China that Japan had displayed for so many years. Rōyama Masamichi said of the thesis that "it is not colonial economics, but a community of destiny based on cooperative relations among the peoples of a region." Further, "Japan itself will be an integral member of the East Asian Community formed under Japanese leadership. To the extent that Japan will, therefore, have to abide by the principles of the community, it must be recognized that there will be limits to Japanese nationalism."[52] It is not difficult to find instances in which writers sought to "restrain" Japanese self-righteousness and despotism with regard to China, but that was the extent of the response Japanese intellectuals were prepared to make to the great tide of Chinese nationalism.

In this connection, however, we should not overlook the particular form of the "East Asian Community" thesis advanced by Ozaki Hotsumi. His analysis of the Sian incident, in which Chiang Kai-shek was kidnapped and spirited off to Red Army headquarters in Sian in December 1936, brought him almost instant fame as an expert on China. By this time he was already in contact with the Soviet spy, Richard Sorge (1895-1944), and his excellent understanding of China and keen intuition regarding the mood of the Chinese people enabled him to predict even then that the Communists would take over after the war. Ozaki was executed for espionage along with Sorge in November 1944, but as can be readily imagined, his conception of a "New Order in East Asia" was quite out of the ordinary. Under interrogation, Ozaki said,

What I called the "New Order in Asia" was . . . based on the fact that revolutionary forces in this nation are extremely weak, and that, therefore, an important turnabout in Japanese society would be difficult for Japanese alone to accomplish; even if they did, the results would not be stable. . . . Complete hegemony [in Asia] would have to be established by the Soviet Union, a Japan divested of its capitalist structure, and a China under the control

---

[51] For a discussion of Kuo Mo-jo, see his *Kō-Nichisen kaisōroku* (Tokyo, 1962) in Japanese translation, and for Ch'en Pu-lei see his *Ch'en Pu-lei hui-i-lu* (Taipei, 1967).

[52] Rōyama Masamichi, "Tō-A kyōdōtai no riron," *Kaizō*, November 1938.

of the Chinese Communist Party. Close cooperation and aid would be necessary among these three nations, and only around the nucleus of their union could a community of the peoples of East Asia be established.[53]

This appearance of Marxism among the so-called East Asian Community theorists reveals an attempt to navigate through the intellectual confusion of the time with clever bits of subterfuge. In Ozaki's case, for example, this deception is evident in his effort "to exploit for his domestic schemes the concepts of an 'East Asian League' and the 'East Asian Community' which arose in an attempt to deal with the China Incident."[54] He was walking a very dangerous tightrope.

The notion of an "East Asian League," referred to in the interrogation report, appeared around the same time as the "Community" idea, and although suppressed by the authorities, retained a group of devotees even after Japan's surrender. Writing about these two concepts, Ozaki said,

> ... the idea of an "East Asian Community" was subscribed to by a number of theorists and scholars, among them Ryū Shintarō and Rōyama Masamichi, but due to the lack of interest displayed by people actively engaged in politics, I believed it to be politically impotent. The "East Asian League" concept, however, seemed to have some political moment, so I judged it the best one to use. As far as actual content was concerned though, the league theories were lacking in brilliance.[55]

The originator of the "East Asian League" concept was also chief planner of the Manchurian incident, and one of the founders of the Kyōwa Kai (Association for Asian Harmony) in Manchuria, General Ishiwara Kanji, and the concept was used in the early stages of formation of Manchukuo. At the time this league thesis took shape, Ishiwara was on the general staff of the Kwantung Army. Later on, he was made chief of the Operations Division, Army General Staff, and at the beginning of war with China, he was a prominent member of the anti-expansionist faction. Eventually, of course, he was defeated by the expansionists.[56] Simply put, Ishiwara was opposed to hostilities

---

[53] See the record of Ozaki's interrogation, "Jinmon chōsho," in *Zoruge jiken* (Tokyo, 1962), vol. 2, pp. 128-29.

[54] Ibid., vol. 1, p. 45.   [55] Ibid.

[56] For a detailed examination, see Tanaka Shin'ichi, "Nikka jihen kakudai ka fukakudai ka," *Bessatsu chisei*, December 1956.

between China and Japan. At a colloquium held in the Tokyo office of the Kyōwa Kai, on May 12, 1938, he said, "The Chiang Kai-shek regime may collapse, but I believe firmly that it will not. Even assuming that Chiang did fall, would that cause four-hundred million Chinese to give up fighting? In my view, it most certainly would not."[57] Many at the time were in sympathy with that view. In *Tō-A Renmei ron* (The East Asian League thesis), Ishiwara's chief theoretical adviser, Miyazaki Masayoshi, stated,

> Inasmuch as the objective of the League would be the liberation of the peoples of East Asia, it must guarantee completely the right of political independence of those who have been liberated. In addition to working for the freedom of Asian peoples who have not yet been liberated, Japan and the other member countries must assure freedom of choice, leaving it entirely up to the newly liberated nation to decide whether to join the League or remain completely independent. The right to secede from the League must also be guaranteed. The East Asian League shall be a firm pledge entered into voluntarily by the nations of East Asia, and based on relations of mutual economic and political reliance among Japan and other members. It will not be a coercive order.[58]

Behind Ishiwara's conception was his supposition, from the perspective of military history, that an apocalyptic world war, the *sekai saishū sen*, was inevitable. He believed the "East Asian League" to be a necessary precondition of Japan's survival in such a war. Thus he considered creation of the League, with Japan, Manchuria, China (and probably Korea) forming its nucleus, to be an urgent task. The founding of the state of Manchukuo was a step in that direction, and incompatible with both the militarist priorities of the army and the profit-seeking of big business. The destiny of Manchukuo, however, was to betray his hopes, and the increasing likelihood of war between Japan and China demolished his conception of an East Asian League. Forced to retire by Tōjō Hideki (1884-1948) in 1941, he remained an enemy of the government throughout Tōjō's regime. At an opposite pole from the Marxists, he became what might be called an ultra-rightist critic of the war.

[57] For a summary of the May 12, 1938 talk by Ishiwara Kanji, see *Ishiwara Kanji shiryō—kokubō ronsaku* (Tokyo, 1967), p. 249.

[58] Miyazaki Masayoshi, *Tō-A Renmei ron* (Tokyo, 1938), pp. 45-46.

Neither of the conceptions Japan formulated vis-à-vis China, the "East Asian Community" or the "East Asian League," ever became a reality. The former was criticized by members of the Imperial Way faction, such as Kanokogi Kazunobu (1884-1949) in *Sumera Ajia* (Asia under imperial rule),[59] and from a capitalist standpoint by such men as Kojima Seiichi (1895-) in *Nihon senji keizai ron* (A discussion of the Japanese war economy).[60] The latter was rejected by the same groups, and also by the so-called Pan-Asianists, men like Matsui Iwane, Nakatani Takeyo, and Nomura Shigeomi, who claimed that "the thesis neglects the position of the Japanese Empire as the leader and the nucleus of Greater East Asia and, further, does not recognize the role of the Empire in world history."[61] Hence, on the eve of the Great East Asian War, Japan had no ideology with regard to China besides that of blanket support for invasion.

In August 1940, the second Konoe cabinet announced the new ideals of the Greater East Asian Coprosperity Sphere. Whereas previously the concept of a New Order in East Asia had functioned to camouflage Japanese self-righteousness, now it was replaced by an ideology harboring hypocrisy on an even grander scale. The Coprosperity Sphere concept was bandied about by military men and politicians who, stimulated by Germany's faraway blitzkrieg advances, were anxious to get on the bandwagon of world trends.

In other words, the Coprosperity Sphere concept meant taking advantage of sweeping Nazi conquests in Europe to "turn away from our present emphasis on the China Incident, toward the south."[62] In that sense, the Coprosperity Sphere idea provided the army with a graceful way to wash its hands of the "China Incident." The "Main Principles of Japan's Policy for Coping with the Situation in Accordance with International Developments" was prepared jointly by the Army and Navy Divisions of Imperial Headquarters and dated July 27, 1940. In the first chapter, "Reasons for Proposal," there was this passage:

> . . . it is urgent for the Empire to break away from its present tendency to rely on England and the United States, to establish a framework for self-sufficiency which centers on Japan, Man-

[59] Kanokogi Kazunobu, *Sumera Ajia* (Tokyo, 1937).

[60] Kojima Seiichi, *Nihon senji keizai ron* (Tokyo, 1938).

[61] See Hashikawa Bunsō, "Dai Tō-A kyōeiken no rinen to genjitsu," in *Iwanami kōza Nihon rekishi* (Tokyo, 1977), vol. 21, p. 280.

[62] Asahi Shinbunsha, ed., *Taiheiyō sensō e no michi* (Tokyo, 1963), supplementary volume on source materials, p. 323.

chukuo and China, and encompasses Mongolia from India eastward and the south Pacific from Australia and New Zealand
northward. The opportunity for achieving this goal is now, and
it will be very difficult at a later time. This is the situation in
view of the probable future Far Eastern policy of the United
States once its arms build-up is complete, and projected moves of
the Soviet Union once its national strength is fully augmented.[63]

The Greater East Asian Coprosperity Sphere, then, would "have at
its core Japan, Manchukuo and China," and be expanded beyond
that to include "the former German trust territory islands, French
Indochina, the South Pacific islands, Thailand, British Malaya, British
Borneo, the Dutch East Indies, Burma, Australia, New Zealand,
India, etc."[64] As territorial designs were broadened in this manner,
however, the content of the plan itself was further diluted. That is
because, rather than an honest effort to achieve its nominal goal of
"coexistence and coprosperity," the Coprosperity Sphere idea merely
served to cover up Japan's diminishing national strength.

I HAVE sought to survey Japan's relations with the rest of Asia from
Fukuzawa Yukichi's "Datsu-A-ron" to the formation of the Greater
East Asian Coprosperity Sphere. I have focused on China policy as
the central problem in that regard, and on the bitter frustrations that
accompanied efforts to arrive at a viable solution. Rather than the
accumulation of particular misinterpretations or blunders, the unsettled state of affairs would seem to have resulted from a more basic
and pervasive inability on the part of the Japanese to comprehend the
Chinese people. That would appear to be consistent with the supposition that the Japanese have always ranked Western Europe above
Asia. But in that case, how are we to interpret the conclusion reached
by John Dewey, and more recently by David Riesman, that Chinese
culture is much closer to that of Europe than is Japan's? If that
cannot be confirmed, then are we to conclude that, regardless of their
other propensities, the Japanese just do not like the Chinese?

The famous Japanese authority on Chinese literature, Takeuchi
Yoshimi (1910-1977), castigated the Japanese for their "slave
mentality" based on an inveterate elitism.[65] This mentality is clearly
evident in the obverse of "Datsu-A-ron" thinking, that is, in a fervent

---

[63] Ibid., p. 324. [64] Ibid., p. 330.
[65] See among others, Takeuchi Yoshimi, "Chūgoku no kindai to Nihon no
kindai," in *Takeuchi Yoshimi hyōron-shū* (Tokyo, 1966), vol. 3, pp. 9ff.

desire to become part of the West. That urge resulted in slavish emulation of the ways of the "advanced countries," which in the Meiji and Taishō periods were represented by Europe, and are now identified with the United States. At the present time, that mentality is manifest not as a military but as a technological and economic version of imperialism. We must continue to ask ourselves whether Japan may again seek to be the leader of an "Asian League." Should it do so, the road ahead will not be an easy one.

INDEX

Library of Congress Cataloging in Publication Data

Main entry under title:

The Chinese and the Japanese.

"Sponsored by the Joint Committee on Contemporary
China of the American Council of Learned Societies and the
Social Science Research Council"
    Includes index.
    1. China—Relations (general) with Japan—Addresses,
essays, lectures.   2. Japan—Relations (general) with
China—Addresses, essays, lectures.   I. Iriye, Akira.
II. Chi, Madeleine, 1930-   III. Joint Committee on
Contemporary China.
DS740.5.J3C399   951   80-378
ISBN 0-691-03126-6
ISBN 0-691-10086-1 pbk.

DATE DUE

1:8204168			
8/18/85			
Nov 3 '88			
GAYLORD			PRINTED IN U.S.A.